Also in the Collected Studies Series:

Holiness and Politics
in Early Medieval Thought

Professor Karl F. Morrison

Karl F. Morrison

Holiness and Politics
in Early Medieval Thought

VARIORUM REPRINTS
London 1985

British Library CIP data   Morrison, Karl F.
                              Holiness and politics in early medieval thought.
                              — (Collected studies series; CS219)
                              1. Sociology, Christian — History — Middle
                              Ages, 600–1500
                              I. Title
                              261.1'094   BT738

                              ISBN 0–86078–167–4

Copyright © 1985 by   Variorum Reprints

Published in Great Britain by   Variorum Reprints
                                   20 Pembridge Mews London W11 3EQ

Printed in Great Britain by   Galliard (Printers) Ltd
                                   Great Yarmouth Norfolk

                                   VARIORUM REPRINT CS219

CONTENTS

This volume contains a total of 302 pages.

INTRODUCTION

The essays collected in this volume address three moments in the formation of Europe: the age of the Church Fathers, the Carolingian era, and the Investiture Conflict, together with its aftermath. The moments were scattered over a range of 900 years; their great dramas were enacted in widely dissimilar circumstances, lands, and cultures. Yet, they were alike. For, at each juncture, Christians were compelled, both to reflect upon their place in the world, and to reform the world according to their doctrines. At the conversion of the Roman Empire, the most decisive revolution in western history before the twentieth century; again, after the fall of Rome, at the grafting of Christianity and the Church hierarchy onto the political order of Germanic tribes; and, finally, in the eleventh and twelfth centuries, at the first great clash between pope and emperor, the two heads of Latin Christendom, Christians heard from the Gospel the same lordly call to transform the political order into an instrument of holiness.

There were constants in the ebb and flow of centuries and cultures. This continuity existed, in large part, because Christians in every age considered Scripture the only infallible rule of life. Thus, at every age, writers invoked the same commandments, parables, and events from Scripture as guides for infusing politics with holiness. However, there were perplexities, even in the constant letter of Scripture. Scripture, for example, commanded Christians both to hate the world that rejected them and to love their enemies, both to withdraw from and to overcome the world, both to lay aside and to acquire the sword. Relating texts from dead societies to living institutions posed other practical difficulties.

Thus, ambiguities and contradictions were part of Scripture itself, and these difficulties at the source ramified through the varied and often mutually repellent interpretations drawn from Scripture. Much depended on the results, including the relation of the secular power of kings to the spiritual authority of bishops, and the place of coercion in the service of faith.

During the long centuries when Europe was formed, therefore, political thinking was for Christians an effort to apply God's eternal truths to the world's changing circumstances; but, departing from the same principles, minds reached different and sometimes contradictory conclusions.

The following essays describe some of the quandaries repeatedly encountered as the tradition of political thought in the West lengthened and matured. Throughout the nine centuries represented here, fundamental questions persisted; conclusions regarding the proper relation between temporal and spiritual orders of government likewise fell within the same range. However, between question and answer came a process of reasoning. How did a given writer reach, verify, and defend his assertions? What method of inference made his conclusions thinkable to him? What formative movement led to up, and was incorporated in, the finished doctrine? While questions and answers remained constant, processes of moving from the one to the other differed. Most of the following essays describe examples of such transitional methods.

It will be readily apparent that my address to those intervening processes has changed over the years. As I reflected on political doctrines and the ways of thinking that they incorporated, I slowly realized that the bewildering array of analogues, metaphors, and allegories in which writers expressed their doctrines actually made up a coherent, if remarkably variable, structure of inference. That structure revolved about the poles of likeness and unlikeness; its dynamic principle was imitation (or mimesis). It gradually became obvious to me that the recognition of likeness and unlikeness, and the play of imitation, fundamental in the mental formation of children, had been taken up into philosophy and theology to elucidate the formation of societies and, indeed, of all human experience, in the panorama of history.

As to political thought, the dynamic of mimesis reconciled what might have appeared to be the contrary demands of eternal truth and changing circumstances. No temporal image could fully reproduce an eternal model. Thus, in the quest for spiritual perfection, Christians believed, history could rush onward, in an ever-widening river of innovation, as mankind grew in likeness to the archetype according to which it had originally been made. Mankind progressed by imitation. As part of the tradition of formal thought (and not simply of everyday experience, endlessly repeated), the mimetic structure of inference was not limited to the centuries represented in this book. It originated in the classical world, matured during the formation of Europe, and persisted, with many variations, to the present day. I attempted to describe its career in my book, *The Mimetic Tradition of Reform in the West* (Princeton, 1982).

Quite understandably, the later essays in this volume express a clearer awareness of the mimetic structure of inference, and of the mimetic tradition as a whole, than do the earlier ones. However, it is instructive to detect, even in the earliest essays, the language and syntax of mimesis. Without my knowing it, the evidence was able even there to speak for itself, demanding continual reform in the interplay of holiness and politics, glorifying want, pain, and death in warfare against spiritual wickedness and unbelief, and still teaching that the kingdom of God was not of this world. Experience in the three ages considered here ingrained this idealist, relentless, and militant questing into the character of Europe.

KARL F. MORRISON

Lawrence, Kansas
March 1985

PUBLISHER'S NOTE

The articles in this volume, as in all others in the Collected Studies Series, have not been given a new, continuous pagination. In order to avoid confusion, and to facilitate their use where these same studies have been referred to elsewhere, the original pagination has been maintained wherever possible.

Each article has been given a Roman number in order of appearance, as listed in the Contents. This number is repeated on each page and quoted in the index entries.

I

ROME AND THE CITY OF GOD

An Essay on the Constitutional Relationships of Empire and Church in the Fourth Century

CONTENTS

"Christianity has been long enough in the world to justify us in dealing with it as a fact in the world's history. . . . It has from the first had an objective existence, and has thrown itself upon the great concourse of men. Its home is in the world; and to know what it is, we must seek it in the world, and hear the world's witness to it."—John Henry Newman, Introduction to *An Essay on the Development of Christian Doctrine.* London, 1848.

INTRODUCTION *

Modern corporative theory owes much to mediaeval thought concerning Church-State relations: out of that early thought ultimately came the present-day legal constructs according to which autonomous institutions coexist in the same society. A critical element in the formulation of those doctrines was the concept of the Church as the City of God; a critical time in their formulation was the fourth century, when that concept first achieved practical importance. When St. Ambrose and his contemporaries wrote that the Church was the City of God, they joined two independent principles of early Christian thought: that the Church, the Kingdom of Christ, was in fact a legal corporation discrete from the civil government, and that its nature was theological. From these premises, the Fathers went on to examine the place of the City of God in this world, and particularly the relationships of the Heavenly Kingdom to the Roman Empire. Their thought in this dimension is complex, for it is both theological and jurisprudential. Its most lasting product was the doctrine of dualism: that Christian society was rightly governed in its religious character by the Church and in its temporal character by the legally discrete institutions of the civil authority.

Theological enquiries and general histories of the Church alike have tended to ignore the legal framework to which the Fathers sought to relate their doctrinal positions. Particularly, they have not taken into account the historical and intellectual continuity and parallels between the Synagogue and the Church, continuity which the Fathers frequently acknowledged. Historians of the Jewish people have pointed out the liturgical, administrative, and juristic analogies—even affinities—which persisted between the New Israel and the Old into the fifth century.

Ecclesiastical historians, however, have been slow to prosecute this line of enquiry; and they have in practice treated the Church *quā* corporation as beginning anew with the conversion of Constantine, striking out in uncharted ways to find a *modus vivendi* with the civil power. This has also been the argument of legal historians, even of Gierke. Seeing analogies

* This essay reviews the background of some ecclesiological positions which came to importance in Western thought through St. Augustine's *City of God* and the later works of mediaeval Latin authors on the relations of ecclesiastical and civil powers. Consequently, it does not consider the works of the Cappadocian Fathers, which were ultimately less influential in the West than were the writings of Athanasius as known in Latin translation and as reflected in the works of St. Hilary. See G. B. Ladner, *The Idea of Reform* (Harvard, 1959), p. 132, and *passim.* On the Cappadocians, see F. Bauer, *Des heiligen Johannes Chrysostomus Lehre über den Staat und die Kirche und ihr gegenseitiges Verhältnis,* Diss. Vienna, 1946. R. E. Carter, "Saint John Chrysostom's Rhetorical Use of the Socratic Distinction Between Kingship and Tyranny," *Traditio* **14** (1958): 367–371. G. F. Reilly, *Imperium and Sacerdotium According to St. Basil the Great* (Washington, 1945). S. Verosta, *Johannes Chrysostomus, Staatsphilosoph und Geschichtstheologe* (Vienna, 1960). L. Welserheimb, "Das Kirchenbild

der griechischen Väterkommentare zum Hohen Lied," *Zeitschrift für Katholische Theologie* **70** (1948): 393–449. I hope to discuss the political thought of the Greek Fathers in a later essay. I acknowledge with pleasant memories an indebtedness to my colleagues at the University of Minnesota, Professors Robert F. Berkhofer, Jr., Ralph E. Giesey, and Darrett B. Rutman; for the present study is the outcome of many enlightening and spirited discussions with those gentlemen, particularly with Professor Giesey. I am also under a heavy obligation to Professor Josef L. Altholz, of the University of Minnesota, for his kindness and patience in revising the initial draft. Professor Stephan Kuttner, of the Catholic University of America, Monsignor Thomas Shannahan, of St. Paul's Seminary, St. Paul, Minnesota, and the Interlibrary Loan Division of the University of Minnesota all gave very generous assistance to me in securing research materials not accessible at the University of Minnesota, and I am glad of this opportunity to thank them for their help.

between Roman municipal administrative order and the Church's local administration, they have ignored the exact parallels in the Synagogue from which the Church historically evolved, and judged that Rome set the pattern for the Church's development. The origin of the Church in their eyes is pagan Rome, not Jerusalem. This attitude denies the early Church a heritage which the Fathers themselves vigorously claimed; it separates the Church from the ground of its institutional development, and from the context within which its juristic attitudes toward the Empire evolved.

The Church is old enough to be regarded as an institution which has shared with other institutions the phenomenon of growth; it is great enough to bear statements of historical truth. When the Fathers claimed for the Church the integrity of her laws and juridical apparatus in the face of encroachments by the civil power, they followed a pattern set by the Synagogue, from which also ecclesiastical doctrines and order principally derived. Like the priestly tribe of the Old Dispensation, the Fathers strove to give legal reality to the realm of the "Lord God, King of the Universe."

This separatist doctrine, originating in the laws of the Synagogue, was strengthened by repeated persecution; the Nicene Fathers and their immediate successors, many of whom bore scars from the harrying under Diocletian, steadfastly witnessed it. It was the great Hosius, adviser to Constantine, president of the Nicene Council, and himself a confessor, who wrote to Constantius II towards the middle of the century that he must content himself with the government of the Empire and leave that of the Church to bishops. The Church continued to preserve its status as an *iso-politeia* in religious matters. To be sure, the Church and the Empire came ever closer in the course of the fourth century, but the imperial powers by which they were approximated were those of Roman law, morally neutral, flexible, directed by the will of the emperor. In the light of theology and institutional development, the Fathers considered these powers totally alien to the Church, which was perfectly good, eternal, unchangeable, and which was governed by immutable laws. Imperial favor was to the Church's good. Still, the Fathers knew that that favor depended entirely upon the will of the particular emperor, and that the Empire could, by the exercise of the same legal powers, either persecute or succour the Church.

For their part, most fourth-century emperors acknowledged the dualistic position of the Fathers in their formal actions. Within a society which recognizes both the Church and the civil government as having legal and moral authority, the two institutions may be correlated in one of three ways: they may exist distinguished but not separated one from the other; they may co-exist in total separation; or they may be commingled. The possibility of any of these relationships between Church and Empire, the possibility

of conflict and correlation, first became real under Constantine, but it was not clearly formulated until much later in the fourth century, under Constantius II and his successors. This was a problem which could obtain only when Church and Empire, as institutions, recognized that each other had legal existence and powers and exercised moral authority. Before the time of Constantine, the Church had acknowledged the existence of the Empire as a legal institution, and according to Scriptural admonitions, it had prayed for the welfare of the civil power and submitted to its acts of force. At the same time, it had, particularly in time of persecution, denied the Empire supreme moral authority over believers. For its part, the Empire had not acknowledged either the legal existence or the moral authority of the Church prior to Constantine. Consequently, before the fourth century, and especially under persecution, the Church and the Empire existed as absolutely discrete institutions, and there was no common ground of acknowledgment on which conflicts over jurisdiction could occur. The persecuted Church enjoyed perfect freedom in its doctrinal formulations and juridical functions because Roman denied it legal existence.

By his laws, Constantine granted the Church legal recognition and in some measure guaranteed the independence it had earlier enjoyed. But in his time, the problem of Church-Empire relations was by no means completely defined. The chief question which determined the course of later Church-Empire relations was only generally apparent under Constantine, for it was not clear whether an alien religion—"alien" because its own laws and juristic apparatus derived from non-Roman institutions—accepted as the Roman State religion should be governed by Roman precedent: that is, whether the Church, as the successor of State paganism, should be governed by the same *ius publicum* which governed its predecessor.

The problem of institutional relationships became distinct only when this question was affirmatively answered, when Christianity came to be considered the State religion, and when an effort was made to subject the Church to government by the civil authority. The crisis was reached when the Empire undertook to secure the Church's definition of a particular creed as "orthodox" and to gain the universal acceptance of that creed, rejecting broad and general toleration in favor of a policy of narrow exclusiveness. With this crisis came the doctrine of Caesaropapism, but this doctrine could obtain only in a militantly Christian Empire, not in a pagan one. Its founder was Theodosius, "the son of the Church," not Constantine, the *pontifex maximus*.

Certainly, true Caesaropapism cannot be averred before Christianity was the State cult: that is, before Gratian rejected the title *"pontifex maximus,"* and, more exactly, before Theodosius I issued the edict *"Cunctos populos,"* requiring universal adherence to

Christian orthodoxy throughout the Empire. For Caesaropapism involved not only the affirmation that the emperor possessed certain powers in sacred affairs, but also the formal acknowledgment of that tenure by the Church. As long as the Emperor was not a Christian, the Church could not grant that acknowledgment to him as an individual; as long as a non-Christian might come to the throne, it could not grant it to the imperial office.

The problem of institutional relationships did not become clear, therefore, under Constantine. For the Empire remained pagan and the Emperor was only quasi-Christian; Constantine continued to hold the title and to discharge the functions of the *pontifex maximus,* and to countenance—even to foster by public grants—pagan institutions and practices. To be sure, he appears to have followed a policy of less broad toleration towards paganism in his later years; but the effects of this manifested themselves in the East, not in the West, and the policy was implemented only in particular cases, and not as a general regulation. Constantine's policy was so ambiguous that at his death he received the pagan honor of apotheosis from a pagan Rome.

The exclusive policy toward which Constantine may have tended, but which he did not implement, was first projected in earnest by Constantius II, Constantine's son. Constantius legislated against pagan practices, threatened to withdraw the civil privileges of pagans in Alexandria, and removed the Altar of Victory from the Roman Senate House. He intervened forcibly in ecclesiastical affairs and attempted to direct episcopal adjudication, to dictate the "canon" of Church order, and to compel the Church's universal acceptance of the creed he himself favored. It seems possible that, to his mind, Christianity, his religion, was *de facto,* though not *de iure,* the State cult; and the problem of defining imperial powers in Church affairs, the problem we have just mentioned, became distinct in his day. Still, the ancient Roman cults were in fact and in law the State religion; Constantius, like his father, discharged his duties as the *pontifex maximus,* the head of the State paganism; he did not implement the exclusive policy he threatened.

He had presented the problem, however, and under Constantius's successors, thought concerning the institutional relations of Church and Empire followed two major courses. From the classical premise that the State and the State religion were distinct, but not separate, some persons, particularly the Fathers, departed very widely, affirming that the two must be fundamentally separate when the State religion was Christianity. Others went beyond the classic proposition and developed the doctrine now called Caesaropapism. The separatist position was constant throughout the fourth century, and consequently it appears far more strongly than the second in ecclesias-

tical writings of that period. The second was not continuous, and indeed, one should entertain grave doubts as to whether it actually existed before the fifth century.

Some of the elements of Caesaropapism were surely present under Constantine. That is, Hellenistic concepts such as those of the emperor as "living law," as the representative of God with whom he had direct communication, and as the image of God still enjoyed great vigor, and many of them appear in the works of contemporary Christian authors. The panegyric of Eusebius on Constantine's tricennalia is a well-known and extreme example of the court literature which embodied these concepts.

Even in Eusebius's works such expressions lack predominantly Christian content. When, for example, he wrote that the Roman Empire was "the imitation of the monarchical power in heaven" and that "the Emperor is one, the image of the one all-imperial God," [1] he was borrowing conventional pagan rhetorical devices. And when, in describing Constantine's feast at the conclusion of the Council of Nicaea, he wrote more explicitly that those who beheld the imperial court felt as though they were beholding an image of the Kingdom of Christ, he was also careful to qualify his remark by saying that the sight was like a dream, and not reality. The Christomimesis of this statement is clearly the Theomimesis of the other two, somewhat Christianized owing to the specifically ecclesiastical nature of the Council and, perhaps, to the principal question it considered: the Arian Christology. In the pagan Empire it had been natural for the emperor, most of whose predecessors had been deified after their deaths, and who himself would probably receive that honor in due time, to receive quasi-divine honors. So too, the first "Christian" Emperor, continuing conventional court ceremonial, could well be called the "friend" or "image" of God, the Pambasileus, without imbuing such rhetorical devices with meaning which would make him the authentic representative of God in the Church. Constantine ruled a pagan Empire, which reverenced many of his predecessors as gods and which granted him also the pagan honor of apotheosis after his death. The ideological and institutional fusion between Church and Empire which would have transmuted Hellenistic into Christian attributions of imperial divinity, which would have changed the pagan form into Caesaropapism, had not occurred by the time of Constantine's death.

There is, in fact, very little evidence that Constantine sought to assume the absolute constitutional

---

[1] De Laud. Const., cc. 5, 7 (Migne, *Patrologia Graeca* **20**: 1336, 1357). On this material see K. M. Setton, *Christian Attitude Towards the Emperor in the Fourth Century* (Columbia, 1941), p. 17 ff. In general, translations from Greek authors have been taken from the *Library of Nicene and Post-Nicene Fathers.*

headship of the Church. It is true that there are two statements in the *Vita Constantini* which indicate the opposite: The *Vita* records that the Emperor himself claimed to be "bishop of those outside"—a text which some scholars have extended to read "bishop of those outside the Church," and which others have interpreted as asserting dominance over the Church itself—and it also comments that "he watched over all his subjects with an episcopal care." [2] But this biography was written after Constantine's death—Seston has proposed that it was actually composed toward the end of the fourth century, very considerably after he died—and scholars have disputed the authorship of Eusebius, which would in some measure authenticate the "imperial episcopate" as truly Constantinian. In any event, the meaning of the passages is not clear; and it is possible that the author meant only to describe an analogy in respect of the etymology of the word "episcopos," an analogy between the consecrated bishops and the Emperor Constantine, the careful overseer of his people. This same analogy appears when Constantine addresses the bishops as "brethren" and "fellow-servants," without claiming either the sacramental powers of the priest or episcopal authority in ecclesiastical government.

In his juridical actions, Constantine scrupulously avoided usurping episcopal authority. Although he summoned synods, he never summoned them arbitrarily, but always at the petition of the clergy for the decision of specific ecclesiastical problems. Even when he attended ecclesiastical assemblies, such as the Council of Nicaea, he allowed the clergy complete freedom to debate and to formulate doctrinal judgments. So far was he from doctrinal pronouncements on his own authority, that whenever doctrine assumed juridical importance (as at times it did in the several stages of the process against Arius), he referred the question to his episcopal advisers or to a full synod. He confirmed and sanctioned the decrees of some synods, but he did not frame them or give them validity in the ecclesiastical context: civil confirmation had only civil effect. Finally, he never presumed to judge the person of a bishop in a matter of faith. He maintained, and the Fathers acknowledged, that in criminal cases, even bishops must be tried by the imperial court. When Constantine dismissed the charges against Athanasius at Psamathia and those against Caecilian at Milan, he sat in judgment over bishops; but the charges which he reviewed were *"crimina,"* civil crimes—murder and rebellion—and not matters of spiritual jurisdiction. His refusal at Nicaea to judge bishops accused of heresy clearly indicates his policy.

Constantine claimed, therefore, the offices of defending and propagating the Faith, but not that of governing it. In his letters and edicts, he strongly and frequently stated his concern to heal schisms and to restore the unity of the Church as an acceptable sacrifice to God, a sacrifice which would bring reciprocally the welfare of the Empire and of the Emperor. But in the characteristic imperial office of legislation, just as in that of adjudication, Constantine took care to preserve the juridical integrity of the Church, and especially to guarantee the legitimacy of episcopal judgment in matters of faith.

Thus, Constantine did not act, or aspire to act, as the earthly head of the Church. In his time, the Hellenistic rhetorical devices which exalted him as quasi-divine entered the vocabulary of Christian courtiers, but they had not yet assumed the explicitly Christian connotations which would later adorn genuine Caesaropapistic thought. Constantine himself limited his actions *vis-à-vis* the Church according to the still pagan character of the Empire and to the precedents of Roman law.

When, under Constantine, Church and Empire acknowledged each other as legal and independent institutions, the potentiality for conflict between them was present. The first crisis in their constitutional relationship came under Constantius II, Constantine's son and successor, and it derived precisely from Constantius's attempt to assume the ecclesiastical headship in law which his father had disclaimed. Lucifer of Cagliari charges that he claimed to be superior to bishops, even bishop of bishops, and that he wished to subject the Church to his royal (or imperial) control. And, as we shall see, the protests of other churchmen against the Emperor's methods center upon his efforts to assert civil authority over the Church.

Yet, the basis of this attempted union was not Caesaropapistic; it rather derived from the relations of the emperor to the State cult in classical Roman law. It is very "probable that, for Constantius, God was the Supreme God without distinctively Christian attributes. That Christ was like God, *homoios,* was the most that he could understand and personally accept. But after all, he too, as an emperor, was in the process of becoming or acting like God, *homoiōsis.*" [3] For him, as for Constantine, the Hellenistic attributes of divinity to the Emperor were not thoroughly Christianized. But unlike his father, he did not consider Christianity an alien cult, and he made it his goal to subject the Church to the same constitutional rule to which State paganism was subjected, without formally supplanting paganism with Christianity as the State religion. The Church was to be under the *ius publicum,* and thus

2 Vita Constantini, IV, 24 (Migne, *Patrologia Graeca* 20: 1172). See W. Seston, "Constantine as a 'Bishop,'" *Journal of Roman Studies* 37 (1947) : 127–131.

3 G. H. Williams, "Christology and Church-State Relations in the Fourth Century," *Church History* 20 (1951), 3: 23. See the extensive critique of Williams's interpretation by P. Beskow, *Rex Gloriae. The Kingship of Christ in the Early Church* (Stockholm, 1962), pp. 315 ff.

under the administration of the emperor. While he preserved the form of juridical freedom for the Church, he used his authority to vitiate the reality of that freedom, and to supersede the old relationship of separatism between Church and Empire with the relationship of distinction, but not separation, which existed between the Empire and State paganism.

He had taken the first step toward the stage where the two institutions would be commingled, and where Hellenistic concepts concerning divine kingship would become Caesaropapism. But the Fathers protested his abuse of the Church's liberties and institutions, which were derived, not from Rome, but from the Synagogue and from theological necessity, and they maintained that he had exceeded the legitimate powers of his office. Shaped in Judaic practice and hardened under persecution, their thought admitted no concept of Church-Empire relations other than that of true separation. And Hilary of Poitiers went so far as to denounce Constantius for enslaving the Church, and

to yearn for the time of the ancient persecutors, Nero and Decius, when torture and death led to freedom.[4]

In the following chapters, we shall examine the constitutional and theological principles which ultimately brought Constantius and the Fathers into opposition, sketching the spheres of legal competence claimed by Church and Empire in their common dealings, and indicating the judgments of three Fathers, SS. Athanasius, Hilary, and Ambrose, upon the juridical relations between Rome and the Church as the City of God. We shall be discussing primarily a legal fiction: the spiritual Kingdom of Christ. Legal fictions are real facts; and after Nicaea, the Fathers strove to secure absolute recognition of this fiction in the imperial courts. Thus, Rome would acknowledge juristically the integrity and independence which the Church claimed for its sacramental government; and civil law would satisfy the demands of theology.

4 Contra Constantium, c. 4 (Migne, *Patrologia Latina* 10: 580 f).

I

PART I

LEGAL PRINCIPLES

1. CIVITAS DEI

Conscious that the Church of their age was morally and constitutionally alien to the Empire, the Fathers demanded that its independence from Roman jurisdiction in matters of faith and inner discipline be confirmed by civil law. The first of their legal principles was that the Church was an integral juridical body, and they required the temporal power to adopt and enforce the premise that the City of God was a true and spiritually autonomous polity. The legal fiction of the City of God was conventional in patristic thought by the fourth century. When they wrote of the Church as the *"gens sancta,"* the *"populus electus,"* the *"civitas sacerdotalis et regia,"* or, simply, the *"civitas Dei,"* [1] the Fathers did more than use pious

[1] *Cf.* the judgment of Pope Leo I (Sermo 82, c. 1. Migne, *Patrologia Latina* **54**: 422 f) : "Isti sunt [sancti Patres] qui te ad hanc gloriam provexerunt, ut gens sancta, populus electus, civitas sacerdotalis et regia per sacram beati Petri sedem caput orbis effecta, latius praesideres religione divina quam dominatione terrena." Salin explicitly denied the juristic content of these terms. See E. Salin, *Civitas Dei* (Tübingen, 1926), pp. V, 68, and his judgment is shared by Zeiller, who maintains that "the kingdom of God" was a purely mystical concept for the Fathers (J. Zeiller, "Le royaume de Dieu et l'unité terrestre aux premiers siècles du christianisme," *Revue Apologètique* **64** (1937) : 515 and *passim*). Enquiring into the conceptual background of St. Augustine's *City of God,* Leisegang also emphasized that Father's debt to Manichaeism and Neo-platonism without commenting upon the juristic reality of his image (H. Leisegang, "Der Ursprung der Lehre Augustins von der Civitas Dei," *Archiv für Kulturgeschichte* **16** (1926) : 127 ff, 136, 152). Other scholars, however, have stressed the legal aspects of the problem without referring to the theological ones. For example, A. Beck, *Römisches Recht bei Tertullian und Cyprian* (Halle, 1930), pp. 133, 141, 151, has shown that the concept of the Church as a polity was quite fully developed in the time of Tertullian and Cyprian, and F. Leifer ("Christentum und römisches Recht seit Constantin," *Zeitschrift für Rechtsgeschichte*, Röm. Abt.,**58** (1938) : 187), and A. Ehrhardt ("Constantins des Grossen Religionspolitik und Gesetzgebung," *Zeitschrift für Rechtsgeschichte*, Röm. Abt., **72** (1955) : 147, 179) have discussed the effects of Constantine's religious policy upon the Church as an institution. They have tended, however, to consider Constantine the creator of the Church as a polity, rather than the fosterer of an already existing institution. One must also mention Ehrhard's theory—so relevant to the image of the Church as a "city"—that the government of the early Church developed precisely upon the pattern of the Roman *municipium* ("Das Corpus Christi und die Korporationen im spätrömischen Recht," *Zeitschrift für Rechtsgeschichte*, Röm. Abt., **70** (1953) : 304, and **71** (1954) : 34, 39) : "So entwickelte sich die Rechtsfähigkeit der Bishöfsgemeinde nach dem Vorbild der antiken Polis"). The perspective of this view is, however, distorted by leaving out of account the Church's Jewish heritage and the influence of theology upon the political thought of the Fathers; for the hierarchy of the Church first evolved from the hierarchy of the Synagogue, not

rhetorical images; they observed what was for them a juristic reality. The concepts *"gens," "populus,"* and *"civitas,"* were familiar in Roman law as legal corporations which, by virtue of their separate ethnic or national character, were entitled to live according to their own laws and customs so long as their practices did not impede Roman interests, the *"utilitas publica."* The Fathers argued that the Church was such a corporation, governed by its peculiar laws and coexisting as an *isopoliteia* with the Roman Empire.

They claimed sole jurisdiction over the faithful in religious matters, and they particularly maintained that the definition of the Faith and the trial of religious charges against bishops fell wholly within the legal competence of the Church. The warrant for this claim lay in the theological construct of the Kingdom of Christ, which removed matters of faith from the judgment of nonbelievers. Constantine the Great and his successors tended to acknowledge the legal fiction and to admit it into Roman jurisprudence. This tendency was at times very weak, as under Julian the Apostate; it was dangerously jeopardized by Constantius II; and it did not produce full and permanent guarantes of ecclesiastical jurisdiction until the reigns of Gratian and Theodosius I.

Still, it was always present, and the usual practice of fourth-century emperors was to disclaim jurisdiction in religious matters, referring them to the proper ecclesiastical courts. As early as the third century, Aurelian remanded the case of property ownership in the church of Samosata to the "Italian prelates of the Christian religion and the Roman bishop." [2] And, after Licinius had attempted to destroy the Church's juridical structure by prohibiting synodal assemblies,[3] Constantine restored it in full force. He was concerned that the Church enjoy undisturbed its "own

from Roman civic government. Likewise without any reference to Jewish religious practices, Ehrhardt describes as a precedent for the Church's liturgical baptism the oath of fidelity toward the emperor taken by the Roman legions. A. Ehrhardt, "Christian Baptism and Roman Law," *Festschrift Guido Kisch* (Stuttgart, 1955), esp. p. 162 f. The tendency to discount Judaic influence in the institutional development of the Church, or to pass over it in silence, and to begin the constitutional history of the Church in the age of Constantine is common. For further examples of this treatment, see C. Boucaud, *Pax Romana* (Paris, 1930), **1** : p. 118 and *passim*, and R. M. Honig, "The Nicene Faith and the Legislation of the Early Byzantine Emperors," *Anglican Theological Review* **25** (1943) : 304 ff.

[2] Eusebius, Historia Ecclesiastica, VII, 30 (Migne, *Patrologia Graeca* **20** : 719).

[3] Vita Constantini I, 51 (Migne, *Patrologia Graeca* **20** : 966).

8

law";[4] and, when the Donatists appealed to him from the proper ecclesiastical court, he expressed very considerable vexation:

> They seek worldly things, casting aside heavenly. O mad boldness of insanity! They have interposed an appeal, as is the custom in the cases of Gentiles. Thus are the nations accustomed sometimes to flee minor jurisdiction, where justice can be had quickly, and to betake themselves by appeal, through interposed authority, to greater jurisdiction. What do these detractors of the law think of Christ, the Saviour, when they reject the heavenly judgment meaning to implore mine?[5]

There is much to support the contention that the words Rufinus attributes to him during the Council of Nicaea accurately state his legal attitude toward the Church and the episcopacy. Given written charges against bishops, the Emperor caused the petitions to be burned, saying:

> God has established you bishops and has given you power of judging us; thus are we rightly judged by you. But you cannot be judged by men. Wherefore, look for the judgment of God among yourselves, and let your disputes, whatever they are, be reserved to that divine review.[6]

Even Constantius II, in his most extreme actions, did not assume for himself the prerogative of judging bishops or deciding matters of faith; he rather followed the letter of the canons, however much he perverted their spirit. His successors, including Julian the Apostate, also continued to acknowledge the separate legal order of the Church. Valentinian I, for example, declared that, as a layman, he could not judge priests, and issued an edict reserving the judgment of priests (or bishops) to the priesthood.[7] Valentinian's son, Gratian, removed ecclesiastical matters entirely from civil jurisdiction.[8] Sacred matters and, in religious affairs, those who judged of sacred matters were to be judged according to the peculiar law of the Church and by the authorities which that law prescribed.

The analogy of all this to the relationship between Jewish and Roman courts is exact and allows one to surmise that Rome's legal attitude toward Christians may have derived historically from her attitude to-

ward the Jews, or at least that the same principle held in the two cases: namely, that they were discrete nations, or peoples, entitled to the full enjoyment of their laws and customs so long as the exercise of this right did not conflict with the *"utilitas publica."* Significantly, even in the later years of the fourth century, when the imperial government imposed new and increasingly restrictive measures upon the peculiar rights of the Jewish community, it honored the right to decide religious matters according to Hebraic law. "Let all Jews," reads the interpretation of an edict issued by Arcadius and Honorius,

> who are known to be Romans, carry before the elders of their religion only what pertains to the discipline of their religion, in such a way that they may preserve among themselves the establishments of Hebrew laws.

All other matters which pertained to Roman law must, the Emperors decreed, be decided by imperial judges according to that law.[9]

The words of St. Augustine are, in this context, most instructive. He praises Christ, the eternal King, and writes that the Jews, though themselves resisting the truth, have carried witness to it throughout the world.

> O glory of our King! Rightly were the Jews conquered by the Romans, but not destroyed. All nations (*gentes*) subjected by the Romans went over to the laws (*jura*) of the Romans: this nation (*gens*) was both conquered and remained in its own law (*lege*) preserving, in as much as pertains to the cult of God, ancestral customs and ritual (*patrias consuetudines ritumque*). Even though their temple has been cast down and the early priesthood extinguished, as the prophets had said, the Jews still preserve the circumcision and the certain custom by which they are distinguished from other nations. Wherefore this, unless because of their testimony to the truth?[10]

In patristic writings of the fourth century, no theme is more persistent than that her laws and customs must be preserved to the *gens sancta,* the Church. For, in exact parallel to Jewish practice, the Church had her *patriae consuetudines,* Apostolic tradition, and her law, the Scripture and the canons; like the Synagogue, she claimed that these customs and this law, which reserved the adjudication of sacred matters to religious courts, must be honored and protected by the civil power.

I

The imperial attitude toward the Church—and, indeed, the concept of the Church held by the Fathers themselves—was certainly influenced very heavily by the Jewish origin of the Church and by the continued Hebraic influence in its religious and social practices. Of course, the historical connection between Church and Synagogue was precise, and St. Paul spoke not only for himself but for many others when he wrote, "I say then, hath God cast away his people? God

---

[4] Constantine, Ep. 2 ad Anulinum (Migne, *Patrologia Latina* 8: 481).

[5] Constantine, "Aeterna, religiosa et incomprehensibilis," (Migne, *Patrologia Latina* 8: 488).

[6] Rufinus, Historia Ecclesiastica, X, 2 (In E. Schwartz, ed., *Eusebius Werke* (Berlin, 1906): 2, 2, p. 961).

[7] Ambrose, Ep. 21, 2 (Migne, *Patrologia Latina* 16: 1005). *Cf.* Cod. Th. XVI, 2, 12, an edict of Constantius II and Constans (355): "Mansuetudinis nostrae lege prohibemus in iudiciis episcopos accusari. . . . Si quid est igitur querellarum, quod quispiam defert, apud alios potissimum episcopos convenit explorari, ut opportuna adque commoda cunctorum quaestionibus audientia commodetur."

[8] Mansi, *Collectio Conciliorum* 3: 626: "Judiciis publicis . . . quibus sacerdotale caput lex vestra summovit." After making this statement, the members of the Roman synod (382) continued to acknowledge certain instances in which the Bishop of Rome might appear before the Emperor for judgment.

[9] Cod. Th. II, 1, 10 int.

[10] Sermo 374 (Migne, *Patrologia Latina* 39: 1667).

I

10

forbid. For I also am an Israelite, of the seed of Abraham, of the tribe of Benjamin" (Romans 11:1). In the post-apostolic period, authors like St. Ignatius of Antioch continued to emphasize this connection claiming that the Israelite prophets had lived in accordance with the principles Jesus was later to teach in His ministry. They claimed the patriarchs and Moses as forefathers of the Christian community, and called themselves "Jews" and "Israelites" in observance of their religious heritage. St. John Chrysostom records at the end of the fourth century that Christians were still going to law and praying in synagogues;[11] the Marcionites called their churches "synagogues"[12] and observed the Jewish Sabbath; many Christians observed Easter on the Jewish Passover;[13] and it was not uncommon for Christians to be buried in Jewish cemeteries.[14] The comments of Julian the Apostate in this regard are important, as they illustrate the attitude of a reigning emperor, educated at a Christian court, toward the two religious groups. He observed that

. . . the Galilaeans say that, though they are different from the Jews, they are still, precisely speaking, Israelites in accordance with their prophets, and that they obey Moses above all and the prophets who in Judaea succeeded him . . . .[15]

While he strongly condemns the "Galilaeans" for rejecting the more cultivated practices of "Hellenism," Julian's major charge is that the Christians had "gone

---

[11] Adv. Iud. IV, 7 (Migne, Patrologia Graeca 48: 881).
[12] L. Duchesne, Early History of the Christian Church (London, 1922) 2: p. 514, n. 1.
[13] Below, note 38.
[14] For a discussion of the conscious perpetuation of Jewish practices by Christians see S. W. Baron, A Social and Religious History of the Jews (2d ed., New York, 1952) 2, 2: p. 188; M. Simon, Verus Israël (Paris, 1948), passim; and W. H. C. Frend, "The Gnostic Sects and the Roman Empire," Journal of Ecclesiastical History 5 (1954) : 25–37. Simon himself states that his study was written to redress in part—or rather, to protest against—the "antisémitisme raciste" of the 1940's, and his approach is, in general, apologetic. He does not consider the effect of the legal relationship between Empire and Synagogue upon that of Empire and Church (see p. 125), and he regularly cites sources from the first five centuries of our era as though they were exactly contemporary, without regard for differences in meaning and in historical context. His treatment of the ideological affinity of the Church and the Synagogue, however, is excellent, and he interprets quite accurately the patristic sentiment when he writes: "L'Ancien Testament en effet, pour qui sait le lire, relate l'histoire non pas du peuple juif, mais de l'Eglise, préexistante au même titre que son chef, réalité spirituelle dont Israël selon la chair n'a jamais été que la grossière enveloppe. . . . Ainsi, Eglise et Israël sont synonymes, christianisme et judaïsme authentique se confondent" (p 104). See also pp. 91, 102 f., 118, and 120 ff.
[15] Against the Galilaeans, 253B, ed. W. C. Wright, The Works of the Emperor Julian (London, 1923) 3: p. 392. Modern scholars have tended to ignore the fact that Julian was thoroughly disciplined in Christian doctrine by Eusebius of Nicomedia, and consequently to discount the evidence he offers concerning Christian attitudes.

over to the corpse of the Jew [i.e., Christ]," [16] that preferring the Jewish belief to the pagan, they had "transgressed their own law," [17] abandoned the religion of their forefathers, and given themselves over to the predictions of the prophets.[18] In short, they were to his mind an errant Jewish sect.

The connection between the Church and the Synagogue was more than a matter of record in the fourth century, for the debt of Christians to Jewish institutions and practices in the most critical religious matters was clear and immediate. For example, the organization of the clergy was strikingly similar in the two groups. Excluding the exegetes, who were not properly members of the Jewish hierarchy, the Synagogue clergy consisted of the "archisynagogus" (perhaps equivalent to the Rabbi), priests, sacristans, lectors, and translators. The duty of the translators, to render Scriptural readings into the vernacular for the benefit of those who had no Hebrew, was unnecessary in Christian churches, but the other offices were perfectly familiar and usual in the "new Israel." The archisynagogus was the overseer of the community, who gave religious instruction to his people and superintended the Divine Service and the material affairs of the Synagogue. With the destruction of the Temple, the priests lost their sacrificial functions, at the same time preserving the name of the priesthood, and the power to bless. Their principal duty was seeing to the collection of tithes. The sacristan preserved order in the Synagogue and executed corporeal punishments imposed by the Jewish court. Finally, the lector read from the Scriptures during the Divine Service.[19] The comment of St. Ambrose upon Ephesians 4:11, 12 establishes the striking analogy between the archisynagogus and the bishop, who supervised all aspects of the particular church's life; between the Jewish priests, in their material duties, and Christian deacons; between the synagogue readers and the ecclesiastical lectors; and between the sacristans and the magistri, the officers who restrained and beat those who were noisy in the Church, "sive ii qui litteris et lectionibus imbuendos infantes solebant imbuere, sicut mos Iudaeorum est, quorum traditio ad nos transitum fecit, quae per negligentiam obsolevit." [20]

---

[16] Ibid., 197C, p. 372.
[17] Ep. 47, 432D, ibid., p. 142.
[18] Against the Galileans, 238B, ibid., p. 388. See, for example, G. Downey, "Julian and Justinian and the Unity of Faith and Culture," Church History 28 (1959) : 339–349, and F. Dvornik, "The Emperor Julian's Reactionary Ideas on Kingship," Studies in Honor of A. M. Friend, Jr. (Princeton, 1955), p. 78.
[19] See J. Juster, Les Juifs dans l'Empire romain (Paris, 1914) 1: pp. 450–456.
[20] Migne, Patrologia Latina 17: 387. Cf. the comment of J. Schmitt, "Sacerdoce judaïque et hierarchie écclesiale dans les premières communautés palestiniennes," Revue des sciences religieuses 29 (1955) : 250: "Le sacerdoce lévitique fut l'âme de la théocratie juive restaurée après l'Exil: dès la fin du siècle apostolique une valuer parallèle de sens ainsi que de nom, le sacerdoce chrètien apparaît comme le fondement de la nouvelle

I

Equally important was the conciliar organization which prevailed in both communities. The actual governance of the Synagogue lay with a council of elders (*presbyteroi*), over which in most instances the archisynagogus presided. This council superintended the financial affairs of the Synagogue, judged on membership in it, adjudicated disputes among Jews, and represented the interests of the religious group before civil authorities.[21] The analogy between this order and that of the bishop presiding in his council of presbyters—which St. Ambrose acknowledged explicitly as a borrowing from the Synagogue[22]—is obvious and needs no elaboration. By way of emphasis, however, it may be added that just as the Jewish councils judged local religious disputes and expelled the heretical, acting as "autocephalous" courts, so did the Christian bishops and their presbyters judge doctrinal disputes locally, as self-sufficient corporations.[23]

On another level, the orders of communal worship in the two communities were closely related. Readings from the Scriptures, followed by sermons occur in both services, and in both the sermons were most often used to explain the content of the readings in their relation to the circumstances of the particular day, if it were a feast day, or in a more general moral context, on ordinary days. As we know them, the sermons in the Church, like those in the Synagogue, tended to be Scriptural exegeses. More important was the concept of sacrifice and oblation which marks the two orders so strongly and characteristically, a similarity which caused St. Jerome in a typically wrathful denunciation to declare that, though the Jews might believe they were offering oblations to God, God in fact hated and rejected their religious observances because they denied Christ, while, on the other hand, He received the offerings of the Church, which confessed the Father, the Son, and the Holy Spirit.[24] From

its Hebrew heritage, the Church took prayers, liturgy and liturgical music, the hours of prayer, and feast days—in short, the basic apparatus of its ritual.

The Church, therefore, shared—albeit in modified form—the jurisdictional structure and the religious character which distinguished the Jews as a nation apart. It also shared those attitudes toward the Roman Empire which sharpened that distinction into absolute moral separation. For Church and Synagogue, the only significant community was the community of believers, sacramentally expressed in Christian terms as the "communion of believers." The Law of God governed this community. The Law was in every regard superior to the law of man; and the community was part of a wider community of which God was the ruler. Christian and Jewish exegetes similarly interpreted two famous visions in the Book of Daniel, the one a dream of Nebuchadnezzar, the other a dream of Daniel himself. In the King's dream appeared a statue whose parts, in descending order from the head downward, were made of gold, silver, bronze, iron, and iron mixed with clay. It was destroyed suddenly by a great stone which grew until it filled the whole world. Daniel interpreted the dream as referring to four great kingdoms destroyed and succeeded by a fifth, which would itself stand forever. The second vision expresses the same eschatological concept. Four beasts appear in succession, and they are followed by "one like the Son of man," to whom. "was given dominion and glory, and a kingdom, that all people, nations, and languages, should serve him. His dominion is an everlasting dominion which shall not pass away, and his kingdom that which shall not be destroyed" (Daniel 2:31–45, 7:1–14). These visions originated in the middle of the second century B.C., when the Jewish kingdom was defending its existence against the Seleucids.[25] They state allegorically the enmity of the Jews against those who would enslave them; and when Palestine fell to the Romans, this significance was transferred to the new "oppressor." Rome was the "kingdom of wickedness," and exegetes glossed the apocalyptic texts to proclaim the ultimate victory of Adonai and "the ultimate Jewish victory over Rome—not through Rome—in the messianic age and the eternity of the Jewish people." [26]

---

communauté culturelle, l'Eglise. Entre ces deux institutions, et malgré leurs différences par bien des côtés essentielles, la continuité ou plus exactement la progression s'avère certaine: le sacerdoce ecclésial est à vrai dire la replique spiritualisée et sublimée, en d'autres termes l'achèvement eschatologique du sacerdoce juif." See A. Guillaume, "Is Episcopacy a Jewish Institution? *Bulletin of Oriental and African Studies* (London) 13 (1949) : 23–36. On possible relations between Jewish and Christian ordination ceremonies, see A. Ehrhardt, "Jewish and Christian Ordination," *Journal of Ecclesiastical History* 5 (1954) : 125–138, and E. Ferguson, "Jewish and Christian Ordination: Some Observations," *Harvard Theological Review* 56 (1963), 13–20.

[21] Juster, *op. cit.* 1: p. 438 ff.

[22] Below, Chapter IV, n. 37.

[23] E. Schwartz, "Die Conzilien des IV. Jahrhunderts," *Historische Zeitschrift* 104 (1909) : 1–37.

[24] Comment in Amos 5: 12 (Migne, *Patrologia Latina* 25: 1054). On the conceptual similarity between the sacrifice in the Synagogue and that in the Church, see C. W. Dugmore, "Sacrament and Sacrifice in the Early Fathers," *Journal of Ecclesiastical History* 2 (1951), 27 ff. P. Smulders ("Le mot et le concept de 'tradition' chèz les Pères grecs," *Recherches de science religieuse* 40 (1952) : 51) points out one further critical

similarity between Church and Synagogue: the authority of tradition. The posthumously published essays of Bartlett are quite sketchy on the Judaic background of Christian liturgical practices (J. V. Bartlett, ed. C. J. Cadoux, *Church Life and Church Order During the First Four Centuries* [Oxford, 1943]), but the studies by F. L. Cirlot (*The Early Eucharist* [London, 1939], p. 15 and *passim*), C. W. Dugmore (*The Influence of the Synagogue upon the Divine Office* [Oxford, 1944]), and especially F. Gavin (*The Jewish Antecedents of the Christian Sacraments* [London, 1928]) are more complete.

[25] J. W. Swain, "The Theory of the Four Monarchies: Opposition History under the Roman Empire," *Classical Philology* 35 (1940) : 1–21.

[26] Baron, *op. cit.* 2, 2: p. 153.

Christian authors from Hippolytus onwards employed the same images with generally the same construction. Rome was the last kingdom before the coming of Antichrist and the terrible sufferings of the end of all things, the last human kingdom before Christ would return in glory and establish His eternal kingdom. Like the Jews, they saw the Roman Empire as evil in itself—it was Babylon, the harlot sitting upon a beast, "the great city which had dominion over the kings of the earth" (Apoc. 17:18)—but for the Christians the Empire served one positive good: it delayed the terrors of the end of the world.

To Christian apologists, this good emphasized the obligation imposed equally upon the Jews and the Christians by Jeremiah and repeated upon Christians by St. Paul and by the author of I. Peter to pray for the benefit of their land and ruler. For, as Tertullian wrote:

There is another and a greater need for us to pray for the emperor, and, indeed, for the whole estate of the Empire and the interests of Rome. For we know that the great upheaval which hangs over the whole earth, and the very end of all things, threatening terrible woes, is only delayed by the respite granted to the Roman Empire. Because we would not experience these things, we favor Rome's long continuance when we pray that they be delayed. . . .[27]

The performance of these prayers as a sacred duty in the Christian liturgy found its precedent in Jewish practice. Although Rome did not relieve the Jews of all symbolic acts of allegiance to the emperor, it did allow them, from the time of Augustus onward, to offer sacrifices each day in the emperor's name at the temple in Jerusalem instead of sacrificing directly to the genius of the emperor. Augustus is reported to have established a subsidy for the support of this sacrifice; but, with the destruction of the Temple, the Emperor commuted this duty to prayers in the synagogues for the sake of the emperor.[28] It is important to observe that, when Galerius issued his edict of toleration for the Christians, he explicitly required this same service of them:

In return for this indulgence of ours, it will be the duty of Christians to pray to God for our recovery, for the public weal, and for their own; that the state may be preserved from danger on every side, and that they themselves may dwell safely in their homes.[29]

The performance of this conventional duty, in the Church as well as in the Synagogue, merely illustrated the religio-juristic separatism of Christians and Jews. The common historical background of the two groups, their similar constitutional and liturgical practices deriving from that background, the contempt for the Roman Empire which the two shared, their attribution of first allegiance to a higher king than Caesar and to a higher law than imperial law, and the self-identification of Christians as "Israelites," all severed Christians and Jews as one block from the main body of Roman imperial society.

For the Jews, Julius Caesar had formulated this severance in legal terms (47 B.C.), when he commanded as "Imperator and Pontifex Maximus, Dictator for the second time," that "whatever high-priestly rights or other privileges exist in accordance with their laws, these he and his children shall possess by my command. And if, during this period, any question shall arise concerning the Jews' manner of life, it is my pleasure that the decision shall rest with them." [30] Afterwards, the imperial government continued Caesar's policy that "the national customs and sacred rites" [31] should be preserved for the Jews; imperial law guaranteed "their laws and freedom." [32] Before the destruction of the Temple (A.D. 70) the Emperor followed this policy on the ethnic premise that the Jews were a discrete people or nation. During the Great Diaspora (i.e., after A.D. 70) this premise continued in force with one very important change: that is, the confession of faith became the principal distinguishing character of the Jew. The Hebrew nation as a territorial power was destroyed; it survived as a religious community, as a *religio,* which continued to exercise as a people its national laws and liberties.

In this context, the early Church developed; from it, the Church took its character as a *"civitas"* or *"gens."* The ease with which a Jew might convert to Christianity unimpeded by the initiatory requirements asked of others,[33] represents in some measure the deep affinity of the two *gentes.* For in both, the central element of union was the Faith, expressed in liturgical practices. Both peoples were scattered and had no effectual supreme government; on the other hand, both claimed the necessity of determining matters of faith among themselves according to their traditional laws and institutions. This separatism from the State in internal matters was necessary to preserve the Faith and thus to preserve the identity of the community. No outsider, no one ignorant of the Scriptures and of relevant tradition, could rightly determine questions of belief; such a person could not assume the office of the religious rulers in the communities. In

---

[27] Apologia, c. 32 (*Corpus Scriptorum Ecclesiasticorum Latinorum* 69: 81). On this obligation in the Church and in the Synagogue, see L. Biehl, *Das liturgische Gebet für Kaiser und Reich* (Paderborn, 1937), p. 25 ff.

[28] Baron, *op. cit.* 1: p. 244 f. Juster, *op. cit.* 1: p. 346 f.

[29] Lactantius, De Mortibus persecutorum c. 34 (*Corpus Scriptorum Ecclesiasticorum Latinorum* 27: 213).

[30] Josephus, Jewish Antiquities, XIV, 195, ed. R. Marcus, *Josephus* (London, 1943) 7: p. 550.

[31] *Ibid.,* XIV, 213, p. 562.

[32] *Ibid.,* XIV, 260, p. 588. The conclusion of Balanos that fourth-century Christians tended not to identify with a particular temporal nation emphasizes the similarity of attitude which existed on this point in Church and in Synagogue. D. S. Balanos, "Ekklesia kai Ethnos," *Praktika tēs Akademias Athenōn* 13 (1938): 210 f. I am indebted to Professor T. G. Stavrou for this citation.

[33] Juster, *op. cit.* 1: p. 110.

the hierarchy of both groups, orthodoxy was a qualification for office; heterodoxy, grounds for exclusion from office. For example, the title of the bishop or of the archisynagogus to direct the spiritual life of his congregation and to administer the temporal property it had ceded to the church or synagogue was conditional upon his ability to teach and to enforce true doctrine. This became particularly clear on the Christian side among the Donatists and later among the orthodox in the Arian dispute, when it was maintained that lapse from orthodoxy *ipso facto* negated the episcopal title. The purity of the Faith was consequently inseparable from the religious jurisdiction of the Church or the Synagogue; none could judge whether a bishop had deviated from the true Faith and become unworthy of his office, no one could depose him, except those who could establish the canon of faith.

Clearly, the jurisdictional system which arose from the necessity of maintaining true religious practices within the community and of assuring the orthodoxy of its leaders was virtually as critical to continuing the integral existence of the community as was the Faith itself. The existence of the *gens sancta*, like that of the Jewish nation, depended upon its power to determine and to enforce the Faith according to its own laws and within its own juridical bodies. The Empire, as we have said, recognized this necessity, and even in an age of repression allowed the Jews the right to "bring before the elders of their religion what pertains to the discipline of their religion in such a way that they may preserve among themselves the establishments of Hebrew laws" (Cod. Th. II, 1, 10 int.). But in other matters, concerning public life and regulated by Roman law, Jews who were also Roman citizens were required to submit to imperial jurisdiction. At the same time and in the same tenor, Roman law prescribed,

Whenever a case concerning religion arises, it is fitting that bishops convene; but other cases, which pertain to ordinary judges (*cognitores*) or to the use of public law, (*ius*) must be heard according to the laws (*legibus*). (Cod. Th. XVI, 11, 1.)

The new Israel had attained through its religious character and its historical connection with the Jewish kingdom, the status of a *gens*, a *populus*, a *civitas*.

II

Much of the controversial literature by the Fathers centers upon the concept of the Church as an *isopoliteia*. This is most evident during the reign of Constantius II, who attempted by force to secure universal approval of an Arian creed and to obtain the ecclesiastical deposition of orthodox bishops. The Fathers protested vehemently that the Emperor was wrongfully restricting the *"libertas"* of the Church, intruding imperial sovereignty into its constitution, and transforming it into a "civil senate" by violating its peculiar laws.

Yet, the Empire did honor the constitutional integrity of the Church at least in form. Civil officers did not define the Faith or pass judgment on bishops. For these purposes, councils met: some of them gathered in response to imperial summonses; some of them were scrupulously obedient to the imperial will; but all of them preserved at least the façade of independent jurisdiction in matters of faith and episcopal administration. Significantly, one of the heaviest charges St. Athanasius entered against Constantius II was, not that he destroyed the canons, but that he subverted them, keeping their letter, but vitiating their spirit.[34]

Two judicial activities of the fourth century illustrate most clearly the constitutional separatism of the Church and imperial respect for it: the definition of the orthodox Faith, and the trial and deposition of bishops. It is true that the emperors took a lively and personal interest in both, and that many of the synods and councils which debated these issues gathered at imperial command and under the patronage of the emperor himself or of his envoys. This intervention was invited by the Church, not imposed upon it, and the imperial action was considered as an enabling or sustaining factor, rather than a constitutive element in ecclesiastical affairs. The emperor confirmed synodal edicts; he did not frame or promulgate them. Even extreme ecclesiastical purists thought this role of the emperors entirely proper. The emperor was for the Church, as he was for the Synagogue, the executor of ecclesiastical sentences which required secular action— as for example, the expulsion of deposed bishops from their sees—and the reviewer of appeals from religious courts. In these two characters, he must know the canon of Faith so as to act justly and to uphold the liberties of the religious community, so as to distinguish the true Christian from the false, so as to determine whether the ecclesiastical court of first instance had judged fairly and whether the case might be justly reopened before another ecclesiastical court. He discharged a very necessary function in legal review, as the visible Church itself lacked one supreme and commonly acknowledged juridical head. The ecclesiastical constitution at the provincial level and below was clearly defined, at least by the time of the Council of Nicaea (325); but as yet, the greatest provincial bishops had no juridical superior. Consequently, there was no one to whom disputes involving more than one ecclesiastical province might be submitted; though it had spread throughout the Roman world, the Church did not have a supreme and comprehensive government to which it might look for definitive judgment of legal controversy. It did not acknowledge

---

[34] Historia Arianorum, c. 54 (Migne, *Patrologia Graeca* 25: 760), with more than a touch of irony: "In doing this, Constantius certainly upheld ecclesiastical canons."

the emperor as representing such a government in religious matters, but it rather saw him as having the power to refer general questions to proper and authoritative courts qualified to judge them. In this light, the imperial power supplemented the juridical organs of the Church, without itself being one of them or altering them in any way.

Historians have been inclined to judge that the role of the emperors in fourth-century synodal history was incipient Caesaropapism, and that theology and ecclesiastical institutions were twisted to serve either greater imperial interests or merely the personal convictions of the emperors. This is only partially true. St. Athanasius clearly sensed the dangers of imperial intervention when he maintained that Constantius was transforming the Church into a civil senate. But the transformation was then far from complete. Relations between Church and Empire had not yet come to the point they reached under Justinian, when synodal decrees were declared to have the force of imperial law, and the Emperor on his own authority gave the canons of the ecumenical councils the same legal character as the Holy Scriptures.[35] Indeed, of all the synods in the century, only the two which tradition established as ecumenical, Nicaea (325) and Constantinople (381), received on petition imperial confirmation of their decrees. (One may also mention that Constantius II gave imperial corroboration to the creed of Rimini, as revised at Nicaea-Thrace, when he sent it throughout the Empire commanding bishops to sign it or be deposed. Similarly, Valentinian I gave his support to the Synod of Illyricum (365–372), when he ordered that the doctrine of the *Homoousios* be taught by all bishops. Neither act was explicity a confirmation of synodal decrees.) The *"libertas"* of Roman citizens,[36] the *"libertas"* of the Church was still paramount in the fourth century; and the predominant image of the emperor was not that of the head of the Church, but that of the guardian of his subjects' liberties.

Credal formulations of the century illustrated the constitutional relationship between the Church, as an *isopoliteia*, and the imperial government, as an enabling but extra-constitutional element. As we have indicated, the definition of the Faith was critically important in matters of ecclesiastical jurisdiction; and in the period under review, creeds were, for the greater part, juridical instruments framed to serve immediate purposes. They were formulated to establish a canon by which true bishops could be distinguished from false, and the false, deposed. They were professions of Faith; but creeds were also, more practically, canons of ecclesiastical law, drafted and approved by bishops for the governance of the Church.

During the period in question, there were three major credal formulations: the two orthodox symbols of Nicaea (325) and Constantinople (381) and the Arian creed of Rimini-Seleucia. It may be useful to mention how the formulation of these professions manifested the correlative principles just described.

In his work, *De Synodis*, St. Athanasius observed with great acuteness that the Council of Nicaea

... was not a common meeting, but convened upon a pressing necessity and for a reasonable object. The Syrians, Cilicians, and Mesopotamians, were out of order in celebrating the Feast, and kept Easter with the Jews; furthermore, the Arian heresy had risen up against the Catholic Church and found supporters in Eusebius and his fellows, who were both zealous for the heresy, and conducted the attack upon religious people. This gave occasion for an ecumenical council that the feast might be everywhere celebrated on one day, and that the heresy which was springing up might be anathematized. It took place then; and the Syrians submitted, and the Fathers pronounced the Arian heresy to be the forerunner of Antichrist and drew up a suitable formula against it.[37]

In this statement, Athanasius, who himself assisted in the Council of Nicaea, states very precisely that the purpose of the Nicene Faith was juridical and immediate—the condemnation of Arianism. He further records that the profession was the work of "the Fathers" and neglects to mention the role of the Emperor Constantine in the Council and particularly in the framing of the Creed.

The omission is significant, for it emphasizes Athanasius's statement that the Council was allowed perfect freedom to consider the problems before it: "It was no compulsion," he writes, "which led the judges to this decision [against Arius], but they all deliberately vindicated the truth. And they did so justly and rightly." [38] Indeed, there is every indication that Constantine left the great doctrinal problems to the bishops for solution, and that he did not attempt in any way to alter the due constitutional process of the Church.

The Emperor's actions were three: he summoned the Council, he attended and participated in the debates, and he enforced the conciliar decisions in the temporal sphere. But in none of these actions did he move on his own initiative or assume the episcopal duty of judging questions of the Faith. Rufinus informs us that Constantine summoned the Council at the insistence of his bishops;[39] and a much later and generally unreliable account maintains that he summoned it in response to Arius's appeal to Caesar.[40] Likewise,

---

[35] Nov. 131, 1 : 545.

[36] Cf. Orosius VI, 1, 8 (*Corpus Scriptorum Ecclesiasticorum Latinorum* 5: 351): "Inter cives Romanos . . . tuta libertas."

[37] *De Synodis*, c. 5 (Migne, *Patrologia Latina* 26: 688). See V. C. LeClercq, *Ossius of Cordova* (Washington, 1954), p. 222 ff.

[38] *Ad episcopos Aegypti*, c. 13 (Migne, *Patrologia Graeca* 25: 568).

[39] Historia Ecclesiastica X, 1, ed. E. Schwartz *cit.*: 2, 2, p. 960: "ille ex sententia sacerdotum apud Nicaeam episcopale concilium convocat. . . ."

[40] Mansi, *Collectio Conciliorum* 2: 705.

while Constantine took a very notable part in the discussions of the Council, he did not preside,[41] nor did he prescribe decisions for the bishops or join them in making them. The debates were in Greek, which was somewhat less familiar to Constantine than Latin, but Constantine's biographer affirms that the Emperor was able to follow them, "hearing everything most patiently," asking questions of both sides, and ultimately to bring all the bishops to his point of view.[42] This participation was critical in the consideration of the Faith. Eusebius of Caesarea offered a creed to the Council for consideration. Constantine was present and received the profession with great enthusiasm, suggesting the addition of the word *"homoousios"* to describe the relationship of the Son to the Father. The bishops accepted this one suggestion and drafted the creed in its final form.[43] Decisive as this intervention was, it did not violate the juristic competence of episcopal courts. Constantine did not himself formulate the creed, and when it was presented to him, he declared that it was inspired by God, revealed by the Holy Spirit speaking through the saints.[44] In this connection, one must also recall the very strong affirmation which Rufinus attributes to him that bishops cannot be judged by men; "for God has given you to us as gods, and it is not meet that man should judge of gods." Further, in accordance with the anathemas which the Council appended to the Creed, Constantine threatened to exile all those who refused to sign the profession, and he implemented these threats immediately by banishing Arius, and his supporters, Bishops Secundus and Theonas, together with the clergy who accompanied them. Finally, he commanded that Arius's books be burned and forbade their concealment on pain of death. The Council subsequently deposed Eusebius of Nicomedia and Theognis of Nicaea for Arianism, and Constantine enforced this judgment with edicts of banishment and invitations to the two sees to elect orthodox successors. His action against Eusebius was the more determined because that Bishop had assisted Licinius against Constantine and, since Licinius's defeat, had intrigued against the Emperor. But even in this instance, as in that of Theognis, the act of deposition was the Council's, and banishment was simply a secular corroboration of the effectual sentence.

Sixty years later, the assertion by the Church of its autonomy in doctrinal matters and the Empire's recognition of that independence received clear expression again at the Council of Constantinople (381).

Like Nicaea, the Council of Constantinople met to decide specific disputes—the conflict among Demophilus, Gregory Nazianzenus, and Maximus over the episcopal throne of the eastern capital, and the controversy between the Macedonian clergy and the orthodox. Like Nicaea, it was summoned by the Emperor upon the petition of his clergy, after Maximus had appealed to him for confirmation of his election, and, more important, after Ulfilas and other Arian bishops had asked Theodosius for a synod to hear their case and had received his promise that a synod would be summoned for that purpose.[45] According to one account, Theodosius changed his mind after he had promised Ulfilas a synodal hearing and forbade all discussion of the Faith.[46] But, as the definition of the orthodox Faith was one of the chief works of the Council of Constantinople, this prohibition can scarcely have been complete or final.

Theodosius participated in the opening ceremonies of the Council, but Melitius of Antioch presided even then. The Emperor greeted Melitius, Theodoret tells us, as a loving son seeing his father after a long absence; and "after he had welcomed all the other bishops lovingly, he asked them as fathers to take counsel about the matters set before them."[47] In the major deliberations of the Council, Theodosius took no formal part, although he made strong personal efforts to bring the Macedonians into agreement with the orthodox; his participation in the Council did not become more formal even after the sudden death of Melitius and the election by the bishops of Gregory Nazianzenus as their president. Indeed, far from dominating the discussions, Theodosius sustained two very great disappointments because of the freedom he allowed the Fathers: the Macedonians refused to adopt the orthodox position, and the Council, contrary to the Emperor's declared opinion, accepted the resignation of Gregory Nazianzenus from the see of Constantinople. It is true that in one important ecclesiastical matter Theodosius intervened directly and definitively. He chose Gregory's successor. But the choice was made from a list prepared by the Council and was canonically approved by the people of the See.[48] In all its legal deliberations—including the definition of the Faith, which separated true bishops from false—Theodosius scrupulously allowed the Council the freedom to exercise the peculiar laws of the Church.

The terms under which the Emperor confirmed the decrees of the Council emphasize this point. Upon concluding its deliberation, the assembly wrote to Theodosius thanking God that He had granted him the Empire "for the common peace of the Churches and the confirmation of the salutary Faith." It was neces-

[41] J. Hefele- H. LeClercq, *Histoire des Conciles* (Paris, 1907) 1: p. 425.

[42] Vita Constantini, III, 13 (Migne, *Patrologia Graeca* 20: 1070).

[43] Eusebius, Ep. I, 4 (Migne, *Patrologia Graeca* 20: 1540).

[44] Socrates, Historia Ecclesiastica I, 9 (Migne, *Patrologia Graeca* 67: 86). See also Rufinus, Historia Ecclesiastica, X, 5 (ed. E. Schwartz *cit.* 2, 2: p. 965).

[45] See Hefele-LeClercq, *op. cit.*, 2, 1: p. 3, n. 3.

[46] *Loc. cit.*

[47] Theodoret, Historia Ecclesiastica, V, 7 (Migne, *Patrologia Graeca* 82: 1208).

[48] Hefele-LeClercq, *op. cit.*, 2, 5, 1: p. 10.

sary, the bishops wrote, to report their decisions to the Emperor: they had renewed harmony among themselves, pronounced certain "brief definitions" (i.e., the canons), confirmed the Faith of Nicaea, and condemned those who deviated from that Faith. They asked Theodosius to confirm these decisions by edict in the same zeal for the Church's honor with which he had summoned the Council. The bishops did not present their decisions to the Emperor for review or judgment; the validity of their decrees did not depend upon imperial approval. As the text of the imperial edict confirming the acts of the Council indicates, the civil corroboration was intended merely to give force in the temporal sphere to the sentences the clergy had imposed in the spiritual. For, in complete accord with the ecclesiastical judgment, Theodosius commanded that churches be given over to bishops who confessed the orthodox faith, and that those who dissented from "the communion of the Faith," from the Nicene Creed, be expelled from the churches as manifest heretics (Cod. Th. XVI, 1, 3). The act is corroborative, but not constitutive. The judgment was the bishops'; the material enforcement, the Emperor's.

The Councils at Nicaea and Constantinople were sympathetic to the religious views of the reigning emperor, and it could be objected that the freedom of deliberation and decision which they enjoyed in religious matters derived from imperial certainty of the final decision, rather than from genuine constitutional independence of the Church in those matters. The Synod of Rimini, however, resisted the Arian Constantius II in the name of orthodoxy. It failed and ultimately adopted an Arian creed; but its failure gives important evidence of the Church as a theoretical legal *isopoliteia*. The extreme measures Constantius employed to extort the creed he wanted from the Synod clearly indicate the episcopal position that no creed could be established by imperial edict, and that legal competence for such establishment lay only in episcopal jurisdiction.

Technically, the role Constantius played in the Synod was as narrowly circumscribed as those Constantine adopted at Nicaea, and Theodosius, at Constantinople. He summoned the assembly at the petition of his bishops,[49] for the purpose of settling some explicit disputes by considering *"de fide et unitate."*[50] He himself was far from Rimini when the Synod met; and although he named the prefect Taurus protector of the assembly, its presidency was held by the bishops (probably successively by Restitutus and Musonius). In the edict which summoned the dual synod of Rimini-Seleucia, Constantius specified that a commission of ten bishops from each assembly should inform him of their decisions, and that, in case of irreconcila-

ble dispute between the two bodies, deputies from Rimini should report the judgment of their synod to the Emperor and then enter into discussions with the eastern bishops. There is nothing in these conditions to suggest that the freedom of the bishops to discuss questions of Faith and ecclesiastical unity was in any way restricted. Indeed, Constantius expressed in his summons very great concern that "due order be observed in ecclesiastical affairs," a condition which, he rightly observed, hindered the western bishops from exceeding their competence in the cases immediately under review by issuing judgments against the eastern bishops.[51]

Constantius had offered, in the pattern set by his father, to pay the expenses of assisting bishops; all save three impoverished bishops from Britain refused the offer, apparently to maintain in conscience the freedom which was theirs in law.[52] They proceeded to implement that freedom at once. An Arian creed which Constantius had approved (not by any formal action) was read to the Synod. The orthodox members immediately protested that the Nicene Faith was sufficient and suspended the Arian bishops from communion. Considering its work done, the Synod reported these actions to Constantius, urging him to acknowledge the apostolic Faith, established by Christ, the Saviour of the Empire and the grantor of the Emperor's salvation, and to allow its members to return to their sees, as their commission had been discharged.[53]

This report displeased the Emperor, who resolutely designed to secure the Synod's approval of an Arian confession. In the affairs of the Synod which followed, we must distinguish carefully between Constantius's constitutional acts and the coercive measures by which he finally achieved his goal. These latter were crude in the extreme. He refused to grant the orthodox legates audience until, after four months of indoctrination by Arians under painful conditions, the envoys actually violated their mission and subscribed the heretical creed. Upon returning to their brethren, who had been held at Rimini, they were at first repudiated by them. But the prefect Taurus, whom Constantius had ordered to hold the Synod "until all had consented to one faith,"[54] remained true to his commission; the advancing winter, the physical frailty of some assisting bishops, the shortage of provisions, and the incessant and deceptive cajoling of the Arians at length gained the unanimity Constantius had sought. The Arian profession was adopted with unimportant changes; the Synod reported this decision to the Emperor and dispersed, praising Constantius's

---

[49] See Athanasius, De Synodis, cc. 1, 7 (Migne, *Patrologia Graeca* 26: 681, 690).
[50] Hilary of Poitiers, Frag. Hist. VIII, 1 (*Corpus Scriptorum Ecclesiasticorum Latinorum* 65: 94).

[51] *Loc. cit.*
[52] Sulpicius Severus, Chron. II, 41 (*Corpus Scriptorum Ecclesiasticorum Latinorum* 1: 94).
[53] Hilary, Frag. Hist. V, 1 (*Corpus Scriptorum Ecclesiasticorum Latinorum* 65: 84).
[54] Sulpicius Severus, *loc. cit.*

piety and asking his support.[55] Constantius had won his victory by crude and illicit coercion.

But, in form, he had preserved the canonical liberty of the Synod. At the same time that the orthodox members of the Synod had sent him their envoys, the Arians had sent him theirs. It was clear that the Synod had not fulfilled its charge; the problems before it had not been decided. If Constantius could not receive the orthodox envoys immediately, it was, he said, because he was oppressed by burdens of state which he had to settle first so as to approach "matters of Divine Law" with a "soul clear from every care." He himself did not undertake to decide the conflict between the orthodox and the Arians; indeed, when the legates of the orthodox faction were received in audience, they accepted the Arian position, and there was no apparent dispute. It was Constantius's pious wish that, when they returned to the Synod, the assembly "might be able to bring to a close matters which so deeply affect the well-being of the Catholic Church."[56] Technically, the Synod was commissioned to "agree upon one Faith," and the Emperor merely afforded it his protection until it should have discharged that commission. Formally, the debate was free, and the unanimous decision was free; the Emperor had taken no part in the process except to guarantee the Fathers the full exercise of the peculiar law of the Church.

The Synod of Seleucia, the companion synod to that of Rimini, does not require additional discussion. The same pretence of freedom was maintained there to attain the same end. Allowing the assembled bishops the specious exercise of the canons, Constantius deliberately sowed dissent and, upon reducing the Synod to a rump and applying extraordinary pressures, he gained its "free" profession of the Arian creed.

Juristically, Constantine at Nicaea, Theodosius at Constantinople, and Constantius at Rimini-Seleucia, acknowledged that the power to define the Faith and, consequently, to adjudicate disputes in which the Faith was a critical factor rested in the episcopacy alone. It was, in fact, the acknowledgment that, like the old Israel, the new had *patriae consuetudines* which must be maintained. The Faith was the fundamental element in those *consuetudines;* it was the great treasure of apostolic tradition, "the faith enduring from ancient times, the Faith which the prophets, the Gospels, and the Apostles preached through God Himself and our Lord, Jesus Christ."[57]

When he declared that the Jews had preserved their distinctive national law and, "in as much as pertains to the cult of God, ancestral customs and ritual," St. Augustine described the Jewish polity in the very terms in which he himself and the Fathers before him construed the legal structure of the Church. For they demanded that the City of God enjoy the integrity of its laws and spiritual administration. The "ancestral customs" in Christian dress—apostolic tradition—transmitted the Faith; but they also transmitted the canons, the peculiar law by which the *gens sancta* was to be governed in spiritual matters.[58] These too, the Fathers argued, must be maintained; over them, the civil government had no power.

Perhaps the most critical extension of this claim was that the trial of bishops must be conducted by ecclesiastical, not civil, law, and accordingly before episcopal, not secular, judges. Among the episcopal trials in the fourth century, none was so celebrated as that of St. Athanasius, which lasted nearly half a century in all its various stages. It may stand as a paradigm of the ecclesiastical claim to juridical integrity.

In general, the trial moved at different times on two levels, the civil and the religious. Athanasius freely accepted imperial jurisdiction in the first, and strongly rejected it in the second. The earliest appearance of civil charges came when, after his condemnation by the Synod of Tyre on ecclesiastical charges, Athanasius fled to Constantinople and requested a new hearing from Constantine. His enemies arrived shortly after, and, intent upon securing the Bishop's fall, they neglected the accusations of sacrilege and murder on which he had been tried and entered a civil charge against him: "inventing another accusation *which concerned the Emperor himself,* they declared before him that Athanasius had threatened to cause the grain to be withheld which was sent from Alexandria to his home [Constantinople]."[59] Constantine was enraged and banished Athanasius immediately, without reviewing the condemnation of the Synod. Athanasius does not deny that Constantine was entirely within his legal rights to inflict this penalty, given the civil charge. When his enemies charged him before Constantine's sons with murder and civil disorder, he tacitly accepted the jurisdiction of the imperial court.[60] Later, when the Arians accused him before Constantius of treasonable acts, he again openly recognized the adjudication of the Emperor. He urges Constantius to review the evidence, to declare his enemies false accusers, and to condemn them. Against the charges of poisoning the mind of Constans toward his brother, of conspiring with the usurper Magnentius, of showing contempt for the imperial dignity by celebrating divine offices in an unfinished church being constructed by Constantius, and

---

[55] Hilary, Frag. Hist. VI, 2 (*Corpus Scriptorum Ecclesiasticorum Latinorum* 65: 87 f.).

[56] Athanasius, De Synodis, c. 55 (Migne, *Patrologia Graeca* 26: 792).

[57] Hilary, Frag. Hist. V, 1 (*Corpus Scriptorum Ecclesiasticorum Latinorum* 65: 79).

[58] Athanasius, Ep. Encyclica, c. 1 (Migne, *Patrologia Graeca* 25: 225).

[59] Apologia contra Arianos, c. 87 (*ibid.*, 405).

[60] Ep. encyclica, c. 5, Apologia contra Arianos, c. 3 (*ibid.*, 232 f, 252 f).

of being contumacious towards an imperial order, he presents the most thorough and precise defense. It was a defense written by a fugitive, for Athanasius had fled from possible violence at the hands of the Arians, who claimed imperial authority for their actions. Athanasius feared the heat of the moment, and wrote to the Emperor:

Would you have had me, Lord, appear before your magistrates in order that though you had written merely in the way of threatening, they might not understand your intention, but being exasperated against me by the Arians, might kill me on the authority of your letters, and on that ground ascribe the murder to you?

Far from denying the imperial competence in this case even to the point of capital punishment, Athanasius acknowledges it; the possibility that the law might take its full course was his greatest fear and the cause of his flight.

In matters which did not concern the imperial interest, Athanasius regarded the imperial court as an interlocutory court, a court of review. Accusations and synodal processes and judgments might be appealed to the emperor for review, and if the cause for opening or reopening the trial were sufficient, the emperor might refer the case to a synod for retrial, summoning the synod and commanding bishops to attend. Accordingly, Athanasius appeared before Constantine in Psamathia to answer the charges which the Arians had brought against him in hope of submitting the case to formal trial. The Arians had entered the charges before Constantine, who, upon hearing the charges and the defense, found no sufficient reason for opening the process and condemned the Arians as false accusers. In this attitude, Athanasius also appealed the decision of the Synod of Tyre, requesting "either that a lawful council of bishops might be assembled, or that the Emperor would himself receive his defense concerning the charges they brought against him." [61] Constantine himself explicitly wrote that the role of the Emperor would be to enquire whether "an impartial and uncorrupt judgment" had been passed.[62] That he intended to do no more is indicated by his intention to summon yet another synod to hear the case.[63] But when, as we have observed, the charges were changed from ecclesiastical to civil matters, the necessity of synodal hearing was removed and Constantine proceeded to immediate civil sentence. Athanasius did not consider such interlocutory hearings before the Emperor to be genuine trials, for he omitted the hearing at Psamathia from the list of processes in which he had been acquitted.[64] And yet, he did regard them as valid, if limited, participation by the imperial power in ecclesiastical processes.

Finally, Athanasius in no way contradicted the

power of the Emperor to repudiate and banish bishops, when the civil power acted in accord with canonical processes. His objection to the intrusion of Gregory of Cappadocia was that Constantius had broken the spirit of the canons while preserving their letter. In accordance with the canons, Constantius secured the approval of the Alexandrines to his renunciation of Athanasius, but the approval had come, not from the Christian, but from the pagan citizens. When Constantine had earlier threatened him with the same punishment, Athanasius did not in any way contest the Emperor's power and right to make the threat good.[65] And in the later incident, his only objection was that the canons had been wrongly used. In short, Athanasius accepted the Emperor as the due executor of canonical sentences which required the action of the secular arm. The effectual deposition and exile of a bishop was such a sentence, rightly enforced by the civil office.

Once, however, Constantius overstepped his limits and aroused a response which is most enlightening for our purposes. At the Synod of Milan (355), the proposal to condemn Athanasius met such vigorous and persistent resistance that Constantius intervened personally. He summoned the recalcitrant bishops Paulinus of Trier, Lucifer of Cagliari, Eusebius of Vercelli, and Dionysius of Milan—three of them, Paulinus, Lucifer, and Dionysius, were metropolitans —to his presence and commanded them to sign the condemnation and to enter communion with the Arians. The Bishops refused, saying that there was no ecclesiastical canon which warranted such action; the Emperor responded that they should accept his word as a canon and conform or go into exile. With solemn admonitions, the Bishops stood fast and "warned him against infringing ecclesiastical order and mingling Roman sovereignty with the constitution of the Church." [66]

The basis for this claim to juridical independence was stated most plainly in a letter which Pope Julius wrote to the Arian bishops on behalf of St. Athanasius. The Arians had written to Julius requesting that he summon a synod to judge the case against Athanasius, and Julius acceded to their request. But, upon learning that Athanasius himself would be present at the Roman synod, the Arians demurred and, excusing themselves on questionable grounds, they declined to attend. The Synod convened all the same, adjudged

---

[61] Apologia contra Arianos, c. 9 (ibid., 264).
[62] Ibid., c. 86 (ibid., 401 ff.).
[63] Ibid., c. 9 (ibid., 264).
[64] Ibid., c. 1 (ibid., 248 f.).

[65] Ibid., cc. 59, 60 (ibid., 357 ff.).
[66] Athanasius, Historia Arianorum, cc. 33, 34 (Migne, Patrologia Graeca 25: 732, 733). See K. F. Hagel, Kirche und Kaisertum in Lehre und Leben des Athanasius (Borna-Leipzig, 1933), p. 66: "Damit ist das göttliche Gesetz aufgehoben und des Kaisers Wille an seine Stelle getreten." Peeters's discussion shows very clearly that even the preliminary charges which Constantine heard at Psmathia dealt with homicide, a civil crime. P. Peeters, "Comment S. Athanase s'enfuit de Tyr en 335," Académie royale de Belgique: Bulletin de la classe de lettres et de sciences morales et politiques 30 (1944) : 137.

Athanasius innocent of the charges against him, and received him into communion. Moreover, it directed Julius to write to the Arians stating the grounds for its judgment.

Throughout his letter runs the theme that the canons must be preserved inviolate, that "a custom which has once obtained in the Church and been established by councils should [not] be set aside by a few individuals." [67] The canons have been handed down by the Apostles; they are the "traditions of the Fathers," [68] and comprise "the Canon of the Church." [69] Observance of the Apostolical Canons preserves order in the Church;[70] their breach tears asunder the limbs of Christ.[71] When review of synodal decisions is necessary, it can be legitimately discharged by other synods,

. . . to the end that the judges, having before their eyes that other trial which was to follow, might be led to investigate matters with the utmost caution, and that the parties concerned in their sentence might have assurance that the judgment they received was just, and not dictated by the enmity of their former judges.[72]

Julius charges that in the case of Athanasius, the canons had been violated by the intrusion of the civil power, albeit at the invitation of Arian clergy. Constantius II had expelled Athanasius and sent Gregory of Cappadocia to assume his episcopacy. "What canon of the Church, or what apostolical tradition warrants this," Julius asks, "that, when a Church was at peace, and so many bishops were in unanimity with Athanasius, the bishop of Alexandria, Gregory should be sent thither, a stranger to the city, not having been baptized there, nor known to the general body, and desired neither by presbyters, nor bishops, nor laity— that he should be appointed at Antioch and sent to Alexandria, accompanied not by presbyters, nor by deacons of the city, nor by bishops of Egypt, but by soldiers? . . . The canons received from the Apostles ought not thus to be set aside." [73] In contravention of the law of the Church, laymen and heathen, not ecclesiastical authorities, had conducted the preliminary investigation of the charges against Athanasius. One of the principal charges was that of sacrilege against a cup used in the Eucharist and against an altar table. Julius observes that the enquiry "was carried on before the Prefect and his band and in the presence of heathens and Jews," although priests who wished to attend were barred. And he expressed astonishment that

. . . Presbyters who are the ministers of the Mysteries are not permitted to attend, but an enquiry concerning Christ's

blood and Christ's body is carried on before an *external judge*, in the presence of catechumens, nay, worse than that, before heathens and Jews, who are in ill repute in regard to Christianity. Even supposing that an offense had been committed, it should have been investigated legally in the Church and by the clergy, not by heathens who abhor the Word and know not the Truth.[74]

The basis for the juridical integrity of the Church could not be stated more plainly; the status of the Church as an *isopoliteia*, as an institutionally discrete body, derived from its sacramental nature, from the Faith and the sacraments through which the Mysteries of the Faith were expressed. Cases touching the Faith and other sacred matters must be judged by those qualified to determine the true Faith, and not by external judges who had no knowledge of it. The Fathers did not question the competence of imperial courts in civil cases; that is, in cases in which imperial interests were directly involved. But in matters pertaining to the "cult of God," the Empire could not intervene, except to enable the proper ecclesiastical courts to discharge their duties. The Church was not in any sense part of the Empire. Her laws were not imperial laws; her ruler was not Caesar.

It was in this spirit that Hosius of Cordova, the adviser of Constantine, wrote to Constantius that God had granted the Empire to the Emperor, and the Church to the clergy. "If any man stole the Empire from you, he would be resisting the ordinance of God: in the same way you on your part should fear lest, in taking upon yourself the government of the Church, you incur the guilt of a grave offense." [75] And in the same spirit, St. Hilary wrote of the Church as the kingdom of God, commenting upon the verse (I Peter 2.9), "Ye are an elect generation (*genus electum*), a royal priesthood (*regale sacerdotium*), a holy nation (*gens sancta*)." He writes:

The laws (*leges*) of the world are one thing; the offices (*munera*) of God are another. When the devil dares to tempt the Lord, he boasts that the world is his. But the Lord commands us to die to the world that we may live to Him. With the Lord, contempt of riches is wealth; with the Lord, rejection of earthly honor is the kingdom of heaven.[76]

The Church was "the most glorious city of God . . . living in these transitory times, a pilgrim among the impious," later to "dwell in the fixed stability of the eternal seat, which it now awaits through patience until 'Justice shall return unto judgment. . . .'" [77] Her members were a discrete *gens* or *populus*, governed by their own laws and courts in matters of religion. The new Israel had taken on the juristic mantle of the old.

[67] Athanasius, Apologia contra Arianos, c. 22 (Migne, *Patrologia Graeca* 25: 286).

[68] *Ibid.*, c. 35 (col. 307).

[69] *Loc. cit.*

[70] *Ibid.*, c. 21 (col. 284).

[71] *Ibid.*, c. 34 (col. 305).

[72] *Ibid.*, c. 22 (col. 284).

[73] *Ibid.*, c. 30 (col. 300).

[74] *Ibid.*, c. 31 (col. 300 f.).

[75] Historia Arianorum, c. 44 (*ibid.*, col. 745 f.). On this letter, see LeClercq, *op. cit.*, p. 449 ff.

[76] Tractatus in CXVIII Psalmum, Nun, 9 (*Corpus Scriptorum Ecclesiasticorum Latinorum* 22: 479).

[77] Augustine, De civitate Dei I, praef (*Corpus Scriptorum Ecclesiasticorum Latinorum* 40, 1: 3).

2. THE ALIEN EMPIRE

I

The first principle of patristic thought about Church-State relations was that the Church was an autonomous corporation in spiritual matters. The second, to which we must now turn, was that the Empire remained supreme in civil matters. As in the Synagogue, believers held, so to speak, two citizenships; they submitted in religious matters to their "ethnic" law, and in criminal, to civil law, under which they fell as Roman citizens.[1]

The fusing of Church and Empire into one institution was only begun in the fourth century; as we have suggested, the two still remained fundamentally independent in the minds of orthodox thinkers until the end of that period. At the same time, they had approximated one another, and their relations under Theodosius were far different from those under Constantine. Constantine regarded Christianity as a favored cult, but he tolerated the other religions within the Empire. While he entertained bishops in splendor which some praised as an image of the heavenly kingdom,[2] he also functioned as the *pontifex maximus* of the State paganism, supplying members to its priestly colleges and public funds for its sacrifices and rituals.

Thus he enforced the lenient terms of the Edict of Milan, by which he and Licinius granted Christianity the status of a *religio licita* and specified that

. . . all others are to be allowed the free and unrestricted practice of their religions; for it accords with the good order of the realm and the peacefulness of our times that each should have freedom to worship God after his own choice; and we do not intend to detract from the honor due any religion or its followers.[3]

Constantine was not baptized until he lay dying, nearly thirty years after his conversion. Toward the end of the century, Theodosius was baptized within a year of his accession, and he followed the religious policy of Gratian, renouncing the title and functions of the *pontifex maximus* and issuing the most stringent edicts against pagans and heretics. He went further; upon the petition of the Council of Constantinople (381), he established the Nicene profession as the true religion over "all peoples which the government of Our Clemency rules." [4] Indeed, he went so far in identifying the interests of the Church with those of the Empire as to decree that the same capital punishment prescribed for sedition and *lèse majesté* should be imposed for disturbing the peace of the Church.[5]

This transition from broad toleration to the establishment of a State religion, exclusive of all other cults, must be explained with reference to three factors: the emperor, the imperial power, and the Empire. These were distinct elements in the Roman constitution. The Empire was the scene of the action; imperial power, the instrument; the emperor, the motivator and director. By the end of the fourth century, the emperors had used their powers not merely to acknowledge the Christian community as a legitimate part of the Empire, but much more, to make the Empire a Christian community. Though stated in law, this adjustment was unstable; it rested wholly upon the steadfastness of succeeding emperors in the orthodox profession and their inclination to use their powers for the benefit of the Church.

The imperial power was morally neutral, and Christian authors argued that, although it was held with the assent of God, it could be turned to good or evil purposes depending upon the nature of the ruler. Accordingly, it could be used to the benefit or to the detriment of the Church at the choice of the particular emperor. St. Augustine's famous sentence that both good and wicked rulers held their power by the providence of God, the good to reward the people and the wicked to punish it, is a patent statement of this fact.[6] And as we shall see in a later chapter, St. Am-

---

[1] See E. R. Goodenough, *The Jurisprudence of the Jewish Courts in Egypt* (New Haven, 1929), p. 245 ff. In this chapter, we shall examine the remarkably keen—and unfortunately neglected—suggestion by Biehl (L. Biehl, *Das liturgische Gebet für Kaiser und Reich* [Paderborn, 1937], p. 36): "Da die altrömische Staatpraxis, die Religion lediglich vom Standpunkt des Staatsinteresses zu betrachten fortwirkte, und auch die alte Rechtsanschauung, dass das *ius sacrum* ein Teil des *ius publicum* sei, weiterlebte, müsste sich das Verhältnis von Kirche und Staat in der Form des Staatkirchentums ausprägen. Daran scheiterte die Verwirklichung des christlichen Grundsatzen von der Verschiedenheit und Selbstständigkeit der beiden Gewalten trotz seiner wenigstens theoretischen Anerkennung durch die byzantinischen Kaiser. Das *ius publicum* und das *ius sacrum* fanden im Kaiser ihren höchsten Träger." Our position, however, is that the principle of independence survived and was acknowledged in fourth-century Roman law, though its sharpness was very considerably modified in later times.

[2] *Vita Constantini*, III, 15 (Migne, *Patrologia Graeca* 20: 1074). Bauer and Muller both emphasize the gradualness of change in imperial religious policy under Constantine the Great, and they reject the position that Constantine's actions were caesaropapistic. C. Bauer, "Die Anfänge des byzantinischen Cäsaropapismus," *Archiv des katholischen Kirchenrechts* 140 (1931): especially p. 113: "Einen grundsätzlichen 'Cäsaropapismus' in dem Sinne, dass die byzantinischen Kaiser selbst ein formelles Recht, die Kirche zu lehren und zu regieren beansprucht hätten, hat es nie gegeben. Praktisch haben sie fast alle tief in das kirchliche Personen- und Verwaltungsrecht eingegriffen. . . ." H. Muller, *Christians and Pagans from Constantine to Augustine* (Pretoria, 1946) 1: pp. 23, 34 ff. But see Biondi, who does not consider in detail the juristic bases of Church-Empire relations in the fourth century. B. Biondi, *Il Diritto Romano Christiano* (Milan, 1952) 1: p. 185: "Per designare questa situazione, in cui l'imperatore interviene liberamente nell' ambito della Chiesa in questioni di fede, si è escogitato il termine di cesarismo o cesaropapismo. . . . Constantino si qualifica come fondatore del cesaropapismo."

[3] Lactantius, De mortibus persecutorum, c. 48 (*Corpus Scriptorum Ecclesiasticorum Latinorum* 27: 230 f).

[4] Cod. Th. XVI, 1, 2, 3.

[5] Cod. Th. XVI, 1, 4.

[6] De civitate Dei, V, 19 (*Corpus Scriptorum Ecclesiasticorum Latinorum* 40, 1: 253.

brose harbored the same concept of instability in imperial policy when he wrote that temporal power was but a dream. The imperial power was also a creature and a creator of law. Its purpose was to guard public order, or, as Symmachus wrote, "to preserve for each his own."[7] Abiding in the person of the emperor, who exercised it, the power transferred its character to the man, who became in the language of the panegyricists, "*lex animata*" or "*lex loquens*," the very personification of law.[8] For, as Ulpian wrote, "What has pleased the prince has the force of law, in as much as with the royal law (*lex regia*) which was established concerning his command (*imperium*), the people ceded to him and *into him* all its command (*imperium*) and power."[9] Others preferred to think of the emperor as a priest of the law, the intermediary between the divine principles and their earthly reflections.[10] But in practice, the "living law" and the "priest of the law" held the same absolute powers: the legislator was free of the laws, though, as Paulus observed, he was under a moral obligation "to preserve the laws of which he himself is seen to be freed."[11]

The imperial power made the emperor the guarantor of his subjects' liberties, giving him two means for discharging that office: the power over persons and the power over laws and things created by laws. Both of these were in some instances validly exercised over the clergy, and even on petition of the clergy.

The distinction between cases of religion, which must be tried before bishops, and civil, or criminal cases, which must be tried by civil judges, subjected all persons to the criminal jurisdiction of the Empire, and, when exercised against bishops, that latter jurisdiction stood as lawful in itself. Seditious bishops incurred the penalties of banishment and death as lawfully as did traitorous laymen.

The instrument most often used by the imperial government against the episcopacy was banishment. It was sometimes used to implement a synodal sentence of deposition, but more frequently, as under Constantius II and Valens, it was an act of the imperial government alone. Launched against the most dis-

tinguished prelates, including bishops of Rome, Constantinople, and Alexandria, the decree of banishment took its force from the criminal jurisdiction proper to the Empire. The banished were disturbers of the peace, and, as Julian wrote in his edict banishing Athanasius from Alexandria,

. . . a troublesome man is unfit by nature to be leader of the people. But if the leader is not even a man, but only a wretched puppet, like this great personage who thinks he is risking his head, this surely gives the signal for disorder.[12]

The fear of Athanasius that he was "risking his head" derived from the knowledge that he had defied Julian's express orders: although the Emperor had forbidden him to return to his see, Athanasius had in fact resumed his residence in Alexandria and had even performed baptisms there. In this disobedience he had incurred a penalty more severe than banishment: capital punishment, the penalty of *lèse majesté*. Though a bishop, he was liable to civil prosecution and execution on this charge. Athanasius had actually been in danger of such prosecution earlier, under Constantius II. About 356/7, the Bishop's enemies persuaded Constantius to indict him on numerous grave civil crimes, including sedition, conspiracy, and contumacy. The Emperor issued an edict for his immediate apprehension and imprisonment[13] and declared that "he would only suffer the punishment he deserves if one were to kill him ten times over. . . ."[14] Although he professed that Constantius himself did not wish to harm him, but that only inferior civil officers designed his death, Athanasius still envisaged himself imprisoned, brought before imperial judges, tried by them, and executed. He fled. "It would neither have been becoming in me to surrender and give myself up that my blood might be shed, nor in you, as a Christian King, to have the murder of Christians, even of bishops, imputed to you."[15] But he did not question the legitimacy of a civil process in the matters charged against him; indeed, he was at one time ready to defend himself personally before the Emperor.[16]

The possibility that this process might lead to execution was very real. In the year 385, the heretic Priscillian, Bishop of Avila, appealed his case to the Emperor Maximus from the Synod of Bordeaux, which had been summoned to hear the charges against him. The indictment was fundamentally doctrinal, and St. Martin, who was then at the imperial court, protested "that it was brutal and unheard-of impiety for a temporal judge to judge a Church trial."[17] Never-

---

[7] Relatio, c. 16 (Migne, *Patrologia Latina* 16: 971).

[8] K. M. Setton, *Christian Attitude Towards the Emperor in the Fourth Century* (New York, 1941), pp. 26, 112.

[9] Inst. I, 1.

[10] See Symmachus, Relatio, c. 13 (Migne, *Patrologia Latina* 16: 969): "Oro vos, justitiae sacerdotes, ut urbis vestrae sacris reddatur privata successio." Julian the Apostate, Panegyric in Honor of Constantius, 33B (ed. W. C. Wright, *The Works of the Emperor Julian* (London, 1913) 1: p. 84): ". . . your [victory] was stainless and unalloyed, and was more like the act of a priest going to the temple of his god than of an emperor going to war." Gregory Nazianzenus, Orat. contra Iulianum, IV, 35 (Migne, *Patrologia Graeca* 35: 561): Constantius held "the imperial priesthood."

[11] Sent. V, 12, 9a (ed. P. Krüger, *Collectio Librorum Iuris Anteiustiniani* (Berlin, 1878) 2: p. 121): "Decet enim tantae majestati eas servare leges quibus ipse solutus esse videtur."

[12] Ep. 47, 435C (ed. W. C. Wright *cit.* [London, 1923] 3: p. 150).

[13] Apologia ad Constantium, c. 29 (Migne, *Patrologia Graeca* 25: 632).

[14] *Ibid.*, c. 30 (Migne, *Patrologia Graeca* 25: 636).

[15] *Ibid.*, cc. 32, 34 (*ibid.*, 637, 641).

[16] *Ibid.*, cc. 29, 32 (*ibid.*, 632, 637).

[17] Sulpicius Severus, Chronicon II, 50 (*Corpus Scriptorum Ecclesiasticorum Latinorum* 1: 103).

theless, the civil process proceeded with two assisting bishops, and *"gemino iudicio"* Priscillian was condemned as a malefactor, on the civil side, and as one who indulged in obscene doctrines, on the ecclesiastical. The Bishop was sentenced to death and executed, together with two of his supporters.[18]

The legal principles at work in the processes against Athanasius and Priscillian are perhaps most clearly stated in documents from a third similar process: that against Pope Damasus about the year 371. The circumstances of this trial are not entirely clear, but it is known that a Jew, Isaac, who had converted to Christianity and subsequently lapsed, charged Damasus before the Emperor Gratian (or Maximus?) with certain crimes for which the punishment was death. "He sought the head of our holy brother," a later Synod wrote, "and the spilling of the blood of innocent persons." [19] Caspar suggests, with very great probability, that the charge was related to the disorders attending Damasus's election, in which several persons lost their lives. Damasus himself charged his enemies with "homicide" in those disorders;[20] and they would have been very likely to accuse him of the same crime. At first heard by the prefect Maximin, the case was removed to the Emperor himself, who declared Damasus innocent and gave Isaac his "just deserts." [21] A Roman Synod, which reviewed the process in 378, declared that it was proper for a Roman bishop to defend himself before the imperial court if a case should not fall within the competence of his own court: cases which "pertain to public laws" might justly be tried by imperial authority, but those which touch the conscience of a bishop must be judged by bishops.[22]

From the case of Damasus came a very considerable widening of the papal jurisdiction by Gratian's edict *"Ordinariorum sententiae."* We shall return to this in a later context; for the present, it may suffice to observe that the principles actually stated in the process against Damasus, and patent in those against Athanasius and Priscillian, subjected even bishops to imperial jurisdiction in criminal cases, and that the power of life and death the Emperor held over his subjects extended also to those who were princes of the Heavenly Kingdom.

The power of the sword extended over all subjects in criminal matters; we need not elaborate upon the nature of the coercive authority. Like it, the emperor's power over laws and things created by laws was general and constitutionally unlimited. For, as Ulpian said in his statement on the *lex regia*, whatever the emperor established "by letter and subscription," decreed in adjudging a case, issued as interlocutory pronouncements, or commanded by edict was law.[23] This was true, wrote Gaius, because the emperor himself had acceded to the Empire by law.[24] By virtue of this legal construct and the comprehensive legislative powers of his office, the emperor administered without accountability the whole structure of the *ius publicum.*

This point of classical Roman law came to be particularly relevant in the constitutional relations of Church and Empire. Ulpian defines the *ius publicum* as "what regards the state of Roman interest" (*quod ad statum rei Romanae spectat*), and continues to say that the *ius* abides *"in sacris, in sacerdotibus, in magistratibus."* [25] That is, sacred matters and priests as well as civil processes and magistrates fell under the rubric of *ius publicum;* and this elision between sacred and temporal matters before the imperial power extended to the ownership and control of property. For the emperor was the effectual owner not only of State property, but also of holdings consecrated to the gods. The *ius divinum,* which regulated ownership of temples, temple furniture and the like was a branch of the *ius publicum.* Technically, the ownership of property consecrated to divine service fell to the particular divinities to whom it had been ceded; but practically, its administration devolved upon the Roman people and thus upon the emperor.[26] Gaius distinguishes once between private, divine, and public law: cases involving private ownership are to be decided by private law; churches, including the temples of God and the patrimonies and sustenance which belong to ecclesiastical *iura,* fall under the divine law; and walls, *fora,* gates and similar works belong to the public law.[27] But this distinction did not alter the classic concept by which imperial administration was admitted over all three *iura,* and the emperor accepted as the supreme arbiter in all matters of property ownership, whether private, "divine," or public.

In the pagan context, these classical extensions of imperial authority to priests as well as civil magistrates and to sacred property as well as temporal continued to be observed throughout the fourth century, although the legislation of Gratian and Theodosius against paganism considerably lessened their relevance.

---

[18] *Loc. cit.,* and II, 51 (*ibid.,* p. 103 f.).

[19] Mansi, *Collectio Conciliorum* 3: 626. See A. Hoepffner, "Les deux procès du pape Damase," *Revue des études anciennes* 50 (1948): 288–304, who shows that the trial of Pope Damasus was conducted entirely by ecclesiastical bodies. *Cf.* M. Radin, *The Trial of Jesus of Nazareth* (Chicago, 1931), where it is shown that Pontius Pilate "waived his rights" and allowed the Jewish courts to try Jesus according to their own laws and customs, although the Roman court ultimately executed the Jewish sentence (pp. 204, 230 ff., 253 ff.). On the juristic structure of imperial appeals and interlocutory decisions, see J. M. Kelley, *Princeps Judex* (Weimar, 1957), p. 70 ff.

[20] Col. Avellana I, 12 (*Corpus Scriptorum Ecclesiasticorum Latinorum* 35: 4).

[21] Mansi, *Collectio Conciliorum* 3: 626: "Isaac quoque ipse ubi ea quae detulit probare non potuit, meritorum suorum sortem tulit."

[22] Mansi, *Collectio Conciliorum* 3: 626 f. On this see E. Caspar, *Geschichte des Papsttums* (Tübingen, 1930): p. 203 ff.

[23] Inst. I, 2.

[24] Gaius, I, 5.

[25] Inst. 1, 2.

[26] Gaius, 2, 3, 6.

[27] Ep. II, 1, 1.

For our purposes, it is important to observe that, within limits, they were considered valid in the Christian context from the conversion of Constantine onwards, and that they admitted of very considerable imperial authority over the persons of priests and the property of churches.

Upon the exercise of that authority over the Church, there was one check: namely, the concept of the Church as a discrete people, subject in religious matters to its own laws and to the operations of its own juristic apparatus. In those matters, the Church both claimed and enjoyed the status of an *isopoliteia*. But in matters which came under imperial jurisdiction (as, for example, criminal prosecution), the full force of the imperial power in its legislative, as well as in its coercive, character could lawfully be brought to bear.

Indeed, the Church acknowledged these sweeping powers and frequently petitioned the Emperor to exert them on its behalf. To be sure, St. Ambrose insisted that the letter of the law regarding *res sacrae* be observed, and that the Empire forswear all authority over property consecrated to God, leaving administration of that property to God's vicars, the bishops. But until he protested on sacramental grounds that church buildings did not come under imperial jurisdiction, the imperial administration of ecclesiastical property as *res sacrae* had proceeded unhindered, and heretics and orthodox alike in their times petitioned the emperor to transfer churches into their hands from those of their doctrinal enemies. Similarly, churchmen besought the temporal sovereign to review ecclesiastical sentences passed against them, to enforce synodal decisions by the power of the sword, and to confirm ecclesiastical privileges by original legislation.

The episcopate of St. Ambrose provides two incidents which illustrate how the classical Roman concept of the emperor as the administrator of *res sacrae* survived to enter the Christian Empire: namely, Gratian's confiscation of the temporalities belonging to the Vestal Virgins and the pagan priestly colleges, and Valentinian II's attempt to transfer basilicas from the orthodox to the Arians. St. Ambrose is very explicit in saying that Gratian did not disturb the legal privileges of the Vestals and the priestly colleges, but merely withdrew their sustenance: "Their lands have been taken away, not their rights." [28] The pagan Symmachus protested against the withdrawal of that property with the argument that the holdings of the religious associations in question were under private law, rather than public. Asking "Does not the religion of Rome appertain to Roman law?" he asserted that Gratian had violated the customs of his predecessors by denying to the priestly *collegia* the right to property they had earlier inherited. "What name," he asks,

"shall be given to the taking away of property which no law nor accident has made to fail?" The lands which the State granted to the colleges ceased to be public property and fell under private law; the emperors who ruled over all were responsible for preserving his own for each individual, and they could not lawfully resume to the fisc property once alienated and not duly restored to public domain by law or accident. [29]

In his response, St. Ambrose took the opposite view: that the disposition of the property in question did fall under the jurisdiction of the emperor and so under the rules of public law. He indicates that the precepts of private law have not been prejudiced for the Vestals and the priestly colleges, and that they still enjoy the benefits of gifts to shrines and legacies to soothsayers. "Their land only," he writes, "had been taken away, because they did not use religiously that which they claimed in right (*ius*) of religion." [30] In the most dogmatic terms, he affirms that this deprivation satisfied the principles of equity and the *ius gentium*,[31] and that it was well within the competence of imperial authority. "Had these things not been abolished, I could prove that they ought to be done away with by your authority," he wrote to Valentinian II.

But since they have been forbidden and prohibited by many princes throughout nearly the whole world, and were abolished at Rome by Gratian of august memory, the brother of your Clemency, in consideration of the true faith, and rendered void by a rescript, do not, I pray, either pluck up what has been established in accordance with the faith, nor rescind your brother's precepts. In civil matters, if he established anything, no one thinks that it ought to be treated lightly, while a precept about religion is trodden under foot.[32]

This argument contrasts nicely with the one Ambrose stated when the imperial authority used the same powers of *res sacrae* to transfer basilicas from the Bishop's control to that of the Arians. His objection is fundamentally sacramental, as we shall see in a later chapter. To surrender the church buildings would be to surrender the altars of God, for they contained the symbols of the very body of Christ. But in law, he took up an argument analogous to Symmachus's position that the property in question fell under private, not public law. He wrote that he could not lawfully surrender the basilica, and the Emperor could not suitably receive it. "By no right can you violate the house of a private person, and do you think that the House of God may be taken away?" [33] The basilica was for Ambrose the inheritance of his fathers, and it could not be given up.[34] The Bishop explicitly denied the public character of the church when he wrote

---

[28] Ep. 18, 16 (Migne, *Patrologia Latina* 16: 977). On the following argument, see P. Batiffol, "De la dédicace des églises. Dédicace païenne et dédicace chrétienne," *Revue des sciences philosophiques et théologiques* 1939: 58–70.

[29] Relatio, c. 13 (*ibid.*, 970).
[30] Ep. 18, 16 (*ibid.*, 977).
[31] *Ibid.*, c. 13 f. (*ibid.*, 976); Ep. 17, c. 4 (*ibid.*, 962).
[32] Ep. 17, c. 5 (*ibid.*, 962).
[33] Ep. 20, c. 19 (*ibid.*, 1000).
[34] Sermo contra Auxentium, c. 17 f. (*ibid.*, 1012).

that the Emperor had authority over public, not sacred buildings.[35]

What interests us especially, however, is the argument against which Ambrose spoke, the argument that the church building did in fact fall under imperial power. Unfortunately, this argument is known only in fragments from Ambrose's refutation, but its tenor is sufficiently clear. Valentinian II issued an imperial order commanding Ambrose to surrender the basilica, which was at the same time draped with imperial hangings to mark it as state property.[36] Upon the Bishop's resisting, a court official accused Ambrose of contumacy in acting contrary to the Emperor's command,[37] denounced him by implication as a usurper (*tyrannus*),[38] and threatened him with capital punishment.[39] The crisis ended when the imperial order was rescinded.[40]

Still, the claim to power over the churches, which Gaius attributes to the *ius divinum,* had been made, patently on the basis of the classic attribution of the *res sacrae* to imperial administration. St. Ambrose's protest recalls the technical distinction that the *res sacrae* belong, not to the Emperor, but to the god to whom they were dedicated, and it is an important step in the development of the concept of ecclesiastical liberties and immunities. But the implications of this were not well established, and the older claim that the effectual management of *res sacrae* belonged to the Roman people and the emperor is apparent in the imperial demand he resisted. Ambrose freely admitted the legitimacy of imperial requirements upon the lands and nonconsecrated movables of the Church. "If [the Emperor] demand tribute, we do not refuse it. The lands of the Church pay tribute. If the Emperor wants the lands, he has the power to claim them; none of us will interfere."[41] That is, just as he upheld the power of the Emperor over the sustenance of the pagan colleges, so he also acknowledged it over the sustenance of the Church, admitting to that extent the traditional claims of the Empire over *res sacrae,* but denying them over objects explicitly consecrated to divine service. The Empire had no claim over what was God's, though it might lawfully demand what was the Church's.

The exercise of these conventional powers is also well attested in the writings of St. Athanasius, who protests repeatedly against Constantius II that the Emperor ought not to transfer the churches from the control of the orthodox to that of heretics. But Athanasius never disputes the legitimacy of the Emperor's power to do so. Indeed, he reconciled himself to the fact, by thinking that while the Arians might have the churches, the orthodox had the true Faith: "And aliens indeed had held the Place, but knew not the Lord of the Place, while in that He neither gave answer nor spoke, they were deserted by the truth. What profit then is the Place to them?"[42] And one may recall that among the civil charges against which the Bishop defended himself in flight was one that he had abused the imperial prerogatives by conducting worship in an undedicated church.[43]

Just as churchmen petitioned the emperors to use the legitimate imperial powers over consecrated property—as the examples of the Arians and St. Athanasius show equally well—so they also petitioned them to use their legislative and jurisdictional powers on behalf of the Church.

Petitions for the confirmation of ecclesiastical decrees and privileges by imperial law are rare in the fourth century; but they occur in critical contexts and indicate the urgency with which the petitioners sought that corroboration which would make their decrees executable by civil officers within the general competence of temporal courts. Two of the most important instances have already been mentioned in another context: Constantine's confirmation of the decisions of Nicaea and Theodosius's of the decrees of Constantinople (381). The documents issuing from these two councils show very clearly that the decisions rested with the assembled bishops, that, as synodal decrees, they had a validity of their own, and that imperial confirmations were intended to add a quality which would otherwise be absent: temporal sanctions against offenders. The ferocious edicts Constantine issued after Nicaea amply illustrate this. The bishops had pronounced the Arian doctrines heretical and had expelled Arius and his followers from the Church. Constantine accepted this judgment and added the further sentence that the books by Arius must be given up to be burned on pain of death, and he corroborated the sentences of episcopal deposition with that of civil banishment. "Whatever is decided in the sacred councils of bishops," he wrote, "ought to be ascribed to Divine Will."[44] The decrees of Nicaea were, for him, the "sentence of the Son of God,"[45] and as a "cham-

[35] Ep. 20, 19 (*ibid.*, 999).

[36] *Ibid.,* 4, 20, 24 (*ibid.,* 995, 1000, 1001).

[37] Sermo contra Auxentium, c. 18 (*ibid.,* 1012).

[38] Ep. 20, 22 (*ibid.,* 1001).

[39] Ep. 20, 28 (*ibid.,* 1002), Sermo contra Auxentium, c. 16 (*ibid.,* 1012).

[40] Ep. 20, 26 (*ibid.,* 1002).

[41] Sermo contra Auxentium, c. 33 (*ibid.,* 1017).

[42] Frag. (survives only in Latin translation) Migne, *Patrologia Graeca* 26 : 1189 f.

[43] Apologia ad Constantium, c. 14 ff. (Migne, *Patrologia Graeca* 25 : 612 ff.). It may be added that the imperial claim over *res sacrae* did not extend merely to pagan and Christian property. The Jews dedicated their synagogues to the emperor; prior to the reign of Claudius, they were compelled to keep and to honor imperial insignia—and under Claudius, even images of the Emperor—in the synagogues. Afterwards, these later requirements were lifted, and the Empire contented itself with receiving the dedication of synagogues. See J. Juster, *Les Juifs dans l'Empire romain* (Paris, 1914) 1: p. 348 ff.

[44] "Cum ex florenti," Mansi, *Collectio Conciliorum* 2: 926.

[45] Mansi, *Collectio Conciliorum* 2: 922.

pion of the holy mysteries of His grace," [46] Constantine sought to implement that sentence through the imperial power. The decree of Theodosius confirming the decision of Constantinople revealed the same attitude. The Emperor accepted the decision of his bishops in defining the Faith and gave it temporal force by commanding that heretics be expelled from the churches. And, as we have observed, he later imposed capital punishment upon those who violated the established Faith and disturbed the peace of the Church. [47]

At least toward the end of the fourth century, the clergy sought imperial confirmation of ecclesiastical processes as well as of the Faith. The petition of the Roman Synod of 378 to Gratian is a distinguished example of this. The Synod praised Gratian for removing priests from the jurisdiction of civil judges in religious matters, and urged him to re-enforce the earlier edicts by which he had established that exemption, reaffirming their principles. In particular, it asked that if a bishop who had been deposed by the judgment of the Roman bishop or of true believers should attempt to retain his church, or if a bishop should contumaciously disobey a summons to appear before an ecclesiastical court, the imperial prefect of Italy or the vicar of Rome be required to force him to go to Rome for judgment. If the case should arise at a great distance from Italy, it should be remanded to the metropolitan over the see in question; but if the accused were himself a metropolitan, the case should be referred to Rome. Further, if the trial should fall under the jurisdiction of a metropolitan suspected of bias towards the accused, the latter might appeal his case to the bishop of Rome or to a synod of fifteen neighboring bishops. The condemnation issued by either was to be accepted as final. In his response, the famous edict "Ordinariorum sententiae," Gratian granted the petition of the Synod, and, extending its terms, obliged the prefects of Gaul as well as of Italy, the proconsuls, and the vicars to enforce the process the bishops had described. [48]

Bishops accepted the authority of imperial edicts, or pronouncements in the ius publicum, as authoritative corroborations of their judgments; they also implicitly accepted the proposition that the ius publicum was in some sense valid in ecclesiastical processes, that even in cases which were not civil or criminal by nature the imperial power could act authoritatively. This action was interlocutory, and it was exercised in reviewing charges intended for definitive trial by synodal courts or in reviewing appeals for retrial from judgments already issued by the proper courts. This was the legal power which the emperors exercised in summoning synods, when they judged that ecclesiastical

cases which had been appealed to them were worthy of trial or retrial, or when they dismissed charges without trial, as Constantine dismissed the charges against Athanasius at Psamathia. When the emperor granted permission for retrial, he, in effect, nullified the earlier synodal decision. St. Ambrose expressed some chagrin at this state of affairs when he complained that the imperial power had abrogated the judgment of the Synod of Capua against Flavian of Antioch.

When we had begun to hope that these most equitable decrees of the Synod had provided a solution and put an end to discord, your Holiness [Theophilus of Alexandria] wrote once more that our brother Flavian had again sought help from entreaties and from the support of imperial rescripts. The toil of so many bishops has been spent in vain; we must turn again to temporal judgments, to [imperial] rescripts; once more will aged bishops be put upon to cross the seas; once more, though weak in body, must they exchange their native land for foreign soil; once more must holy altars be abandoned that we may travel to distant places. . . . [49]

But Ambrose did not protest against the interlocutory powers of the Emperor; indeed, he accepted as legitimate the recourse to civil tribunals and imperial rescripts.

Even St. Hilary, one of the strongest advocates of the constitutional separatism of the Church, appealed to Valentinian I for an imperial hearing of his charges against Auxentius, the Arian bishop of Milan. When Hilary's agitation in Milan against Auxentius was forbidden by Valentinian's "grievous edict," Hilary petitioned the Emperor directly for a hearing, which was granted. Valentinian appointed a commission consisting of a questor and a magister, with "about ten bishops sitting with us." Auxentius succeeded in convincing the commission and the Emperor of his orthodoxy; the commission dismissed Hilary's charges without trial, and commanded him to leave Milan or be remanded into custody. [50]

The Church accepted the powers which classical Roman law ascribed to the emperor, powers of legislation, powers over all matters comprehended in the ius publicum. These were, the Fathers acknowledged, morally neutral, but they might be enlisted to defend the interests of the Church. Still, the exercise of imperial power over persons and over laws, even at the behest of the clergy, did not touch the essence of the Church. It did not define the Faith, decide cases of discipline on sacramental matters, or in any way alter the Church's administrative structure or its peculiar laws; the Empire remained potestas exterra.

II

The Church could not enter into closer relations with the Empire because, in the final analysis, the use of the

[46] Athanasius, Apologia contra Arianos, c. 86 (Migne, Patrologia Graeca 25: 403).
[47] Cod. Th. XVI, 1, 3, 4.
[48] Mansi, Collectio Conciliorum 3: 624 ff.

[49] Ep. 56, 3 (Migne, Patrologia Latina 16: 1170).
[50] Contra Auxentium, cc. 7-9 (Migne, Patrologia Latina 10: 613 ff.).

imperial power fell to the irresponsible discretion of the emperor. Recognizing the authority of imperial legislation, the clergy might well petition the emperors for confirmation of synodal decrees, but the emperors were not obliged to honor the petition. Constantius II, for example, impounded the sentence of the Synod of Rimini against his favorites, the Bishops Valens and Ursacius;[51] and although a Roman Synod (369) declared Auxentius of Milan deposed, Valentinian I refused to implement the sentence or to corroborate it with an edict of banishment. The personal convictions of the emperor were of paramount importance; for, as he willed, he might enable and enforce ecclesiastical sentences, or not; he might grant privileges or withdraw them.

In a famous passage, the historian Theodoret described the mutations of religious policy which occurred in the fourth century as a result of this variable and extra-legal element.

Constantine the Great, most worthy of all eulogy, was indeed the first to grace his empire with true religion; and when he saw the world still given over to foolishness, he issued a general prohibition against the offering of sacrifices to the idols. He had not, however, destroyed the temples, though he ordered them to be kept shut. His sons followed in their father's footsteps. Julian restored the false faith and rekindled the flame of the ancient fraud. On the accession of Jovian, he once more placed an interdict on the worship of idols, and Valentinian the Great governed Europe with like laws. Valens, however, allowed every one else to worship any way they would and to honor their various objects of adoration. Against the champions of the Apostolic decrees alone he persisted in waging war. Accordingly during the whole period of his reign, the altar fire was lit, libations and sacrifices were offered to idols, public feasts were celebrated in the forum, and votaries initiated in the orgies of Dionysus ran about in goat-skins, mangling hounds in Bacchic frenzy, and generally behaving in such a way as to show the iniquity of their master. When the most faithful Theodosius found all these evils, he pulled them up by the roots, and consigned them to oblivion ["publishing edicts in which he ordered the shrines of the idols to be destroyed."][52]

Throughout these very great changes, the imperial powers described above continued to be exercised lawfully by reigning emperors, although they were directed toward the most widely different goals. Constantius II and Valens, for example, used their authority over *res sacrae* to transfer church buildings from the orthodox to the Arians, whom they favored; and they employed their powers of legislation to force the Christian clergy to choose between conforming to the Arian profession or going into banishment. If correctly rendered by Athanasius, Constantius's assertion at the Synod of Milan (355) that bishops should accept his word as canon may be taken as an affirmation of the emperor's character as *lex animata;* and the Emperor's statement

that the Syrian (i.e., Arian) bishops received his word as canon indicates that, to some of the clergy, the absolute powers of imperial legislation extended into the Church. But when Constantius pressed his claims to this length, the orthodox clergy resisted, as we have seen; Lucifer of Cagliari denounced him as presuming to act as the "bishop of bishops."[53] Similarly, when Valens attempted to enforce conformity to the Arian creed, Eulogius of Edessa asked, "Has he then received the priesthood as well as the Empire?"[54] Still, the powers those emperors exercised were lawfully theirs; and when later emperors used them to transfer churches from the heretics to the orthodox and to enforce conformity to the Nicene creed, orthodox writers praised their wisdom and piety.

The clearest evidence that such powers did belong to the emperor and that they could be used by him at will comes from the reign of Julian the Apostate. That Emperor overturned the religious policy of his predecessors, the Christians Constantine and Constantius II, and proposed to reform State paganism and to restore it to its former prominence. Accordingly, he withdrew by law the privileges which the Christian clergy had been granted in using the imperial post, barred Christians from publicly supported teaching positions, and deprived the clergy of the right to draw up wills and of immunity from public taxation. Like Christian emperors, he held authority over *res sacrae* and used it to further his religious policy. Under a decree which orders "public property" to be restored to municipal government,[55] he compelled the restoration to pagan cults of pagan temples which had been turned into Christian churches.[56] Gregory Nazianzinus denounced Julian for despoiling the churches of their furniture,[57] and the Emperor himself has left a biting statement of purpose regarding the spoliation of the church at Edessa.

Therefore, since by their most admirable law they are bidden to sell all they have and give to the poor so that they may more easily reach the kingdom of the heavens, I have ordered—so as to aid them in that effort—that all their funds, namely the funds of the church of the Edessenes, are to be taken over to be given to the soldiers, and that its property be expropriated to the fisc. This is in order that poverty may teach them to behave properly and that they may not be deprived of that heavenly kingdom for which they still hope.[58]

---

[53] Moriendum esse pro Dei filio (*Corpus Scriptorum Ecclesiasticorum Latinorum* 14; 311, 25).

[54] Theodoret, Historia Ecclesiastica, IV, 15 (Migne, *Patrologia Graeca* 82: 1156).

[55] Cod. Th. X, 3, 1.

[56] Libanius, Orat. 18, 126.

[57] Orat. contra Julianum, IV, 86 (Migne, *Patrologia Graeca* 35: 613).

[58] Ep. 40, 424C (ed. W. C. Wright, *cit.* 3: p. 126). Dvornik does not consider this evidence when he writes that Julian was hostile to the convention that the king was superior to law. F. Dvornik, "The Emperor Julian's Reactionary Ideas on Kingship," *Studies in Honor of A. M. Friend, Jr.* (Princeton, 1955), p. 74.

---

[51] Hilary of Poitiers, Contra Constantium, c. 26 (*ibid.*, 601).

[52] Historia Ecclesiastica, V, 20 (Migne, *Patrologia Graeca* 82: 1242).

These examples will suffice to illustrate the fundamental instability which marked the use of their constitutional powers vis-à-vis the Church by the emperors of the fourth century. There was not an imperial religious policy in this period; rather, there were the religious policies of the several emperors. The edicts of one emperor might modify or completely overturn those of his predecessor, and, as actually happened, pagan, heretical, and orthodox emperors, each in his turn, might pick up or cast down religions or sects as they pleased.

III

The example of Julian the Apostate shows the potential insecurity of Christianity in the Empire and, more important, the fallacy of speaking of a Christian Empire until long usage together with law had firmly established Christianity as the religion of the whole Empire. That did not occur in the period under review. Its clear beginnings came when Gratian divorced the imperial office from paganism by rejecting the office and the functions of *pontifex maximus* (379) and when, by the decrees *Cunctos populos* and *Episcopis tradi*, he, Valentinian, and Theodosius commanded the adherence of all peoples within the Empire to the Nicene profession.

From the conversion of Constantine until the last two decades of the fourth century, the relations of the emperor to the Church did not change the relations between the Church, the particular institution, and the Empire, the general institution in the midst of which the Church existed. The attitudes of the Christian emperors in this period are roughly comparable to those of Heliogabalus and Alexander Severus who attempted to establish a syncretic religion embracing Judaism, Orphism, Christianity, and other mystery religions.[59] Neither the early syncretist emperors nor the later Christian, before Gratian, elevated their private devotions to the dimension of a State religion. Indeed, they appear to have observed the legal strictures which Paulus records forbidding the introduction of foreign religions on pain of death;[60] and it is important to notice that after Gratian had broken definitely with paganism and formally adopted Christianity in its place, the pagans charged him explicitly with that legal violation.[61]

Constantine the Great and his Christian successors until Gratian followed deliberately ambivalent policies. They accepted and discharged the office of *pontifex maximus*, allowed State support for the pagan priestly colleges and for pagan rituals, and themselves witnessed the ancient barbarities at their triumphal celebrations. The researches of Professor Alföldi have shown most convincingly that Theodoret's remarks on Constantine's anti-pagan legislation are somewhat overdrawn, and that Constantine made every effort to continue good relations with the pagans in the Empire, particularly with those in Rome.[62] Although Constantius II issued fierce edicts against pagan practices, he did not enforce them. Indeed, Symmachus praised him for maintaining the State paganism for the Empire, although the Emperor himself held to another religion.[63] The Emperor once used his tolerant policy toward the Alexandrine pagans to sustain the intrusion of his favorite, Gregory of Cappadocia, into Athanasius's see. He threatened "that, unless they complied with the instructions contained in his letters, their bread should be taken away, their idols overthrown, and the persons of many of the city-magistrates and people delivered over to certain slavery." The pagans did comply and with great violence attended Gregory's entrance, "singing the praises of their idols and saying, 'Constantius has become a heathen and the Arians have acknowledged our customs.'"[64] Valentinian I granted general toleration to all his subjects and honored it so scrupulously that even the pagans praised him for it. And, as Theodoret says, Valens persecuted only the orthodox, allowing the pagans full religious freedom.

The edicts of Gratian did not abolish paganism; as St. Ambrose observes, the Emperor deprived the priestly colleges of their lands, but not of their legal rights. Theodosius first made a determined effort to stamp out pagan religious practices and to establish orthodox Christianity as the unchallenged State religion. He commanded the expulsion of heretics and their harrying by civil officials, and struck vigorously at the pagan cult. He forbade the holding of the Olympic Games and removed to Constantinople the sacred statue of Zeus, sculptured by Pheidias eight hundred years before; in a series of fierce decrees, he closed pagan temples for purposes of worship, while leaving them open for the display of art treasures, denied all public support to heathen rituals, and restricted pagan practices, public and private, to the purely social and non-religious. He cancelled all privileges of the priestly colleges, and in 394, officially abolished paganism in the city of Rome.

At this point, the Emperor had employed his powers over laws and over the persons of priests to impose Christianity upon the whole Empire. The history of the Christian Empire had begun. But to contemporaries, who still recalled the reigns of the heretics Constantius and Valens and the pagan Julian, this change was not apparent. For they realized that another emperor of a different persuasion might turn the powers of his office to reverse Theodosius's judgments and edicts,

---

[59] Lampridus, *Ant. Heliogab*, 3, 5: 28, 4, and *Al. Sever*. 29, 3.
[60] Sentent. V, 21, 2 (ed. Krüger *cit.*, p. 127 f.).
[61] Relatio Symmachi, c. 16 (Migne, *Patrologia Latina* 16: 971).

[62] See especially A. Alföldi, trans. H. Mattingly, *The Conversion of Constantine and Pagan Rome* (Oxford, 1948), p. 110 ff.
[63] Relatio, c. 8 (Migne, *Patrologia Latina* 16: 968).
[64] Historia Arianorum, cc. 54, 56 (Migne, *Patrologia Graeca* 25: 757 ff.).

to abrogate his laws, and to follow a totally different course. This fundamental instability made churchmen hesitant to accept imperial edicts in their favor as integral parts of ecclesiastical law. They welcomed imperial support, but they continued to construe Church and Empire as two discrete institutions, each under its own law, each under its own ruler.

PART II

THEOLOGICAL PRINCIPLES

3. SS. ATHANASIUS AND HILARY

Thus far, we have examined the legal implications of the statement, "the Church is the City of God." We have seen that Church and Empire were considered alien to each other; that the Church claimed absolute jurisdiction in its sacramental life (including discipline of the clergy in purely religious cases), at the same time acknowledging the sole competence of civil courts in criminal, or "external," jurisdiction; and that, from the time of Constantine onwards, civil law confirmed this separation of competences. In this chapter and the one which follows, we shall examine the doctrinal warrant for this juristic division: that the nature of the Church as a polity was theological.

Although they condemned the Jews as "ignorant of the truth" and as "murderers of Christ," the Fathers were aware of the Church's historical and doctrinal affinity to the Synagogue. For example, St. Athanasius, following St. Paul, regarded Christ's advent as the final consummation of the "ancient ordinances" of the Jewish people. The Jews received the "divine food" of Christ "through the type when they ate a lamb in the passover. But not understanding the type, even to this day they eat the lamb, erring in that they are without the city and the truth." [1] St. Hilary also saw these

relationships when he wrote that "Christ, in His kingdom, is between the Law and the prophets," [2] and when he wrote of the two Israels, "Israel carnalis," the Synagogue, and "Israel spiritualis," the Church. [3] He realized that both were composed of many peoples, [4] and that both were scattered throughout the world. The Word of Truth had gone first to the Jews, but despite the earnest efforts of the Apostles, Israel carnalis had rejected the Gospel. [5] Still, the Synagogue was the prefiguration of the Church, [6] and the the Church grieved for the loss of the Jews; [7] so, in the fullness of time, would the faithful remnant of that people be gathered into the Church. [8]

Finally, despite his frequent and vigorous denunciations of the Jews—he calls the Synagogue "the place of perfidy, the house of impiety, the shelter of madness, which God Himself has damned" [9]—St. Ambrose was keenly sensitive to the Church's institutional debt to the Synagogue. Indeed, the Church was the direct and true continuation of the Synagogue. The Synagogue, which had neither beginning nor end, [10] was the first "congregatio" of God; [11] its head was Christ. [12] But when the chosen people proved faithless and rejected

---

[1] Ep. heor. I, cc. 7, 8; Ep. heor. 19, c. 1 (Migne, *Patrologia Graeca* 26: 1364 f., 1424). Scholars have, in general, neglected the connection between theology and political thought with which we shall be concerned here. The article by G. H. Williams is a brilliant exception ("Christology and Church-State Relations in the Fourth Century," *Church History* 20 [1951]: no. 3, pp. 3–33; no. 4, pp. 3–26), but Professor Williams did not attempt to relate his conclusions to contemporary legal principles. On the other hand, A. Beck (*Römisches Recht bei Tertullian und Cyprian* [Halle, 1930], pp. 27–175) focused his attention entirely upon principles of Roman law, without any reference to theology or general political thought, and in his monograph on Athanasius, Hagel failed to enquire into the legal warrant for imperial actions vis-à-vis the Church and into the sacramental and legal concepts which directed Athanasius's thought (K. F. Hagel, *Kirche und Kaisertum in Lehre und Leben des Athanasius* [Borna-Leipzig, 1933], pp. 48 ff., 51 ff.). Specialist studies of fourth-century theology have likewise failed to establish the connection between the Fathers' sacramental and soteriological thought and their broader intellectual activity. C. W. Dugmore, "Sacrament and Sacrifice in the Early Fathers," *Journal of Ecclesiastical History* 2 (1951): 24–37, does not discuss the Eastern Fathers in detail, or Atha-

nasius and Hilary at all, when he does describe the general sacramental thought of their day. The same can be said of the less scholarly essay by J. Zeiller, "Le royaume de Dieu et l'unité terrestre aux premiers siècles du christianisme," *Revue apologétique* 64 (1937): 513–535, esp. 533. Voisin and, more recently, Berchem, in his fine study, comment particularly upon Athanasius's Christological thought, but they do not extend their remarks to his soteriology, to his concepts about the sacraments, or to the significance of all this in his position on Church-State relations. G. Voisin, "La doctrine christologique de S. Athanase," *Revue d'histoire ecclésiastique* 1 (1900): 226–248; J. B. Berchem, "Le Christ sanctificateur d'après S. Athanase," *Angelicum* 15 (1938): 515–558. See especially Berchem, pp. 521, 525 (on the Incarnation), and 543 ff. (on baptism).

[2] Comment. in Matt. XVII, c. 2 (Migne, *Patrologia Latina* 9: 1014).

[3] Tractatus in psalmum CXXI, cc. 7–10; Tractatus in psalmum LII, 19 f. (*Corpus Scriptorum Ecclesiasticorum Latinorum* 22: 574 ff, 132).

[4] Cf. Tractatus in psalmum II, 7 (*ibid.*, p. 41).

[5] Comment. in Matt. XV, c. 9; XXIV, c. 8 (Migne, *Patrologia Latina* 9: 1006, 1050 f.).

[6] Supra, note 3, and Tractatus in psalmum LIX, c. 13 (*Corpus Scriptorum Ecclesiasticorum Latinorum* 22: 201 f.).

[7] Comment. in Matt. I, c. 7 (Migne, *Patrologia Latina* 9: 923).

[8] Ibid., X, c. 14; XVII, cc. 2–8; XXVI, c. 5 (*ibid.*, 971 f., 1013 ff., 1057 f.).

[9] Ep. 40, 14 (Migne, *Patrologia Latina* 16: 1106).

[10] Exposit. in psalmum CXVIII, Sermo. XX, 3 (Migne, *Patrologia Latina* 15: 1484). In the published outline of his dissertation, Figueroa sketches St. Ambrose's concept of God's rejection of the Synagogue, the growth of the Church out of the Synagogue, and the ultimate sterility of the Synagogue. G. Figueroa, *The Church and the Synagogue in Saint Ambrose* (Washington, 1949), pp. 1, 15, 27 ff.

[11] Ibid., Sermo II, 9 (*ibid.*, 1212 f.).

[12] Enarratio in psalmum XLIII, 62 (Migne, *Patrologia Latina* 14: 1118): "Lex autem Synagogae caput non a principio, quia Christus erat caput veteris Synagogae quam Moyses fundavit et condidit."

its Head, the Church arose out of the Synagogue,[13] and seized its "kingdom."[14] From Jewish practice, the Church took its form of juristic debate,[15] its conciliar government,[16] and some offices.[17] As for the Jews, they saw their spiritual inheritance without receiving it;[18] they must not be counted among the heathen, but among the apostates.[19] Their wrongdoing had profited the Gentiles, and the faith of the Gentiles had freed the people of Israel by converting it to the Truth.[20] The Church had arisen in the context of the Synagogue; it had deserted the rites of the Jews, forsaking the shadows to follow the sun.[21] Still, it preserved constitutional and doctrinal elements of its Jewish heritage; and at length the two Israels would again be one.

This awareness of affinity to the Synagogue had considerable relevance in the Church's dealings with the Empire; for the legal status of the Jewish people was both the status of the early Church and, by the fourth century, a precedent for establishing the legal status of Christians who "were, in some sense, Israelites."[22] When they claimed juridical independence from the Empire, the Fathers argued on theological grounds that the Church, the Body of Christ, must be distinct from civil government; but they also argued on the implicit assumption that the juristic privileges of the Old Israel belonged also to the New, and that just as the Jews, though ignorant of the truth, were allowed to preserve their ancestral customs and laws because of their imperfect testimony to the truth, so should the Church, which knew the truth, enjoy its own tradition and its own law.

In this intellectual context, the two great defenders of orthodoxy in the mid-fourth century, Athanasius and

Hilary, condemned the intrusion of the civil power by Constantius II into ecclesiastical affairs. The terms of their condemnation indicate that the Fathers were actually maintaining the independence of the Church from the Empire; but that independence was not absolute. The juristic division they sought—the division which, in their eyes, Constantius had overstepped—was the division between "ethnic" and imperial jurisdiction. They were simply maintaining that the privileges of legal competence which the Church had enjoyed as a distinct people at least from Aurelian onwards (at times surreptitiously) should be continued. It must be acknowledged, Athanasius and Hilary were saying, that matters of faith and legal processes deriving from them, cases in which the imperial government had no interest, were to be adjudicated by the established courts of the religious group in question. Such cases might be appealed to the emperor for hearing and referred by him to a duly constituted court; but their judgment fell within ecclesiastical, not civil, competence. The division they sought in legal matters was, so to speak, a division of legal competences, and not a thorough and absolute separation of one government from another.

On the other hand, the Fathers did seek complete doctrinal freedom for the Church, and it is here that the interpretation of their thought in constitutional terms is most relevant. Athanasius and Hilary were concerned to repel Constantius's efforts to supersede the Nicene faith with the Arian profession which had found his favor. Imperial practice had been to leave doctrinal matters to the particular religious group. As we have seen, Constantius paid lip service to that form while he vitiated it in practice, and the Fathers besought him in this, as in juristic matters, to return to the letter and the spirit of earlier usage. In doctrine, the Church was to be absolutely discrete from the Empire. But, in the judgment and execution of cases arising from doctrinal disputes, the Church and the Empire were to work in concord.

To approach the Fathers' work purely from the standpoint of political philosophy or even from that of institutional integrity is to set up a framework of interpretation foreign to them. For both Athanasius and Hilary met the problems of their day primarily with theological and ecclesiological predispositions, rather than with philosophical and institutional. Church law expressed theological truths. For the Fathers, the Church was in the first instance the mystical body of Christ, and only derivatively a legal construct. Its first essence was sacramental, not administrative. In their eyes, the fundamental operations of the Church were motivated and sustained by the charismatic relationship between Christ and the true believers, between Christ and the Church. The critical point in human history was the crucifixion, when mankind was freed from the Law and from sin; the critical element in human thought was soteriology, for man's noblest goal was union with his Redeemer.

[13] Exposit. in Lucam, X, c. 6 (*Corpus Scriptorum Ecclesiasticorum Latinorum* 32, pt. 4: 457), and especially De Jacob et vita beata II, 2, 9 (*ibid.*, pt. 2: 36).

[14] Exposit. in Lucam, V, c. 113 (*ibid.*, p. 229 f).

[15] Comment. in Ep. I. ad Cor. XIV, v. 31 (Migne, *Patrologia Latina* 17: 258).

[16] Comment. in Ep. I ad Tim. V, v. 1 (*ibid.*, 475): "Unde et Synagoga et postea ecclesia seniores habuit, quorum sine consilio nihil agebatur in ecclesia."

[17] Comment. in Ep. ad Ephes. IV, vv. 11, 12 (*ibid.*, 387 f.): "Magistri vero exocristae sunt, quia in ecclesia ipsi compescunt et verberant inquietos, sive ii qui litteris et lectionibus imbuendos infantes solebant imbuere, sicut mos Judaeorum est, quorum traditio ad nos transitum fecit, quae per negligentiam obsolevit."

[18] Ep. 75, 6 (Migne, *Patrologia Latina* 16: 1258).

[19] Comment. in Ep. ad Rom. IX, v. 27 (Migne, *Patrologia Latina* 17: 139): "Recedentibus Judaeis a merito et promissione patrum dum illam non recipiunt, hi reliquiae sunt, qui credendo in fide promissionis patribus factae persistunt, fideles effecti; a Lege enim recedunt, qui in eum quem Lex solum ad salutem sufficere promisit, non credunt. Igitur apostatae habeantur necesse est, quicum Christum non recipiunt, rei sunt violatae legis."

[20] Enarrat. in psalmum LXI, c. 29 (*Corpus Scriptorum Ecclesiasticorum Latinorum* 64: 395).

[21] Ep. 78, 1 (Migne, *Patrologia Latina* 16: 1268).

[22] Julian the Apostate, Against the Galilaeans, 253B, ed. W. C. Wright, *The Works of the Emperor Julian* (London, 1923) 3: p. 392.

The objections of Athanasius and Hilary to the intrusion of the civil power into ecclesiastical affairs must be set into this doctrinal context. Although the two Fathers addressed themselves to the same problems with very similar soteriological and ecclesiological premises, they cast their objections differently. Both protested that the doctrinal integrity of the Church must be maintained and that the high-handed actions of Constantius had jeopardized it. Beyond this, Hilary was concerned for the purity of the Faith itself. He stated his primary charge against Constantius in a lapidary sentence: "*Edictis fidem terruisti.*"[23] The Arians have labored, he writes, to the end that the Faith may be destroyed, and that doctrines about the Lord may be established by human judgment and power,[24] rather than by bishops exercising their authority in the apostolic tradition. Throughout, his argument centers upon the word "*libertas.*" The Church must enjoy its liberty; the individual must enjoy his liberty; the Emperor, whose office is to guarantee the liberty of his subjects has connived in its restriction.[25] The legal freedom of the Church to acknowledge and preserve the true Faith as the source of her true freedom has been denied; and the days of persecution have returned.

Like Hilary, Athanasius was an unrelenting fighter for the Nicene Faith, but his primary objection against the Emperor is not corruption of true belief, but the wrongful transformation of the Church into a branch of the civil government, which, in his eyes, led to that corruption. His argument is, in the first instance, doctrinal, but juridical in tenor. For him, the Church was a sacramental body governed in this world by bishops, "stewards of the divine mysteries," according to tradition established by Christ and confirmed by the Apostles. On that account, it was not to be given over to secular rulers. But Constantius "infringed ecclesi-

astical order and mingled Roman sovereignty with the constitution of the Church, introducing the Arian heresy into the Church of God."[26] The Arians, under Constantius's patronage, considered the Church a "civil senate,"[27] and made "the Holy Place a house of merchandise and a house of juridical business for themselves. . . ."[28]

Athanasius's peculiar circumstances—the judicial process which the Arians began against him shortly after his accession (329) and which continued intermittently until the death of Julian the Apostate (363)—clearly made him unusually sensitive to the legal instruments and maneuvers employed against him. And Constantius's claim at the Synod of Milan (355) that the bishops should accept his word as canon, accompanied as it was by the command that the Synod condemn Athanasius, would in itself explain sufficiently the Bishop's acute sense of the juridical transformation which Constantius was introducing into the Church.

Still, his fundamental argument is the same as that of Hilary. The Arian heresy has been introduced into the Church of God; the Holy Place, polluted; the Faith, imperiled.

The two arguments may be considered complementary, variations on a theme; and in the following remarks, we shall attempt to describe both the theme and the variations more fully.

I

For Athanasius, as for Hilary, the Church was simply the body in which "the doctrine of the mysteries" was confirmed, in which the true Faith, revealed by Christ and transmitted unchanged by the Saints from generation to generation, was preserved.[29] It was the community which bore the impress and image of Christ,[30] through which believers were incorporate in Christ through the regeneration of the spirit and participation in fleshly existence,[31] a community whose inner life pagans and heretics could never know.[32] Spread

---

[23] Contra Constantium, c. 11 (Migne, *Patrologia Latina* 10: 588).

[24] De Synodis, c. 4 (*ibid.*, 483).

[25] Ad Constantium, I, c. 2 (*Corpus Scriptorum Ecclesiasticorum Latinorum* 65: 182). Legal historians are agreed that, by the time of the early Empire, the legal concept of *libertas* as a right deriving from membership in political institutions— especially in cities and ethnic groups—had become blurred. As C. Wirszubski comments, it had ceased to be a right and had become a gift, "and ceasing to be a right, lost what had made its essential quality." (*Libertas as a Political Idea at Rome During the Late Republic and Early Principate* [Cambridge, 1950], p. 171.) More recently, E. Levy has reviewed various scholarly judgments on the question, which he formulates as follows: "Keine *civitas* ohne *libertas*. Dass ein Sklave nicht römischer Bürger sein könnte, versteht sich von selbst. Gilt aber auch der Umkehrschluss, 'Keine *libertas* ohne *civitas.*' Genauer: war nach römischer Anschauung jeder ein Sklave, der nicht irgendwo *civis* war?" ("Libertas und Civitas," *Zeitschrift für Rechtsgeschichte*, Röm. Abt. 78 (1961) : 142.) Levy concludes that the dependency of *libertas* upon the *civitas* lost precise legal meaning in late classical antiquity. Still, the relation of the two terms continued in Roman law, though somewhat weakened; and Hilary's claim that the *libertas* of the Church be upheld must be construed with regard for the concept of the Church as a *civitas* or as a discrete people.

[26] Historia Arianorum, c. 34 (Migne, *Patrologia Graeca* 25: 732).

[27] *Ibid.*, c. 78 (*ibid.*, 788).

[28] Migne, *Patrologia Graeca* 26: 1189 f.

[29] Ep. heor., II, 7 (*ibid.*, 1370). See the study by Richard, who concludes that Athanasius tended toward Apollinarianism. M. Richard, "Saint Athanase et la psychologie du Christ selon les Ariens," *Mélanges de science religieuse* 4 (1947) : esp. 38 f, 47.

[30] Orat. II contra Arianos, c. 80 (Migne, *Patrologia Graeca* 26 : 316).

[31] Orat. III contra Arianos, c. 16 (*ibid.*, 353 ff). *Cf.* Orat. II, c. 74 (*ibid.*, 305).

[32] *Cf.* the exclusion of non-Christians from worship services. Apologia ad Constantium, c. 16 (Migne, *Patrologia Graeca* 25: 613 ff), Ep. heor. VII, c. 4 (Migne, *Patrologia Graeca* 26: 1392). On Anthanasius's acceptance of the Nicene Faith, see J. Lebon, "Le sort du *consubstantiel* de Nicée," *Revue d'historie ecclésiastique* 47 (1952) : 485–529: and on the similarities between the theology of Athanasius and that of Hilary, see P. Löffler, "Die Trinitätslehre des Bischofs Hilarius von Poitiers zwischen Ost und West," *Zeitschrift für Kirchengeschichte* 71

throughout the whole world, the Church held to the same worship and maintained the same Faith and the same canons,[33] being sustained by the sacramental union of Saviour and saved.

Hilary makes this concept explicit when he writes that God released man from captivity by remitting his sins, "establishing us in the body of His flesh. For He is the Church holding her all within Himself through the sacrament of His body." [34] He writes again that the Incarnation was "the sacrament of [His] birth and the mystery of the body [He had] taken on." [35] And, in another place, he speaks of the Church as Holy Sion and the heavenly Jerusalem, the body of all the Faithful, the soul sanctified by the sacraments of the Church, in which, through the glory of the Resurrection —that is, through Christ's Incarnation, sacrifice, and resurrection—the very nature of Divinity rests.[36]

Hilary describes the Church in several conventional ways. He calls it the mouth of Christ,[37] the body of Christ,[38] the bride of Christ,[39] the ark of salvation to which many are summoned, but few come.[40] The Church is the inheritance of God,[41] and those who are cast outside her are handed over to the rule of the devil.[42]

But the Father returns again and again to the image of the Church as Christ, or as the body of Christ. She is the Lord in the body.[43] Through her alone is the

way to heaven, in her only is rest; for "all hope of our rest is in the body of Christ." [44] Outside her, apart from the Son of God, there is no true understanding of the Word of Life.[45] From the Church of the Apostles, many churches have sprung up,[46] and they are scattered throughout the world. Yet are they one, for the body of Christ is one.[47] Throughout his body, Christ preserves spiritual unity by the gift of understanding and wisdom [48] and by the revelation of mysteries.[49] Above all, the confession of Christ as the true Son of God,[50] and unfeigned participation in His body through the sacraments were the mark of the true believer, and the token of ecclesiastical unity.

The Fathers are quite explicit in affirming that the Church is the body of Christ and that the sacraments, Baptism and the Eucharist, are the instruments by which the true believer participates in that Body, sharing its holiness and the glory of its resurrection. Indeed, the distinction between Church and sacrament is not clear, so predominant is the concept of the Church as a sacramental union, so close is the identity between the Faith, the Word of Life, and Christ, the Word of God.

The Festal Letters of Athanasius illustrate this conceptual elision. In those letters, written at Eastertide for the instruction of the clergy under Athanasius's direction, Christ is the bread, the food of saints.[51] He promised that the believers should no longer eat the

---

(1960) : 26–36, and P. Smulders, *La doctrine trinitaire de S. Hilaire de Poitiers* (Rome, 1944), p. 293.

[33] E.g., Ep. encyclica, c. 1 (Migne, *Patrologia Graeca* 25: 224).

[34] Tractatus in psalmum CXXV, c. 6 (*Corpus Scriptorum Ecclesiasticorum Latinorum* 22: 609): "Ipse est enim ecclesia, per sacramentum corporis sui in se universam eam continens."

[35] De Trinitate IX, 55 (Migne, *Patrologia Latina* 10: 326).

[36] Tractatus in psalmum CXXXI, c. 23 (*Corpus Scriptorum Ecclesiasticorum Latinorum* 22: 679 f).

[37] Tractatus in psalmum CXXXVIII, c. 29 (*ibid.*, p. 764 f).

[38] Tractatus in psalmum CXXVIII, c. 9 (*ibid.*, p. 643).

[39] Tractatus in psalmum CXXVII, c. 9 (*ibid.*, p. 634).

[40] Tractatus in psalmum CXLVI, c. 12 (*ibid.*, p. 852).

[41] Tractatus in psalmum LXVII, c. 12 (*ibid.*, p. 287).

[42] Tractatus in psalmum CXVIII, Ain, c. 5 (*ibid.*, p. 497 f).

[43] Tractatus in psalmum CXXIV, c. 3 (*ibid.*, p. 598). There are several quite good, recent studies of St. Hilary's theology. J. E. Emmenegger, *The Functions of Faith and Reason in the Theology of Saint Hilary of Poitiers* (Washington, 1949), esp. p. 163 f, describes very well the quality of Faith in Hilary's thought, without extending his remarks to the relationship between Faith and the Sacraments. J. F. McHugh, *The Exaltation of Christ in the Arian Controversy* (Shrewsbury, 1959), esp. p. 25 f, describes lucidly the Father's doctrine concerning the Incarnation and man's sharing in Christ's divinity. And P. T. Wild, *The Divinization of Man According to Saint Hilary of Poitiers* (Mundelein, Illinois, 1950), affords an excellent précis of Hilary's soteriology which is particularly clear on the union of the believer and Christ through faith (p. 85 f), baptism (p. 93 f), and the Eucharist (p. 106 ff). None of these works, however, relate Hilary's theology to his political thought, on which the essay by J. Lécuyer must be consulted. ("Le sacerdoce royal des chrétiens selon Saint Hilaire de Poitiers," *L'année théologique* 10 [1947]: 302–325.) See especially p. 305: "L'alliance de la Royauté et du Sacerdoce dans le Sauveur est un des thèmes essentiels de la pensée d'Hilaire." And p.

324 f: "Sacrement, signe de la foi en la Résurrection du Christ, l'Eucharistie est plus que cela: c'est un gage de notre propre résurrection et de notre montée au ciel avec le Christ. . . . Bref, par l'Eucharistie, le Christ nous communique sa propre divinité et nous prépare à cette union ineffable qui se réalisera un jour au ciel. Le sacrifice des chrétiens est ainsi un nouveau principe d'unité entre le Christ et l'humanité, unité plus intime, plus profonde que celle fondée sur l'unité de nature: communication de la vie divine présente dans la chair du Christ que nous mangeons; participation toujours plus étroite au Sacrifice de notre grand-prêtre céleste, et à son Sacerdoce royal." *Cf.* J. Leclercq, "L'idée de la royautée du Christ dans l'œuvre de Saint Justin," *L'année théologique* 7 (1946): 91, 95. See below, pp. 34 f. The recent essay by T. Camelot, "Le Sens de l'eglise chez les Pères latins," *Nouvelle Revue théologique* 83 (1961): 367–381, is a very useful summary of terms used by the Latin Fathers to describe the Church, but it attempts no thorough analysis of patristic soteriology or ecclesiology.

[44] Tractatus in psalmum XIV, c. 5 (*ibid.*, p. 87).

[45] Comment. in Matt. XIII, c. 1 (Migne, *Patrologia Latina* 9: 993).

[46] Tractatus in psalmum CXXXI, c. 14; Tractatus in psalmum CXXXVIII, c. 40 (*Corpus Scriptorum Ecclesiasticorum Latinorum* 22: 673, 773).

[47] Tractatus in psalmum XIV, c. 3; Tractatus in psalmum CXXXI, c. 14 (*ibid.*, pp. 85 f, 673).

[48] De Trinitate, VI, 36 (Migne, *Patrologia Latina* 10: 186 f).

[49] Tractatus in psalmum CXXXVIII, 30, 31 (*Corpus Scriptorum Ecclesiasticorum Latinorum* 22: 765 f).

[50] De Trinitate, VI, 38 (Migne, *Patrologia Latina* 10: 188 f).

[51] Ep. heor. I, c. 5 (Migne, *Patrologia Graeca* 26: 1363). On the general problem of Athanasius's Christology, see E. Weigl, *Untersuchungen zur Christologie des heiligen Athanasius* (Paderborn, 1914). Weigl limits his discussion to the particular theological point of the relation of Christ to God the Father, and he does not discuss Athanasius's soteriology.

flesh of the sacrificed lamb, "but His own, saying, 'Take, eat and drink; this is my body and my blood.' " [52] He is both the giver of the Feast and the Feast itself, who gathers and unites the Faithful,[53] and He is also the living Word, which vivifies the Church. "He by His living Word quickens all men and gives Him to be food and life to the saints; as the Lord declares, 'I am the bread of life.' . . . The bread of Wisdom is living fruit, as the Lord said: 'I am the living bread which came down from heaven. If any man eat of this bread, he shall live forever.' " [54] The new Passover, Christ, unified the Saints; but those outside the orthodox community, the pagan and the heretic, could not participate in the feast, they could not partake of the bread of life.[55]

The effect of baptism was similar, "for as we are all from earth and die in Adam, so being regenerated from above of water and Spirit, in the Christ, we are all quickened; the flesh being no longer earthly, but being henceforth made Word by reason of God's Word who for our sake 'became flesh.' " [56] Christ in human form received baptism in the stead of all men, and his unction in the Holy Spirit is the unction of the true believer. He has confirmed the sacrament of regeneration for mankind, and to those who truly believe He gives the joy of redemption. But the sacrament is ineffectual when performed by heretics, and brings pollution rather than redemption.[57] By His Incarnation, Christ brought man freedom from sin and the Law; and joining man to God through His human body, He vouchsafed immortality to him [58] with the sign and seal of baptism.

Hilary is equally emphatic in construing the Eucharist and baptism as necessary sacraments of unity in the Church; as we have observed, he once defined the Church as those souls which the sacraments had sanctified. That he also defined it as the body of Christ was no exercise of rhetorical license, for his ecclesiological concepts, like those of Athanasius, were truly mystical. The profession of faith was itself the body and blood of Christ, and by accepting the true Faith, "we are in Christ, and Christ, in us." This union was formalized in the Eucharist: mankind shares fleshly existence with Christ, and through the mystery of the sacraments, Christ enters the believers.[59] Christ is the

bread by which the Faithful are prepared for fellowship with God,[60] and those who are not to enter the kingdom of God are excluded from the communion.[61] He is the living bread in the Eucharist whose property it is to vivify those who receive Him.[62]

Like Athanasius, Hilary saw baptism as a sacrament which transformed man and brought him into union with the Divine. He agreed that, depending for its validity as it did upon faith in the nature of Christ as perfect man and perfect God, baptism was without effect when performed by those who denied Christ's proper attributes.[63] When duly performed, it brought the power of resurrection.[64] It transformed the body and soul of the recipient, and conferred free will, the freedom of power, upon him.[65] Related to Christ through human form, he entered by baptism into the fellowship of Christ's flesh (in consortium Christi carnis), and his body was no longer his, but Christ's.[66]

For Athanasius and Hilary, the mystical character of the Church was paramount. The Eucharist and Baptism were, to use a later phrase, the channels of grace, by which the believer came to physical and spiritual union with Christ, by which the souls of the Faithful were sanctified and redeemed. To this, all else was subordinate. The first duty of the Church was to preserve the pure Faith, that element which made the sacraments effectual means of salvation, and to guard the "doctrine of the mysteries."

The Fathers knew very well that there was a visible Church, an administrative order in which bishops ruled. But to their eyes, the whole purpose of that order was the preservation of the Faith, the sacramental content of religion. We have already observed that Hilary considered the profession of Faith to be in some sense the body and blood of Christ, a bond of mystical union between Christ and the Faithful. That profession, with its sacramental cast, was at the center of the thought which both Athanasius and Hilary set forth about the episcopacy. Christ had enunciated the Faith to the Apostles, who had confirmed it; and since their time, it had been handed down unchanged from generation to generation of bishops, the successors of the Apostles. The foremost duty of the bishop was

[52] Ep. heor. IV, c. 4 (ibid., 1379). On the soteriological thought of Athanasius, see the brilliant article by D. Unger, "A Special Aspect of Athanasian Soteriology," Franciscan Studies 6 (1946) : esp. pp. 31, 45, 191 f. Unger does not mention the relation of Athanasius's soteriology to his thought about the sacraments.

[53] Ep. heor. X, c. 2 (ibid., 1397 f).
[54] Ep. heor. VII, c. 5 (ibid., 1393).
[55] Ibid., c. 4 (ibid., 1392).
[56] Orat. contra Arianos III, c. 33 (ibid., 396).
[57] Orat. contra Arianos I, c. 47 (ibid., 108 f). Cf. Orat. contra Arianos II, c. 41 (ibid., 233 ff).
[58] Orat. contra Arianos II, c. 67 ff (ibid., 289 ff).
[59] De Trinitate VIII, 13, 14 (Migne, Patrologia Latina 10: 245 ff). For similar thought, see Ignatius, Trall. VIII, "Faith is the flesh of Christ, and love is His blood," and Ambrose, "Splendor Paternae Gloriae," 'Christus nobis sit cibus potusque noster sit Fides.'

[60] Tractatus in psalmum LXIV, c. 14 (Corpus Scriptorum Ecclesiasticorum Latinorum 22 : 245).
[61] Comment. in Matt. XXX, c. 2 (Migne, Patrologia Latina 9 : 1065).
[62] Tractatus in psalmum CXXVII, c. 10 (Corpus Scriptorum Ecclesiasticorum Latinorum 22 : 635 f).
[63] Cf. De Synodis, c. 91 ff (Migne, Patrologia Latina 10: 544 ff).
[64] De Trinitate, IX, 9 (ibid., 288).
[65] Comment. in Matt. XI, c. 24 (Migne, Patrologia Latina 9 : 976 f).
[66] Tractatus in psalmum XCI, c. 9 (Corpus Scriptorum Ecclesiasticorum Latinorum 22 : 353) : "Istius modi enim corpora configurabit in transformationem corporis sui, et horum humilitatem in gloriam carnis suae transferet, qui contundentes omnes cupiditatum aculeos, et voluptatum sordes abluentes post novae nativitatis sacramentum, meminerint se non carnem suam habere, sed Christi."

to guard and teach the Faith, to remain steadfastly true to the Apostolic tradition.

One negative example will suffice. Both Athanasius and Hilary were familiar with the decrees of the Synod of Sardica (348), which attributed very great powers of appellate jurisdiction to the bishop of Rome. Hilary seems to have devoted a very considerable treatment to that Synod in his now fragmentary ecclesiastical history, and Athanasius was intimately concerned with the Synod itself, as it judged the Arian charges against him. The Synod decreed that a bishop deposed by a synod of the bishops in his province might appeal his case to Rome either on his own initiative or through the judges who had condemned him. The bishop of Rome might reject or receive the appeal, either confirming the initial judgment or summoning a synod to hear the case a second time. The second court would be composed of bishops summoned by Rome from provinces neighboring that of the accused, and it would be presided over by papal legates. No disposition of the accused's see could be made until the pope had confirmed the initial judgment or the appellate decision had been issued.[67]

These canons were critical in the institutional development of the Church; and as they sustained in some measure the process which had been followed in Athanasius's case, the process in which a Roman synod had acquitted the Bishop of Alexandria of the Arian charges against him (342), they were quite important to Athanasius himself. Yet neither Athanasius nor, so far as we can tell, Hilary construed these canons as establishing a juridical hierarchy in the Church. It is true that Athanasius pled his case before the Roman Synod; but the Arians, not he, had appealed the process to Rome, and once the Synod had been summoned, the Arians tacitly denied its competence by not attending.[68] For Athanasius, the Roman synod and the Synod of Sardica which came after it were simply two in an extended series of hearings to judge a particular case, and they did not impose a jurisdictional hierarchy upon the universal clergy.[69] In legal matters, his attitude was non-ecumenical; the clerical order was not well defined in juridical terms. Bishops judged cases of their lower clergy; greater cases and appeals from episcopal judgments were heard by provincial synods, from which appeal might be made to still other synods. In rendering his judgment in Athanasius's case, Pope Julius affirmed that the decisions of one synod might be reviewed by those of another, a statement which admits of an interminable series of hearings in the absence of one supreme court from whose decisions there is no appeal.[70] The long and wearisome sequence

of judgments and appeals which is the history of Athanasius's forty-year process is evidence enough that both Athanasius and his enemies were of this same opinion. The juristic thought of the Fathers was conciliar and particularistic, and not yet monarchical and ecumenical.

It was the Faith, and not the law, which gave the Church its cohesiveness; and the element which unified the episcopacy was the common sacramental office of preserving the Faith. In Athanasius's mind, God raised bishops to the episcopate,[71] and, as Christ was "Bishop of Souls,"[72] the Church was His bride, so was the mortal bishop set over the Faithful for their spiritual welfare and married to his Church.[73] The bishop was the "steward of God's mysteries," trustee of the Faith,[74] and no one who denied the true Faith could rightly ·claim the episcopal title.[75]

Athanasius's letter to Dracontius, urging the monk to take up the episcopacy to which he had been elected, strongly affirms the spiritual responsibility of the bishop. It is an answer to those beseeching Dracontius not to imperil his soul by leaving the monastic life to assume the responsibilities of teaching and government. Arguing that those elected to be stewards of the mysteries may, like SS. Paul and Timothy, press all the more earnestly toward the higher spiritual goals in their own lives, Athanasius directs Dracontius's attention beyond concern for his own salvation. God has advanced him to the episcopacy so that he may care for the Church.

> Before you had received the grace of the episcopate, no one knew you; but after you became one, the laity expected you to bring them food, namely instruction from the Scriptures. When then they expect, and suffer hunger, and you are feeding yourself only, and our Lord Jesus Christ comes and we stand before Him, what defense will you offer when He sees His own sheep hungering? . . . If Dracontius does not think the episcopacy has its rewards, he despises the Saviour Himself. He must acknowledge the grace given him in baptism and accept the summons God has sent him, preserving the "little ones" from danger and defending the Church from her enemies.[76]

This concept of the episcopacy as being primarily an office of teaching and defending the true Faith is precisely that held by Hilary. Bishops are "princes of the people," and they must watch over their flocks, confirming the weak by the truth of doctrine, converting the depraved, and dispensing the Word of Life as the bread of eternity.[77] Like the Apostles, they are the eyes of the Church, "the eyes of the body," and they must turn

[67] J. Hefele-H. LeClercq, *Histoire des Conciles* (Paris, 1907) 1, 2: p. 759 ff.
[68] Apologia contra Arianos, c. 20 (Migne, *Patrologia Graeca* 25: 280 f.).
[69] *Ibid.*, cc. 1, 20, 36 ff (*ibid.*, 248 f, 280 f, 308 ff).
[70] *Ibid.*, c. 21 (*ibid.*, 284). For Athanasius's belief that tradition proved the legitimacy of doctrine, see P. Smulders, "Le

Mot et le concept de 'tradition' chez les Pères grecs," *Recherches de science religieuse* 40 (1952) : 56 f.
[71] *Ibid.*, c. 6 (*ibid.*, 257).
[72] Ep. de sententia Dionysii, c. 8 (*ibid.*, 482).
[73] Apologia contra Arianos, c. 6 (*ibid.*, 256).
[74] Ep. encyclica, c. 1 (*ibid.*, 224 f).
[75] Apologia contra Arianos, c. 49 (Synod of Sardica) (*ibid.*, 334 ff) and Historia Arianorum, c. 75 (*ibid.*, 784).
[76] Ep. ad Dracontium (*ibid.*, 524 ff).
[77] Comment. in Matt., XXVII, c. 1 (Migne, *Patrologia Latina* 9: 1058).

their sight from the cares of this world to God, from what is imperfect to what is perfect,[78] to the end that they may have true knowledge of the faith which they preach and guard.[79]

From this common sacramental office derived the common law and the common Faith of the Church; the bishops, standing in the Apostolic tradition as stewards of the mysteries, maintained the Faith, that single element which united the many churches into one mystical body. *"Ecclesia"* and *"Fides"* are virtually synonymous when Hilary writes that the Church was instituted by Christ and confirmed by the Apostles,[80] instituted by the revelation that Christ was by nature the Son of God and confirmed by the confession of St. Peter, "Thou are Christ, the Son of the Living God." Upon the fact of Christ's true Sonship rested the Faith, the Church, the Apostleship; the heterodox confession which denied it was not proper to the Church or to Christ.[81] Witnesses of the mystery of the Incarnation, the Apostles transmitted unchanged what they had received to their disciples and successors. And in this way, the Faith was confirmed by one generation for the next, and true belief was preserved through the fidelity of bishops to their predecessors' establishments. Rejection of those establishments, alteration of the Apostolic Faith, would discredit as teachers those who deviated from the Faith, for, as Athanasius asks, "How are they themselves to be trusted by those whom they teach to disobey their teachers?" The Fathers who had died true to the Faith would be condemned as heretics, and consequently, the episcopal consecrations the Fathers had performed—including those of the innovators—would be called into question.[82] The apostolic tradition would be broken, and the Church thrown into chaos.

More than ecclesiastical order depended upon maintaining the true Faith. The validity of the sacraments was conditional upon the acknowledgment of the divine and the human nature of Christ; unity of mind with the Church, the body of Christ, must precede mystical union, spiritual sanctification, through the sacraments.[83] Personal salvation depended upon unfeigned confession of the true soteriological role of Christ. This was the very ground of ecclesiological thought for Athanasius and Hilary, the basis on which rested their concepts of relationships within the Church and of the place of the Church in this world. It was an inexpressibly sacred matter. "But," Hilary wrote,

the errors of heretics and blasphemers force us to deal with unlawful matters, to scale perilous heights, to speak unutterable words, to trespass on forbidden ground. Faith

ought in silence to fulfill the commandments, worshipping the Father, reverencing with Him the Son, abounding in the Holy Ghost, but we must strain the poor resources of our language to express thoughts too great for words. The error of others compels us to err in daring to embody in human terms truths which ought to be hidden in the silent veneration of the heart.[84]

Struggling to express the inexpressible, the Fathers still wrote much which is both lucid and important. Their arguments center upon two points: that the purpose of Christ's coming was to free man from the bondage of sin, and second, that that purpose could be fulfilled perfectly only by the perfect union of divine and human natures in the person of the Saviour, a union which would enable man to share in the divine nature of Christ by sharing first in His human nature. The mystical, or sacramental, character of these premises is clear: the salvation of mankind, Christ's work, is possible because Christ participated in humanity and because, in consequence, humanity can participate through Him in divinity.

It was this great premise which Hilary found "too great for words," and which Athanasius described in a luminous passage:

For here [John 6: 62–64] also He has used both terms of Himself, flesh and spirit; and He distinguished the spirit from what is of the flesh in order that they might believe not only in what was visible in Him, but in what was invisible, and so understand that what He says is not fleshly, but spiritual. For how many would the body suffice as food, for it is to become meat even for the whole world? But this is why He mentioned the ascending of the Son of Man into Heaven; namely, to draw them off from their corporeal idea and that from henceforth they might understand that the aforesaid flesh was heavenly from above and spiritual meat, to be given at His hands. For "what I have said unto you," He says, "is spirit and life;" as much as to say, *"what is manifested and to be given for the salvation of the world is the flesh which I wear. But this and the blood from it shall be given to you spiritually at My hands as meat, so as to be imparted spiritually in each one, and to become for all a preservative to resurrection of life eternal."* [85]

The emphasis upon the verity of the two natures of Christ and upon the mystic union of the believer with Him which Athanasius revealed in this comment on the Eucharist also occurs in his thought about baptism. When Christ was baptized, he writes, the true believers were baptized in Him and by Him. And when He was anointed with the oil of gladness by the Holy Spirit, mankind shared in His sanctification and anointing.[86] Because the Word was incarnate, man is deified; and because the Word assumed all the attributes of the flesh, man is delivered from these attributes. Otherwise, man would have remained mortal and corruptible. But because the Word has become a new origin of hu-

---

[78] Tractatus in psalmum CXXXVIII, c. 34 (*Corpus Scriptorum Ecclesiasticorum Latinorum* 22 : 768).

[79] De Trinitate, VIII, 1 (Migne, *Patrologia Latina* 10 : 236 f).

[80] De Trinitate, VII, 4 (*ibid.*, 202).

[81] *Ibid.*, VI, 32 ff (*ibid.*, 183 ff).

[82] De Synodis, c. 13 (Migne, *Patrologia Graeca* 26 : 703). *Cf.* Hilary, De Synodis, c. 91 (Migne, *Patrologia Latina* 10 : 543 ff).

[83] *Supra*, notes 37, 43, 64.

[84] De Trinitate II, 2 (Migne, *Patrologia Latina* 10 : 51).

[85] Ep. ad Serapionem IV, 19 (Migne, *Patrologia Graeca* 26 : 665 ff).

[86] Orat. contra Arianos I, 47 (*ibid.*, 108 f).

man existence, the former origin and infirmity of flesh has passed away,

. . . the curse of sin being removed, because of Him who is in us, and who has become a curse for us. And with reason; for as we are all from earth and die in Adam, so being regenerated from above of water and Spirit, in the Christ we are all quickened; the flesh being no longer earthly, but being henceforth made Word by reason of God's Word who for our sake "became flesh." [87]

These theological principles occur again and again in the writings of Athanasius. Christ came to witness the truth and thereby to destroy the works of the devil; [88] He came to gather the tribes, freeing all men from sin and making all sons of God.[89] His purpose has been accomplished through the sacrifice of Himself. But He accomplished man's liberation only because He was truly God and truly man, and because man can now be joined to God through His intermediacy.

The Word was made flesh in order to offer up this body for all, and that we, partaking of His Spirit, might be deified, a gift which we could not otherwise have gained than by His clothing Himself in our created body, for hence we derive our name, "men of God" and "men in Christ." But as we, by receiving the Spirit, do not lose our own proper substance, so the Lord, when made man for us, and bearing a body, was no less God; for He was not lessened by the envelopment of the body, but rather deified it and rendered it immortal.[90]

Mankind is "bound together in Him through the likeness of the flesh," [91] and "we all, partaking of the Same, become one body, having the one Lord in ourselves." [92]

Hilary declared as definitely as Athanasius that mankind's salvation was through Christ alone,[93] and that it was secure because by assuming human flesh He had enabled man to participate in the saving divinity through His intermediacy.[94] Salvation is in the body of Christ,[95] and man attains to it through true Faith and through the sacraments. By partaking of the Eucharistic elements, truly the body and blood of Christ "both from the declaration of the Lord Himself and our own faith," "He Himself is in us through the flesh and we in Him, and together with Him we ourselves are in God." Man is united with the Saviour, and so with the Father, "corporeally and inseparably." [96] Again, the sanctification of man came through the baptism of Christ, and through their baptisms, the faithful "put on one Christ," [97] their bodies no longer theirs, but Christ's.[98]

At the center of Hilary's argument is the confession of St. Peter, "Thou are Christ, the Son of the Living God," the confession that Christ was truly God, truly the Son of God, the incarnate and saving Word.[99] Eternally God, Christ condescended to assume the form of a servant and to sacrifice Himself for the redemption, the "libertas," of man.

These were the mysteries of the secret counsels of heaven, determined before the world was made. *The Only-begotten God was to become man of His own will, and man was to abide eternally in God.* God was to suffer of His own will, that the malice of the devil, working in the weakness of human infirmity, might not confirm the law of sin in us, since God has assumed our weakness. God was to die of His own will, that no power, after that the immortal God had constrained Himself within the law of death, might raise up its head against Him or put forth the natural strength which He had created in it. Thus God was born to take us into Himself, suffered to justify us, and died to avenge us; for our manhood abides forever in Him, the weakness of our infirmity is united with His strength, and the spiritual powers of iniquity and wickedness are subdued in the triumph of our flesh, since God died through the flesh.[100]

Through this sacrifice and the glorification of the ascended Christ, man is made the perfect image of God. The perfect humanity and the perfect divinity of Christ are necessary to the divine plan of salvation; "for, being conformed to the glory of the body of God, he is exalted to the image of the Creator, after the pattern assigned to the first man." [101]

This was the article of Faith from which radiated the ecclesiological thought both of Athanasius and of Hilary. It was this article which gave purpose and meaning to the mission of the Church, which defined its character, which expressed its highest mysteries. This was the Faith whose true confession gave the sacraments their validity; this was the Faith which Hilary once called, of itself, a sacrament of flesh and blood. Revealed by Christ to the Apostles, confirmed and transmitted by them to their disciples, the mystery of the Incarnation was the treasure of which bishops were stewards, the hope of salvation for all men.

II

The ecclesiological, or soteriological, position which we have just described was the position of the Homoousians, and it was, of course, from that stand-

---

[87] Orat. contra Arianos III, 33 (*ibid.,* 393 ff).

[88] Orat. contra Arianos II, 51 ff (*ibid.,* 253 ff).

[89] *Ibid.,* II, 72 (*ibid.,* 300 f).

[90] Ep. de Nicaenis decretis, 14 (Migne, *Patrologia Graeca* 25: 440).

[91] Orat. II contra Arianos, 74 (Migne, *Patrologia Graeca* 26: 304 f).

[92] Orat. III contra Arianos, 22 (*ibid.,* 368 f).

[93] Tractatus in psalmum CXLIII, 21 (*Corpus Scriptorum Ecclesiasticorum Latinorum* 22: 826); De Trinitate, I, 16 (Migne, *Patrologia Latina* 10: 37).

[94] Tractatus in psalmum LIII, 8 (*Corpus Scriptorum Ecclesiasticorum Latinorum* 22: 140 f), and Tractatus in psalmum CXLI, 1 (*ibid.,* p. 799 f).

[95] Tractatus in Psalmum XIV, 4, 5 (*ibid.,* p. 86 ff).

[96] De Trinitate VII, 13–17 (Migne, *Patrologia Latina* 9: 210 ff).

[97] *Ibid.,* VIII, 8 (Migne, *Patrologia Latina* 10: 242).

[98] *Supra,* note 47.

[99] De Trinitate, II, 23 ff (Migne, *Patrologia Latina* 10: 65 ff).

[100] *Ibid.,* IX, c. 7 ff (*ibid.,* 285 ff).

[101] *Ibid.,* XI, 49 (*ibid.,* 432).

point that Athanasius and Hilary approached the major disputes of their day. In particular, it was the standpoint from which they regarded the operations of the civil power in ecclesiastical matters, and we shall have to enquire how their ecclesiology affected their political views.

In the previous discussion, we have mentioned that, for Athanasius and Hilary, the Church was above all the mystical body of Christ, in which believers participated corporeally through the sacraments of the Eucharist and baptism. Further, the visible Church, the episcopal order, was also construed in this light, not as a juristic organization, but as the vessel in which the sacrament of Faith, the doctrine of the Incarnation of God, was preserved. Upon the continuance of this one doctrine, integral and unchanged, depended the validity of the sacraments performed, the verity of union between believer and Saviour, and the salvation of mankind. If Christ were not truly God and truly man, the Fathers argued, the liberation of man from sin through His death would be imperfect, and the actual mystic union of God and the Church would be impossible.

The Fathers set their ecclesiological thought against the Arians, who did in fact dispute the premise that Christ and God were identical in substance and glory. Both Athanasius and Hilary were arguing on two levels: on the doctrinal level, against the Arian theologians, and second, on the political level, against the civil government which fostered Arianism. We are particularly concerned with the second level, the conflict of Homoousios and Homoiousios in the political context of Church-State relations.

Had Constantius undertaken the support of the Homoousians, Athanasius and Hilary might have regarded his efforts with the same favor which orthodox bishops later showed orthodox emperors in their attempts to stamp out heresy. But Constantius fostered the Arians, and the Fathers, not being able to reject the Roman Empire, were forced to emphasize the distinction between the Empire and the Church and to maintain the position which Hosius of Cordova had expressed in his famous letter to Constantius:

Intrude not yourself into ecclesiastical matters, neither give commands to us concerning them; but learn them from us. God has put into your hands the kingdom; to us He has entrusted the affairs of His Church. And as he who would steal the empire from you would resist the ordinance of God, so likewise fear on your part lest by taking upon yourself the government of the Church, you become guilty of a great offence. It is written, "Render unto Caesar the things that are Caesar's, and unto God the things that are God's." Neither therefore is it permitted to us to exercise an earthly rule, nor have you, Lord, any authority to burn incense.[102]

Christ was King over the Church; the Emperor over the Empire. Hosius admonished Constantius with the

example of Ozias, the King of Israel, who was struck with leprosy when he broke into the Holy of Holies and burned incense. Athanasius compared the Arians to the Jews who cried out at the trial of Jesus, "We have no king but Caesar," and he accused Constantius:

He, being without arguments of reason, forces all men by his power, that it may be shown to all, that their wisdom is not according to God, but merely human, and that they who favor the Arian doctrines have indeed no king but Caesar; for by his means these enemies of Christ accomplish whatever they wish to do.[103]

Hilary states the charge more crisply. Homoousios is the ancient faith of the Church, he writes; by denying the Incarnation of God, Constantius has thrown the Church into confusion; he has "set his hands against Christ Himself." [104]

Both Athanasius and Hilary were deeply alarmed that, by imposing the Arian doctrine upon the Empire, Constantius was in fact violating the very body of Christ. But, as we have already suggested, their protests differ in focus. Athanasius objected primarily to the liberties Constantius took with the juridical structure of the Church so as to secure submission to the Arian creed. The nature of this protest was juristic, but its basis was sacramental: The Bishop maintained that cases in which the Empire had no interest should not be tried in Imperial courts, and particularly, that cases in which matters of faith and doctrine were at issue should be heard by ecclesiastical judges, not by secular men, heathen, and infidel. In his effort to win universal recognition for the Arian creed, Constantius overstepped these limits and made, in Athanasius's eyes, a civil senate of the Church. Again, Hilary's objection is more direct. He protests against the actual establishment of the Arian creed by imperial power and affirms that this violates the primary duty of the Emperor, to guard the liberty of his subjects.

Although Athanasius charges Constantius primarily with transgressing the competence of ecclesiastical courts and Hilary accuses him of jeopardizing the Faith itself, the Fathers differ in emphasis more than in sentiment. Athanasius was as vitally concerned as Hilary to defend true doctrine from its enemies. Unlike Hilary, he did not consider the Emperor a font of heresy. For him, Constantius was a willing—even enthusiastic—instrument in the hands of the Arian bishops; and although he often censured the Emperor for abusing the imperial power on behalf of the Arians and their creed, he never charged, as Hilary did, that he was an originator of the heretical profession.[105]

---

[102] Athanasius, Historia Arianorum c. 44 (Migne, *Patrologia Graeca* 25: 745 f).

[103] *Ibid.*, cc. 32, 33 (*ibid.*, 729 ff).

[104] Contra Constantium, c. 11 (Migne, *Patrologia Latina* 10: 589): "In ipsum Christum manus missae." Cf. *ibid.*, c. 26 (*ibid.*, 600).

[105] Cf. Historia Arianorum, c. 32 (Migne, *Patrologia Graeca* 25: 729): "He knows not, nor has he ever read, how that the Sadducees and the Herodians, taking unto them the Pharisees, were not able to obscure the truth; rather it shines out thereby more brightly every day, while they crying out 'We have no

Athanasius's impeachment of Constantius is that he has tried to alter the "times," "laws," and "customs," of the Church; but the perverting of doctrine was the work of others, whom Constantius only assisted.[106] The Emperor's great wrong was transgressing the rightful limits of civil jurisdiction, imposing the imperial will upon ecclesiastical judgments, and transforming the Church into a "civil senate" or a "place of judicial business." If the cases concerned the Empire, then the Emperor might intervene and issue definitive testimony.[107] But the civil power had intruded itself into actual matters of ecclesiastical jurisdiction, matters which touched the sacraments.

Precedents for this had been set in the time of Constantine the Great, and Athanasius had objected to them as vigorously as he objected to the procedures under the son of Constantine. In the early days of his struggle, Athanasius had been accused of sacrilege, and Constantine had sent an imperial commission to investigate the charges. Athanasius and his loyal bishops had condemned the investigation because the commission had barred the Faithful and "summoned heathen witnesses during the enquiry concerning a cup belonging to the mysteries."[108] Later, upon the testimony of Athanasius and others, Pope Julius had restated this protest.

Athanasius positively asserted that Macarius was kept at Tyre under a guard of soldiers while only his accuser accompanied those who went to the Mareotis; and that the presbyters who desired to attend the enquiry were not permitted to do so, while the said enquiry respecting the cup and the Table was carried on before the Prefect and his band, and in the presence of heathens and Jews. This at first seemed incredible, but it was proved to have been so from the reports, which caused great astonishment to us, as I suppose, dearly beloved, it does to you also. Presbyters, who are the ministers of the mysteries, are not permitted to attend, but an enquiry concerning Christ's blood and Christ's body is carried on before an external judge, in the presence of catechumens, nay, worse than that, before heathens and Jews, who are in ill repute in regard to Christianity. Even supposing that an offense had been committed, it should have been investigated legally in the Church and by the clergy, not by heathens who abhor the Word and know not the Truth.[109]

The enquiry had been continued at the Synod of Tyre. But when Athanasius saw that "a Count presided, an executioner attended, an usher instead of the deacons of the Church introduced us into court, and the Count only spoke, while all present held their peace, or rather obeyed his directions,"[110] he had appealed to Constantine for a review of the process,[111] at the same time

denying that the assembly was a true synod because of secular intervention.[112]

Subsequently, Athanasius entered the same objection when Constantius disclaimed him as bishop and intruded Gregory of Cappadocia into his see. He protested that he had been denounced on the testimony, not of true churchmen, but on that of Arians, to whom he denied the name "Christian." Heathen magistrates forced Gregory upon an unwilling church.[113] To give the appearance of legitimacy to his act—that is, to give the appearance that he was acting to execute the will of the Alexandrines[114]—Constantius had "the senators, the heathen magistrates, and wardens of the idol temples" subscribe his rejection of Athanasius and transferral of the churches to the Arians and agree to receive as bishop whomever Constantius should appoint. Even Athanasius admits with irony that the Emperor was upholding the strict letter of the canons when he did this, at the same time as he violated the order which the canon prescribed, and the Bishop records with some satisfaction the chant which the pagans sang in the violence which accompanied Gregory's entrance: "Constantius has become a heathen, and the Arians have acknowledged our customs."[115] The appearance of legality did not confer legitimacy on Gregory's rule which began in contravention of the canons; "for one that was sent from him [Constantius] cannot be a bishop (God forbid!), and so indeed his [Gregory's] conduct and the circumstances which preceded his entrance sufficiently prove."[116] The wrongful assent of the marketplace and the temple warders could not take the place of the canonical will of the Church and the Faithful.[117]

Athanasius also contests Constantius's establishment of eunuchs as competent judges in ecclesiastical cases, for the canons forbid them to be admitted into any ecclesiastical council.[118] And he recounts with great fervor the part Constantius took in the process against him, particularly at the Synod of Milan (355), where the Emperor himself assumed the role of accuser and, due process failing to secure unanimous condemnation, commanded all to sign the judgment against Athanasius on pain of banishment. The passage of arms which Athanasius attributes to the Emperor and the reluctant bishops is particularly instructive. When Constantius ordered immediate condemnation, the bishops

. . . were astonished at this novel procedure and said that there was no ecclesiastical canon to this effect. He immediately said, "Whatever I will, be that considered a canon; the bishops of Syria let me thus speak. Either obey, or go into banishment." When the bishops heard this, they

---

king but Caesar,' and obtaining the judgment of Pilate in their favor, are nevertheless left destitute, and wait in utter shame, expecting shortly to become bereft, like the partridge, when they shall see their patron near his death."
[106] *Ibid.*, c. 74 (*ibid.*, 784).
[107] *Ibid.*, c. 76 (*ibid.*, 785).
[108] Apologia contra Arianos, c. 14 (*ibid.*, 272).
[109] *Ibid.*, c. 31 (*ibid.*, 300 f.). *Supra*, p. 19.
[110] *Ibid.*, c. 8 (*ibid.*, 264).
[111] *Ibid.*, c. 86 (*ibid.*, 401 ff.).

[112] *Ibid.*, c. 8 (*ibid.*, 264).
[113] Ep. encyclica, c. 2 (*ibid.*, 225 f.).
[114] *Loc. cit.*, and Historia Arianorum, c. 33 (*ibid.*, 729 ff.).
[115] Historia Arianorum, cc. 54, 56 (*ibid.*, 757 ff.).
[116] *Ibid.*, c. 48 (*ibid.*, 752 f.) and Ep. encyclica, c. 2 (*ibid.*, 225 ff.).
[117] Historia Arianorum, c. 54 (*ibid.*, 757 f.).
[118] *Ibid.*, c. 38 (*ibid.*, 737).

were utterly amazed and stretching forth their hands to God, they used great boldness of speech against him, teaching him that the kingdom was not his, but God's who had given it to him, whom also they bade him fear, lest He should suddenly take it away from him. And they threatened him with the day of judgment, and warned him against infringing ecclesiastical order and mingling Roman sovereignty with the constitution of the Church and against introducing the Arian heresy into the Church of God.[119]

When Athanasius came to sum up his charges against Constantius, they all derived from the one premise that the Emperor had in fact "infringed ecclesiastical order and mingling Roman sovereignty with the constitution of the Church." The Bishop asked, "Why, while pretending to respect the canons of the Church, has he ordered the whole course of his conduct in opposition to them?" He has presumed to intrude bishops into sees, to allow soldiers to invade churches, to set counts and eunuchs over ecclesiastical cases, and to declare by imperial edict the judgments of bishops.

When was such a thing heard of before from the beginning of the world? When did a judgment of the Church receive its validity from the Emperor, or rather, when was his decree ever recognized by the Church? There have been many councils held heretofore; and many judgments passed by the Church. But the Fathers never sought the consent of the Emperor to them, nor did the Emperor busy himself with the affairs of the Church.[120]

Athanasius considered the Church an institution juristically discrete from the Empire, an institution in which the canons and the processes which they prescribed held sole legal validity. And in the contemporary documents which Athanasius quotes—the letter of Hosius, to which we have already referred, a letter of Pope Julius, an argument of Pope Liberius, and letters of the Synod of Sardica—as well as in his own comments, the separation of ecclesiastical courts from civil is repeatedly emphasized.

Like the Faith, the canons were preserved through Apostolic tradition; like the Faith, the canons were the same for all true believers. Referring to the Arians, Athanasius wrote, "We have a common Saviour, who is blasphemed by them, and canons belonging to us all, which they are transgressing."[121] Divine law and the canons were the supreme criteria by which religious matters might be judged,[122] and Athanasius manifestly was of the same mind as Pope Liberius, who demanded that matters of faith and cases deriving from them be considered, according to the canon and Apostolic tradition, by a synod free of imperial intervention.[123] As we have seen, his attitude was the same as that of the Synod of Sardica, which petitioned the Emperors to "command that none of the magistrates whose duty it is to attend only to civil cases, give judgment upon clergy, nor henceforth in any way, on pretense of

providing for the churches, attempt anything against the brethren."[124]

The separation for which he called was by no means complete. For him, the imperial tribunal was the most solemn court on earth,[125] and he himself appealed to it on occasion. The distinction in his mind between civil and ecclesiastical courts was a distinction of causes, or competences, rather than a distinction of persons. He acknowledged the imperial court as a court of first instance in cases touching the emperor, whether the accused were cleric or layman; but in purely ecclesiastical matters, he considered it a court of review. When Constantius stood as the accuser of Athanasius, the Synod of Milan rejected his action as inappropriate, since the case did not involve imperial interests. The implication is that, had the charges been political crimes rather than ecclesiastical offenses, the Emperor would have been quite in order.[126]

The distinction which Athanasius drew between civil and ecclesiastical courts was, therefore, the distinction between competence in religious and competence in public cases. We have mentioned this distinction in an earlier chapter and found that it was applied to Jewish legal institutions from a very early time. It is the distinction which Theodosius I formalized, albeit disadvantageously for the Jewish courts, when he decreed that Roman Jews had full jurisdiction over religious matters in their own courts, but that matters touching the public interest must be tried by Roman Law.[127] Far from being novel, it was perfectly conventional, and it was Constantius's breach of this convention which disturbed Athanasius most. The Father admitted that the Emperor might intervene decisively in processes against ecclesiastics when imperial interests were involved; but he strongly denied that the Emperor might direct processes which touched matters of faith.

Rendering to Caesar the things which were Caesar's implied the full acknowledgment of Rome's claim in civil trials; but rendering to God the things which were God's meant the exclusion of extra-ecclesiastical powers, powers not comprehended in the Apostolic tradition, from processes which concerned the Body of Christ. As Roman citizens, bishops owed loyalty to the Emperor; but as stewards of the mystery of Faith, they owed their first duty to their heavenly King. When he attempted to "mingle Roman sovereignty with the constitution of the Church," to make of the Church a "civil senate," with the purpose of imposing the doctrine of the Homoiousios, Constantius challenged that higher duty, he transgressed the canons by which it was to be discharged, and he jeopardized the Faith it guarded.

Like Athanasius, Hilary admits that the imperial power may rightly intervene in some ecclesiastical proc-

[119] Ibid., cc. 33, 34 (ibid., 729 ff).
[120] Ibid., cc. 51, 52 (ibid., 753 ff).
[121] Ep. encyclica, cc. 1, 6 (ibid., 221 f, 233 f).
[122] Apologia ad Constantium, c. 1 (ibid., 595 f).
[123] Historia Arianorum, c. 36 (ibid., 736).

[124] Apologia contra Arianos, cc. 39, 43 (ibid., 346, 321).
[125] Ibid., 3 (ibid., 252 f).
[126] Supra, note 91.
[127] Cf. J. Juster, Les Juifs dans l'empire romain (Paris, 1914) 2: p. 152.

esses. For example, he does not contest the legality of the banishment imposed upon him by the Empire in execution of his earlier synodal condemnation.[128] He admits, with Athanasius, that the Empire has due claims on all subjects and that its dignity is very great. Nevertheless, he shows a contempt for it unequalled in the writings of the other Father. In his commentary upon the first Psalm, he glosses the verse "and he shall not sit in the seat of the scornful" as follows:

Now the third condition for gaining happiness is not to sit in the seat of pestilence. The Pharisees sat as teachers in Moses's seat, and Pilate sat in the seat of judgment: of what seat then are we to consider the occupation pestilential? Not surely that of Moses, for it is the occupants of the seat and not the occupation of the seat that the Lord condemns. . . . That then must be really pestilential the infection of which Pilate sought to avoid by washing his hands. For many, even God-fearing men, are led astray by the canvassing for worldly honors; and desire to administer the law of the courts, though they are bound by those of the Church. But although they bring to the discharge of their duties a religious intention, as is shown by their merciful and upright demeanor, still they cannot escape a certain contagious infection arising from the business in which their life is spent. For the conduct of civil cases does not suffer them to be true to the holy principles of the Church's law, even though they wish it.[129]

Hilary's charges against Constantius are chiefly an elaboration of this thought. In the first two of his three addresses to the Emperor, the Father considers him a man wishing to know the true Faith, but hindered from it by the perversity of the bishops about him, who write "what is theirs, and not what is God's."[130] In the last of the addresses, Hilary is more straightforward in condemning the Emperor; Constantius was dead, and the Bishop felt free to compose a vigorous denunciation. Yet, however different in tone the third address is from the others, it is like them in essence. Throughout them all runs the same thought: the power of the "seat of pestilence" has endangered both the souls of those who sit in it and the Faith of the whole Church.

In the first address, Hilary complains that the freedom of the Church to follow the true Faith has been severely limited; for, although it is the Emperor's duty to insure his subjects the benefits of liberty, civil judges have intruded themselves into ecclesiastical affairs, usurping the right to try clerics and tormenting innocent men. He beseeches the Emperor to set heretics in the place of orthodox teachers, but rather to allow his people the power to follow those who taught orthodoxy, to celebrate the divine mysteries, and to pray for the welfare of the Emperor. Further, Constantius should restore the banished clergy to their sees, "so that

there may be everywhere free liberty and glad rejoicing." With particular regard for the processes against Athanasius and Eusebius of Vercelli, Hilary charges that the Arians have wrongly used the civil power against the true Faith.[131]

He continues this argument in the second address. The hope, life, and immortality of all men have been endangered by the Arian heresy which retains baptism but denies that Christ was truly God, "as though baptism could be something without faith in Christ." With apparent sincerity, Hilary addresses Constantius as "most pious," "good and religious," and "most gracious," and offers to teach him the true Faith in the hearing of the Council of Constantinople, then in session (360). He asks this audience for the Emperor's sake and for that of God's churches; the welfare of mankind is at stake, and Hilary extends the name Antichrist and the sentence of anathema over anyone—Constantius not excluded—who refuses to confess the "only-begotten God."[132]

These thoughts culminate in the furious third address, in which Hilary condemns (the dead) Constantius as the fomentor of Arianism, as Antichrist himself. The Emperor has used every means to undermine the Faith. But his persecution is more subtle than those of old; for he burdens the Church with public revenues and the spoil of pagan temples, lavishes immunities and remissions of taxation upon the clergy, builds churches, and honors bishops, all to the end that Christ may be denied.[133] Violence also serves his purpose, and he has torn bishops from the altar in Milan, banished and abused the bishops of Trier and Rome, and desecrated the church and clergy at Toulouse.[134] He pretends loyalty to Christ, but his unswerving purpose is to prevent Christ from being honored equally with the Father.[135] It was he who moved the successive revisions of the creeds which deviated from the Faith of Nicaea, rejecting each one in its turn, and descending to the lowest pit of blasphemy.[136] Most heinous of all, it was he who starved the Synod of Rimini into accepting the Arian formula, and with threats and violence splintered the synod of Seleucia and snatched the Arian profession out of the ruins.[137] In this, he had done nothing else than make a present to the devil of the world for which Christ died.[138] Constantius is responsible: "unfaithful, you promulgate the Faith; impious, you dissemble piety." "Edictis fidem terruisti."[139]

Constantius had violated his first duty, that of preserving their liberty to all his subjects. But more im-

---

[128] Ad Constantium, c. 2 (Corpus Scriptorum Ecclesiasticorum Latinorum 65: 197 f). K. M. Setton, Christian Attitude Towards the Emperor in the Fourth Century (New York, 1941), p. 99 f.
[129] Tractatus in psalmum I, c. 6 (Corpus Scriptorum Ecclesiasticorum Latinorum 22: 23).
[130] Ad Constantium, c. 4 (Corpus Scriptorum Ecclesiasticorum Latinorum 65: 198).

[131] Ibid., cc. 1, 2, 4, 6, 7, 8 (ibid., p. 197 ff).
[132] Ibid., cc. 3–5, 7, 8, 11 (ibid., p. 198 ff).
[133] Contra Constantium, cc. 5, 10, 11 (Migne, Patrologia Latina 10: 581 ff).
[134] Ibid., c. 11 (ibid., 589).
[135] Ibid., c. 5 (ibid., 581).
[136] Ibid., cc. 23, 24 (ibid., 598 ff).
[137] Ibid., cc. 7, 13–15 (ibid., 583 f, 591 ff).
[138] Ibid., c. 15 (ibid., 593).
[139] Ibid., cc. 9, 11 (ibid., 585 f, 587 f).

portant, he had denied the true divinity of Christ; setting his hands against Christ Himself, he had imperiled that greater liberty, "the liberty of the Faith," which Christ won by His death and in which the believers participated through confession of his perfect divinity and perfect manhood. The "liberty of the Church," and "steadfastness of our hope," and "the confession of God" were all virtually synonymous for Hilary.[140] Constantius's rejection of the true and Apostolic confession, formulated at Nicaea,[141] struck at the body·of Christ, and jeopardized the liberty from sin secured through His sacrifice.

On another level, the heretical revision of the Creed endangered the free will of the individual, received through regeneration in baptism and the confession of faith which accompanied it.[142] For, as we have seen, Hilary denies the validity of baptism in which the true Incarnation of God was not confessed. The Emperor's office, the "seat of pestilence," was external to the Church, and bore towards her only that responsibility it bore toward all subjects: to guarantee her liberty. Constantius had exceeded this office. He had profaned the very mystery of the Incarnation, and, contravening Christ's liberation of mankind, he had given over to the bondage of the devil the world for which He died.

III

SS. Athanasius and Hilary held that the emperor as emperor had nothing to do with the Church; on the other hand, they did not hold that the emperor was within the Church as its subject.[143] As the guarantor of liberties and the head of the most solemn tribunal in this world, the Emperor was critically important in resolving nonsacramental disputes within the clergy. These were duties he owed to all·ethnic groups under his dominion who were allowed to retain their juristic integrity; and the protests of Athanasius and Hilary indicate how scrupulously he was expected to exercise them on behalf of the Church.

The sacramental separation of the Church from the Empire was absolute; its juristic separation was not. And the point of the Fathers' objections is that the Emperor had extended his juridical rights into the sacramental functions of the Church. With regard to the other position, there is in the works of the two Fathers no indication that they proposed the imposition of ecclesiastical censures against him. Indeed, Constantius II, like his father, unbaptized until he lay on his deathbed, was not formally a member of the Church and not subject to ecclesiastical discipline until just before he died. Athanasius and Hilary offer themselves freely

enough for martyrdom; but they do not threaten any action against Constantius or his office. The goal of the Fathers was not the absolute severing of Church from Empire, and not the establishment of ecclesiastical power over imperial. Rather, it was the reestablishment of the conventional relationship between Empire and ethnic group, validated for the Church under Constantine, and disturbed by Constantius's overzealousness in religious matters.

Athanasius and Hilary were the first to meet the problem of a friendly Empire: their solution was the same which the confessors before them advanced toward a hostile one. The Empire was an external power, and however great its authority over Christians in external matters, it had no place in the inner, the characteristic, functions of the Church.

4. S. AMBROSE

SS. Athanasius and Hilary witnessed the Empire in transition from paganism to Christianity; S. Ambrose saw the Christian Empire established.

The year after Athanasius died, Ambrose, the consularis, became Bishop of Milan. In his episcopate (374–397), Ambrose observed the culmination of the tendencies in Church-Empire relations which began with the conversion of Constantine. He saw the Empire itself converted by imperial edict from a pagan state tolerating many religious cults to an orthodox Christian state, which prohibited paganism and heresy. The imperial effort to establish a uniform creed for the Church, so strong and so painful under Constantius, exceeded itself under Gratian and Theodosius I, when the Nicene confession was declared legally binding on all peoples under Roman domination. Gratian abandoned the title and functions of the *pontifex maximus,* withdrew public support from pagan sacrifices, and confiscated the property and revoked the privileges of the priestly colleges and of the Vestal Virgins. Theodosius continued and extended this work, abolishing the Olympic Games and desecrating the shrines at Olympia, renewing the old prohibitions against pagan sacrifices, and closing pagan temples for purposes of worship. He forbade absolutely all pagan religious practices; and legislating against heretics, he established the orthodox as the only true Christians and the Nicene Faith as the creed of the Empire. Blood was shed in enforcing these new laws; law and the Empire were on the side of the Christian God. Orthodoxy in the Faith was identical with loyalty to the Empire, and heresy or paganism, with treason.

It was exactly this revolution which Julius Firmicus Maternus, himself a convert to Christianity from philosophic paganism, had urged upon Constans and Constantius toward the middle of the century. God had committed the Empire to them, he wrote, for the specific purpose of extirpating paganism. And he appealed to their steadfastness in the Faith to strike the Devil

---

[140] E.g., Tractatus in psalmum CXIX, c. 11 (*Corpus Scriptorum Ecclesiasticorum Latinorum* 22: 551 f).

[141] Contra Constantium, c. 23 (Migne, *Patrologia Latina* 10: 598 f).

[142] Comment. in Matt. XI, 24 (Migne, *Patrologia Latina* 9: 976 f). But *cf.* In Cantic. quind. grad., prologus, c. 4 (*ibid.,* 641).

[143] Setton, *op. cit.,* p. 107 f.

low with their laws and so destroy the wickedness of idolatry. "Lift up the standard of venerable law; sanction, promulgate what is beneficial." Then, God would make them joyous partakers in His glory and will; joining their happiness with the strength of God—for Christ was fighting for the salvation of man—they would win the victory.[1]

Yet, living at the time when the Emperors won the victory Firmicus desired, St. Ambrose did not give imperial legislation a major place in his concept of relations between the Church and the Empire. Even laws of consummate importance, like the edict *Cunctos populos* by which Theodosius made the Nicene Faith legally binding throughout the Empire, are either passed over in silence or referred to obliquely. And when, in the particular case of the Altar of Victory, Ambrose had to cite the relevant enactments of Gratian, his citations were of the most superficial nature: he invoked the tenor, but not the letter of the law. The victory for which Firmicus had appealed was won, but Ambrose did not acknowledge it.

It is true that the official letters of the Synod of Aquileia, attributed to Ambrose, show very great reverence for the imperial power and for the Emperor as legislator and executor of the laws. The Synod was held in the same year that *Cunctos populos* was promulgated, the year of the Council of Constantinople (381). With great unction, the bishops in their letters commended Theodosius's zeal for the Church, professed themselves the Emperor's debtors for his assistance, promised to preserve the honor due the imperial power, petitioned Theodosius to summon a new synod and to exclude Arian priests from their ministries, and finally urged him to "give orders to have reverence shown first to the Catholic Church and *then to your laws*, so that, with God as your patron, you may triumph while you provide for the peace and tranquility of the churches."[2] Still, if Ambrose held the pen which wrote these letters, it is not at all certain that he held without reserve the thoughts they express. The dual restriction of writing a ceremonial letter in the name of a synod imposed responsibilities and limits not necessary in autonomous writings.

The great legal changes of his day did not alter for Ambrose the fundamental relationship between Church and Empire. His concept of that relationship was essentially the position maintained by Athanasius and

Hilary before him. The Church was a spiritual, or sacramental, institution, whose very being was the Faith; and only persons initiated into her mysteries and consecrated to preserve and to teach the Faith might rule her people and administer her inner discipline. External to this mystical order, the Empire might place its juridical structure at the service of the Church, acting as a court of review in matters which ecclesiastical courts could not definitively resolve without recourse to external powers, and executing ecclesiastical sentences which required the use of armed force. But it could in no instance enter judgment upon a matter of the Faith, or in any other way usurp the sacramental authority of episcopal administration.

Soteriological and mystical concepts were as central to Ambrose's thought as they were to Athanasius's and Hilary. God had voluntarily humbled Himself and taken on human form so that by His sufferings and death He might free mankind from the bondage of the law and the burden of sin. The Church is the body of the Saviour; and through her sacraments—baptism and the Eucharist—the true believer participates corporeally and spiritually in His human and divine natures, attaining salvation in union with God. This is the great mystery, this is the Faith, which was for Ambrose the Church and the Church's sole possession. It was this which made the Christian a member of a kingdom higher than the earthly, which made him subject to a higher king than Caesar, which bound him under a higher law than the imperial.

Yet, Ambrose's thought on the problem of Church-Empire relations went further than that of his predecessors. So long as their argument touched only law and legal relationships, the Fathers were forced to write negatively: the Empire was external to the Church, and it could not rightly intrude into the constitutional structure of the Church. When his remarks turned to the relative legal competences of ecclesiastical and legal courts, Ambrose himself took this negative position and defended with all his eloquence the juristic integrity of the Church. But his arguments went beyond this restricted framework. When he found positive law insufficient for his position or contrary to it, he swept law aside and appealed to higher moral sanctions. Athanasius and Hilary had opposed an unbaptized Arian Emperor, with whom they had no communion and over whom they claimed to spiritual authority. By contrast, the emperors with whom Ambrose had chiefly to deal, Gratian and Theodosius I, were baptized and orthodox, and Ambrose entered communion with them and asserted very considerable moral powers over them. Likewise, he appears to have exercised great influence over the young Valentinian II, who died while still a catechumen. Accordingly, Ambrose's most cogent appeals are not to the imperial office, but to the men who held it, and they are not legal, but moral.

---

[1] De errore profanae religionis, cc. 17, 21 (Migne, *Patrologia Latina* 12: 1019, 1029). *Cf. ibid.*, cc. 25, 29, 30, cols. 1037, 1045, 1048, and Augustine on the *imperatores felices*, De civitate Dei, V, 24 (*Corpus Scriptorum Ecclesiasticorum Latinorum* 40: 260 f). On the philosophical debt of Augustine to Ambrose, see G. A. McCool, "The Ambrosian Origin of St. Augustine's Theology of the Image of God in Man," *Theological Studies* 20 (1959): 62–81.

[2] Epp. 10, 11, 12 (Migne, *Patrologia Latina* 16: 940 ff). On the date of the Synod, see J. Zeiller, "La date du Concile d'Aquilée (3. Sept. 381)," *Revue d'histoire ecclésiastique* 33 (1937): 39–44.

Ambrose's thought about the relations between the Church and the civil power—and consequently, his thought concerning the Christianization of the Empire by law—moved in two dimensions. It moved in the dimension of positive law, where it found of primary importance, not the recent Christianizing edicts, but the conventional guarantees of integrity for religious courts and institutions. And it moved in the dimension of moral considerations, where the Emperor, as a man and a member of the Church, fell under the direction and the censure of ecclesiastical authority.

Though dogmatically expressed, Ambrose's political thought was a fragile structure, and the Bishop did not attempt to establish a lasting system by which the relation of Church and Empire might be conducted. Throughout, he expressed only two unalterable premises: that the Church was juristically discrete from the Empire, and that her members were subject to her discipline. There are no lofty and general rules here. Even the statement, *"Imperator intra ecclesiam, non supra ecclesiam est,"* which some historians have exalted as a general principle, was a direct comment upon the particular status of Valentinian II as a catechumen. Ambrose's great moral claims were claims of his own authority over particular rulers, though later generations considered them precedents expressive of general truths. The Bishop saw numerous emperors in his day —Constans and Constantius II, Julian, Jovian, Valens and Valentinian I, Gratian, Valentinian II, Theodosius I, Eugenius, Arcadius and Honorius—emperors whose religious convictions ranged between philosophic paganism and rigid orthodoxy, and whose religious policies varied just as widely. The attempt to establish any firm principle relating the imperial office to the Church would perforce have seemed impracticable to him; for the accession of a pagan or apostate would void such a principle. Indeed, Ambrose witnessed a change of this sort when the pagan Eugenius succeeded Valentinian II. By the same token, the Bishop placed no lasting trust in imperial laws; for he acknowledged that the emperor was not bound by law, and that he might freely abrogate the establishments of his predecessors. Consequently, the edicts of Theodosius in favor of Christianity might be overturned as easily as Eugenius overturned Gratian's edict against pagan sacrifices, the priestly colleges, and the Vestal Virgins, as easily as he restored to the Roman Senate the Altar of Victory against whose restoration Ambrose had successfully argued before Valentinian II.

The Bishop's protests went further than those of Athanasius and Hilary, not because he advanced any new principle, but because particular historical circumstances gave him the opportunity to invoke spiritual sanctions against his emperors. His arguments are occasional pieces, and their fundamental premises are the same as those the earlier Fathers maintained: that the Church is a sacramental institution, exercising discipline over her members, and that the juristic integrity she enjoys as a sacramental body must be maintained. Though they express no new principles, Ambrose's arguments in legal and moral thought deserve to be studied as logical and opportune developments of the protests of Athanasius and Hilary, and further, as continuations of Jewish doctrines concerning the relations between the Synagogue and the Empire.

I

When he sent Ambrose out to assume his duties as consular prefect in Milan, the imperial prefect instructed the young man, "Go and act, not as a judge, but as a bishop." [3] Probus's meaning is not clear, but he can scarcely have intended Ambrose to act with the disregard for the emperor and for imperial law which he showed after he had indeed become bishop. Then, he claimed a higher king than Caesar, a higher law than Rome's; and when the emperor acted within the law, but against those superior claims, Ambrose preferred open resistance to obedience. [4] For "all power of this world is not verity, but a dream." [5]

There were two critical points in Ambrose's thought when he addressed himself to the problems of the imperial office: first, that the ruler was not bound by law; and second, that a distinction should be drawn between governmental power and the holder of that power.

Despite its importance, the Father never treated the first point fully. It occurs twice, once in his commentary upon the Gospel of Luke, and again in his *Apologia Prophetae David.* The first passage deals with Christ's miraculously healing a leper (Luke 5:12, 13). Christ touched the leper to heal him although, as Ambrose recalls, the law forbade the touching of lepers. "But," the Father comments, "he who is lord of the law does not serve the law, but makes the law." [6] Here, Ambrose clearly had in mind the role of Christ as the establisher of the Old Testament, the "Law," ascribed to Him commonly by the Fathers: the particular "law" in question is a passage in the book of Leviticus. [7] But that the statement had a more general implication is indicated by the second passage. Commenting—possibly for the instruction of Theodosius I—upon Psalm 51:

[3] Paulinus, Vita S. Ambrosii, c. 8 (Migne, *Patrologia Latina* **14**: 29).

[4] E.g., Ep. 20, cc. 22, 23 (Migne, *Patrologia Latina* **16**: 1000 ff).

[5] Liber de Joseph Patriarcha, c. VI, 30 (*Corpus Scriptorum Ecclesiasticorum Latinorum* **32**: 94): "Sed hoc somnium est, et omnis potentia seculi somnium, non veritas, est." Studies of St. Ambrose's theology have, in general, not considered the ramifications of that Father's doctrinal convictions in his political thought. E.g., J. Huhn, *Ursprung und Wesen des Bösen und der Sünde nach der Lehre des Kirchenvaters Ambrosius* (Paderborn, 1937). J. Rinna, *Die Kirche als Corpus Christi Mysticum beim hl. Ambrosius.* Rome, 1940. K. Schwerdt, *Studien zur Lehre des heiligen Ambrosius von der Person Christi* (Diss. Freiburg-i.-B.). Bückeburg, 1937.

[6] Expositionis in Lucam V, 7 (*Corpus Scriptorum Ecclesiasticorum Latinorum* **32**, 4: 181): "Lex tangi leprosos prohibet, sed qui dominus legis est, non obsequitur legi, sed legem facit."

[7] Leviticus 13:3.

I

14, "Deliver me from bloodguiltiness, O God, thou God of my salvation," Ambrose writes that this verse could apply to the death of Uriah, which David had countenanced and for which he suffered great spiritual agony; "although the king is free of the laws, he is still a criminal to his conscience" (quamvis rex legibus absolutus, suae tamen reus sit conscientiae.")[8] Here, Ambrose is in perfect accord with the legist Paulus, who wrote that the emperor was morally obliged to obey the laws "of which he himself is known to be freed" (Sent. V, 12, 9).

The king (or emperor) was free of the laws; for he who makes the law does not serve the law. Further, he was free to use his power for good or for evil. The distinction between the ruler and the power to rule is an important one, for it denies the assumption of any particular moral character or responsibilities upon accession to the supreme temporal office. Ambrose writes that God ordains all powers; that is, He allows them to be held. But He does not actually grant them, and even the devil can boast of having dispensed them. Power is neither good nor evil in itself; but ambition is evil, and the ambitious man, who abuses power, is evil. On the other hand, he who uses power rightly is a minister of God, "a minister of God unto thee for good." (Romans 13:4)[9]

These two points, the freedom of the Emperor from laws and the moral neutrality of power, tell us much about Ambrose's indifference toward the Empire as a legally Christian institution. The Empire had become Christian precisely because the emperors were free to overturn the edicts of their predecessors, to turn persecution into acknowledgment and sanction, and because

they had chosen to use the imperial power for good purposes.

This is the burden of the Bishop's famous comments upon the imperial conversion of Constantine, inserted in his funeral eulogy of Theodosius. The Empress-dowager Helena, concerned for the salvation of her son, the Emperor Constantine, instituted diligent search for the relics of Christ's body. The Holy Cross and Nails were recovered, and she mounted the Nails in a bridle and in a crown which she sent to Constantine. Using both, he began the line of Christian emperors "and transmitted the Faith to succeeding kings." Ambrose elaborates upon the significance of the imperial crown and bridle, set with such holy relics. The crown with its Holy Nail was fitting for Christian rulers, "so that, in imitation of the Lord, it might be said of the Roman emperor, 'Thou hast set upon his head a crown of precious stone' " (Psalm 20:4). The crown from the Cross, so that the Faith may shine forth; the bridle also from the Cross, so that power may rule." The bridle was particularly significant, for through it the Holy Spirit seemed to call the emperors to check their own excesses and to govern their subjects. Before, the imperial power had seemed prostrate in iniquity, and emperors had polluted themselves with wanton license after the fashion of brute animals.

They did not know God. The Cross of the Lord restrained them and recalled them from the error of impiety.

After Constantine, all the emperors had followed the true Faith, "except the one, Julian, who abandoned the author of his salvation in giving himself to the error of philosophy." [10]

In this account, two points are clear: that the conversion was due to Helena's personal initiative (supported to be sure by the Holy Spirit), and second, that perseverance in the Faith was due to the particular inclination of the emperors themselves, just as Julian's defection was due to his voluntary rejection of "the author of his salvation." Ambrose acknowledges that emperors in the past, like Nero and Caligula, had exercised the imperial power with the unchecked license of tyrants; and from his comments on the neutral moral character of power, one is perfectly warranted in surmising that he considered the bridle of the Faith a restriction upon the imperial office which might be cast off by any ruler without altering the fundamental nature of his office.

Concomitantly, the deviation of an emperor from the Faith might well invalidate the edicts by which Gratian and Theodosius had made the Empire legally Christian. The emperor was legibus solutus, and Ambrose was

---

[8] C. 77 (Corpus Scriptorum Ecclesiasticorum Latinorum 32, 2: 350): "Sequitur: 'Libera me de sanguinibus, Deus, Deus salutis meae.' Et ad Uri mortem potest referri, quod mandatae necis ejus conscius, veniam tanti poscat admissi, et quamvis rex legibus absolutus, suae tamen reus sit conscientiae. . . ." Cf. the forged Apologia altera, c. 3, 8 (ibid., p. 363). "Non enim solvit potestas justitiam, sed justitia potestatem; non legibus rex solutus est, sed leges suo solvit exemplo." P. De Francisci accepts this second passage as genuine, proving that Ambrose thought the Emperor under the law. Arcana Imperii (Milan, 1948) 3, 2: p. 221. To be sure, Ambrose appears to imply in his famous comment to Valentinian II that the emperor is under the law (Ep. 21, 9. Migne, Patrologia Latina 16: 1004 f): "Quod cum prescripsisti aliis, prescripsisti et tibi. Leges enim imperator fert, quas primus ipse custodiat." But his meaning is clearly that of Paulus (Sent. V, 12, ed. P. Krüger in Collectio Liborum Iuris Anteiustiniani (Berlin, 1878) 2: p. 121): "Ex imperfecto testamento legata vel fideicommissa imperatorem vindicare inverecundum est: decet enim tantae maiestati eas servare leges, quibus ipse solutus esse videtur."

[9] Expos. in Lucam, IV, 29 (Corpus Scriptorum Ecclesiasticorum Latinorum 32, 4: 153) " 'Qui resistit potestati, Dei, inquit, ordinationi resistit.' Hic quoque licet dicat dare se diabolus potestatem, omnia tamen illa ad tempus permissa sibi esse non abnuit. Itaque qui permisit, ordinavit; nec potestas mala, sed is qui male utitur potestate. Denique, 'Vis non timere potestatem? Fac bonum, et habebis laudem ex illa.' Non ergo potestas mala, sed ambitio. Denique eo usque a Deo ordinatio potestatis, ut Dei minister sit, qui bene utitur potestate: 'Dei, inquit, minister est tibi in bonum.' " Cf. Romans 13: 1–4.

[10] De Obitu Theodosii, cc. 40–51 (Corpus Scriptorum Ecclesiasticorum Latinorum 73: 392 ff). Cf. G. Bardy, "Chrétiens et païens à la fin du IV siècle," L'année théologique 4 (1943): esp. 462. On St. Ambrose's metaphysical distinction between the kingdom of this world, governed by Satan, and the Kingdom of Heaven, see J. E. Niederhuber, Die Lehre des hl. Ambrosius vom Reiche Gottes auf Erden (Mainz, 1904), esp. pp. 47 ff, 61 ff, 75 ff.

44

acutely aware that edicts of toleration had overturned edicts of persecution, and that edicts of positive constitution and privilege had superseded edicts of mere toleration. The principle of legal reversal was patent, and Ambrose acknowledged it. Consequently, he is silent toward the momentous legal processes of his day by which the constitutional forms of Church and Empire were being ever more closely correlated; and his is a silence all the more remarkable in his conflicts with Arians and pagans.

In view of Ambrose's concept of instability in imperial policy and in edicts as statements of policy, it is not surprising that he seldom appeals to imperial edicts as authorities, and never appeals to them without relating them to more abstract legal principles. To be sure, the Bishop was fully aware that bad laws could be modified or supplanted by good. Accordingly, he petitioned Theodosius after the slaughter at Thessalonica to prescribe a mandatory interim of thirty days between the issuance and the execution of a decree in cases of confiscation and/or capital punishment. He also praised Gratian's abolition of pagan practices in Rome "by rescript." [11] But in the second instance, he also acknowledges the possibility that Gratian's act could be rescinded and the pagan cult restored. He advances the possibility that a "heathen Emperor" might build an idolatrous altar "today" and, directly counter to the edict of Gratian, compel Christians to witness the sacrifices upon it. He puts the impermanence of civil law most succinctly in his appeal to Valentinian II's fraternal piety. Valentinian must not restore the practices his brother had abolished. Otherwise, Gratian's spirit would be distressed and might say to him:

I did not feel that I was overcome, because I left you as Emperor. I did not grieve at dying, because I had you as my heir; I did not mourn at leaving my imperial command, because I believed that my commands especially those concerning divine religion, would endure through all ages. I had set up these memorials of piety and virtue; I offered up these spoils gained from the world, these trophies of victory over the devil, these I offered up as gained from the enemy of all, and in them is eternal victory. What more could my enemy take from me? You have abrogated my decrees, which so far he who took up arms against me did not do. Now do I receive a more terrible wound in that my decrees are condemned by my brother.[12]

Because of their natural instability, Ambrose appealed beyond imperial edicts when he appealed to temporal law at all: he appealed to the great and general legal

principles of equity which lay behind valid positive law. On the premise that "equity confirms commands, and injustice dissolves them," [13] the Bishop sought primarily the implementation of equity itself rather than that of particular decrees. This is illustrated by his appeals over positive law to the *ius gentium* and to the principle of religious liberty.

In the great disputes of his episcopate, Ambrose invoked the *ius gentium* twice: once in his conflict with Symmachus on the issue of the Altar of Victory, and again in the case of the Synagogue at Callinicum. Both times, the Bishop's point was that Christians should not be constrained to indemnify those who had harmed them in the past. Interestingly, he did not in either case seek the support of imperial edicts; and in fact, he was contesting the strong argument Symmachus advanced on the basis of legal precedent, the precedent of the imperial office itself, and the particular regulations concerning public order to which the Jews of Callinicum had appealed. It is these arguments which have been regarded, in particular, as unworthy of Ambrose by virtue of their great vindictiveness and intolerance. In both cases he swept aside cogent legal arguments; but he swept them aside by invoking a principle higher than the particular precedent and the particular edict. That his argument rested on the *lex talionis* did him small credit, but it did not invalidate his position.

It was only equitable he said, that the decree against pagan practices be upheld and the Altar of Victory excluded from the Senate House; for "they are complaining of their losses who never spared our blood, who destroyed the very buildings of the churches. And they petition you to grant them privileges who by the last Julian law denied us the common right of speaking and teaching. . . ." [14] It was only equitable that the Jews not be indemnified for the loss of their Synagogue, which Christians had burnt; for "If I were pleading according to the law of the nations, I would mention how many of the Church's basilicas the Jews burned in the time of Julian. . . . But the Church was not avenged, and shall the Synagogue be avenged?" [15]

Ambrose wrote contemptuously of the Jews in Callinicum, referring to the juristic integrity they preserved within the Empire.

Although they refuse to be bound by the laws of Rome, thinking them outrageous, they now wish to be avenged, so to speak, by Roman laws. Where were those laws when they set fire to the domes of the sacred basilicas? If Julian

---

[11] Ep. 17, 5 (Migne, *Patrologia Latina* 16: 962).

[12] *Ibid.*, 16 (*ibid.*, 965). *Cf.* Hans von Campenhausen, *Ambrosius von Mailand als Kirchenpolitiker* (Berlin-Leipzig, 1929), p. 275 f: "Er [Ambrosius] versichert höchstens, dass fromme Fürsten für die Kirche ein Gewinn sind, und dass ihre Frommigkeit auch umgekehrt nicht ohne politischen Lohn bleibt, aber alle Wohltäten und Gesetze, mit denen die Kaiser die Kirche unterstutzen, nimmt er lediglich als eine Beweis ihrer privaten Frommigkeit entgegen, ohne deren Betätigen von den eigentlich politischen Pflichten zu unterscheiden." Campenhausen does not, however, draw any conclusions from Ambrose's position that the emperor was *legibus solutus*.

[13] De Officiis, II, 19 (Migne, *Patrologia Latina* 16: 128): "Claret ergo quoniam et aequitas imperia confirmet, et injustitia dissolvat."

[14] Ep. 17, 4 (Migne, *Patrologia Latina* 16: 962). For a review of the evidence concerning the affair of the Altar of Victory, see N. Casini, "Le Discussioni sull' *Ara victoriae* nella Curia Romana," *Studi Romani* 5 (1957): 501–517.

[15] Ep. 40, 15 (Migne, *Patrologia Latina* 16: 1107): "At certe si jure gentium agere, dicerem quantas ecclesiae basilicas Judaei tempore Juliani incenderint. . . ."

did not avenge the Church, because he was an apostate, will you, O Emperor, avenge the harm done the Synagogue, because you are a Christian? [16]

But this argument, this appeal to the *lex talionis* as superior to positive law, and Ambrose's contempt for the Jews, who were privileged to live according to their own religious laws, ring hollow when the Bishop appeals to the principle of religious liberty on his own behalf.

In his dispute with the pagan, Symmachus, Ambrose acknowledged the principle of religious freedom, the principle that "everyone ought freely to defend and maintain the faith and purpose of his own mind." [17] But, referring to the particular case at issue, he observed that there were many pagan altars and shrines in Rome, and that the pagans' maintenance of their religious freedom should not be so broad as to force Christian senators to be party to pagan rites in the Senate House. As indicated above, his objection to the exercise of their religious liberty by the Jews is more comprehensive.

When the interests and articles of his own Faith were at issue, however, Ambrose did not hesitate to claim the full religious exemptions sanctioned by Roman practice, or even to deny the binding power of Roman laws when they jeopardized those exemptions: "We, by the law of the Lord Jesus Christ, are dead to this [worldly] law. The law did not gather the Church together, but the Faith of Christ." [18]

The affair of the basilicas is a paradigm of Ambrose's thought in this regard. In 384 the Arian Empress Justina, through the mouth of her young son, Valentinian II, requested the Bishop to give up two basilicas for Arian worship. Upon Ambrose's refusing, Justina had him summoned before the imperial consistory to defend his action; but the Bishop appeared accompanied by so large a company of Milanese that he was allowed to depart before the hearing had been formally opened. Subsequently, the Court attempted to take the basilicas by a show of armed bravado, but it retreated in the face of Ambrose's unswerving resistance.

Ambrose's comments center principally upon two questions: whether he could rightfully be tried before the imperial consistory, and whether the basilicas could be surrendered. Claiming religious exemptions, he answers both negatively. With regard to the first question, the Bishop acknowledged that Valentinian I had established by law

that priests should judge concerning priests. Moreover, if a bishop were accused of other matters also, and a question of character was to be enquired into, it was also his will that this should be reserved for the judgment of bishops. [19]

Ambrose goes further. Valentinian's establishment was merely the statement in positive law of a general and more binding principle; for a matter of faith must be tried by a religious court (in this case, by an episcopal court). The rights of the priesthood must not be subjected to the scrutiny and judgment of heathen or laymen, and least of all to the judgment of Valentinian, who is still only a catechumen, a youth, ignorant of the sacred writings. Valentinian I had said,

"It is not my business to judge between bishops." Your Clemency [Valentinian II] now says: "I ought to judge." And while he, though baptized in Christ, thought himself unequal to the burden of such a judgment, does your Clemency, who have yet to earn for yourself the sacrament of baptism, arrogate to yourself a judgment concerning the faith, though ignorant of the sacrament of that faith? [20]

The bishops must consider matters of faith as at Nicaea, where Constantine "did not promulgate any laws beforehand, but left the decision to the bishops." Still, Valentinian has presumed to issue a decree on the case at issue, banishing Ambrose from his see. The Bishop refuses to obey the edict, for imperial law cannot be set above the law of God; furthermore, if Valentinian desires a legitimate discussion of the problem, he must rescind his edict and allow a proper ecclesiastical assembly to gather.

Just as his rejection of imperial competence in matters of Faith rests upon his concept of the Church as a mystic union into which secular power might not justly intrude, so also his refusal to surrender the basilicas derives from the principle of religious exemption. When he writes that *divina* are not subject to the imperial power, and that the palaces belong to the Emperor he is merely stating this principle. [21] With great emphasis, Ambrose observes that the Church pays tribute to the Emperor when he requires it, and that if the Emperor should lay claim to the lands or to the silver and gold of the Church, the Church would surrender it. As for his own personal property, the Bishop would willingly give up his lands, his dwelling, his plate, and anything in his power to give, if that should be demanded.

On the other hand, the command to surrender the basilicas was, for Ambrose, precisely the command to "surrender the altars of God." [22] It was the command to surrender the places consecrated to mystic service of

---

[16] *Ibid.*, 21 (*ibid.*, 1108 f) : "Et cum ipsi Romanis legibus teneri se negent ita ut crimina leges putent, nunc velut Romanis legibus se vindicandos putant. Ubi erant istae leges cum incenderent ipsi sacratarum basilicarum culmina? Si Julianus non est ultus ecclesiam, quia praevaricator erat, tu, imperator, ulcisceris synagogae injuriam, quia christianus es?"

[17] Ep. 17, 7 (Migne, *Patrologia Latina* 16: 962) : "Libere enim debet defendere unusquisque fidele mentis suae et servare propositum."

[18] Sermo contra Auxentium, 24 (Migne, *Patrologia Latina* 16: 1014) : "Non lex ecclesiam congregavit, sed fides Christi."

[19] Ep. 21, 2 (Migne, *Patrologia Latina* 16: 1003).

[20] *Ibid.*, 5, Sermo contra Auxentium, 29 (Migne, *Patrologia Latina* 16: 1004, 1016).

[21] Ep. 20, 8 (Migne, *Patrologia Latina* 16: 996 f) : "Respondi, si a me peteret, quod meum est, id est, fundum meum, argentum meum, quidvis hujusmodi meum, me non refragaturum: quanquam omnia quae mei sunt, essent pauperum, verum ea quae sunt divina, imperatoriae potestati non esse subjacta."

[22] Ep. 20, 16 (Migne, *Patrologia Latina* 16: 998) : "Mandatur: Trade altaria Dei."

the Church,[23] to give up to the enemies of Christ the places where His sacrifice of Himself was reenacted, to abandon the very form of the body of Christ.[24] The claim made in the Emperor's behalf that all things belong to him was erroneous; for the Church (i.e., the altars) belong to God and not to Caesar.[25] By offering all the earthly goods of the Church to the Emperor, Ambrose acknowledged the rightful claim of the imperial government over temporal property. It should be observed particularly that the Bishop does not deny that the Emperor might legally receive the church building. His words explicitly state his claim to the benefits of religious exemptions: "The command is given then: 'Hand over the basilica.' I answer, 'It is not *lawful* (*fas*) for me to hand it over, nor, O Emperor, is it *advantageous* (*nec . . . expedit*) for you to receive it.' " [26] The property of God (*divina*) is not his to give; but he does not object that the Emperor might not, in terms of Roman law, rightly confiscate the building by force or even execute Ambrose for his resistance: "Let the Emperor act as he must. He must take my life rather than my Faith." [27]

Even the principle of equity which sustained the imperial laws has at this point proven inadequate for Ambrose's argument, and the Bishop's break with temporal law becomes complete. "The law of God has taught us what to follow; human law cannot teach us this." [28] The tension in his mind between temporal law and theology is clear. He abandons edicts and legal principles

alike, and appeals to the higher law of Faith, and to moral judgment against the Emperors who infringed it. Worldly law must be abridged when necessary; for the maintenance of civil law should be secondary to religion.[29]

II

The burden of Ambrose's thought is, therefore, extra- or supra-legal. It is, in fact, moral or sacramental, and derives principally from Ambrose's concept of the Church, and of the bishop's functions within the Church. He shared with Athanasius and Hilary the concepts that the Church was a mystic union of the true believers with God, that the end of this union was the salvation of the individual through participation in the human and divine natures of Christ, and that the sacraments, sustained by a true confession of faith in the Incarnation, were the means by which the Faithful achieved that corporeal and spiritual union. Likewise, he shared with the earlier Fathers the belief that the Church was an effective kingdom, that this Kingdom of God was superior to all earthly kingdoms, and, as we have seen, that its law was superior to civil law.

To this structure, Ambrose added two elements which made it positive, dynamic, and even aggressive toward temporal rulers where it had been largely negative and defensive in the hands of earlier writers. Athanasius and Hilary contented themselves with denying the right of the imperial government to intervene in the sacred matters of the Church and in the juridical processes related to them. Their argument was almost entirely, as we have seen, a demand that the convention of religious exemptions continue to be observed in the Church's favor. But Ambrose adapted the image of the Church as the Kingdom of God to immediate circumstances and carried this argument to a far greater height.

The first element by which he transformed the earlier argument was a loftier concept of the episcopal office. Professor G. H. Williams has shown how the images of the priestly bishop and the prophetic bishop combined in Ambrose's mind to increase the vigor of his appeals against actions of the imperial power.[30] But the basis of this combination was even loftier than the constructions of the priestly or prophetic offices alone. It was the concept of Christ as King, and of the bishop as the representative of the royal Saviour. Commenting upon I Corinthians 11:8–10, where women are admonished to cover their heads in Church, Ambrose remarks that this command is just:

Since she is not the image of God a woman ought, therefore, to veil her head, to show herself subject. And since falsehood began through her, she ought to have this

---

[23] *Cf.* Ambrose's defense of his selling sacred vessels to redeem captives. De Officiis, II, 28, 143 (Migne, *Patrologia Latina* 16: 142).

[24] De Sacramentis, IV, 3, 8, V, 2.7 (*Corpus Scriptorum Ecclesiasticorum Latinorum* 73: 49, 61): "Quid est enim altare, nisi forma corporis Christi?"

[25] Sermo contra Auxentium, 35 (Migne, *Patrologia Latina* 16: 1018): "Ecclesia Dei est, Caesari utique non debet addici, quia jus Caesaris esse non potest Dei templum." On St. Ambrose's application of private law to the House of God, see S. Calafato, *La Proprietà Privata in Sant'Ambrogio* (Turin, 1958), p. 63 ff.

[26] Ep. 20, 19 (Migne, *Patrologia Latina* 16: 999): "Mandatur denique: Trade basilicam. Respondeo: Nec mihi fas est tradere, nec tibi accipere, imperator, expedit."

[27] Sermo contra Auxentium, 18 (Migne, *Patrologia Latina* 16: 1015): "Respondi ego, quod sacerdotis est; quod imperatoris est, faciat imperator. Prius est ut animam mihi, quam fidem auferat." Palanque remarks that Ambrose was "avant tout un juriste," but he never refers to the precise legal context of the *ius publicum* in which the Bishop's conflicts occurred, nor does he ever observe the tension in Ambrose's mind between classical Roman law and Christian theology. The chief weakness in his approach is that he considers Ambrose as acting in a Christian Empire, and as making no distinction between the Empire and the emperor. Further, he considers the Empire a "personne morale," although Ambrose himself explicitly comments upon the moral neutrality of imperial power (above, note 9). As he writes, "Les devoirs de l'Etat chrétien, ce sont pour Ambroise les devoirs du prince chrétien. Il ne distingue jamais l'Etat—personne morale—et la personne du souverain." J. R. Palanque, *S. Ambroise et l'Empire romaine* (Paris, 1933), p. 355. This is also the position of Campenhausen, *op. cit.*

[28] Ep. 21, 10 (Migne, *Patrologia Latina* 16: 1005): "Legem enim tuam nollem esse supra Dei legem. Dei lex nos docuit quid sequamur, humanae leges hoc docere non possunt."

[29] Ep. 40, 11 (Migne, *Patrologia Latina* 16: 1105): "Sed disciplinae te ratio, imperator, movet. Quid igitur est amplius? Disciplinae species an causa religionis? Cedat oportet censura devotioni."

[30] "Christology and Church-State Relations in the Fourth Century," *Church History* 20 (1951), no. 4, p. 9 f.

sign, that her head be not free, but covered with a veil out of reverence for the bishop. For the bishop has the role (*personam*) of Christ. Because of the beginning of crime, she ought to appear subject before a bishop, since he is the vicar of the Lord, just as she would before a judge.[81]

The image of the bishop as "vicar of the Lord" is, of course, a legal one; Ambrose implies that the relation of the bishop to Christ is that of the judge to the emperor. It was the ecclesiastical counterpart of the relationship between the framer of law and its executor. The Father also expressed that relation in priestly or sacramental contexts. Christ was the type of all future priests, Himself both priest and victim, and it was He who established the earthly priesthood by summoning Aaron to serve Him and continued it by summoning Aaron's successors.[32] This summons bishops shared with Christ, who had Himself been called to the sacrificial office,[33] just as they shared with Him and the Apostles the headship of the Church.[34] Christ is the High Priest;[35] the bishop is the *"summus sacerdos,"*[36] combining in the one office of bishop all inferior clerical offices.[37] But most important, just as Christ was the author of salvation, which could be attained through His body, the Church, so did the salvation of the whole people lie in the person of the bishop.[38] "In him is the life of all formed."[39] Ambrose gave this relationship symbolic expression when he spoke of burying saints and bishops beneath the altar :

Let the triumphant victims [the martyrs Gervasius and Protasius] take their place where Christ is the victim. Let Him be upon the altar who suffered for all; let them be beneath the altar who were redeemed by His suffering. This is the spot that I had destined for myself, because it is fitting that a bishop rest where he was wont to offer [the Sacrifice].[40]

The altar was "the form of the body of Christ." Christ was upon it, the Sacrifice and Sacrificer; His vicar, who had enacted His priestly rôle was beneath it.

The basis of episcopal authority was, therefore, the nature of Christ, who gathered the Church and sustained it through His self-sacrifice. Accordingly, the Faith, which defined the nature of Christ, and the sacraments, which brought the benefits of His passion to the true believer, were critically important in Ambrose's construction of the episcopal office. In regard to both, as we have indicated, Ambrose shared the convictions of Athanasius and Hilary; and a brief review of their *loci communes*, as held by Ambrose, will suffice.

When he wrote, "the Church has no possessions of her own except the Faith,"[41] Ambrose was in perfect accord with the earlier Fathers. The true Faith, the Faith of Nicaea,[42] was the center of his ecclesiological thought. He once mentions belief in the Resurrection as the fundamental article of Faith;[43] but his more usual position was that the mystery of the Incarnation of God was primary. Faith in this latter article was, in fact, the price paid for the divine mysteries[44] (one of the Father's less appropriate figures of speech) ; it was the gift of God's mercy,[45] and attained its fulness in the sacrament of the passion.[46] Where Faith is, there is the freedom from sin bought by Christ's self-sacrifice : for the victory of Christ is the victory of freedom.[47]

---

[81] Migne, *Patrologia Latina* 17 : 240 : "Mulier ergo idcirco debet velare caput, quia non est imago Dei, sed ut ostendatur subjecta ; et quia praevaricatio per illam inchoata est, hoc signum debet habere ; ut in ecclesia propter reverentiam episcopalem non habeat caput liberum, sed velamine tectum : nec habeat potestatem loquendi ; *quia episcopus personam habet Christi.* Quasi ergo ante judicem, sic ante episcopum, quia *vicarius Domini est,* propter reatu originem subjecta debet videri." *Cf.* Tertullian, *Virg. Vel.,* c. 1, "Paracletus . . . vicarius domini" (Migne, *Patrologia Latina* 2 : 937).

[32] Ep. 63, cc. 45–49 (Migne, *Patrologia Latina* 16 : 1201 f). De Fide Christiana, III, 11, 84–88 (*ibid.,* 606 f).

[33] Ep. 63, 48 (Migne, *Patrologia Latina* 16 : 1202) : "Et ita Christus non exegit, sed accepit sacerdotium."

[34] Comment. in Epist. I. ad Cor. 12:28 (Migne, *Patrologia Latina* 17 : 249) : "Caput itaque in ecclesia apostolos posuit, qui legati Christi sunt, sicut dicit idem Apostolus : 'Pro quo legatione fungimur' (II Cor. 5:20). Isti sunt episcopi, firmante istud Petro apostolo et dicente inter cetera de Juda : 'Et episcopatum ejus accipiat alter.' " *Cf.* Comment. in Epist. ad Ephes. 4 : 11, 12 : "Apostoli episcopi sunt" (*ibid.,* 387).

[35] De Fide christiana III, 11, 85 (Migne, *Patrologia Latina* 16 : 607), quoting *Hebrews* 3 : 1, 2).

[36] De Mysteriis, c. 2, 6 (*Corpus Scriptorum Ecclesiasticorum Latinorum* 73 : 90).

[37] Comment. in Epist. ad Ephes. 4:11, 12 (Migne, *Patrologia Latina* 17 : 387). *Cf.* Comment. in Epist. I. ad Timoth. 3 : 8–10 (*ibid.,* 470).

[38] Comment. in Epist. I. ad Timoth. 6 : 13–16 (Migne, *Patrologia Latina* 17 : 483) : "Magna vigilantia atque providentia praecepta dat rectori ecclesiae ; in hujus enim persona totius populi salus consistit."

[39] Ep. 63, c. 46 (Migne, *Patrologia Latina* 16 : 1201). "Itaque cum in omni actu, tum maxime in episcopi petitione, abesse debet malignitas, in quo vita formatur omnium. . . ." *Cf.* Cyprian, Ep. 33, 1 : "Ecclesia in episcopo." On this text, see J. Zeiller, "La conception de l'Eglise aux quatre premiers siécles," *Revue d'histoire ecclésiastique* 29 (1933) : 582.

[40] Ep. 22, 13 (Migne, *Patrologia Latina* 16 : 1023) : "Succedant victimae triumphales in locum ubi Christus hostia est. Sed, ille super altare, qui pro omnibus passus est. Isti sub altari qui illius redempti sunt passione. Hunc ego locum praedestinaveram mihi ; dignum est enim ut ibi requiescat sacerdos, ubi offerre consuevit."

[41] Ep. 18, 16 (Migne, *Patrologia Latina* 16 : 977) : "Nihil Ecclesia sibi, nisi fidem possidet."

[42] De Fide Christiana, I, 5, 18 (Migne, *Patrologia Latina* 16 : 536, 555).

[43] De Joseph Patriarcha, c. 13, 80 (*Corpus Scriptorum Ecclesiasticorum Latinorum* 32, 2 : 120) : "Primum et maximum fidei fundamentum, in resurrectionem Christi credere."

[44] *Ibid.,* c. 8, 45 (*ibid.,* p. 104) : "Non enim pecunia emitur Christus, sed gratia. Pretium tuum fides est. Hac emuntur divina mysteria."

[45] Comment. in Epist. ad Rom., prologus (Migne, *Patrologia Latina* 17 : 47).

[46] *Cf.* De Spiritu Sancto, III, 17, 124 (Migne, *Patrologia Latina* 16 : 806).

[47] Ep. 75, 5 (Migne, *Patrologia Latina* 16 : 1258). On St. Ambrose's soteriology, see A. Madeo, *La Dottrina Soteriologica di Sant'Ambrogio* (Bergamo, 1943), pp. 31 (the doctrine of the Sacrifice), 71 ff (the doctrine of man's participation in the divine nature), and 87 ff (the doctrine of the believers as the body of Christ).

For Ambrose, the Incarnation was "the pledge of our salvation." [48] To secure the redemption of man, God must humble himself by taking on human form, the form of a servant,[49] and die, and rise again.

For seeing that God could not die, Wisdom could not die; and inasmuch as that could not rise again which had not died, flesh is assumed, which can die, so that although that, whose nature it is, dies, that which had died should rise again. For the resurrection could not be effected except by man; since, "as by man came death, so too by man came the resurrection of the dead." [50]

In accomplishing man's salvation, Christ discharged the dual office of priest and victim.

How then, but in His body did He expiate the sins of the people? In what did He suffer, save in His body. . . . In what is He a priest, save in that which He took to Himself from the priestly nation? It is a priest's duty to offer something, and according to the Law, to enter into the holy places by means of blood. Seeing then, that God had rejected the blood of bulls and goats, this High Priest was indeed bound to make passage and entry into the Holy of Holies in heaven through His own blood in order that He might be the everlasting propitiation for our sins. Priest and victim then, are one; the priesthood and the sacrifice are, however, exercised under the conditions of humanity, for He was led as a lamb to the slaughter, and He is a priest after the order of Melchesedech.[51]

Christ still offers Himself, priest and victim, in the sacrament of the Eucharist.[52] Ambrose's veneration for the two sacraments, the Eucharist and Baptism, was fully as great as was that of Athanasius and Hilary, and for the same reasons. Faith alone, unaided by participation in the sacraments, by corporeal and spiritual participation in the body of Christ, was insufficient to attain perfection.[53] To restore the Church, Christ took on the "mystery of the human body," and instituted the sacraments by which he continually fed the Church, offering to the believer mystic participation in His true humanity and true divinity.[54] A faulty profession of

Faith, which dishonored the Trinity or impugned either of Christ's two natures, would invalidate the sacrament; the Arians, for example, had destroyed baptism by confounding Christ's manhood with His divinity.[55] But it was only through a true profession, sustained by participation in the sacraments, that one was joined in Christ, to sit in and with Him at the right hand of the Father; [56] for "when we eat the body of Christ, we share in His divinity and humanity." [57]

At His passion, Christ prepared the heavenly kingdom. He was dressed in royal robes, crowned, and given a sceptre; He ascended His Cross as a triumphant king mounts his chariot; he received royal acclamations.[58] By His sacrifice, he took upon Himself the weakness of mankind,[59] and He also established His city, the Church,[60] gathering all nations into it and taking for it the former *"regnum"* of the Synagogue.[61]

re-immolation is present in the teaching of Ambrose himself, yet the realism which eventually gave rise to them both derives from him so far as the West is concerned." C. W. Dugmore, "Sacrament and Sacrifice in the Early Fathers," *Journal of Ecclesiastical History* 2 (1951) : 37. Other writers emphasize the largely representative quality of the Eucharist in Ambrose's thought. See F. R. M. Hitchcock, "The Holy Communion in Ambrose of Milan," *Church Quarterly Review* 140 (1945) : 140 and *passim*. L. Lavorel, "Oblats et corps du Christ sur l'autel d'après S. Ambroise," *Recherches de théologie ancienne et médiévale* 24 (1957) : 223 f. and J. Lécuyer, "Le sacerdoce chrétien selon S. Ambroise," *Revue de l'Université d'Ottowa* 22 (1952) : 123 f. On the genuineness of *De Mysteris* and *De Sacramentis*, see Hitchcock's discussion, p. 127 ff.
    [55] E.g., De Fide Christiana, V, 10, 116 (Migne, *Patrologia Latina* 16 : 672).
    [56] Ep. 76, 8 (Migne, *Patrologia Latina* 16 : 1261) : "Non ergo sedimus, sed in Christo consedimus, qui solus sedet ad dexteram Dei Filius hominis. . . ."
    [57] De XLII Mansionibus Filiorum Israel, X (Migne, *Patrologia Latina* 17 : 20) : "Cum igitur Christi corpus manducamus, divinitatem et humanitatem participamus. . . ."
    [58] Expositio in Lucam Lib. X, 103 ff (*Corpus Scriptorum Ecclesiasticorum Latinorum* 32, 4 : 494).
    [59] De Sacramentis, II, 4, 11 (*Corpus Scriptorum Ecclesiasticorum Latinorum* 73 : 30).
    [60] Expositio psalmi CXVIII, 15, 35 (*Corpus Scriptorum Ecclesiasticorum Latinorum*, 62 : 349) : "Civitas Dei ecclesia est, ecclesia corpus est Christi. Peccat in caelum, qui caelestis civitatis jura contaminat, et immaculati corporis violat sanctitatem suorum conluvione vitiorum."
    [61] Expositio in Lucam, V, 113 (*Corpus Scriptorum Ecclesiasticorum Latinorum* 32, 4 : 229). De Jacob et vita beata, II, 2, 9 (*Corpus Scriptorum Ecclesiasticorum Latinorum* 32, 2 : 36) : "Hanc stolam ecclesiae typo Rebecca protulit, et dedit filio juniori stolam Veteris Testamenti, stolam propheticam et sacerdotalem, stolam regalem illam, Dauiticam, stolam Solomonis, Ezechiae, et Josiae regum, et dedit populo christiano, qui uti amictu sciret accepto quoniam populus Judaeorum eam sine usu habebat, et proprios nesciebat ornatus." This quotation and others which we have cited above allow one to question the thesis of Campenhausen that Ambrose did not consider Christians a distinct people like the Jews. Campenhausen writes: "Bei dieser psychologischen Einstellung ist est doppelt wichtig zu betonen, dass Ambrosius nie daran gedacht hat, die Kirche zu einer politischen Grosse im eigentlichen Sinne zu machen und ernsthaft mit dem Staat in Parallele zu stellen. . . . Die Kirche ist für Ambrosius kein Gegenstück zu Platos Staat, und wenn er das Volk Gottes ein Volk nennt, so doch in einem

    [48] De Fide Christiana, IV, 12, 164 (Migne, *Patrologia Latina* 16 : 648).
    [49] See *ibid.*, V, 12, 152 (*ibid.*, 678).
    [50] De Excessu Satyri, II, 91 (*Corpus Scriptorum Ecclesiasticorum Latinorum* 73 : 299), commenting upon I. Cor. 15:21.
    [51] De Fide Christiana III, 11, 86, 87 (Migne, *Patrologia Latina* 16 : 607).
    [52] De Officiis, I, 48, 238 (Migne, *Patrologia Latina* 16 : 94).
    [53] Ep. 7, 20 (Migne, *Patrologia Latina* 16 : 911) : "Nec enim fides sola ad perfectionem satis est, nisi etiam baptismatis adipiscatur gratiam, et sanguinem Christi redemptus accipiat."
    [54] De Viduis, III, 17 (Migne, *Patrologia Latina* 16 : 240) : "Domini enim est perpetuitatem sacramentorum spondere coelestium, et non defuturam spiritalis exsultationis gratiam polliceri, largiri munimenta vitae, fidei signacula, dona virtutum." De Mysteriis, IX, 54 (Migne, *Patrologia Latina* 16 : 407) : "Ipse clamat Dominus Jesu, 'Hoc est corpus meum.' Ante benedictionem verborum coelestium alia species nominatur, post consecrationem corpus significatur. Ipse dicit sanguinem suum. Ante consecrationem aliud dicitur, post consecrationem sanguis nuncupatur." In recent years, scholars have devoted much study to Ambrose's doctrine of the Eucharist. Their judgment is, in general, that stated by Dugmore: "Neither the fully-fledged doctrine of transubstantiation nor yet the idea of

The Church is His kingdom, which shall last forever; [62] it is His body; [63] it is the union of true believers, who reign with Him. [64]

It was in this kingdom that bishops functioned as vicars of the Lord; to its law they appealed as superior to imperial law; to its King they appealed as superior to Caesar. In it, their relationship with Christ was closest in their sacramental functions. Ambrose wrote:

We have seen the Prince of priests coming to us. We have seen and we have heard Him offering His blood for us. We priests follow as we can to offer the sacrifice for the people. Although weak in merit, we are still honorable in the sacrifice; for even though we do not now see Christ offering [the sacrifice], yet is He offered on earth when the body of Christ is offered. Rather, *He is clearly offering in us*, for His word sanctifies the sacrifice which is offered. [65]

The image of Christ acting in the persons of His bishops when they offered the Eucharist, the image of the King sustaining His vicars in the performance of their rightful duties, is very rèlevant to the positions Ambrose took in disputes with his earthly sovereigns. As we have seen, Church and State were for the Bishop constitutionally separate. Maintenance of the laws and administration of the one did not depend upon the vigor of the other. They could even be set at odds, as, for example, in time of persecution. But they could conflict as institutions only when the vicar of the Lord had moral or sacramental authority over the person of the

emperor, when the emperor was, in fact, "within the Church," and a subject of Christ in His heavenly realm. [66] Then, Ambrose's maxim that "although kings have laws in their power, they ought to be the more subject to God," [67] could receive practical importance; then, the emperor could be directed to turn the imperial power to righteous goals and to make of himself a minister of God.

These circumstances obtained in Ambrose's episcopate; for all the emperors with whom he dealt, with the exception of Eugenius, were either baptized members of the Church or catechumens. Accordingly, the appeals he directed to them, and the measures he took against them, derived principally from sacramental grounds. He excluded Maximus "from the company of the communion" for the murder of Gratian; [68] he refused to offer the Sacrifice before Theodosius until the Emperor had promised not to require Christians to indemnify the Jews of Callinicum for the destruction of their synagogue; he declined to admit Theodosius to the Sacrifice until he had done penance for the massacre at Thessalonica and had established legal checks against similar incidents in the future; and when Valentinian II seemed likely to restore the Altar of Victory, Ambrose threatened that the bishops would not "contentedly suffer it and take no notice; you indeed may come to the church, but you will find either no priest there, or one who will resist you." [69]

Ambrose feared, as he said, the Lord of the universe more than the earthly emperor. [70] For him, imperial law was not above the law of God; [71] the imperial power was great, but God was greater. [72] His moral arguments are all *ad hominem*. In them, he did not attempt

---

grundsätzlich anderen Sinne, als Ägypter und Äthiopier, Syrer, Juden, und Araber nach ihrer irdischen Heimat als ein Volk bezeichnet werden könne. Dieser Ausdruck ist für Ambrosius ein reines Bild ohne politischen Nebensinn und das Gleiche gilt, wenn er, wie schon längst üblich, die Kirche als himmlisches Jerusalem und Stadt Gottes zu verherrlichen liebt" (*op. cit.*, p. 263). This position makes Ambrose's position in his conflicts with Valentinian II and Theodosius I wholly incomprehensible; for he explicitly says in all such disputes that he is defending the rights of the Church, which are absolutely discrete from those of the civil government. Still more explicitly, Campenhausen denies that the concept of the Church had significant legal connotations for Ambrose (*op. cit.*, p. 264 f): "Die Verfassungsfrage ist für den religiösen Begriff der Kirche nicht konstitutiv. Die Kirche, von der Ambrosius als Theologe spricht, ist eine rein geistige Gemeinschaft, und an ihre äussere an den Aufbau des Staats erinnernde Organisations Form wird dabei nicht gedacht."

[62] E.g., Expositio in Lucam VII, 91 (*Corpus Scriptorum Ecclesiasticorum Latinorum* 32, 4: 320): "Et ideo regnum ecclesiae manebit aeternum, quia individua fides, corpus est unum."

[63] *Supra*, note 59.

[64] *Supra*, note 55. The reference to believers as co-rulers with Christ is frequent in Ambrose's works.

[65] Explanatio psalmi XXXVIII, 25 (*Corpus Scriptorum Ecclesiasticorum Latinorum* 64: 203): "Sed iam discessit umbra noctis et caliginis Iudaeorum, dies appropinquavit ecclesiae. Videmus nunc per imaginem bona et tenemus imaginis bona. Vidimus principem sacerdotum ad nos venientem, vidimus et audivimus offerentem pro nobis sanguinem suum. Sequimur, ut possumus, sacerdotes ut offeramus pro populo sacrificium etsi infirmi merito, tamen honorabiles sacrificio, quia etsi nunc Christus non videtur offerre, tamen ipse offertur in terris quia Christi corpus offertur. Immo ipse offerre manifestatur in nobis cujus sermo sanctificat sacrificium quod offertur."

[66] *Cf.* De Obitu Theodosii, c. 27: "Bene hoc dicit, qui regnum suum Deo subiecit, et paenitentiam gessit et peccatum suum confessus, veniam postulavit." C. 36: "Domine . . . da requiem perfectam *servo tuo Theodosio*, requiem illam, quam praeparasti sanctis tuis . . ." (*Corpus Scriptorum Ecclesiasticorum Latinorum* 73: 385, 389).

[67] Expositio in Psalmum CXVIII, Ain, 32 (*Corpus Scriptorum Ecclesiasticorum Latinorum* 62: 369): "Non potest hoc justus negare, quia nemo sine peccato, non potest rex, quia etsi leges in potestate habet, ut impune delinquat, Deo tamen subditus est; imo plus ipse debet, cui plus commissum est." Neither of the two standard analyses of St. Ambrose's political thought —those of Campenhausen and Palanque—consider the effects of his ecclesiology and sacramental concepts upon his attitude toward the Roman Empire.

[68] Paulinus, Vita S. Ambrosii, c. 19 (Migne, *Patrologia Latina* 14: 33): "Ipsum vero Maximum a communionis consortio segregavit, admonens ut effusi sanguinis domini sui [Valentiniani II], et quod est gravius, innocentis, ageret poenitentiam, si sibi apud Deum vellet esse consultum."

[69] Ep. 17, 13 (Migne, *Patrologia Latina* 16: 964).

[70] Sermo contra Auxentium, 1 (Migne, *Patrologia Latina* 16: 1007): "quia plus Dominum mundi quam saeculi hujus imperatorem timerem."

[71] Ep. 21, 10 (Migne, *Patrologia Latina* 16: 1005): "Legem enim tuam nollem esse supra Dei legem."

[72] *Cf.* Ep. 57, 7 (Migne, *Patrologia Latina* 16: 1176): "Etsi imperatoria potestas magna sit, tamen considera, imperator, quantus sit Deus."

to establish general principles, and when he declared that it was very respectful to call the emperor a son of the Church, "for the Emperor is within the Church, not above it," [73] he meant precisely that the Emperor Valentinian II, to whom the remark was addressed, was within the Church as a catechumen.

When one seeks a general framework for Ambrose's protests in favor of ecclesiastical liberty, as they relate to his concept of the imperial office, one will not find it in positive law or in general theories by which the civil and the ecclesiastical powers were correlated. The Father discounted positive law and the imperial attitudes it expressed as secondary and impermanent; and the Empire had not yet followed a settled religious policy long enough for the theoretical synthesis of the two powers. One does find it, however, in two arguments, one of occasional application and the other of constant. The first is the argument that the Church is a sacramental body, a spiritual kingdom quite apart from earthly realms and laws. If a temporal ruler is also a member of this kingdom, he must acknowledge its superior claims and submit to the discipline of its King and His vicars. The other is the classic argument that articles of Faith and related problems should be determined by the religious corporation involved rather than by imperial action. This juristic argument, as Ambrose knew, was valid under any emperor, and as we have indicated, it was critical in his concept of Church-Empire relations. But in many of his works appears the elision between *fas* and *ius* which made Ambrose's thought fundamentally supralegal, and which transcends his legal arguments. This elision was most eloquently stated in the Bishop's remarks on the incident of the basilicas.

See how much worse than the Jews the Arians are. They [the Jews] asked whether [Christ] thought that the right of tribute should be given to Caesar; these want to give to Caesar the right of the Church. But as these faithless ones follow their author, so also let us answer as our Lord and Author has taught us. For Jesus seeing the wickedness of the Jews said to them: "Why tempt ye me? Show me a penny." When they had given it, He said: "Whose image and superscription hath it?" They answered and said: Caesar's." And Jesus said to them: "Render unto Caesar the things that are Caesar's, and unto God, the things that are God's." So, too, I say to these who oppose me: Show me a penny. Jesus sees Caesar's penny and says: "Render unto Caesar the things that are Caesar's and unto God the things that are God's." Can they in seizing the basilicas of the Church offer Caesar's penny?

In the Church I only know of one Image, that is the Image of the unseen God, of which God has said: "Let us make man in our image and our likeness;" that image of which it is written, that Christ is the Brightness of His glory and the Image of His person. . . . We pay to Caesar, we do not deny it. The Church belongs to God; therefore, it ought not to be assigned to Caesar. *For the temple of God cannot be Caesar's by right.*[74]

Perhaps Ambrose refers again in this last sentence to the basilicas as falling under private, not public law, and as being administered in the name of God, their owner, by the clergy, His vicars. As we have seen, Ambrose refuted an analogous argument when it was advanced by Symmachus on behalf of the pagan colleges, and in the last analysis, he acknowledged that his own argument was based, not on *ius*, but on *fas*. Here the two—what positive law directed and what religious practice required—elided in Ambrose's mind in a fashion important as foreshadowing the time when the law of God would have legal validity in the courts of Caesar. But in the immediate circumstances which produced it, it was a natural issue of conventional thought tempered by the settled conviction of Ambrose himself that *ius* should be defied when *fas* conflicted with it.

More important, Ambrose was pressing home the distinction in classical law that whatever was consecrated to the service of a god belonged to that god. As a Christian, his view was explicit: altars where Christ's body was sacrificed, and the chalices which held His consecrated blood could never be given over to profane persons by God's chosen servants, His priests. Such things fell under *fas*, the *ius* of the Church. In the incident of the basilicas, Ambrose challenged the *ius* of the emperor over church buildings, *ius* warranted by classical Roman law, because, to his mind, *fas* forbade their surrender. He denied the relevance of Roman law over church buildings because their altars represented the body of Christ, over which the civil power had no competence. Consequently, Ambrose was arguing in the

---

[73] Sermo contra Auxentium, c. 36 (Migne, *Patrologia Latina* 16: 1018): "Quod cum honorificentia imperatoris dictum nemo potest negare. Quid enim honorificentius, quam ut imperator ecclesiae filius esse dicatur? Quod cum dicitur, sine pecato dicitur, cum gratia dicitur. Imperator enim intra ecclesiam non supra ecclesiam est." Scholars have tended, however, to consider this a general maxim, divorced from the particular circumstances to which it was addressed. See for example, G. H. Williams, *op. cit.* (*Church History* **20**, 3 (1951): 28 n. 31; and Palanque (*op. cit.*, p. 377) found it "la formule fameuse, d'un laconisme si expressif," because he did not relate it to the precise state of Valentinian II as a catechumen.

[74] Sermo contra Auxentium, 31, 32, 35 (Migne, *Patrologia Latina* **16**: 1016 ff): "Et tamen videte quanto pejores Ariani sint, quam Judaei. Illi quaerebant utrum solvendum putaret Caesari jus tributi; isti, imperatori volunt dare jus ecclesiae. Sed ut perfidi suum sequuntur auctorem; ita et nos quae nos Dominus et auctor noster docuit, respondeamus. Considerans enim Jesus dolum Judaeorum, dixit ad eos, 'Quid me tentatis? Ostendite mihi denarium.' Et cum dedissent, dixit, 'Cujus imaginem habet et inscriptionem?' Respondentes dixerunt: 'Caesaris.' Et ait illis Jesus, 'Reddite quae sunt Caesaris, Caesari, et quae sunt Dei, Deo.' Ergo et ego dico illis qui mihi objiciunt, 'Ostendite mihi denarium,' Jesus Caesaris denarium vidit, et ait, 'Reddite Caesari, quae Caesaris sunt, et quae Dei sunt, Deo.' Numquid de ecclesiae basilicis occupandis possunt denarium offerre Caesaris? Sed in ecclesia unam imaginem novi, hoc est imaginem Dei invisibilis, de qua dixit Deus, 'Faciamus hominem ad imaginem et similitudinem nostram,' illam imaginem de qua scriptum est quia Christus 'splendor gloriae et imago substantiae ejus.' . . . Solvimus quae sunt Caesaris, Caesari, et quae sunt Dei, Deo. Tributum Caesaris est, non negatur. Ecclesia Dei est, Caesari utique non debet addici, quia jus Caesaris esse non potest Dei templum."

terms of Athanasius and Hilary, that the sacramental body of Christ was exempt from external rule, and he went beyond their position by identifying the basilica, a material holding, with the mystical qualities of that body. The property of God and the property of the Church were not necessarily the same: he admitted imperial claims over all ecclesiastical possessions other than the sacramental, just as he admitted the power of the civil government to execute capital punishment upon him for his contumacy in denying the basilicas to the Emperor.

For him, there were two laws, religion—the law of Faith—and the civil law. The first must be maintained even at the expense of the second; the bishop must uphold *fas* at the risk of incurring lawful punishment prescribed by *ius*.[75] Positive law and the legal principles underlying it were, ultimately, irrelevant, even those which insured the Church her liberties. Clerical immunities, especially the right of bishops to be tried in matters of Faith by other bishops, and the freedom of the Church from external intervention in its sacramental affairs might be guaranteed by imperial law, but they were established and sustained by a higher law. Ambrose therefore elaborated somewhat the ecclesiology of his predecessors, at the same time holding with them that Empire and Church were discrete institutions, that the laws of one were not constitutionally one with the laws of the other, and that Rome claimed honor, but full loyalty belonged only to the City of God.

CONCLUSION

By the time of Ambrose, the Empire had fully acknowledged the legal fiction of the City of God; this acknowledgment proved the permanent basis for the co-existence of the Church and the Roman Empire, the alien community and the commonwealth. Sacramental matters of the Church must henceforth be tried by ecclesiastical law and courts, whose integrity the Christian emperors guaranteed. Civil law had satisfied the demands of Christian theology, and more than satisfied it, for beginning with Theodosius I the Empire followed a repressive policy against heretics and non-Christians. Ecclesiastical jurisprudence and Roman jurisprudence would grow ever closer in the next centuries.

In the fourth century, they were still discrete. The emperors exercised powers deriving from the ancient Roman constitution: the power of the sword, the power of legislation, the power of administration under the *ius publicum*. For its part, the Church claimed exclusive authority over its spiritual functions, a claim deriving from the Synagogue and strengthened by Christian theology. It held, to use St. Ambrose's figure, that in its

inner discipline the royal, prophetic, and priestly stole of the Hebrews had descended to the Christian people. Accordingly, the legal competences of the Church and Empire were divided by causes and not by persons: the doctrine of clerical privileges was not yet completely formulated, and a bishop might be tried by an ecclesiastical court for heresy or by a civil court for sedition.

Throughout the period, there is nothing to substantiate the view that, in law, any emperor actually assumed the headship of the Church. There is, in short, no warrant for the assumption that Caesaropapism, or explicit Christomimesis, as distinct from the pagan Theomimesis, had any genuine influence in determining imperial religious policy; rather, it seems apparent that that policy was consistently framed with reference to principles of classical jurisprudence, and not to Hellenistic rhetorical devices. Under later emperors—as, for example, under Justinian—those devices would have true ideological force in a Christian context, and they would accurately describe the emperor in his legal character as the "likeness" of Christ, or as the general overseer of the Church. But in the fourth century, the Hellenistic concept of emperorship had not been Christianized, just as the Empire had not been thoroughly Christianized, and it had not been adopted into the conceptual framework of the Church. We have seen clearly that the imperial office lacked any explicitly Christian characteristics in the mind of St. Ambrose, the former provincial governor, and indeed he thought it possible that pagans (like Julian the Apostate) might again sit on the throne of Caesar.

As long as this concept prevailed, the Church could never acknowledge any emperor, *qua* emperor, as its earthly head. That could only occur after Church and Empire had co-existed for some time on mutually advantageous terms, and after an unbroken succession of orthodox Christian emperors had acted as patrons of the Church. The memory of Diocletian and of Constantine before his conversion, of Julian, of the heretics Constantius and Valens, and of the pagan Eugenius, were vivid for Christians of the fourth century; for them, the bearer of the purple was clearly not *ipso facto* the head, or even the trustee, of the Church in this world. The welfare of the body of Christ, and the defense of its sacred mysteries, could never be entrusted to an office until the Church was certain that the tenant of that office would not defile his trust.

Consequently, the Fathers of the fourth century did not attempt to correlate Church and Empire as one institution. With the precedent of the Synagogue ever before them, they rather sought independent juristic existence for the two, with the Empire guaranteeing the Church's institutional integrity and, when necessary, yielding it the support of temporal force to execute its judgments. Beyond this, they did not go. They accepted the legitimacy of imperial jurisdiction over all persons, even bishops, in civil or criminal cases, and,

---

[75] It is interesting to compare the classical concepts of *fas* and *ius* as defined in the posthumous collection of essays by P. Noailles, *Fas et Ius* (Paris, 1948).

on the whole, they freely confessed the Empire's lawful control over ecclesiastical properties. In general, they did not dispute the classical privileges of the emperor in the *ius publicum*. Their goal was reached when Roman Law acknowledged the legal fiction of the Kingdom of Christ; for then, the faithful might lead quiet and peaceable lives as citizens of two realms, the human and the divine, rendering to Caesar the things that were Caesar's, and to God the things that were God's.

BIBLIOGRAPHY

ALFÖLDI, A., H. MATTINGLY trans. 1948. *The Conversion of Constantine and Pagan Rome* (Oxford).

BALANOS, D. S. 1938. "Ekklesia kai Ethnos." *Praktika tēs Akademias Athenōn* 13 : 208–218.

BARDY, G. 1943. "Chrétiens et païens à la fin du IVe siècle." *L'Année théologique* 4 : 457–503.

BARTLET, J. V., ed. C. J. CADOUX. 1943. *Church Life and Church Order During the First Four Centuries* (Oxford).

BATIFFOL, P. 1939. "De la dédicace des églises. Dédicace païenne et dédicace chrétienne." *Revue des sciences philosophiques et théologiques*, 58–70.

BAUR, C. 1931. "Die Anfänge des byzantinischen Cäsaropapismus." *Archiv des katholischen Kirchenrechts* 140 : 99–113.

BECK, A. 1930. *Römisches Recht bei Tertullian und Cyprian* (Schriften der Königsberger Gelehrten-Gesellschaft, geisteswiss. Kl. VII, fasc. 2, Halle), pp. 27–175.

BELL, H. I. 1924. *Jews and Christians in Egypt* (London).

BERCHEM, J. B. 1938. "Le Rôle du verbe dans l'œuvre de la création et de la sanctification d'après Saint Athanase." *Angelicum* 15 : 201–232.

—— 1938. "Le Christ sanctificateur d'après Saint Athanse." *Angelicum* 15 : 515–558.

BESKOW, P. 1962. *Rex Gloriae. The Kingship of Christ in the Early Church* (Stockholm).

BIEHL, L. 1937. *Das liturgische Gebet für Kaiser und Reich* (Görres-Gesellschaft, Heft 75, Paderborn).

BIONDI, B. 1952. *Il Diritto Romano Christiano* (Milan) 1.

BOUCAUD, C. 1930. *Pax Romana* (1, *L'ordre romain et le droit des gens*, Paris).

BRANDON, S. G. F. 1951. *The Fall of Jerusalem and the Christian Church* (London).

CALAFATO, S. 1958. *La Proprietà Privata in Sant'Ambrogio* (Turin).

CAMELOT, T. 1961. "Les sens de l'Eglise chez les Pères latins." *Nouvelle Revue théologique* 83 : 367–381.

CAMPENHAUSEN, H. VON. 1929. *Ambrosius von Mailand als Kirchenpolitiker* (Arbeiten zur Kirchengeschichte, XII, Berlin).

CARRINGTON, P. 1957. *The Early Christian Church* (2 v., Cambridge).

CASINI, N. 1957. "Le Discussioni sull' *Ara victoriae* nella Curia Romana." *Studi Romani* 5 : 501–517.

CHADWICK, H. 1958. "Ossius of Cordova and the Presidency of the Council of Antioch (325)." *Journal of Theological Studies*, N.S., 9 : 292–304.

CIRLOT, F. L. 1939. *The Early Eucharist* (London).

COHEN, B. 1944. "The Relation of Jewish to Roman Law." *Jewish Quarterly Review* 34 : 267–280, 409–425.

CROSS, F. L. 1945. *The Study of Athanasius* (Oxford).

DECLERCQ, V. C. 1954. *Ossius of Cordova* (Washington).

DÖLGER, F. 1932. "Zur antiken und frühchristlichen Auffassung der Herrschergewalt von Gottes Gnaden." *Antike und Christentum* (3, Münster), p. 117 ff.

DOWNEY, G. 1959. "Julian and Justinian and the Unity of Faith and Culture." *Church History* 27 : 339–349.

DUDDEN, F. H. 1935. *The Life and Times of Saint Ambrose* (2 v., Oxford).

DUGMORE, C. W. 1944. *The Influence of the Synagogue upon the Divine Office* (Oxford).

—— 1951. "Sacrament and Sacrifice in the Early Fathers." *Journal of Ecclesiastical History* 2 : 24–37.

DVORNIK, F. 1955. "The Emperor Julian's 'Reactionary' Ideas on Kingship." *Studies in Honor of Albert M. Friend, Jr.* (Princeton), 71–81.

EHRHARDT, A. 1953, 1954. "Das Corpus Christi und die Korporationen im spätrömischen Recht." *Zeitschrift für Rechtsgeschichte*, Röm. Abt. 70 : 299–347 ; 71 : 25–40.

—— 1954. "Jewish and Christian Ordination." *Journal of Ecclesiastical History* 5 : 125–138.

—— 1955. "Constantins des Grossen Religionspolitik und Gesetzgebung." *Zeitschrift für Rechtsgeschichte*, Röm. Abt. 72 : 127–190.

—— 1955. "Christian Baptism and Roman Law." *Festschrift Guido Kisch* (Stuttgart), pp. 147–166.

EMMENEGGER, J. E. 1947. *The Functions of Faith and Reason in the Theology of Saint Hilary of Poitiers* (Washington).

FERGUSON, E. 1963. "Jewish and Christian Ordination : Some Observations." *Harvard Theological Review* 56 : 13–20.

FIGUEROA, G. 1949. *The Church and the Synagogue in Saint Ambrose* (Washington).

FRANCISCI, P. DE. 1948. *Arcana imperii* (Milan) 3, 2.

FREND, W. H. C. 1954. "The Gnostic Sects and the Roman Empire." *Journal of Ecclesiastical History* 5 : 25–37.

GARDNER-SMITH, P. 1932. *The Church in the Roman Empire* (Cambridge).

GAUDEL, A. 1929, 1931. "La théologie de Λόγος chez saint Athanase." *Revue des sciences religieuses* (Strassbourg) 9 : 1–26 ; 11 : 524–539.

GAUDEMET, J. 1947. "La législation religieuse de Constantin." *Revue d'histoire de l'Eglise de France* 33 : 25–61.

—— 1954. "L'Empereur, interpret du droit." *Festscrift für Ernst Rabel* (Tübingen) 2 : pp. 169–203.

GAVIN, F. 1928. *The Jewish Antecedents of the Christian Sacraments* (London).

GIERKE, O. 1881. *Die Staats- und Korporationslehre des Alterthums und das Mittelalters und ihre Aufnahme in Deutschland.* (*Das deutsche Genossenschaftsrecht*, 3, Berlin.)

GIGLI, G. 1949. *L'Ortodossia, l'Arianesimo, e la Politica di Constanzo II (337–361)* (Rome).

GILSON, E. 1953. "Eglise et Cité de Dieu chez Saint Augustin." *Archives d'histoire doctrinale et littéraire du moyen âge* 28 : 5–23.

GLAESENER, H. 1957. "L'Empereur Gratien et Saint Ambroise." *Revue d'histoire ecclésiastique* 52 : 466–488.

GRÉGOIRE, H. 1938. "Note sur l'edit de tolérance de l'Empereur Gallien." *Byzantion* 13 : 587–588.

GUILLAUME, A. 1949. "Is Episcopacy a Jewish Institution?" *Bulletin of the School of Oriental and African Studies* (London) 13 : 23–26.

HAGEL, K. F. 1933. *Kirche und Kaisertum in Lehre und Leben des Athanasius* (Diss. Tübingen, 1932, Leipzig).

HITCHCOCK, F. R. M. 1945. "The Holy Communion in Ambrose of Milan." *Church Quarterly Review* 140 : 127–153.

HOEFFNER, A. 1948. "Les deux procès du pape Damase." *Revue des études anciennes* (Bordeaux) 50 : 288–304.

HONIG, R. M. 1943. "The Nicene Faith and the Legislation of the Early Byzantine Emperors." *Anglican Theological Review* 25 : 304–323.

HUHN, J. 1933. *Ursprung und Wesen des Bösen und der Sünde nach der Lehre des Kirchenvaters Ambrosius* (Forschungen zur christlichen Literatur- und Dogmengeschichte, Bd 17, Hft 5, Paderborn).

KELLY, F. J. 1928. "Athanasius and the Arian Controversy." *Ecclesiastical Review* 79 : 173–181.

KELLY, J. M. 1957. *Princeps Judex. Eine Untersuchung zur Entwicklung und zu den Grundlagen der kaiserlichen Gerichtsbarkeit* (Forschungen zum römischen Recht, fasc. 9, Weimar).

LADNER, G. B. 1959. *The Idea of Reform* (Harvard).

I

54

LAVOREL, L. 1957. "Oblats et corps du Christ sur l'autel d'après Saint Ambroise." *Recherches de théologie ancienne et médiévale* 24 : 205–224.

LECLERCQ, J. 1946. "L'Idée de la royauté du Christ dans l'œuvre de Saint Justin." *L'Année théologique* 7 : 83–95.

LEBON, J. 1952. "Le Sort du consubstantiel nicéen." *Revue d'histoire ecclésiastique* 47 : 485–529.

LÉCUYER, J. 1949. "Le Sacerdoce royal des chrétiens selon Saint Hilaire de Poitiers." *L'Année théologique* 10 : 302–325.

—— 1952. "Le Sacerdoce chrétien selon Saint Ambroise." *Revue de l'Université d'Ottowa* 22 : 104–126.

LEIFER, F. 1938. "Christentum und römisches Recht seit Konstantin." *Zeitschrift für Rechtsgeschichte,* Röm. Abt. 58 : 185–201.

LEISEGANG, H. 1926. "Der Ursprung der Lehre Augustins von der Civitas Dei." *Archiv für Kulturgeschichte* 16 : 127–158.

LEVY, E. 1961. "Libertas und Civitas." *Zeitschrift für Rechtsgeschichte,* Röm. Abt. 78 : 142–172.

LÖFFLER, P. 1960. "Die Trinitätslehre des Bischofs Hilarius von Poitiers zwischen Ost und West." *Zeitschrift für Kirchengeschichte* 71 : 26–36.

McCOOL, G. A. 1959. "The Ambrosian Origin of St. Augustine's Theology of the Image of God in Men." *Theological Studies* 20 : 62–81.

McHUGH, J. F. 1959. *The Exaltation of Christ in the Arian Controversy* (Shrewsbury).

MADEO, A. 1943. *La Dottrina Soteriologica di Sant'Ambrogio* (Bergamo).

MEYER ZU BURGHOLZ, H. 1956. *Das Verhältnis von Glauben und Denken bei Athanasius* (Theologische Diss., Heidelberg).

MULLER, H. 1946. *Christians and Pagans from Constantine to Augustine* (Pretoria) 1.

NIEDERHUBER, J. E. 1904. *Die Lehre des hl. Ambrosius vom Reiche Gottes auf Erden* (Forschungen zur christlichen Literatur und Dogmengeschichte, Bd 4, Hft 54, Mainz).

NOAILLES, P. 1948. *Fas et jus: Etudes de droit romain* (Paris).

PALANQUE, J. R. 1933. *Saint Ambroise et l'Empire romaine* (Paris).

PEETERS, P. 1944. "Comment Saint Athanase s'enfuit de Tyr en 335." Académie royale de Belgique, *Bulletin de la classe de lettres et des sciences morales et politiques* 30 : 131–177.

PIETRO, L. 1956. *Fede e Grazia in Ilario di Poitiers* (Pontificia Facoltà theologica 'S. Luigi' Posillipo-Naples, Reggio Calabria).

PIPPIDI, D. M. 1939. *Recherches sur le culte impériale* (Coll. scientifique de l'Institut roumain d'études latines, 2, Paris).

RADIN, M. 1931. *The Trial of Jesus of Nazareth* (Chicago).

RICHARD, M. 1947. "Saint Athanase et la psychologie du Christ selon les Ariens." *Mélanges de science religieuse* 4 : 5–54.

RINNA, J. 1940. *Die Kirche als Corpus Christi Mysticum beim hl. Ambrosius* (Rome).

RIVIÈRE, J. 1939. "Le sacrifice du Père dans la redemption d'après Saint Ambroise." *Revue des sciences religieuses* 19 : 1–23.

RUSSEL, A. G. 1937. "The Jews, the Roman Empire, and Christianity." *Greece and Rome* 6 : 170–178.

SALIN, E. 1926. *Civitas Dei* (Tübingen).

SCHMITT, J. 1955. "Sacerdoce judaïque et hiérarchie ecclésiale dans les premières communautés palestiniennes." *Revue des sciences religieuses* 29 : 250–261.

SCHWARTZ, E. 1909. "Die Conzilien des IV. Jahrhunderts." *Historische Zeitschrift* 104 : 1–37.

—— 1904, 1905, 1908, 1911. "Zur Geschichte des Athanasius." *Gesellschaft der Wiss. zu Göttingen, Nachrichten,* phil.-hist. Kl., 1904, pp. 333–401, 518–547; 1905, 165–187, 257–299; 1908, 305–374; 1911, 369–426, 469–522. Reprinted in E. Schwartz. 1959. *Gesammelte Schriften* (Berlin) 3.

SCHWERDT, K. 1937. *Studien zur Lehre des hl. Ambrosius von der Person Christi* (Diss. Freiburg-i.-B, Bückeburg).

SESTON, W. 1947. "Constantine as a 'Bishop'." *Journal of Roman Studies* 37 : 127–131.

SETTON, K. M. 1941. *Christian Attitude Towards the Emperor in the Fourth Century* (Columbia).

SIMON, M. 1948. *Verus Israël: Etude sur les relations entre chrétiens et juifs dans l'Empire romaine (135–425).* (Bibliothèque des Ecoles françaises d'Athènes et de Rome, fasc. 166. Paris.)

SMULDERS, P. 1944. *La Doctrine trinitaire de S. Hilaire de Poitiers* (Analecta Gregoriana 32, Rome).

—— 1952. "Le Mot et le concept de 'tradition' chez les Pères grecs." *Recherches de science religieuse* (Paris) 40 : 41–62.

TAYLOR, L. R. 1931. *The Divinity of the Roman Emperor* (Middletown, Conn.).

TELFER, W. 1946. "When Did the Arian Controversy Begin?" *Journal of Theological Studies* 47 : 129–142.

UNGER, D. 1946. "A Special Aspect of Athanasian Soteriology." *Franciscan Studies* 6 : 30–53, 171–194.

VOGELSTEIN, M. 1930. *Kaiseridee-Romidee und das Verhältnis von Staat und Kirche seit Constantin* (Breslau).

VOISIN, G. 1900. "La Doctrine christologique de Saint Athanase." *Revue d'histoire ecclésiastique* 1 : 226–248.

WEIGL, E. 1914. *Untersuchungen zur Christologie des hl. Athanasius* (Forschungen zur christlichen Literatur- und Dogmengeschichte, Bd. 12, Hft 4, Paderborn).

WILD, P. T. 1950. *The Divinization of Man According to Saint Hilary of Poitiers* (Pontificia Facultas Theologica Seminarii Sanctae Mariae ad Lacum, Diss. ad Lauream nr. 21, Mundelein, Illinois).

WILLIAMS, G. H. 1951. "Christology and Church-State Relations in the Fourth Century." *Church History* 20, 3 : 3–33; 4 : 3–26.

WIRSZUBSKI, C. 1950. *Libertas as a Political Idea at Rome During the Late Republic and Early Principate* (Cambridge).

ZEILER, J. 1933. "La Conception de l'Eglise aux quatre premiers siècles." *Revue d'histoire ecclésiastique* 29 : 571–585, 827–848.

—— 1937. "La Date du concile d'Aquilée (3. Sept. 381)." *Revue d'histoire ecclésiastique* 33 : 39–44.

—— 1937. "Le Royaume de Dieu et l'unité terrestre aux premiers siècles du christianisme." *Revue apologétique* 64 : 513–535.

ZIEGLER, A. W. 1953. "Der byzantinische Religionspolitk und der sogenannte Cäsaropapismus." *Münchener Beiträge zur Slavenkunde, Festgabe für Paul Diels* (Munich).

I

INDEX

Alexandria, pagans of, 5. See also Gregory of Cappadocia
Altar of Victory, 41; removed by Constantius II, 5; restored by Eugenius, 42. See also Ambrose, St., Bishop of Milan
Ambrose, St., Bishop of Milan, 7, 10, 20f, 25, 27; and imperial control of Church property, 23, 24; on Church and Synagogue, 28f; similarities with and divergences from SS. Athanasius and Hilary, 41f, 50f; on the nature of civil law and power, 42f, 45, 46, 49; on the conversion of Constantine, 43; on the massacre at Thessalonika, 44, 49; dispute with Symmachus about the Altar of Victory, 23f, 44f; controversy over synagogue at Callinicum, 44f; dispute over the basilicas, 23f, 45f, 50f; on Constantine I and the judgment of bishops, 45; soteriology of, 46ff; concept of episcopal office, 46f; ecclesiastical punishment ot secular rulers, 49
Aquileia, Synod of (381), 41
Arians, 13, 14, 15, 23f, 26, 30, 33, 36, 38, 45
Athanasius, St., Bishop of Alexandria, hearing at Psamathia, 6, 18, 25; on Council of Nicaea, 14; legal process against, 17ff, 30, 33, 37f; banishment of by Julian, 21; on imperial control of Church property, 24; on the Synagogue, 28; protest against Constantius II, 30, 36, 37f; soteriology of, 30ff; on the episcopal office, 33
Augustine, St., Bishop of Hippo, 9, 17, 20
Aurelian, 8

Caesaropapism, 4ff, 14, 51
Christomimesis, 5, 51. See also Theomimesis
Church, the One Holy, Catholic, and Apostolic, as the City of God, 3, 8; as the Heavenly Kingdom, 3, and passim; as an isopoliteia, 4, 8, 13, 14, 16, 19, 23; relations with the Empire before Constantine, 4; Jewish precedent for legal relations with the Empire, 9ff; libertas of, 13, 14, 30. See also Soteriology; Synagogue
Constantine I, conversion of, 3, 43; laws in favor of the Church, 5, 24f, 26; as pontifex maximus, 4, 20, 27; apotheosis of, 5; Vita of, 6, 15; and bishops, 5, 9. See also Athanasius, St., Bishop of Alexandria; Eusebius of Caesarea; Nicaea, Council of
Constantinople, Council of (381), imperial confirmation of, 14, 15f, 24; Theodosius I at, 15, 17

Constantius II, 4, 5, 6, 7, 9, 13, 21, 26, 27, 36, 39; religious policies, 5; as pontifex maximus, 5; and the Synods of Rimini-Seleucia, 16f, 26; protests of the Fathers against, 30; and Gregory of Cappadocia, 37. See also Athanasius, St., Bishop of Alexandria; Hilary, St., Bishop of Poitiers; and Lucifer of Cagliari

Damasus, Bishop of Rome, 22
Donatists, 9, 13
Dualism, defined, 3; of the Fathers, 4; of legal relations between Church and Empire, 4

Eschatology, Jewish and Christian, 11f
Eugenius, 42, 49
Eusebius of Caesarea, panegyric on Constantine, 5; at Nicaea, 15. See also Nicaea, Council of

Gaius, 22, 24
Galerius, 12
Gratian, 8, 9, 22, 25, 27, 40, 43; Ordinariorum Sententiae, 22, 25
Gregory of Cappadocia, 18, 27, 37

Hilary, St., Bishop of Poitiers, on Constantius, 7; on the nature of the Church, 19; appeal to Valentinian I, 25; on the Synagogue, 28; protests against Constantius, 29f, 34, 36, 38f; soteriology of, 31, 32; on the episcopal office, 33f; on the nature of civil office, 38f
Hosius of Cordova, 4, 19, 36

Ignatius of Antioch, 10
Illyricum, Synod of (365–372), 14
Ius publicum, as applied to the Church, 4, 6f, 22f, 25, 51

Jerome, St., 11
John, St., "Chrysostomos," 10
Jovian, 26
Julian the Apostate, 8, 9, 10, 21, 26, 43f, 51
Julius I, Bishop of Rome, 18f, 33, 37
Justinian, 14, 51

Kingship, Hellenistic concepts of, 5, 7, 51

Licinius, 8, 20
Lucifer of Cagliari, 6, 18, 26

Marcionites, 10
Martin, St., Bishop of Tours, 21

Maximus, 21, 22
Melitius of Antioch, 15
Milan, Edict of, 20
Milan, Synod of (355), 18, 26, 37f

Nicaea, Council of (325), Constantine I at, 6, 9, 13f, 17; imperial confirmation of, 15, 24; St. Athanasius on, 14; Eusebius of Caesarea at, 15; Creed of, 14, 20
Nicaea-Thrace, Conclave of (359), 14

Paul, St., Apostle, 9f, 12, 28, 33
Paulus, legist, 21, 27, 43
Priscillian of Avila, 21f
Psamathia, hearing at, 6, 18, 25

Rimini-Seleucia, Synods of (359), 14, 16f, 26, 39
Roman law, contrasted with ecclesiastical laws, 4; demands of the Fathers upon, 7, 8; imperial decrees in support of the Church, 9, 20; powers of the emperor in religious matters, 20ff, 26f. See also Ambrose, St., Bishop of Milan; ius publicum
Rome, Bishop of, 8, 33

Sardica, Synod of (348), 33, 38
Soteriology, effect of on political thought, 29ff. See also Ambrose, St., Bishop of Milan; Athanasius, St., Bishop of Alexandria; Hilary, St., Bishop of Poitiers
Symmachus, 21, 23, 24, 27, 44
Synagogue, continuity of with Church, 3f, 7, 9ff, 20, 28f, 38, 51; Roman laws in behalf of, 12f. See also Ambrose, St., Bishop of Milan; Athanasius, St., Bishop of Alexandria; Church, the One, Holy, Catholic, and Apostolic; Hilary, St., Bishop of Poitiers

Tertullian, 12
Theodosius I, 4, 8, 20, 26, 27, 38, 40, 41, 42, 44, 51; Cunctos populos, 4; Council of Constantinople (381), 15, 24. See also Ambrose, St., Bishop of Milan
Theomimesis, 5, 51. See also Christomimesis
Tyre, Synod of (335), 17, 37

Ulfilas, 15
Ulpian, 21, 22

Valens, 21, 26
Valentinian I, 9, 14, 25, 26, 27, 45
Valentinian II, 23, 24, 41, 44, 45, 50

II

"UNUM EX MULTIS": HINCMAR OF RHEIMS' MEDICAL AND AESTHETIC RATIONALES FOR UNIFICATION

CONTENTS

Introduction

Analogy is one of the weakest methods of argument, but it is also one of the most inventive. Across the broad sweep of culture, fateful advances and even discoveries of entire sciences have begun with a vague intuition of likeness. The premise of this essay is that such a transition took place in the Carolingian age, when men applied aesthetic principles to political action.

It is a striking fact that all the Carolingian authors of treatises on kingship (or *Fürstenspiegel*) also wrote about the visual or the literary arts [1]. At first blush, one might plausibly suspect dilettantism, and thus seek no structural connection between aesthetics and government. However, a bridge between those two areas of thought had been constructed in the patristic era. In so far as Carolingian political writers drew guiding principles from ecclesiology, we should take some brief notice of the patristic experiment in analogy.

* I take this occasion to thank Professors Richard Kieckhefer, Emmet Larkin, and Richard Pervo, and Mr. James Melton for assistance during composition of this essay.

(1) The aesthetic doctrines of each major Carolingian writer would reward individual investigation. In this regard, I can mention an article by J. ALLEN CABANISS, 'Saint Agobard as Art Critic', in GEORGE MYLONAS and DORIS RAYMOND ed., *Studies Presented to David Moore Robinson*, II (St. Louis 1953), pp. 1023-28, and, in so doing, thank Professor Cabaniss for introducing me to Carolingian studies.

Throughout classical antiquity and the patristic age, unity was regarded as an aesthetic matter. It involved such issues as form, proportion, and the co-ordination of parts, all subsumed under the term, « beauty ». The aesthetic doctrines that the Fathers applied to the Church were specifically mimetic: that is, they hinged on a mediated tension between image and archetype. In this sense, mimesis had been a term of art ever since Plato applied it to the cosmos and to the structure and functions of the human mind. It described the ambiguous separateness and kinship, the paradoxical similarity in dissimilars, running between the Idea and the actual: that is, between the orders of Being and becoming. The basic principle that mimesis related those antithetic orders persisted through many variations in the schools of Neoplatonists, as they described the assimilation of the soul to God. Quite unsystematically, it figures in St. Paul's theology of baptism and the Eucharist, and, rather more fully developed, in the doctrines of Alexandrine Fathers concerning the soul, the Church, and the Trinity.

From the beginning, the concept of mimesis had been a complex tissue of enigmas, resolved in paradox. It had been grasped by an intuitive and non-rational faculty, which Plato called madness, and theologians, faith. Pseudo-Dionysius, « the Areopagite », captured the inherent tensions of the concept when he portrayed Church order and rituals as replicating celestial hierarchies and, by likeness, participating in the angelic liturgies. Other patristic writers, especially Augustine, projected them from the synchronic into the diachronic dimension, that is, into the realm of historical writing, when they described the movement of events as a slow realization of an archetypal plan in the mind of God, like a garment taking shape on the loom [2].

It would not be surprising to find that Carolingian writers, steeped as they were in patristic doctrines, used rationales of art to elucidate questions of Church unity. However, the distinctive achievement of the Carolingians was that they worked these basically Neo-platonic principles into incomplete, yet coherent, teachings about actual government, secular, as well as ecclesiastical.

In the present essay, I propose to consider one instance. My subject is Archbishop Hincmar of Rheims (ca. 806-882, reigned 845-882), and I wish to identify the mimetic theories out of which he drew his ideas about social order [3]. In his interior life, as in his public actions, Hincmar sought a magic key by which one could be made out of many [4]. As we shall see, he thought that he found the solution to this compositional problem in the doctrine of the Incarnation. Hincmar's career as a ruler, canonist, and statesman is well-known; but the impact of aesthetic doctrines on all those rôles has gone largely unnoticed, even though they were basic to the theme of correction that dominated the Carolingian « Renaissance » and of which Hincmar was a major exponent. An integrative

(2) AUGUSTINE, *Sermo* 53, c. 6, *P. L.*, XXXVIII, col. 366. *De Civitate Dei*, XI, 29. *C.S.E.L.*, XL, pt. 1, p. 556. See my essay ' From Form into Form: Mimesis and Personality in Augustine's Historical Thought ', American Philosophical Society, *Proceedings*, CXXIV (1980), pp. 276-294.

(3) The most complete review of the bibliography on Hincmar is in the footnotes of JEAN DEVISSE's magisterial biography, *Hincmar, Archevêque de Rheims (845-882)*, 3 vols. (Geneva 1975-76), with a comprehensive list, topically arranged, in vol. III, pp. 1141-1234. JANET L. NELSON's article, ' Kingship, Law and Liturgy in the Political Thought of Hincmar of Rheims ', *English Historical Review*, XCII (1977), pp. 241-79, contains an excellent summary of scholarly literature on that subject.

(4) *De praedestinatione, diss. post.*, *P. L.*, CXXV, col. 419. On Hincmar's unusual abilities to synthesize patristic authorities into coherent and original political doctrines, HANS HUBERT ANTON, *Fürstenspiegel und Herrscherethos in der Karolingerzeit* (Bonn 1968), pp. 318 f.

element running throughout the Archbishop's life and thought may thus have been left in the shadows.

Our first task, therefore, will be to establish the general filiation relating Hincmar's ideas about the arts and those about the episcopal office. We shall then identify several aesthetic rationales of unity characteristic of his thought, and we shall describe how those rationales gained expression in a work of art with which the Archbishop was most intimately concerned: his tomb. Finally, we shall locate them in the context of his political thought, especially that regarding consensus.

Throughout his life, Hincmar of Rheims taught unity and practiced controversy. We shall attempt to demonstrate that this contradiction was not merely the familiar disparity between thought and action, but, instead, that the practice of dispute was the logical consequence of his theory of unity. Hincmar's theory of unity, like his politics, was a structure of antitheses. Our discussion will lead us to some aspects of Hincmar's thought that are perhaps less familiar than others: to his theology, as well as to his canonistic knowledge, to his monastic ethos as well as to his political machinations, to his vulnerability as well as to his dominance. The Hincmar whom we shall encounter in this way was a man who felt himself, not the serene « chief theoretician of the Frankish episcopacy », but rather the object of suspicion, defiance, and hatred. It was in the soil of such feelings that his antitheses took root and grew and that his use of terror for political ends found its justification [5].

(5) Cf. DEVISSE, *Hincmar, Archevêque*, II, p. 1124. ' Nous avons sans cesse ressenti le poids, dans la vie et l'œuvre d'Hincmar, de la tension entre des logiques contraires, de la contradiction, au moins apparente, entre situations, attitudes, analyses du prélat. Bien sûr au niveau idéologique toutes ces tensions, toutes ces contradictions se résolvent dans le dessein divin concernant l'homme. Mais ce point de vue ne peut nous retinir ici. Au niveau historique,

I. *Hincmar and the Analogues of Art*

Hincmar wrote at least two treatises on sacred images. Those texts are lost, however, and we shall have to recover his doctrines of aesthetic unity from less direct evidence. The trail that we must follow begins at the monastery of St. Denis, where, as a boy, Hincmar received his education, and at the court of Louis the Pious, where he spent « no little time » as a young man in the service of the Emperor. For some years, his life oscillated between these two poles [6], and, until the end of his days, he continued to refer to, and even to quote, texts that he had read at that time [7]. Hincmar's elder contemporary, Bishop Jonas of Orléans, recalled that Louis the Pious had imitated, and even surpassed, Charlemagne in fostering the liberal arts, patristic studies, and Scriptural exegesis « to cast out the poisoned doctrines of heretics » [8].

tensions et contradictions sont l'essence même du personnage hincmarien, de son action, de la société dans laquelle vit l'archevêque '. We are concerned with the historical stage of ideology. I borrow the phrase,' chief theoretician of the Frankish episcopacy ', from JACQUES BOUSSARD, FRANCES PARTRIDGE trans., *The Civilization of Charlemagne* (New York 1976), p. 115 f.

(6) Hincmar's treatises are mentioned by Flodoard, *Historia Remensis Ecclesiae*, III, 18, 29, *M.G.H.*, *SS.*, XIII, pp. 510, 554. On his early life, see the brief autobiographical excursus in a letter to Pope Nicholas I, *ep.* 11, *P. L.*, CXXVI, col. 81f.

(7) For example, the Synod of Attigny (822), under Louis the Pious (*De divortio, responsio* 5, *P. L.*, CXXV, col. 655); the Synod of Paris (829), (used in the *De regis persona*, ANTON, *Fürstenspiegel*, pp. 224f); Adalhard of Corbie's *de ordine palatii* (used in Hincmar's treatise of that title, see HEINZ LÖWE, ' Hinkmar von Reims und der Apocrisiar. Beiträge zur Interpretation von *De ordine palatii* ', *Festschrift für Hermann Heimpel*, Bd. III (Veröffentlichungen des Max-Planck-Instituts für Geschichte, 36/III. Göttingen 1972), pp. 201 f, 221 f); the *Libri Carolini* (*Libellus Expostulationis*, c. 20. *P. L.*, CXXVI, col. 360 f quoting *Libri Carolini* IV.28); and the life and acts of St. Sanctinus, a putative disciple of St. Denis (*ep.* 23, *P. L.*, CXXVI, col. 153 f. Cf. DEVISSE, *Hincmar, Archevêque*, II, p. 1007. PATRICK J. GEARY, *Furta Sacra. Thefts of Relics in the Central Middle Ages* (Princeton 1978), p. 85).

(8) *M. G. H.*, *Epp.* V, K. A. III, no. 32, p. 354. For a celebrated example of Louis the Pious' court art, see WALTHER LAMMERS, ' Ein karolingisches

588

As he enriched monasteries with gifts of books, vestments, and liturgical furniture, he encompassed them in the stream of artistic magnificence that emanated from his court, and enlisted them in the militant cause that he intended the arts to serve. Louis had a pronounced affection for St. Denis, upon which, after several frustrated attempts, he imposed reform, and where, in 834, he was restored to the imperial office following a brief, but cruel, degradation [9]. His son and successor, Charles the Bald, acted as abbot of St. Denis and lavished his sumptuous patronage of the arts upon it. Three centuries later, even Abbot Suger – himself given to splendid and costly ornamentation – was struck with wonder by the art of this period [10]. To « flee from the world », as Hincmar did by embracing the monastic life at St. Denis [11], was to enter a militant community of reform at whose center stood a church built « at great cost and with exceptional refinement » [12/13].

From the middle of the eighth century on for 100 years, the Byzantine Iconoclastic Dispute served as a foil against which the Franks developed their own conceptions of religious art. Indeed, this conflict provided another long strand of continuity in Hincmar's intellectual life. His predecessor, Tilpin, was present at the Synod of

Bildprogramm in der Aula Regia von Ingelheim ', *Festschrift für Hermann Heimpel*, Bd III (Veröffentlichungen des Max-Planck-Instituts für Geschichte, 36/III. Göttingen 1972), pp. 226-289. On Louis the Pious' patronage of the monastic life, see GERT HAENDLER, *Epochen karolingischer Theologie. Eine Untersuchung über die karolingischen Gutachten zum byzantinischen Bilderstreit (Theologische Arbeiten, Bd X. Berlin 1958), p. 130 f.*

(9) Below, nn. 386 a, 404.

(10) ERWIN PANOFSKY ed., *Abbot Suger on the Abbey Church of St. Denis and its Art Treasures* (Princeton 1946), pp. 33, 60.

(11) *Ep.* 11, *P. L.* CXXVI, col. 82, *saeculum fugiens.*

(12/13) HILDUIN, *Passio Sanctissimi Dionysii*, c. 36. *P. L.*, CVI, col. 49. JOHANN HEINRICH SCHRÖRS, *Hinkmar, Erzbischof von Reims. Sein Leben und seine Schriften* (Freiburg-i.-B. 1884), p. 11.

Rome (769), and, probably, at the Synod of Frankfurt
(794), where important decrees concerning sacred images
were issued. Hincmar himself read, and quoted from, the
Libri Carolini, written slightly before the Synod of Frankfurt [14]; he can hardly have been unaware of the Byzantine
legation to Louis the Pious, and the Synod of Paris (825),
both concerned with religious art; as a protégé of Abbot
Hilduin of St. Denis, and, evidently, a collaborator with
him in writing texts about the Areopagite, he certainly
knew of the Byzantine legation in 827, and he may well
have held in his own hands the codex containing the
Pseudo-Dionysian treatises that the envoys presented to
Louis the Pious, and that Hilduin later had translated.
Toward the end of his life, the middle stages of the Photian
dispute again pressed the function of sacred images to
the front of Hincmar's mind. Normally, the Archbishop
was suspicious of Byzantine practices [15], but the new
crisis was particularly delicate. For, Hincmar wrote, not
only did the judgments issued by the Council of Constantinople (869-70) depart from orthodox teachings, but
Pope Hadrian II (867-872) had assented to its decrees,
contrary to the ancient canons and self-contradictory as
Hincmar judged them to be. Probably between 867 and
872, a number of bishops asked Hincmar to compose a
treatise on « how images of our Savior and His Saints are

(14) On Tilpin, see *Gallia Christiana* (n. s.) IX, coll. 28-32. SIGURD ABEL
and BERNHARD SIMSON, *Jahrbücher des fränkischen Reiches unter Karl dem
Grossen*, 2d ed. Bd I, (Leipzig 1888), p. 63 f. On the *Libri Carolini*, above n. 7,
and PAUL MEYVAERT, ' The Authorship of the *Libri Carolini* ; Observations
Prompted by a Recent Book ', *Revue bénédictine*, (1979), p. 29 ff. On the doctri-
nal issues of the Byzantine controversy, see the general discussion by JOHN
MEYENDORFF, *Le Christ dans la théologie byzantine* (Paris 1969), pp. 235-263.
On the Frankish positions during the reign of Louis the Pious, see HAENDLER,
Epochen, pp. 48, 54 f, 121, 135, and passim.

(15) *M. G. H.*, *Epp.* VIII, K. A., VI, no. 201, p. 225.

to be venerated » [16], a lost contribution at the end of a dispute that Tilpin had seen open a century earlier.

And this was appropriate, for his experience at St. Denis and at the court of Louis the Pious had convinced Hincmar that knowledge and cultivation of the arts was a religious duty, especially for the prelates and teachers of the Church. Of course, he recalled the celebrated letter of Pope Gregory I to Serenus of Marseilles, urging the Bishop neither to destroy sacred images nor to allow them to be adored, but rather to use them for instructing the ignorant [17]. Taking this counsel to heart, Hincmar initiated detailed surveys of the churches and monasteries in his diocese, inventorying « treasure, and vestments, and books » [18], to see that the buildings were in good order [19], and supplied with all necessary liturgical vessels and ornaments [20]. As for the intellectual arts, he insisted that rural priests be adequately educated to « imbue [their scholars] with letters » though, to avoid ill-repute, priests were forbidden to admit girls to the schools [21].

(16) FELIX GRAT et al. ed., Annales de Saint-Bertin (Paris 1964), ad an. 872, p. 187. Flodoard, III, 29, M. G. H., SS. XIII, p. 554; the work also included a metrical dialogue.

(17) LV Cap., c. 25. P. L., CXXVI, col. 389.

(18) Synod of St. Macra, c. 4. P. L., CXXV, col. 1073.

(19) WILHELM GUNDLACH, « Zwei Schriften des Erzbischofs Hinkmar von Reims », Zeitschrift für Kirchengeschichte, X (1889), pp. 10 ff. 135. Hincmar's very detailed knowledge of church property is apparent in references, such as that to a plundered chapel, P. L. CXXVI, col. 539.

(20) On the results of the capitula requiring such census (P. L., CXXVI, coll. 777 ff), see DEVISSE, Hincmar, Archevêque, II, pp. 892 ff. See also the de officiis episcoporum, P. L., CXXV, col. 1087, and the comment by ROSAMOND McKITTERICK that these texts represent ‘ an increasing preoccupation with the minutiae of ecclesiastical discipline, and the exaltation of the priestly and episcopal office... ’, The Frankish Church and the Carolingian Reforms, 789-895 (London 1977), p. 63.

(21) De ecclesiis et capellis, in GUNDLACH, op. cit., p. 121 ff. Cf. ep. 36, P. L., CXXVI, col. 255, ‘ vos, fratres ac filii, qui litteras non didicistis, scitote quid sonat in nostra lingua anathema, id est alieniato... ’.

Employing the arts in the Church's teaching came easily to Hincmar. He delighted in the glint of sunlight on gold, especially on flashing sequins [22]. He knew how greatly moved men could be by the visual pomp of splendid raiment [23]. His eye was keen to illusory or real discolorations [24], and metaphors of painting and the other arts [25] crept unobtrusively into his discourse [26]. If he was not able to join John Scotus Eriugena in conceiving of theology as poetry, at least he could see that, by deploying his textual citations, he worked as an artist did, painting black under white to make his point clear by contrast [27]. Some sense of poetic license entered into his observation that the divine word was like a pearl that could be drilled at any point. Thus, he wrote, even if he interpreted a text of Scripture in a way quite different from the intent of its author, the theologian would not be a « craftsman of falsehood » (*fabricator mendacii*), so long as he remained true to the understanding of his elders [28].

We have sketched in the background. Let us now begin to be specific. Artistic analogies entered directly into Hincmar's concept of the episcopal office. His title

(22) *Pro ecclesiae libertatum defensione, P. L.*, CXXV, col. 1049. *De regis persona, praefatio. P. L.* CXXV, col. 833.

(23) *De cavendis vitiis*, c. 6. *P. L.*, CXXV, col. 906.

(24) *Ep.* 30, c. 33. *P. L.*, CXXVI, col. 208. *De praedestinatione, diss. post.*, c. 16. *P. L.*, CXXV, col. 147.

(25) *E. g.*, suffering as like a refiner's fire, *ep.* 11, *P. L.*, CXXVI, col. 77 f; letter to Hincmar of Laon, *P. L.* CXXVI, col. 552.

(26) E. g., use of the verb *depingere* : *ep.* 11, *P. L.*, CXXVI, col. 78; letter to Hincmar of Laon, *P. L.* CXXVI, col. 511; *LV Cap.*, c. 53, *P. L.* CXXVI, col. 492.

(27) On John Scotus, PETER DRONKE, ' *Theologia veluti quaedam Poetria* ; Quelques observations sur la fonction des images poétiques chez Jean Scot », *Colloques Internationaux du C.N.R.S.* no. 561 (Paris 1977), p. 243. Hincmar's reference occurs in *de praedestinatione, diss. post.*, c. 27, *P. L.* CXXV, col. 282.

(28) The citation occurs in *ep.* 25 (to Hildegar of Meaux) and *De divortio, responsio* 6. *P. L.* CXXVI, col. 165; *P. L.*, CXXV, col. 667. A variant is in *De praedestinatione. diss. post.*. c. 5. *P. L.* CXXV, col. 87.

592

was frequently in hazard; resort to analogy was part of his defence. Almost from the beginning of his pontificate, clerics ordained by Hincmar's predecessor, Ebo, challenged his legitimacy as archbishop of Rheims, taking their case to the papal court. The tortured litigation stretched over sixteen years; before his life ended, Hincmar had been threatened with excommunication by three popes in this and other matters [29]. The integrity of his episcopal ordination had been challenged. Rome, to which he always looked as the oracle of Christian unity, threatened to repudiate him. During the dispute over predestination (in the 850's), some of his episcopal brethren accused him of teaching doctrines that ran contrary to the faith [30]. Given his education and temperament, it was natural that, through all the attacks upon him, he found symbolic reassurance in the power of the arts to correct discord and establish harmony.

Broadly speaking, he found analogues for his episcopal functions in three arts: the gradual achievement of unity, as in building according to a blueprint; re-integration, as in restoration to health through medicine; and organic amplification of something toward its inherent potentiality, as in the expansion of the mind through verbal instruction.

For nearly seventeen years, Hincmar superintended the reconstruction of the cathedral which his ill-starred predecessor, Ebo, had begun. He devoted a massive proportion of his see's resources to the fabric and adornment of this building, with lavish ornaments of gold and

(29) The seriousness of Hincmar's danger is quite apparent in the letter of Leo IV to all bishops of Gaul (*M. G. H.*, *Epp.* V, *K. A.* III, no. 36, p. 605), and in Hincmar's letter to Nicholas I (*ep.* 2, *P. L.* CXXVI, col. 39).

(30) JAROSLAV PELIKAN, *The Growth of Medieval Theology (600-1300)* (vol. III in *The Christian Tradition. A History of the Development of Doctrine.* Chicago 1978), p. 85.

windows of glass. None of his extant letters deal with the cathedral; Hincmar's only surviving reference to it occurs as a brief entry in the *Annales Bertiniani*, recording the consecration of « the mother church of this province » to the Virgin in the presence of Charles the Bald and a large company of bishops [31]. And yet, this protracted and costly work illuminates the mentality behind the persistent references in *Annales* to precious ornaments, furniture, and vessels [32]; it casts into sharp relief Hincmar's contempt for the young man who despaired of being remembered among the good and burned the temple of Diana at Ephesus, so as to be remembered at least among the evil [33]. By constructing the new cathedral with all splendor, Hincmar proclaimed the legitimacy of his own title, but he also expressed connotations that played in his mind when he wrote that Christ founded the episcopal order to build, and not to destroy [34]. He struck an analogy between the bishop and God, that « masterful and skilled mason », who determines where each living stone will fit in His city, Jerusalem, as clear and light as pure gold and glass [35].

Amidst his trials, Hincmar could take some comfort in the thought that, as builder, he imitated God, gradually perfecting His city through time [36]. But other

---

(31) *Annales Bertiniani* (862), ed. cit., p. 94. On Hincmar's cathedral, DEVISSE, *Hincmar, Archevêque*, II, pp. 914-917.

(32) *Annales Bertiniani* (868, 869, 876, 877), *ed. cit.*, pp. 144 ff, 151, 155, 201, 204 f, 216, 218 f.

(33) *De praedestinatione, diss. post.*, c. 22; cf. *De una et non trina Deitate*, *P. L.* CXXV, col. 195. *LV Cap.*, c. 5, *P. L.*, CXXVI, 302 f.

(34) To the clergy and people of Laon, *P. L.* CXXVI, col. 514, ' a quo [Christo] et per quem in aedificationem et non in destructionem sacer ordo episcopalis accepit exordium '. Cf. letter to Charles the Bald on predestination, *P. L.* CXXV, col. 50.

(35) *De praedestinatione, diss. post.*, cc. 19, 20. *P. L.*, CXXV, 171, 181.

(36) For other references to God as a maker, cf. *de una et non trina Deitate*, *P. L.*, CXXV, col. 574, ' maker of the world-machine '; *De praedestinatione,*

mimetic paradigms also came to mind that likewise witnessed to the corrective powers of art.

The model of Christ as « the true physician » [37] was perhaps even closer to Hincmar's heart than that of God the builder. Wounded and poisoned by Satan, the serpent, man looked to Christ for the healing balm, the antidote, of grace [38]. Architecture and medicine overlapped. Both aimed at wholeness: the first worked toward realizing the integrity of a design, the second toward re-integration, the recovery of a damaged wholeness. There had always been a close connection between the monastic life and the practice of medicine. This might be sufficient to explain the very detailed attention with which Hincmar recorded various illnesses of Carolingian rulers, their families, and others in the *Annales Bertiniani* [39]. But there were also more personal reasons. Periodically, Hincmar himself was confined by illness. Toward the end of his life, his active and acute mind rebelled, yearning to be released from the « prison » of his « infirm and senile body » [40]. Quite understandably, then, metaphors of

---

diss. post., c. 38, *epilogi* c. 3, *P. L.*, CXXV, col. 438, God as an *artifex*, free from the order of time; *ep.* 21 (Synod of Douzy), *P. L.*, CXXVI, col. 124, as *opifex hominis*. On the parallel between Christ and Beseleel in the *Libri Carolini*, see HAENDLER, *Epochen*, p. 85.

(37) *De praedestinatione, diss. post.*, c. 26. *P. L.* CXXV, col. 269. On the patristic background of this usage, GERVAIS DUMEIGE, ' Le Christ médecin dans la littérature chrétienne des premiers siècles ', *Rivista di archeologia cristiana*, XLVIII (1972), pp. 115-141; and, on Augustine, RUDOLF ARBESMANN, ' Christ the *medicus humilis* in Saint Augustine ', *Augustinus Magister*, II (Paris 1955), pp. 623-629; and JEAN COURTÈS, ' Saint Augustin et la médicine ', ibid., I (Paris 1955), pp. 43-51. ARTHUR STANLEY PEASE, « Medical Allusions in the Works of St. Jerome », *Harvard Studies in Classical Philology*, XXV (1914), pp. 73-86. Abbots are « spiritual physicians »: *Reg. Benedicti*, c. 28.

(38) *Vita Remigii*, c. 8. *M. G. H., SS. Rer. Mer.*, III, p. 284 f. *LV Cap.*, c. 39, *P. L.* CXXVI, 437. Cf. *de praedestinatione, diss post.*, c. 25, *P. L.*, CXXV, col. 231.

(39) *Annales Bertiniani* (864, 865, 870, 875, 876, 877, 878, 879, 880), *ed. cit.*, pp. 105, 125, 175, 197, 209 f, 211, 216 f, 218, 222, 234, 242.

(40) *Ep.* 20, c. 10. *P. L.* CXXVI, 120 f. Cf. *ep.* 2 to Nicholas I; *ep.* 11 to Nicholas I; *LV Cap.*, cc. 4, 39; *Libellus Expostulationis*, cc. 24, 30; *ep.* 38

healing like those of visual arts, entered Hincmar's vocabulary [41]. He frequently employed them to describe the
penitential sanctions imposed by bishops to restore unity
in the Body of Christ [42]. To some prelates of great holiness, such as St. Remigius, God gave the power to heal
the physical bodies of the faithful, and even to raise the
dead [43]. Hincmar also knew of physical cures that had
been performed even by lesser priests through the use of
consacrated salt and oil [44], and by exorcism [45]. Their
prior task, however, was spiritual. While they, like all
men, were enfeebled by sin, priests were spiritual physicians. God's good will gave them the office of healing
sinners [46], applying curative medication [47], or amputating
a rotten member [48], as the case required. The exorbitant
cost of medicine should not deter a patient [49], nor, if

to Anastasius, *P. L.*, CXXVI, coll. 39, 89, 300, 436 f, 606, 618, 257. *De divortio, responsio* 3, *P. L.*, CXXV, col. 645. A letter by Hincmar's confrère,
Pardulus of Laon, concerns a gastric disorder from which the Archbishop was
suffering. JOHN J. CONTRENI, ' The Study and Practice of Medicine in Northern France during the Reign of Charles the Bald ', JOHN SOMMERFELDT and
E. ROZANNE ELDER ed., *Studies in Medieval Culture*, VI and VII (Kalamazoo
1976), p. 537. See also JOHN J. CONTRENI, *The Cathedral School of Laon from
850 to 920. Its Manuscripts and Masters* (Münchener Beiträge zur Mediävistik
und Renaissance-Forschung, Munich 1978), p. 89, further evidence of Pardulus' medical knowledge.

(41) Hincmar's familiarity with the natural sciences would reward additional study. Cf. his references to the *libri physicorum*, or *physica lectio, de divortio, responsio* 12; *de verbis psalmi: Herodii domus dux est eorum, P. L.*, CXXV,
694, 959. His references to animals normally come *via* patristic quotations —e.
g., hedgehogs (*P. L.*, CXXVI, coll. 557, 562), the rhinoceros (*LV Cap.*, c. 46,
P. L. CXXVI, col. 457 f); the unicorn (*P. L.*, CXXVI, coll. 602, 604 f.), and
birds (*Vita Remigii*, c. 5, *M.G.H.*, *SS. Rer. Mer.*, III, pp. 266-268).

(42) Cf. *Ep.* 55, *P. L.*, CXXVI, col. 278.

(43) *Vita Remigii*, c. 31, *M. G. H.*, *SS. Rer. Mer.*, III, p. 332.

(44) *De divortio, responsio* 15. *P. L.*, CXXV, col. 725.

(45) *De divortio, responsio* 15, *P. L.*, CXXV, col. 717, curing sexual impo-
tence.

(46) *M. G. H.*, *Epp.*, VIII, *K. A.*, VI, no. 125, p. 60.

(47) *De divortio, responsio*, 5, *P. L.*, CXXV, col. 655.

(48) *De divortio, quaestio* 7, *P. L.*, CXXV, col. 772.

(49) *De praedestinatione, diss. post.*, c. 24. *P. L.*, CXXV, col. 220.

596

medication failed, should the excruciating pain of the knife stay the physician's hand [50].

We have now considered two mimetic paradigms of the episcopal office. Hincmar illustrated progressively constructed unity of design with reference to the visual arts, especially architecture. He illustrated the restoration of a lost integrity with reference to the art of medicine. There remained the organic expansion of unity, and this he referred to the verbal arts.

The paradigm of Christ, the Word of God teaching His followers with words, shimmered before Hincmar's mind – the Word sent by the Father to propagate the faith, preaching, calling to repentance, and bearing witness even as He underwent the death of the Cross [51]. But as he considered the verbal propagation of the faith, Hincmar also reached for two other paradigms. The one was St. Peter, pontiff and martyr. Pressed onto all bishops, the « form of Peter » conveyed the character of equity [52], as set forth in the written judgments of individual bishops and in the decrees of synods and councils, texts that had been disseminated in the West through churches established by Peter and his successors. The other was the Virgin. The function of the bishop as nourisher (*nutritor*) was crucial to Hincmar [53], but the word « regeneration » had a force that was not included in « nourishment », and that was not exhausted even by

(50) *Libellus expostulationis*, c. 35. *P. L.*, CXXVI, col. 630. This passage from Ambrose's commentary on Ps. 118 also occurs in *de regis persona*, c. 19, *P. L.*, CXXV, col. 846.

(51) See the general discussion of Hincmar's theology in SCHRÖRS, *Hinkmar*, p. 150 ff. Detailed studies of Hincmar's theology are very rare. See, as a welcome exception, L. D. DAVID, « Hincmar of Rheims as a Theologian of the Trinity », *Traditio*, XXVII (1971), pp. 455-468.

(52) Charles the Bald, *ep.* 8. *P. L.*, CXXIV, col. 194. Hincmar, *ep.* 27. *P. L.*, CXXVI, col. 183.

(53) E. g., *LV Cap.*, c. 51. *P. L.*, CXXVI, col. 488 and *passim*.

the concept of the bishop as husband and father, and
of his church as wife and mother [54]. The Archbishop
could, certainly, recall that, when He nourished those
regenerated by his blood, Christ Himself acted as a mother does, feeding a child with her milk [55]. But the Virgin was the exemplar *par excellence* of the propagation
of the Word. Together with the Apostles, the predecessors of bishops, the Virgin had been crowned with tongues of flame by the Holy Spirit at Pentecost; and bishops, like her, were « thrones of God », bearing within
themselves the presence of Divinity, the « flame of fire »,
that engendered Christ [56]. Thus, in a deep sense, Hincmar
could accept the idea, forged by Gregory the Great, of
the penitent fleeing to the mind of his pastor, as to his
mother's bosom [57].

The ultimate object of spiritual birth and growth
was to enter into the « treasures of wisdom and knowledge »,
but the journey began with « the men who wrote the rules
for the art of grammar » and the « doctors of orthography »,
and it went on to « those who treat of sacred Scripture » [58].
Mastery of the verbal arts included study of etymologies
and of such rhetorical devices as metonymy [59], irony and
antiphrasis [60]. It required the ability to clarify doubtful

(54) Cf. *LV Cap.*, c. 44. *P. L.*, CXXVI, col. 454.
(55) *De praedestinatione, diss. post.*, c. 35. *P. L.*, CXXV, col. 375.
(56) On the Virgin at Pentecost, *de divortio, quaestio* 3 *responsio*, *P. L.* CXXV, col. 749. On bishops as thrones of God, see *de divortio, quaestio* 6, and as seats of the flame of fire, *de fide Carolo servanda*, c. 17. *P. L.* CXXV, coll. 758, 971. On the Holy Spirit as fire, *ep.* 33, c. 4, *P. L.*, CXXVI, col. 248. On the Holy Spirit as a ' Holy Flame ', engendering Christ in the womb of the Virgin, see Hincmar's verses, inscribed at her image on the main altar of Rheims cathedral, and his *Carmen de Virgine Maria.* Flodoard, III, 5. *M. G. H., SS.* XIII, p. 479. *M. G. H., Poet.* III, p. 409 no. ii, p. 410 l. 7.
(57) *De divortio, responsio* 1. *P. L.*, CXXV, 635. On other evidence for the veneration of the Virgin in the ninth century, see HAENDLER, *Epochen*, p. 134.
(58) *P. L.*, CXXVI, col. 508; on the rudiments of grammar, ibid., col. 555.
(59) *De una et non trina Deitate, P. L.* CXXV, col. 564.
(60) *P. L.*, CXXVI, col. 546.

readings by various specialized techniques, including the collation of texts [61]. Above all, it demanded a clarity of understanding that permitted an author to set down his words in a rational order [62]: that is, to compose them in a unified, coherent way [63]. If illiterates were ordained as bishops, unable to fathom the wholeness of Scripture and the marvellous harmony of the canons [64], the Church's vigor would perish, and miseries of every kind, including plague and sterility would befall their unhappy people [65].

Accordingly, Hincmar valued his own mastery of the verbal arts, provided for instruction in literacy through the rural parishes of his diocese, and, from time to time, undertook the personal supervision of training in letters [66]. Great mysteries in the fecundity of the word were to be plumbed through the literary arts. For, as the Trinity had made the flesh of Christ in the Virgin's womb, so by words, priests made the body of Christ at the altar. And, God Himself, the paradigm of bishops, had deployed good and evil in the whole course of history as a poet adorns a most lovely song with antitheses [67]. Great prizes were to be won through the use of words in praying, catechizing, exhorting, and calling to repentance. For, through the power of his words, St. Remigius converted Clovis and all the Franks, and, in baptism, brought them forth from «the immaculate womb of the Church» (below, pp. 631, 656).

(61) Below, nn. 442-446. On Hincmar's classical allusions and general facility in the verbal arts, see DEVISSE, Hincmar Archevêque, II, pp. 1056 f, 1067 f, with a valuable discussion of Hincmar's library.

(62) Cf. the charge that Hincmar of Laon, lacking right understanding, had written sine ratione. LV Cap., c. 43. P. L., CXXVI, col. 448 f.

(63) Cf. de praedestinatione, diss. post., c. 22. P. L., CXXV, col. 195 f.

(64) Cf. Libellus expostulationis, c. 11, P. L., CXXVI, 578.

(65) De praedestinatione, diss. post., c. 36, P. L., CXXV, coll. 382, 387.

(66) DEVISSE, Hincmar, Archevêque, II, p. 1084 ff. LV Cap., c. 39. P. L. CXXVI, col. 437, ' litteris per me et per quoscunque potui erudivi... '.

(67) Synod of Quierzy to Louis the German (858), c. 15. M. G. H., Cap. Reg. Fr., II, no. 297, p. 439. De praedestinatione, diss. post., c. 12. P. L., CXXV, col. 115.

As we have discussed mimetic paradigms of the episcopal office, we have also suggested duties of correction, warranted by analogues in the visual, medical, and verbal arts. In fact, we have been dealing with something rather more than scattered metaphors. The metaphors intersect in a coherent doctrine of the episcopacy that made Hincmar one of the most persistent controversialists of his day. The results of considering correction a mimetic function of the bishop can be traced very clearly in one struggle, drawn out for more than a decade: the Archbishop's conflict with his nephew, protégé, and namesake, Bishop Hincmar of Laon, who eventually transgressed against all the paradigms.

The Bishop violated the ideal of the bishop as builder, and offended against yet deeper convictions, when he « deconstructed » (*defabricavit*) the altar of St. Mary at Laon. His predecessor, Bishop Pardulus, had « very beautifully adorned the altar with gold and quantities of gems, and with many precious and varied ornaments composed of gold and gems ». He had also given the church « a chalice of purest gold ». These Hincmar stripped away, melted, and recast into profane finery, such as sword hilts, belts, and spurs, which he gave to his brother and other favorites. He bestowed the gold and silver, and the precious vestments, of his church as bounty on anyone he chose, and he appropriated « the finest consecrated cloth from the altar of St. Mary for wordly uses » [68].

---

(68) Synod of Douzy to Hadrian II, *P. L.*, CXXVI, col. 637. Some of the gold stripped from the altar may have been provided by Hincmar of Rheims. Cf. Flodoard, III, 21, *M. G. H., SS.*, XIII, p. 518. On Pardulus and his friendship with Hincmar, see SCHRÖRS, *Hinkmar*, p. 62; CONTRENI, *Cathedral School*, pp. 19 f, 32, 73. With regard to depredation of religious art (as treasure), Hincmar's charges against Rothad of Soissons coincide interestingly with these against his nephew. *Ep.* 2. *P. L.*, CXXVI, col. 32. DEVISSE, *Hincmar, Archevêque*, II, p. 595 f.

Hincmar of Laon also offended against the ideal of the bishop as a « spiritual physician »; for, in his various undertakings, he had fomented disorder in the body of Christ. He had made up « a death-dealing potion of discord » for his uncle to drink [69], and he had compounded this offence by vaunting himself on the strength and agility of his own body, while mocking the infirmities of his uncle [70], and threatening to clip out his tongue or behead him [71]. Truly, the Archbishop shot back, the young man was blinded by arrogance [72], not realizing that man passes through this world as a shadow (in imagine) [73]. Could he not recall David's triumph over Goliath, or Paul's boasting, « When I am weak, then I am strong and mighty? » For « strength (virtus) is perfected in weakness » [74].

Finally, Hincmar of Laon offended against the idea that bishops must propagate unity through the verbal arts. As a scholar, as well as an athlete, the young man had contrasted his own abilities all too favorably with those of his uncle [75]. In fact, the Archbishop responded, Hincmar of Laon had never outgrown the habit that he had as a boy, eagerly using words that he did not understand. Instead of being corrected by the exercises that the Archbishop assigned, or simply outgrown, the trait persisted. In the treatises, letters, and compilations of which he was so proud, the younger Hincmar merely threw up what he had not even swallowed, much less di-

(69) LV Cap., c. 39. P. L., CXXVI, col. 437.
(70) LV Cap., c. 52. P. L., CXXVI, col. 491.
(71) Libellus expostulationis, cc. 11, 23, 24. P. L., CXXVI, coll. 577-581, 602 f, 606 f.
(72) P. L., CXXVI, col. 507. LV Cap., c. 44; Libellus expostulationis, c. 22. P. L., CXXVI, 454, 597.
(73) LV Cap., c. 54. P. L., CXXVI, col. 493.
(74) LV Cap., c. 52. P. L., CXXVI, col. 491.
(75) P. L., CXXVI, coll. 508, 546, 550.

gested, a mishmash of unfamiliar, exotic words, snatched hither and yon out of glossaries and set down *sine ratione*. Carried away by the momentum of invective [76], Hincmar of Rheims may have exaggerated the unintelligibility of the result. His wider object, of course, was to demonstrate that the Bishop of Laon's arrogant deformation of language and texts had led him into blatant misunderstandings, and that, by twisting the canons to suit his interpretations, he had injured his own diocese and, drawing his people with him into schism, disrupted unity within the province of Rheims [77].

Thus, Hincmar of Laon had flagrantly ignored his duties as builder, physician, and propagator; he had not cared for his people, as a mother hen, warming her chicks beneath her wings [78]. And, forgetting the care entrusted to his metropolitan, he had not returned, humbly and eagerly, to the metropolitan church, as a mother, to « suck wholesome doctrine from her catholic breasts » [79].

Clearly, these charges against Hincmar of Laon illustrate the Archbishop's habit of thinking about the episcopal office in mimetic terms; but they also point toward a further aspect of our subject, an ambiguity that had earlier characterized patristic thought about the arts. The Archbishop accused his nephew of abusing the arts, not of discarding them. Similarly, when he wrote against Gottschalk of Orbais' doctrines of predestination, Hincmar observed that the literary art had no

---

(76) Cf *LV Cap.*, c. 24, *P. L.*, CXXVI, 448 f.

(77) *LV Cap.*, c. 48. *P. L.* CXXVI, 478 f. The development of arguments on both sides of the dispute between the two Hincmars is convincingly unravelled by Peter R. McKeon, *Hincmar of Laon and Carolingian Politics* (Urbana 1978).

(78) *Ep.* 52. *P. L.*, CXXVI, col. 273.

(79) *Ep.* 53. *P. L.*, CXXVI, col. 276. The theme of propagation appears more explicitly in Hincmar of Rheims' charge that Rothad of Soissons was 'sterilis permanens' and had to be replaced. *Ep.* 2. *P. L.*, CXXVI, col. 38.

error of its own, but that Gottschalk had used the art to serve his depraved understanding [80]. What do these instances suggest about the ambiguous, and therefore critical, element at the core of Hincmar's reasoning by analogy?

The teachings of St. Paul cast a mantle of irony around the arts. The visual world, he taught, was like a mirror, seen through darkly, a device by which one might pass from visible and transitory beings to the invisible things of God. As to the arts of healing, the Apostle wrote that the strength of God was perfected in human weakness. Finally, as to the arts of verbal discourse, « the wisdom of this world is foolishness with God ». « If any man among you seemeth to be wise in this world, let him become a fool that he may be wise » (I. Cor. 3:18-19). Working between the contradictory poles of these paradoxes, the Fathers elaborated doctrines that both asserted the practical advantages of the arts and poised delicately on the verge of iconoclasm.

Together with so much else, Hincmar gained this critical ambiguity from his studies at St. Denis and the court of Louis the Pious. Nothing in his writings anticipates the veneration of an object for its age or beauty alone; nothing anticipates the love of art for art's sake. Had not Satan tempted Adam and Eve into the primal fall with an apple, an object beautiful to the eyes [81]? Hincmar yielded to none in his veneration of St. Remigius. And yet, he records that a silver chalice consecrated by the Saint and inscribed with verses by him, survived « until our times », when it was given over to the Northmen, those « ministers of the Devil », for the ransom of

---

(80) *De una et non trina Deitate. P. L.*, CXXV, col. 573.
(81) *LV Cap.*, c. 46. *P. L.* CXXVI, col. 461.

Christian captives [82]. He revered the rule – established
by the spirit of God « through the mouth of St. Benedict » –
that artisan monks should work humbly at their crafts,
with the abbot's permission, and that the abbot should
suspend from practicing his art any monk who prided
himself on his skill [83].

The eyes deceived. They could be captivated by
illusions cast up by demons [84]. The visual arts also lied.
The ornaments of gold and silver, and the precious vestments worn by kings and bishops concealed flesh that was
but stench and dust and ashes [85]. And were not theologians who confirmed their wrongful doctrines with lies
like painters who normally depicted merles with wings
but no feet, because they were so often on the wing [86] ?
The truth of things was never seen through the eyes of
the body, but only revealed to the eyes of the mind,
through a veil of secrecy lest it be cheapened by full
disclosure [87]. What was physically seen was a *figmentum
simulationis, non veritas* [88]. The unwary might easily
mistake a fiction of the devil (*diaboli figmentum,* or *figmentum mendacii*) for a « simulation of truth » [89].

There was the yet more awesome possibility that
God and man would judge differently, even of sacraments,

---

(82) *Vita Remigii,* c. 2. *M. G. H., SS Rer. Mer.,* III, p. 262. According to
Flodoard, a massive gold chalice encrusted with jewels that Hincmar gave to
the cathedral went the same way ' pro redemptione ac salute patriae ', though
its companion-piece, a paten, was still to be seen at Rheims. III, 5. *M.G.H.,
SS,* XIII, p. 479.

(83) *De una et non trina Deitate. P. L.,* CXXV, col. 503. *Regula Sancti Benedicti,* c. 57.

(84) *De divortio, responsiones* 9, 15. *P. L.,* CXXV, 677 f, 725.

(85) *Ad Ludovicum Balbum: De cavendis vitiis,* c. 9. *P. L.,* CXXV, 989.

(86) *De praedestinatione, diss. post.,* c. 6. *P. L.,* CXXV, 93. The word
' mendam ' must be a misreading of ' *merulam* '.

(87) *De divortio, responsio* 6. *P. L.,* CXXV, col. 659 f.

(88) *Ep.* 22. *P. L.,* CXXVI, col. 140.

(89) *De divortio, responsio* 6; *quaestio* 1 and *responsio. P. L.,* CXXV, coll.
660, 664, 669, 747.

and that, for example, what men regarded as a licit marriage would be « neither mystical nor legal in the eyes of
God » [90].

Hincmar also read a critical ambiguity into the medical and the verbal arts. Sometimes the line between
the arts of medicine and magic grew thin [91]. Indeed,
magicians and the wicked angels associated with them
had their power from God [92], as did the 'spiritual physicians'. But, on the one side, there was superstition,
on the other, true religion [93].

It was common among Carolingian writers, as among
the Fathers, to argue that the verbal arts were inadequate
to true knowledge, and that they were even harmful
without formation of the moral character through Christian doctrine [94]. Hincmar, too, considered the 'wisdom
of this world' to be 'hostile to God' [95]. The delusions
of worldly wisdom had reached their most noxious viru-
lence among heretics and philosophers, those organs of the
Devil, who stood arrayed against the teachers of orthodoxy, ' the organs of Christ, who reign with Him in heaven and shine with miracles on earth ' [96]. Men who
confided only in human shrewdness were a real and present danger; they should be not only repressed, but utterly ground out [97]. Even in theology, earthly wisdom

(90) *Ep.* 22. *P. L.*, 126, col. 140.

(91) *De divortio, responsio* 15. *P. L.*, CXXV, col. 717 ff.

(92) *De divortio, responsio* 8. *P. L.*, CXXV, 677.

(93) Cf. *de divortio, responsiones* 9, 15. *P. L.*, CXXV, 678, 719.

(94) Einhard, *ep.* 57. *M. G. H..*, *Epp.* V, *K. A.* III, p. 138. Cf. Hincmar's
de praedestinatione, c. 31. *P. L.*, CXXV, 296.

(95) *De ordine palatii*, c. 31. *M. G. H.*, *Cap. Reg. Fr.*, II, p. 527.

(96) *De divortio, responsio* 15; *quaestio* 7, *responsio. P. L.*, 720, 768.

(97) *De ordine palatii*, c. 31. *M. G. H.*, *Cap. Reg. Fr.*, II, p. 527. Hincmar
was prepared to pay tribute to Charles the Bald as a philosopher-king (*P. L.*,
CXXV, col. 931). PIERRE RICHÉ, ' Charles le Chauve et la culture de son
temps ', *Colloques Internationaux du C.N.R.S.*, no. 561 (Paris 1977), p. 38
and *passim*. At the same time, his attitude toward philosophy could be di-

was ignorance. The humbling truth was that no one could claim to be sole master of the Scriptures or canons so long as he had to learn about them from other men, and not immediately from God [98]. It was in the simplicity of their faith that the Apostles, uneducated fishermen, had instructed orators and subjected emperors to themselves [99].

Idolatry was the great peril that Hincmar saw in the visual, medical and verbal arts. When he converted the Franks to Christianity, St. Remigius tore them away from visible idols just as the Prophet Jeremiah had recalled his people from the service of graven images [100]; but there were still plenty of idolaters about. In fact, a member of the Carolingian dynasty, Pippin II of Aquitaine, drove this fact home by falling into apostasy, absconding to the Northmen, and keeping their rituals [101]. With regard to the visual arts, the strictures of the second commandment therefore retained a quite literal interpretation. This was also true of the medical art – or rather, of magic, its perverted counterpoise – for, as Hincmar read the canons, enchantment could not take place without idolatry [102]. In the verbal arts, the danger lay in the ease with which men made idols out of their

stinctly hostile. He portrayed St. Remigius overwhelming an Arian who confided in his own dialectical powers (*Vita Remigii*, c. 21, *M.G.H.*, *SS. Rer. Mer.*, III, p. 313 f), and, even if the treatise is not his, the sentiment expressed in *de diversa animae ratione* conforms with his outlook: ' et vera ratio et prophetica auctoritas ' gives the laugh to the ' ratiocinatio philosophorum '. C. 8, *P. L.*, CXXV, col. 946. See *de una et non trina Deitate*, *P. L.*, CXXV, col. 481; *de praedestinatione, diss. post.*, c. 30, *P. L.* CXXV, col. 295.

(98) *LV Cap.*, c. 24. *P. L.*, CXXVI, 379.

(99) *De una et non trina Deitate. P. L.*, CXXV, col. 564. *LV Cap.*, c. 24. *P. L.*, CXXVI, 379.

(100) Cf *Vita Remigii*, c. 1. *M. G. H.*, *SS. Rer. Mer.*, III, p. 262.

(101) *Annales Bertiniani* (864), *ed. cit.*, pp. 105, 113. J. M. WALLACE-HA-DRILL, *Early Medieval History* (New York 1976), p. 226 f.

(102) *De divortio, responsio* 16. *P. L.*, CXXV, col. 728.

own words and interpretations [103], an ease that warranted thinking of idolatry as the mother of heresy [104]. There were varieties of idolatry on every hand – in deviant sexual acts [105], and, above all, in avarice whether for wealth or for position [106]. In all its variations, idolatry occurred because the eyes – whether of the body or the mind – did not see the reality veiled within appearances. To be sure, grace could reduce this discrepancy. Thus, when he touched the risen Christ, the Apostle Thomas saw one thing and believed another; he saw a man and confessed God [107]. Still, the discrepancy remained, deluding and enticing, as it had when Satan tempted Adam and Eve from unity – the worship of one God – into the plurality of self-worship with the lying promise, ' Ye shall be as gods ' [108]. The Archbishop judged that, like the parents of the human race, Hincmar of Laon and Gottschalk had lapsed into idolatry. They had not properly subordinated the analogues of art to the higher analogues of faith.

How could one avoid idolatry? Hincmar drew the answer from his monastic roots [109]. The ascetic virtue of humility counteracted the divisiveness of self-worship; it promoted unity. Hincmar incessantly admonished

---

(103) *De praedestinatione, diss. post.*, c. 16. *P. L.*, CXXV, col. 142. *LV Cap.*, c. 36. *P. L.*, CXXVI, 429.

(104) *De una et non trina Deitate*, *P. L.*, CXXV, col. 479 f.

(105) *De divortio, responsio* 12, *P. L.*, CXXV, coll. 693 f, 698.

(106) *LV Cap.*, cc. 47, 51; *Libellus expostulationis*, c. 30. *P. L.*, CXXVI. 465, 485 ff, 618.

(107) *De divortio, responsio* 6. *P. L.*, CXXV, col. 672.

(108) *De una et non trina Deitate*, *P. L.*, CXXV, col. 479 f.

(109) Schörrs, *Hinkmar*, p. 11 f: ' Jedenfalls aber ist das Ringen des alten Ordensgeistes gegen weltliche Erschlaffung nicht ohne Einfluss auf seine Charakterbildung geblieben, da die seltene Willensstärke, der nie erkaltende Eifer für kirchliche Zucht und Ordnung und der ernst-asketische Zug, der von den Jünglingsjahren an durch das ganze Leben des Mannes geht, auf eine frühe Schule von Erfahrungen und Prüfungen hindeuten '.

kings and other bishops to humility and obedience. It is easy to regard these austere rebukes as self-serving tactics. However, another interpretation – not necessarily excluding self-interest – is also plausible. Hincmar grew to adulthood as a monk; he practiced monastic austerities while archbishop [110]. He served as abbot of St. Remi, and considered monks his « brothers and sons » [111]. He resorted to the *Rule* of St. Benedict in an attempt to edify Pope Nicholas I. There is no reason to suspect hypocrisy in his statement that humility was the virtue that safeguarded all the others [112].

Hincmar recognized humility as an antidote to divisiveness when he invoked St. Benedict's provision that the abbot should forbid artisan monks to ply crafts in which they took pride [113]. The same idea led him to quote Augustine's opinion that man should hate his own work, as sin, in order to come to God [114]. In church order, as well as in private spirituality, this ascetic self-denial served the ultimate goal of unification; for it was through humility, and holy obedience, that believers could be one in Him who prayed ‘ that all may be one, as thou, Father, art in me and I in thee, that they may be one in us » [115].

We have seen that Hincmar accepted the arts as important – if not essential – tools in the work of salvation, reversing the primal fall into idolatry, and thus

(110) As witnessed by the letter of Pardulus, oited above, n. 40.

(111) *P. L.*, CXXV, col. 503.

(112) *P. L.*, CXXVI, col. 77, 266. Cf Schrörs, *Hinkmar*, p. 69, on Lothar I's assumption of the monastic habit before his death. One of the most serious charges made by Pope Leo IV against Hincmar was that he had violated his monastic vows when he became archbishop, and, years later, Hincmar found it still necessary to answer this allegation (obliquely) when writing to Pope Nicholas I (*ep.* 11, *P. L.*, CXXVI, 81 f).

(113) *P. L.*, CXXV, col. 503.

(114) *De praedestinatione, diss. post.*, c. 23. *P. L.*, CXXV, col. 215.

(115) *LV Cap.*, c. 16. *P. L.*, CXXVI, col. 337. John 17 : 21.

into pluralism. Correction had been the *Leitmotiv* of the Carolingian ' Renaissance ' under Charlemagne and Louis the Pious [116]; it permeates Hincmar's thought about the bishop as builder, physician, and propagator. We are now prepared to ask: how in general, did mimesis enter the ideas of correction that we have considered, and how did it cause problems?

In the first place, mimesis entered Hincmar's thought because he presupposed models of authenticity for any work. The model might be the ' norm ' of the monastic rule [117], or that set down in papal decrees [118], both of which he considered divinely inspired. ' Form ' was the word that Hincmar most often used to describe the governing standard. Frequently, it appears to imply nothing more than a procedural routine, or protocol. Thus, Hincmar laid down the ' legal and regular form ' for the election of bishops [119] and the ' form ' according to which degrees of pre-eminence were established within the episcopal order [120]. But, to a man convinced that God's creative act – prescribing measure and order – continued through the canons [121], ' form ' implied much more than external observance. The externals of any sacramental act might conceivably be performed without effect. Suppose that a person leaves the baptismal font unregenerate, just as he entered it. The ritual acts would then be all a game. In marriage too, it was possible for

(116) PERCY ERNST SCHRAMM, ' Karl der Grosse. Denkart und Grundauffassungen. Die von ihm bewirkte Correctio (' Renaissance ') ', *Historische Zeitschrift*, CXCVIII (1964), pp. 306-345. JOSEF FLECKENSTEIN, *Die Bildungsreform Karls des Grossen als Verwirklichung der Norma Rectitudinis.* Bigge-Ruhr, 1953. ANTON, *Fürstenspiegel*, pp. 95, 211 f.

(117) *Ep.* 45. P. L., CXXVI, col. 266.

(118) E. g., *ep.* 31. P. L., CXXVI, 221.

(119) *Ep.* 19. P. L., CXXVI, 117. *Ep.* 48, ibid., col. 268 f.

(120) *LV Cap.*, c. 13. P. L. CXXVI, col. 326, one of Hincmar's most frequent patristic citations.

(121) *LV Cap.*, c. 10. P. L. CXXVI, 321.

observance to be all simulation, and no truth. In either case, ' the mere form ', or ' image ', was received, ' without the power of santification ' [122]. This, Hincmar vehemently argued, was true of clerical ordinations performed by his predecessor Ebo, after being deposed and briefly reinstated in Rheims.

Thus, when Hincmar employed terms such as ' the form of royal power ' [123], or ' the form of bishops ' [124], and when he wrote about the ' form of Peter ' set up ' for all rulers of the Church ' [125], to follow in their judgments, he implied something beyond strict adherence to the letter of the law. For him, as for us, ' form ' could mean ' mold '. When he used the term, he implied a creative act by which a given man – king or bishop – was shaped by being pressed into a pre-existent form, and by which he, in turn, became a ' form ', or ' exemplar ', to his people [126]. The greatest difficulty came in distinguishing partial, or probable, forms from true [127], and thus in gauging degrees of analogy.

The three main tests were truth, authority, and reason. A fourth, custom, was subordinate to these [128]. Clearly, reason was pivotal to all the others; it was the mental faculty by which evidence was sifted and decisions reached, and analogies were drawn and appraised,

(122) *Ep.* 22. *P. L.*, CXXVI, col. 145.

(123) *De una et non trina Deitate*, *P. L.*, CXXV, col. 508.

(124) *Ad episcopos admonitio altera pro Carolomanno rege*, c. 4. *P. L.*, CXXV, 1009.

(125) *Ep.* 27, to Hadrian II. *P. L.*, CXXVI, col. 183. Charles the Bald to Hadrian II, *ep.* 8. *P. L.*, CXXXIV, col. 894.

(126) For the phrase, ' forma cui imprimatur ', see *de fide Carolo regi servanda*, *P. L.* CXXXV, col. 966; *Libellus expostulationis*, c. 5, *P. L.*, CXXVI, col. 573; Charles the Bald to Hadrian II, *ep.* 8, *P. L.*, CXXXIV, col. 889. For the bishop as ' forma gregi ', see *de ecclesiis et capellis*, GUNDLACH ed., p. 126. For the king as exemplar, below p. 679.

(127) *P. L.*, CXXVI, 555 f.

(128) *P. L.*, CXXVI, col. 546. *De presbyteris criminosis*, c. 9. *P. L.*, CXXV, col. 1096.

610

in law or theology. Throughout Hincmar's writings, the four terms constantly reappear in pairs, of which *ratio* is the common denominator – *ratio veritatis* [129], *ratio et auctoritas* [130], and so forth. Beneath all the charges against Hincmar of Laon ran the conviction that he 'had acted contrary to reason' [131], rebelling 'unreasonably' against his king [132] and his archbishop [133]. Hincmar of Rheims charged that, in so doing, he had paid no attention to the *ratio* in canonical texts, and that he had attempted to evade or pervert them by compiling his own rules of action, 'frivolous, useless things, lacking in reason' [134].

A second way, then, by which mimesis entered Hincmar's thought about correction was by way of *ratio*. Again and again, Hincmar emphasized that reason was man's distinctive faculty; for human persons, made in the image of God, were defined as 'individual subsistences of rational nature' [135]. God placed all irrational

---

(129) *P. L.*, CXXV, col. 399, c. 35. *LV Cap.*, c. 8. *P. L.*, CXXVI, col. 315: ' contra rationem et veritatem' *Ibid.*, c. 25, col. 387 f., *ratio* and *veritas* are preferable to *consuetudo*. On the general problem, HANS LIEBESCHÜTZ, ' Wesen und Grenzen des karolingischen Rationalismus ', *Archiv für Kulturgeschichte*, XXXV (1952), pp. 17-44, esp. pp. 28, 43. PIERRE RICHÉ, ' *Auctoritas* ', ' *ratio* ', et ' *divina pagina* ' dans la culture théologique à l'époque carolingienne ', *Nascita dell'Europa ed Europa Carolingia : Un'equazione da verificare*, Spoleto 1979) (Settimane di studio del Centro italiano di studi sull'alto medioevo, XXVII),

(130) *Epp.* 15, 20: *LV Cap.*, c. 47; letter to Hincmar of Laon, *P. L.*, CXXVI, 97, 121, 462, 501. *De divortio, responsio* 12, ' contra legem vel rationem '; *Pro ecclesiae libertatum defensione, exposit. prima*, ' ratio est et non obstitit auctoritati... '. *P. L.*, CXXV, coll. 699, 1051.

(131) *LV Cap.*, c. 30. *P. L.* CXXVI, col. 409.

(132) *LV Cap.*, c. 46. *P. L.*, CXXVI, col. 459.

(133) *P. L.*, CXXVI, 504, 509 f.

(134) *LV Cap.*, cc. 43, 47. *P. L.*, CXXVI, 442, 463.

(135) The Boethian definition occurs in *de una et non trina Deitate*, *P. L.*, CXXV, 585 f. Hincmar employed the Augustinian argument that the triune structure of the human mind carried the image of God (*P. L.*, CXXV, col. 541). I would argue that this, rather than a theocratic meaning, was implied when, writing in the name of Charles the Bald, Hincmar referred to the King as ' in imagine tamen Dei ambulantem esse nos hominem '. He then

creatures under Adam's rule [136]. How was *ratio* mimetic?
If we are too Cartesian in understanding the word, we
will overlook something basic, and perhaps surprising.
Ratio has many meanings. One can rightly emphasize
it as serving philosophy. According to the sense that
we have in view, however, it opposes philosophy, and
this sense is borne out by Hincmar's quite consistent di-
sparagement of philosophy and philosophers, a *typos*
that he derived from the Fathers and that we shall consider in the second section of this paper. The sense of a
'right and perfect reason' kept Hincmar from embracing the strict legal formalism to which his canonistic
studies might have led him. For he was convinced that
the 'right and perfect reason' was virtue, a goal that
men perceived imperfectly in this life, but toward which
the good were called to struggle, ascending by imitation
'from virtue into virtue', until they attained the beatific
vision of God [137]. Without rational perception of that
goal, struggle, persecution, and martyrdom contributed
nothing to salvation. Directed to wrong spiritual goals,
human intellect fell into the madness of heretics and

---

invoked Charles' succession to the royal office as a second line of argument
(*P. L.*, CXXIV, col. 881). Cf. Anton, *Fürstenspiegel*, p. 340. All men are of
the same substance, *de una et non trina Deitate, P. L.*, CXXV, col. 524.
   (136) *Vita Remigii*, c. 4. *M. G. H., SS. Rer. Mer.*, III, p. 266.
   (137) *De una et non trina Deitate, P. L.*, CXXV, col. 579. Cf. *de cavendis
vitiis, praefatio, P. L.*, CXXV, col. 857, ' quotidie magis ac magis de virtute
in virtutem proficiendo custodietis '. *Vita Remigii*, c. 31, *M. G. H., SS. Rer.
Mer.*, III, p. 328, ' Videamus etiam, quomodo hic beatus pater et pastor noster, benedictionibus sibi a legislatore Deo datis, ipsius auxilio in seculi huius
convalle lacrimarum ascensiones in corde suo disposuit et de virtute in virtutem gratia Dei provectus excrevit, usquequo eum quem semper desideravit
spiritu facie ad faciem videre promeruit '. I contend that this sense of *mora*
ascent stood between Hincmar and what Devisse has called ' le reproche qui
peut le plus justement être fait à Hincmar, celui de formalisme juridique ',
and that Devisse himself acknowledged as much when he wrote that, for
Hincmar, law was an instrument of social instruction, not an end in itself.
Hincmar Archevêque, II, pp. 617, 1133.

schismatics [138]. Deprived of the exemplary *ratio* that was identical with Christian virtue, pagans were ' monsters ', and violent, lawless men were hardly more than ' brute and irrational beasts ' [139].

Significant as they were in themselves, Hincmar's comments on form and reason had their place in a wider framework. Here, problems begin to appear. When he thought about knowledge as a whole, Hincmar conceived of three discrete structures. He identified them in terms of vision: the eyes of the body, the eyes of the mind, and the eyes of God. Occasionally, Hincmar did argue that the three coincided. But he also recognized vast discrepancies among them. By contrast with the total and immutable wisdom of God, man's knowledge labored under its own fragmentary, shifting character. Change operated only in the structures of human knowledge, and, even there, further discrepancies set the physical apart from the intellectual vision, and the intellectual, unenlightened by grace, apart from the eyes of faith [140].

(138) *P. L.*, CXXVI, col. 551. Cf. Gottschalk of Orbais' self-delusive anticipation of martyrdom, *de una et non trina Deitate, P. L.*, CXXV, col. 613. *P. L.*, CXXVI, 547 f.

(139) *Vita Remigii*, c. 2., *M. G. H., SS. Rer. Mer.*, III, p. 262; *De Coercendo Raptu Viduarum*, c. 4., *P. L.*, CXXV, col. 1019 f. Cf. *de divortio, responsio* 5. *P. L.* CXXV, col. 658. See also *ep*. 2, to Nicholas I, regarding Rothad of Soissons, *P. L.*, CXXVI, col. 31; ' De eo autem quod benignitas animi vestri pensans non belluinum, sed humanum hominis animum scripsit... sciat dignatio vestra, non illum esse huiusmodi temperantiae '. The Archbishop also wrote of Hincmar of Laon in similar terms, comparing him, in his impaired *ratio*, with a rhinoceros and a unicorn (above, n. 41). The Bishop of Laon alleged that his uncle had planned to capture him, urging Charles the Bald to bring ' tales homines strenuos et peritos, sicut opus est ad talem bestiam capiendam '. *LV Cap.*, cc. 23, 24. *P. L.*, CXXVI, coll. 602, 604. See, further, *ep*. 11, *P. L.* CXXVI, col. 88: ' quia veteres constitutiones jam quasi pro vili apud quosdam habentur, his novis decretis carnales et animales homines territi, quiddam reverentius contra ecclesiam indignitati meae commissam agerent '.

(140) *De una et non trina Deitate*, c. 11 *P. L.*, CXXV, col. 565, distinguishing between the eyes of the mind and those of the body; *De divortio, responsio* 6, ibid., col. 660, the eyes of faith see what the eyes of the body can not (cf. *os*

The importance of form and *ratio* in this overall concept was that they could promote an equilibrium between
the three varieties of human knowledge (the eyes of body,
mind and faith), on the one hand, and divine wisdom on
the other. A complex act was required to achieve some
measure of balance. It combined two sorts of mediation:
ordinary human communication and a second, higher
kind by which – through sacraments – divinity was
mediated to man. Hincmar explicitly described this act
in regard to baptism. He drew its aspects together when
he explained the mimetic act of the Holy Spirit in the
soul. But Hincmar also emphasized that, without the
faith of the baptisand, the ritual was profitless. The
baptisand must, by faith, act as God's fellow-worker [141],
if the cycle were to be complete by which he became incorporate in the Mediator of God and men. The same
emphasis on the recipient led Hincmar to conclude that
the Eucharist was poison to the wicked and salvation
to the good, and that, before the eyes of God, other sacraments and sacramental actions might have effects
very different from what they appeared to have in the
eyes of men [142]. It also entered his general theory of
knowledge, as, for example, when he wrote about Gottschalk of Orbais. How, with all his learning, could Gottschalk have fallen into wrong doctrines about the Trinity?
As a monk, he had sung every day, boy and man, a vesper
hymn that could have kept him from error, and yet his

---

corporis/os cordis, LV Cap., c. 47. P.L., CXXVI, col. 464); De divortio, responsio
12, P. L., CXXV, col. 699 f, ep. 22 and LV Cap., c. 52; P. L., CXXVI, coll.
141, 489, all referring to the disparty between human judgments and those
coram divinis oculis.

(141) Ep. 18, P. L., CXXVI, col. 105 f., quoting I, Cor. 3:9.

(142) Below, nn. 172-176, 408. Cf Cap. Pistensia (862), M. G. H., Cap.
Reg. Fr., II, no. 272, c. 4, p. 310: ' . . . qui participatione nominis Christi christiani vocantur, hoc, quod humano ore dicimur, in divinis oculis esse valemus '.

614

heart did not perceive its meaning; for wisdom could not
enter his wicked soul [143].

Where thought led, action followed. In his great
commentary on *Genesis*, Augustine had explored three
levels of vision as stages in man's ascent toward the con-
templation of God. Hincmar followed a more prosaic
line of inquiry. The ' eye ', he wrote, was action; it was
the turning of the heart (*inclinatio cordis*). (The eye was
the light of the heart). If one's ' eye ' were single, then
one's whole action would be full of light. But, if the intention of the heart were dark, no words could express
the darkness in actions that it caused [143a].

At least in theology, knowledge reflected the mind
of the knower – his light or darkness – rather than the
nature of the thing known. And yet, reason might guide
human structures of knowledge ' from virtue into virtue ',
toward a final balance with what the eyes of God could
see. There was no escape from the discipline of humility
if one remained true to the faith, no abandonment of
relentless self-criticism, always correcting the slow and
hazardous process of equilibration.

Bearing these considerations in mind, we can understand that Hincmar's mimetic concept of unity in human
affairs was really a concept of unification, and that the
modelling process that led to unity took place in the mind
and soul. For Hincmar, the subject of greatest urgency
was not the finished work of art – the new creation that
lay open only to the eyes of God – but the process of
spiritual modelling, or transformation, by which it ap-

(143) *De una et non trina Deitate, P. L.*, CXXV, col. 578.
(143a) *De divortio, praef. M. G. H., Epp.* VIII, *K. A.* VI, p. 77. Hincmar
has adapted Matt. 6:21-23 to read *cor/cordis* instead of *corpus/corporis*. The
equation between *oculus simplex* and *recta intentio* also appears in *Pro Li-
bertate Ecclesiae Defensione, exposit.* I. *P. L.*, CXXV, col. 1037 f.

proached wholeness. The view of life as a continual passage toward *ratio*, a spiritual power or virtue, casts some
light on the paradoxical interplay of imagery and iconoclasm that Hincmar inherited from the Fathers. Progression required that earlier, less complete, stages be
subsumed and replaced until the movement ended, and
man's intellectual vision no longer passed darkly to him
' through a mirror, in an aenigma ', but immediately,
' face to face ' (I Cor. 13:12). Progression demanded humility channelled into self-criticism and denial according
to an elaborate set of inferences drawn from analogy,
inferences to which heretics and schismatics were blind.

We have now reviewed three mimetic functions of
bishops – building, healing, and propagating; and we
have implicitly related those functions to the Incarnation. All of the functions served progressive correction.
In the light of this apparent, and passionate, commitment
to change, it would be difficult to follow Schrörs in concluding that, for Hincmar, dogma and Church order
were permanently closed structures, in which there could
be no further development.

The fact that Hincmar's thought focused as it did
on the Incarnation was decisive. For our purposes, the
important feature of Hincmar's theology of the Incarnation was that it encompassed theories of change, and,
explicitly, of correction. Whatever the precise subject –
the Incarnation itself, the sacraments, or the rebirth of
the soul – the theme was movement from an imperfect
order of being to a perfect one. It was a movement of a
precise kind. It took place by mediation between the
opposite poles of divinity and humanity, a mediation
that did not cease when Christ was born of the Virgin,
but that went on continually through the sacraments of
the Church. As we have yet to see, Hincmar taught that

616

Christ was incorporate, not merely in His own flesh, but also in every believer and in the entire Church.

Among modern scholars, Hincmar's achievements in canon law are esteemed far above those in theology. Schrörs' austere judgment has prevailed: namely, that Hincmar used his comprehensive patristic knowledge to winnow out true from false doctrine, without always clearly perceiving the basic, conceptual issues under debate. There is no evidence in his writings that Hincmar regarded himself as deficient in theology. To the contrary, he wrote indefatigably on all the major theological issues of his day, and he once dropped his guard so far as to mention the delight that he took in such exercises. Over the years, he assembled a large and costly working library in theology, which included both Latin writers and Greek, in translation. The questions whether Hincmar were – as Schrörs wrote – ' less a theologian than a canonist ' [143b], or – as later scholars have sometimes asked – whether his political acts were prompted by moral or juristic principles, emerge from habits of thought foreign to the Archbishop himself. In the next section, we shall examine those habits, particularly as they illuminated the ambiguities of historical continuity and transformation.

II. *Mimetic Rationales and the Analogues of Faith*

We have sketched out some features of Hincmar's mimetic doctrines, but we have not penetrated to their inner structure. Behind the corrective functions of bi-

---

(143b) For the references to SCHRÖRS in this paragraph and the preceding one, see *Hinkmar*, pp. 159, 174.

shops there were rationales; behind the rationales, there
were basic theological propositions. We are at the juncture
where Hincmar's concept of the episcopal office coincided
with his personal spirituality. Let us therefore examine
those deeper rationales and the critical ambiguities that
appeared in them when Hincmar tried to integrate theory
and practice.

We are now in a position to single out three rationales
of progressive correction that Hincmar drew from the
arts, and to consider how they demanded self-criticism.
The rationales parallel what we have said concerning the
medical, visual, and verbal arts. Moving from the least
to the most inclusive, they rest upon principles of wholeness (or *sanitas*), participation, and imitation. For
Hincmar, these rationales were represented by three
symbolic analogues of the Incarnation: wholeness, by
the Old Testament emblem of Moses' brazen serpent;
participation, by the New Testament emblem of the cross;
and imitation, by the apocalyptic emblem of the celestial
tabernacle. As the symbols indicate, Hincmar's rules of
inference had a great deal to do with art, especially with
the progressive realization of a pattern in time. After
we consider them, we shall indicate how these indices of
the Archbishop's habits of thought appeared in a specific
work of art: his tomb.

Pope Leo I expressed Hincmar's first principle in a
lapidary way, so forcefully, indeed, that Hincmar quoted the passage for the instruction of Pope Nicholas I.
In one body, Leo wrote, we have many members, but
not every member acts in the same way. Correspondingly, we, being many, are one body in Christ, all members
one of another. To these Pauline sentences, the Pope
added that ' the organic union (*connexio*) of the entire
body makes one wholeness (*sanitatem*), one beauty (*pul-*

618

chritudinem) [144]. Together with Leo's further statement that the *connexio* required unanimity, especially concord among priests, all this corresponded with Hincmar's view of the Church as one body, functional distinctions setting priests apart from laymen and defining levels in the ecclesiastical hierarchy [145]. No one hates his own flesh, Hincmar wrote, but rather nourishes and fosters it, as Christ does the Church [146].

The difficulty, of course, was that disorders abounded in the earthly body of Christ. Severe discipline was needed – like the wine or olive press, or the refiner's fire – to purify and thus to heal individual members [147], and the spiritual rulers of the people must purge impurities from the bellies of their own minds, burying the fetid waste with the stake of compunction [148]. On a wider level, heresy and insubordination jeopardized the organic unity that Pope Leo had praised. Convinced that the body of Christ had not yet been purged of its dross, Hincmar recalled how God had sent a plague of venomous serpents to punish the Israelites for murmuring against Moses and against Himself, and how, after many died, He had also commanded Moses to make a bronze serpent

(144) *Ep.* 2, *P. L.*, CXXVI, col. 35 f. The full quotation is not indicated by Migne. Hincmar was of course aware of effects that physical mutilation had on priestly functions: ' et sicut in aliqua corporis parte praecisus aut publice poenitens ad ecclesiasticum gradum canonice non potest accedere, vel in ecclesiastico gradu manere... '. *De divortio, responsio* 2, *P. L.*, CXXV, col. 643.

(145) *De divortio, responsio* 2. *P. L.*, CXXV, col. 643 f; *LV Cap.*, c. 48, *P. L.*, CXXVI, 477 f; *Annales Bertiniani* (869), ed. cit., p. 161.

(146) *De divortio, responsio* 5. *P. L.*, CXXV, col. 657, quoting Ephesians 5:29.

(147) *P. L.*, CXXVI, 553.

(148) *De divortio, responsio* 12. *P. L.*, CXXV, col. 703, on Deuteronomy 23: 12-14. Repeated in *Vita Remigii*, c. 5, *M. G. H.*, *SS. Rer. Mer.*, III, p. 271. Cf *de cavendis vitiis*, c. 10. *P. L.*, CXXV, col. 922 f, on removing intestinal obstructions.

and raise it as a standard, so that any who had been bit-
ten, and who looked upon it, would live [149].

What does this figure of speech imply? As we have
said, the analogue between episcopal duties and corrective
medicine held major importance for Hincmar. We can
go on to say that the equation of beauty with a healthy
co-ordination of physical members gave Hincmar a rationale for corrective action.

In the first place, the Archbishop assumed that every
disease required a specific treatment, one that was discovered by trial and error. Obviously, it was best to consult a skilled physician, rather than one who could do
more harm than good through inexperience in combining
medicinal powders, or in applying plasters to wounds [150].

In the second place, it was apparent that new diseases
did appear, calling for additional experiments. By and
large, Hincmar held to the Galenic theory that health
could be restored by applying ' contraries to contraries,
hot to cold and cold to hot ' [151]. But an unfamiliar disease
called for unfamiliar medicine [152], and, as tests went on,
the patient might well consume his resources before the
cure was found, only to clutch at it eagerly then, despite
his poverty [153].

(149) E. g., *de praedestinatione, diss. post.*, cc. 24, 33. *De cavendis vitiis*,
c. 9. *P. L.*, CXXV, coll. 215, 320 f, 916. Cf *Libellus expostulationis*, c. 22. *P. L.*,
CXXVI, col. 599. Hincmar of Laon has presented authorities that vitiate his
own position, and that are as plain to see as Moses' serpent-standard.

(150) *Conc. Duz.*, II, c. 8. *Mansi*, XVII-A, col. 298. *Pro eccles. lib. defens.*,
P. L., CXXV, col. 1060.

(151) *Ep.* 35, *P. L.*, CXXVI, col. 170. *De divortio, responsio* 6, *P. L.*,
CXXV, col. 671.

(152) *Epp.* 11. 17, *P. L.*, CXXVI, 87, 101. *De praedestinatione, diss. post.*,
37.11. *P. L.*, CXXV, col. 413.

(153) *De praedestinatione, diss. post.*, c. 24. *P. L.*, CXXV, col. 220. See Synod at S. Macra, *Mansi* XVII, col. 539: ' quia medicus saepe, quos leni un-
guento medicare non potest, per amarum poculum confectionis reducit ad
hilaritatem sanitatis '.

620

In the third place, if medicines failed to restore wholeness, one had to resort to more drastic means. Should medicine fail to cure a gangrenous foot, or hand, or genital, or should cancer begin to devour the member, amputation would be called for [154]. In other cases of spreading disease, the cutting blade and the cauterizing fire were also needed, and the physician must act, undeterred by the tears of the sick. For it would be ' useless mercy ', if, out of fear of a quick incision or the pain of searing, the body should quite waste away, and life should end [155]. Hincmar did not draw a clear line between medicine and veterinary science. It was easy therefore for him to think of amputation as an analogue of the stern segregation of goats and sheep with contagious maladies from healthy ones, ' lest the latter be impaired, or die, of their disease ' [156].

In fact, Hincmar employed all of his references to medicine and surgery by way of illustrating and justifying his official acts. His references to practical skills built up by experience and applied, if need be, with pitiless severity allude indirectly to the bishop's corrective work. But his rationale for corrective action was also qualified by uncertainties, beyond those of any experimental venture. Hincmar knew many physical and mental disorders. They could come about in the natural course of

(154) *De divortio, responsio* 5. *P. L.*, CXXV, col. 657.

(155) *Libellus expostulationis*, c. 35. *P. L.*, CXXVI, 630.

(156) *De divortio, quaestio* 7 *responsio*. *P. L.* CXXV, col. 762. The analogue between amputation and excommunication was a common one; the methods addressed the problem of contagion. See also *ep.* 33, *P. L.*, CXXVI, col. 245; and, with reference to leprosy, *de una et non trina Deitate*, *P. L.*, CXXV, col. 485; *pro ecclesiae libertatum defensione, exposit. prima*, *P. L.*, CXXV, 1058 f. Cf. the comparison of heresy with pox – ' et velut pustulae humore noxio coalescente de loco in loco scatent in corpore, atque velut putres et corruptae cicatrices ecclesiae membra foedare tentantes, se catholicos esse dicunt... ' *De praedestinatione, diss. post.*, c. 34. *P. L.*, CXXV, col. 353. In this chain of thought, there is a close parallel with *Reg. Benedicti*, c. 28, one that came easily to Hicmar as monk and abbot.

things, or through the malice of demons. There usually was a demon behind mental affliction, he argued [157], and he has left us a description of one incident that exemplified some of the practical ambiguities that his theory posed.

The event occurred toward the end of January, 873. The future emperor, Charles the Fat, was the principal actor. Charles had accompanied his father, Louis the German, to Frankfurt, where Louis hoped to consolidate his control over the former Lotharingian kingdom. While in a royal council there, Charles suddenly arose and exclaimed that he wished to leave the world, and would have no sexual intercourse with his wife. Giving every sign of distraction, he dropped his sword to the ground, and loosened his swordbelt and robes. Bishops and others overpowered him and rushed him into a church, where the Archbishop of Mainz hastily vested and celebrated Mass, as Charles intermittently shouted, ' Woe ! Woe ! ' His father commanded that he be led to the shrines of the martyrs, so that, by their merits and prayers, Charles might be resored to ' a sane mind '.

Hincmar recorded that Louis and the other eyewitnesses were dumbfounded by this event, which appears to have been the first onslaught of the debility that became increasingly pronounced in Charles and that finally incapacitated him, thus leading to his deposition. As far as Hincmar was concerned, the profound ambiguity of appearance and reality lay at the heart of it.

---

(157) *Ep.* 9, *P. L.*, CXXVI, col. 70: Gottschalk's behavior proves him to be either *daemoniacus aut maniaticus*. The only treatment that Hincmar mentions for persons with violent mental disorders is violent restraint (*LV Cap.*, *pref.* and c. 35, *P. L.*, CXXVI, 291, 427); but, in the letter cited, he describes Gottschalk as having food and drink, like the monks (at Hautvilliers, where he was held), clothing (if he wished to accept it), and wood for his fire. He also had water, but he was unwilling to wash his body, hands, or face. Madness was a stock polemical charge – e. g., against Hincmar of Laon in *LV Cap.*, c. 46, *P. L.*, CXXVI, col. 460.

622

Satan, he wrote, had first transfigured himself into an angel of light. So disguised, he appeared to a terrified Charles. Reassuring the Prince, Satan administered ' communion [allegedly] sent by God for him ', and, with that morsel of bread, entered into him (cf. John 13:27). Charles' alarming seizure followed, and it was hoped that, reverently brought into places sacred to martyrs, he could be freed from the demon [158].

There were historical ambiguities in the practice of spiritual medicine yet deeper than discrepancy between appearance and reality. Even if the bread offered to Charles were a sham, Hincmar still knew that the Eucharistic elements brought life to some and death to others. After all, the effects of medicine took hold in the patient, not in the physician. And so it was possible for life-giving wine to turn into poison for some, and for the therapeutic incisions of the surgical knife – penance – to inflict mortal wounds [159]. Since all things happened by God's will or permission [160], it was even possible that Satan had told the truth when he assured Charles that he came from God.

Reference to the Eucharistic elements leads us to our second corrective rationale: unity through participation. Hincmar began with the proposition that one could pass to invisible things through visible. However, the visible elements consecrated by the Church in its sacraments constituted a special case. In them, the visible became identical with the invisible ' by a mystery of action (*operationis*) ', and believers participated directly, and not through likeness conveyed in types and shadows.

---

(158) *Annales Bertiniani* (873), ed. cit., p. 190 f.
(159) Cf *LV Cap.*, c. 38. *P. L.* CXXVI, 435. *De una et non trina Deitate*, *P. L.*, CXXV, 501 f.
(160) Below, n. 215.

Thus, if the brazen serpent appropriately symbolized the trial-and-error of medical practice, the cross symbolized both mediated and immediate participation. Of course, the Gospel of John refers to the brazen serpent as a foreshadowing of the cross, and Hincmar inherited a long and intricate tradition of exegesis about the mutual relationship between the two symbols, the ' figure ' through which temporal life was prolonged, and the ' truth ' through which life without end was given [161].

How could participation be regarded as an aesthetic rationale? From Alcuin, Hincmar learned that sight occurred by intromission: that is, the eye received light from an external source, light that it would not have had in itself if it had not borrowed it from another [162]. The seeing eye retained its integrity, but, after a fashion, it also became the light that it saw, by participating in it. What we might call the subject/object dichotomy persisted; but there was also a sense in which the subject became one with the object. Similarly, a composite number was made up of parts, but each part retained its identity. Like the visible and invisible elements in a sacrament, the many became one, and yet remained individual, loosing nothing by their connection [163].

---

(161) *De cavendis vitiis*, c. 9. *P. L.*, CXXV, col. 916. Cf *de divortio, responsio* 6, *P. L.*, CXXV, 670, ' in cujus ligno crucis omnium hominum ut dicit Ambrosius levatur infirmitas '.

(162) *De una et non trina Deitate*, *P. L.*, CXXV, col. 570.

(163) *Explanatio in Ferculum Salomonis*, *P. L.*, CXXV, col. 821. On number as an aesthetic principle in Carolingian culture, see ' Toward a Medieval Aesthetic ', a symposium consisting of three essays published in *Viator*, VI (1975): CHARLES W. JONES, ' Carolingian Aesthetics: Why Modular Verse ', emphasizing patristic models, pp. 309-340; RICHARD L. CROCKER, ' The Early Frankish Sequence: A New Musical Form ', pp. 341-349; WALTER HORN and ERNEST BORN, ' On the Selective Use of Sacred Numbers and the Creation of a New Aesthetic in Carolingian Architecture ', pp. 351-390. The third essay contains observations on the plan of St. Gall, which will be set forth in a full-length study, to be published in 1979 by the University of California Press.

624

To Hincmar's mind, participating was the essential act of seeing; for the viewer became one with what he saw. In quite another sense, it established ' the mystic kinship ' of numbers, applicable, of course, in architecture, and capable of determining the precise number of verses in a metrical composition [164]. By seeing, the viewer participated in the seen object; by number, the elements of a composition participated in one another, and it might be, in a heavenly archetype.

These senses converge in a discourse on the cross. Hincmar wished to establish that the number of the elect corresponded with divisions of the promised land among the ancient Hebrews. Working his way backward to the cross, he began with the twelve tribes of Israel. To achieve the perfection of this number, he first multiplied it by itself, and then multiplied the result by 100,000, which, being 10 multiplied by itself four times, signified the enduring life of the Church. The final result (144,000) is the number of the saved set down in the *Apocalypse*. At this point, Hincmar returned to the number 12. He recalled that it often symbolized the Church, since it combined three, the number of the Trinity, with four, that of the earth's parts. Twelve was also the number of the Apostles, sent into all four quarters of the world to preach the Trinity and the Lord, incarnate by the Holy Spirit of Mary, the Virgin, and crucified. Signifying by its four dimensions [165] the universal monarchy of the faith, the cross was the mark on the foreheads of the re-redeemed that Ezekiel had seen prefiguratively and John, in truth [166].

(164) *Explanatio in Ferculum Salomonis, P. L.*, CXXXV, 819.

(165) *Explanatio in Ferculum Salomonis, P. L.*, CXXXV, col. 824 f. Cf. *de praedestinatione, diss. post.*, c. 34, *P. L.*, CXXXV, col. 351 f.

(166) *LV Cap.*, c. 15. *P. L.*, CXXXVI, col. 328. Ezekiel 9:4, 6. Apocalypse 7:3-8. Behind this discourse stand Hincmar's thoughts concerning the

Such were the general rules. But actual practice intruded the shadow of historical ambiguity. To a generation unacquainted with corrective lenses, the variations in light admitted to the retina must have emphasized the uncertainty written into the metaphor of sight. Given the fallibility of eyes beyond the age of forty, it is by no means obvious that Hincmar ever saw with full clarity the paintings that adorned his cathedral. On a more exalted level, it was apparent that Ezekiel and John, seeing the same sign on the foreheads of the saved, had practiced two different kinds of vision.

And so it was also with number. From his books on nature, Hincmar learned that the human foetus took shape in four stages, lasting 45 days altogether. Adding one for the very day on which the semen begins to divide into members, he concluded that the entire formative period lasted 46 days, and that, during the balance of pregnancy, the body merely increased in size. He was struck by the fact that building the physical body of Christ required 46 days, the identical number of years taken to construct the Temple; and this correspondence led him to further affinities with the gestation of the body and soul of every believer, and the growth of the Church, as the body of Christ [167]. But Hincmar knew that in particular cases, abortions and miscarriages cut short the formative process, thus evading his general rule. He was also aware of congenital malformations that participated in the full term of gestation, but failed to achieve the full form of the human body [168].

mystic properties of the number ten, on which see *Explanatio in Ferculum Salomonis*, *P. L.*, CXXV, col. 821.

(167) *Explanatio in Ferculum Salomonis*, *P. L.*, CXXV, col. 832.

(168) *De divortio, interrogatio* 12, *responsio* 12, *P. L.*, CXXV, coll. 689, 707. *Annales Bertiniani* (875), ed. cit., p. 197. *De praedestinatione, diss. post*, c. 33. *P. L.*, CXXV, col. 332 f. On other congenital disorders, below, n. 286.

626

When it came down to the individual case, even the sacraments, those supreme means of unity through participation, were haunted by ambiguity. Christ consecrated the mystery of the Church's unity at His table; He himself was daily consecrated at His table, the altar [169]. By participation in the consecrated elements of the Eucharist, one body was made out of many believers [170], just as, ' by participation of the name of Christ ', they were all called Christians [171]. And yet, even these kinds of participation might be deceptive, as we saw with regard to marriage and baptism. Again, if uncanonically performed – even by orthodox men – an episcopal ordination engulfed both the ordinand and his consecrators in heresy; it mediated, not holy orders, but expulsion of all concerned from the episcopal rank [172]. Further, those who embraced heretical beliefs could hold to the outward ritual and discipline of the Church [173], but such virtues as appeared to adorn their acts were simulations, shams, not unlike a reed whose shining exterior hides a hollow core [174]. Many indeed were spiritually dead, although they seemed to be alive [175]. Polluted by crimes, they had no qualms about participating in the secrets of Christ's mysteries. But, as the consecrated bread entered their bellies, filled with iniquity, Satan entered their cruel and impious minds, as he had entered Judas' [176]. The « terrible sacrament » of the altar became their condemna-

---

(169) *De cavendis vitiis*, c. 10. *P. L.*, CXXV, col. 921.
(170) *De praedestinatione, diss. post.*, *P. L.*, CXXV, col. 419.
(171) *Cap. Pistensia* (862), c. 4. *M. G. H.*, *Cap.*, II, no. 272, p. 310.
(172) *Ep.* 19, c. 10. *P. L.*, CXXVI, col. 116.
(173) *Ep.* 33, c. 4. *P. L.*, CXXVI, col. 247.
(174) *De divortio, responsio* 15. *P. L.*, CXXV, col. 720.
(175) *De divortio, responsio* 10. *P. L.*, CXXV, col. 685.
(176) *Ep.* 16. *P. L.*, CXXVI, col. 99 f. *De divortio, responsiones* 6, 13. *P. L.* CXXV, coll. 671 f. 710 f. Synod of St. Macra, c. 5. *Mansi*, XVII, col. 543: ' terribile sacramentum '.

tion, as it became life for the devout. Satan could harm even the innocent in this way, as he had afflicted Charles the Fat.

What did participation require to cut through these ambiguities? It required more than sight; for Pilate could not have asked, ' What is truth ' ? if he had seen, with the eyes of his mind, the Truth standing before the eyes of his body [177]. It required more than the eyes of faith; for even the demons whom Christ cast out confessed Him, ' because they knew Him to be Christ ' [178]. It required even more than grace; for there were believers the eyes of whose minds grace had illuminated, and who yet were worse than the spiritually blind in their unwillingness to do good [179]. Beyond sight, faith, and grace, participation required action. True participation came by works; it was by imitating the works of righteousness or those of iniquity that one became a member of Christ's body, or the devil's [180].

Hincmar began with the hypothesis that Christian unity was incomplete, and that its impairments could, and must, be corrected. He elucidated his hypothesis with corrective rationales of healing and participation, but neither of these exhausted the issue of correction. Their symbols, too, failed to represent the profound and coherent unity that Hincmar envisaged, a perfection that admitted no addition. The brazen serpent belonged among the prefigurations in the Old Testament that had been fulfilled and superseded by the revelations of the New. The cross itself, which Moses's ensign foreshadowed, was limited to time. It appeared late in history, and its

(177) *LV Cap.*, c. 43. *P. L.*, CXXVI, col. 450.
(178) *De divortio, responsio* 7. *P. L.*, CXXV, col. 674.
(179) *LV Cap.*, c. 46. *Ep.* 25. *P. L.*, CXXVI, coll. 459, 171.
(180) Cf *epp.* 17, 55. *P. L.*, CXXVI, 102 f, 277-279.

propitiatory work would cease when the redemption of the world had been accomplished. The rationales of healing and participation were encompassed and completed by that of imitation, in which, as we have already suggested, procreation was an important element. For Hincmar, Moses' tabernacle symbolized this, most comprehensive, rationale of correction. For the tabernacle made by Moses imitated the celestial tabernacle, not made by hands, ' the heavenly Jerusalem, our mother, an abiding city, a building of God ', composed, in distinct orders, of men and angels. Like the brazen serpent and the cross, the tabernacle alluded to the Incarnation; for Christ, the supreme and eternal High Priest, had entered into the true tabernacle above through His own blood, and, sitting there in the glory of His Father's majesty, He interceded for His faithful people [181].

In general, ' to imitate ' meant ' to follow ' [182]; but this apparently simple definition had complex repercussions. To imitate – to follow – was also to form, as children are formed by the examples of their tutors [183], as learned Christians imitate wise and venerable men, like Pope Gregory the Great [184], and as even great, ' imitable ' prelates, including Pope Gregory himself, humbly corrected themselves by imitating what was good in their inferiors [185]. St. Paul had pointed the way to fur-

(181) *LV Cap.*, c. 11. *P. L.*, CXXVI, 325. Cf *LV Cap.*, c. 44. *P. L.* CXXVI, col. 455, where the bishop is described as a tabernacle, containing the rod and manna.

(182) *P. L.*, CXXVI, col. 528.

(183) Alexander the Great was depraved by the bad example of his tutor, Leonidas. *De ordine palatii*, c. 1. *M. G. H.*, *Cap. Req. Fr.*, II, p. 518. *Ad Carolum III.*, c. 2; *ad proceres*, c. 1. *P. L.*, CXXV, coll. 990 f, 993.

(184) Charles the Bald to Hadrian II, *ep.*, 8. *P. L.*, CXXIV, col. 887.

(185) *LV Cap.*, cc. 4, 48. *P. L.*, CXXVI, coll. 302, 477. On ' imitable ' prelates, see *P. L.*, CXXVI, 223 (destructive models), and the letter cited in n. 184, col. 887; ' [Gregorius] toto orbi colendus et imitandus '.

ther ramifications when he defended the claims of Christians to be sons of Abraham after the faith, while Jews were his seed after the flesh. Augustine wove this doctrine into his mimetic theories, teaching that Christians had been engendered by imitating Abraham, and, in parallel fashion, that imitation had likewise procreated Satan's offspring. Hincmar added this idea of imitation as a procreative act to his repertory [186].

When he turned to the sacraments, Hincmar's thought about imitation, as procreation, intersected with his analogues of healing and participation. Hincmar regarded the sacraments as supreme instruments of healing and participation. These functions, however, were secondary to an imitative act in which things that were not one by nature became so by a ' mystery of action ' [187]. We have already mentioned Hincmar's statement that, without the sanctification of the Holy Spirit, the liturgical actions prescribed for baptism or marriage or episcopal ordination remained empty forms [188], and we may now examine Hincmar's doctrines of mimesis in baptism and in the Eucharist, the two sacraments by which, above all, the contagion of sin was healed and the Church's sons, begotten.

Hincmar's theology of baptism presupposed that man had been made in the image of God, that this inherent mimetic relationship had been destroyed by sin, and that, through baptism, the interior man was reformed

---

(186) *LV Cap.*, c. 15. *P. L.* CXXVI, col. 328 f, and *de divortio, quaestio* 6 *responsio. P. L.* CXXV, col. 758 f, a full discussion. Cf *de divortio, quaestio* 7 *responsio, P. L.,* CXXV, col. 762. By imitating their exemplars, heretics become members of Antichrist and sons of the devil. *Ep.* 21; *LV Cap.,* cc. 5, 47. *P. L.,* CXXVI, 131, 303, 467. *De una et non trina Deitate : De praedestinatione, diss. post.,* c. 38 *epilogi* c. 5, *P. L.,* CXXV, coll. 553, 463.

(187) *De divortio, responsio* 6. *P. L.,* CXXV, col. 664. Below, n. 226.

(188) See nn. 90, 122, 408.

630

according to the image of the Creator. The object of the sacrament was therefore to restore, or reform, a lost likeness. But the ritual itself was mimetic. The priest imitated visibly, in water, what the Holy Spirit performed invisibly, in the soul [189]. The visible elements – the priest, the body of the candidate, and the water – were of no avail without the invisible elements of Spirit, soul, and faith [190]. Through the sacramental mimesis of invisible by visible, culminating in the three-fold immersion of the candidate in water, there came yet another imitation: the mimetic participation of the believer in the very death and resurrection of Christ [191].

Hincmar's repertory of corrective analogues coincided in this mimetic act. He expressed in detail the curative effects that participation in Christ was to have, as the candidate was marked with the sign of the cross, exorcised and given exorcised salt – so that demons might be cast out and a habitation prepared for the Lord – as the priest touched his eyes, nose, ears, and, sometimes, his tongue – to free them from the infirmities of sin. Thus, was the heavenly Jerusalem daily built up, even with the souls of infants [192]. Thus, did the Church give birth to the adoptive sons of God.

As baptism recapitulated Christ's death and resurrection, the Eucharist re-enacted His sacrifice [193]. In baptism, the visible actions of the priest imitated the invisible acts of the Spirit. So, too, in the Eucharist, no priestly offices were valid unless Christ, the true Pon-

---

(189) *Ep.* 18. *P. L.,* CXXVI, col. 109. *De una et non trina Deitate, P. L.,* CXXV, col. 555.

(190) *Ep.* 18. *P. L.,* CXXVI, col. 105.

(191) *De praedestinatione, diss. post.,* c. 35. *P. L.,* CXXV, col. 374 ff.

(192) *Ep.* 18. *P. L.,* CXXVI, coll. 105-107.

(193) *Vita Remigii,* c. 15. *M. G. H., SS. Rer, Mer.,* III, p. 300. The same citation occurs in *de cavendis vitiis,* c. 6. *P. L.,* CXXV, 903.

tiff, with all the properties of human nature, acted through them, reconciling men to God [194]. By this mimetic relation, God converted the bread and wine of the Eucharist into the Body and Blood of Christ. By consuming the elements, believers passed over into the flesh of Him who was made their flesh [195]. Through mimesis, the invisible elements of the sacrament – attended, as in heaven by choirs of angels – became one with the visible [196], and the participants in Christ's Body, becoming incorporate Him, were made the sacrifice that He was [197].

Hincmar was able to write of the baptismal font as the Church's immaculate womb [198], whence she delivered all the reborn into one and the same infancy [199]. He read a far more complex set of cross-references into the altar, retaining the same procreative associations. When he contemplated the altar, Hincmar saw it as Christ's very Incarnation and sacrifice [200], but he also identified it with repositories of Christ's human body: the womb of the Mother of God, the sepulchre [201], and that other tabernacle, the body of each believer [202].

---

(194) *Ep.* 26. *P. L.*, CXXVI, col. 172; *de cavendis vitiis*, c. 10, *P. L.*, CXXV, col. 928. *Vita Remigii*, c. 7, *M. G. H.*, *SS. Rer. Mer.*, III, p. 278.

(195) *De cavendis vitiis*, c. 10. *P. L.*, CXXV, coll. 925-927.

(196) *De cavendis vitiis*, c. 6. *P. L.*, CXXV, col. 903. *Vita Remigii*, c. 15. *M. G. H.*, *SS. Rer. Mer.*, III, p. 229.

(197) *De cavendis vitiis*, cc. 7, 9. *P. L.*, CXXV, coll. 910, 916. Cf. *Vita Remigii*, c. 31. *M. G. H.*, *SS. Rer. Mer.*, III, p. 333 f.

(198) *P. L.*, CXXVI, 519.

(199) *Ep.* 10. *P. L.*, CXXVI, 75.

(200) *De cavendis vitiis*, c. 8. *P. L.*, CXXV, col. 912 f. *De ecclesiis et capellis*, Gundlach ed., p. 105. From his patristic sources, Hincmar also was able to identify the cross with baptism and the sepulchre, thus linking the symbolism of womb and tomb. *De divortio, responsio* 6, *P. L.*, CXXV, col. 667.

(201) *De cavendis vitiis*, cc. 6, 8. *P. L.*, CXXV, 904 f, 913 f. *De praedestinatione, diss. post.*, c. 25. *P. L.*, CXXV, col. 229 f.

(202) *De cavendis vitiis*, c. 8. *P. L.*, CXXV, col. 914. See also the *Explanatio in Ferculum Salomonis*, *P. L.*, CXXV, col. 817, for an inventory of related metaphors.

632

Clearly, this network of associations also included the final repository of Christ's body, the celestial tabernacle not made by hands. But, like the rationales of healing and participation that they encompassed, the mimetic analogies were clouded with ambiguity. For the Church, that great ' building of God ', was partly above and partly on earth, yearning for its heavenly fellowship [203]. The procreation of Christ's members from the womb of the Church – so easily identified with the act by which the Trinity ' constructed ' his earthly flesh in the Virgin's body [204] – had not ceased. The incarnation of Christ in His members was still in process in the womb of the Church. The image was not yet at one with its celestial archetype, and this disjunction intruded the familiar need for criticism and correction into Hincmar's thought from yet another point. The source of that need, which we must now face squarely, was historical incompleteness. It was this that plagued all three rationales with practical ambiguities; for while the present life was as night by comparison with the resplendent age that was to come [205], still, the glory of the coming world took form in the dense shadows of this mortal, passing life. The resulting tensions could never be dispelled by objective evidence and proof; but they could be transcended by faith.

* * *

Hincmar's view of the past was Augustinian. Augustine used the concept of mimesis to portray a singularly complicated pattern. At first glance, that pattern might

---

(203) *LV Cap.*, c. 11. *P. L.*, CXXXVI, col. 325.
(204) Cf *de una et non trina Deitate*, *P. L.*, CXXV, col. 552 f.
(205) *De divortio, responsio* 1. *P. L.*, CXXV, col. 633.

appear to be rigorously symmetrical. Christ, the true mediator, the mediator of life, stood on the one side. Satan, the false mediator, the mediator of death, stood on the other. The sons of each were begotten by imitation into two, counterpoised cities. And yet, what appeared to be the bilateral symmetry of opposites turned out to be real unity. For the pride that motivated Satan, and thus his offspring, was, in fact, a perverse imitation of God. Instead of dualism, Augustine saw a pattern in which one archetype was imitated in two ways. However, there was a further complexity. Only one imitation engendered form. The followers, or imitators, of Christ were reformed into the image of God, while those of Satan were engulfed in formless confusion. Therefore, only in the City of God did events signify something beyond their own temporal present. Those in the city of man signified nothing beyond themselves. Only the City of God had a history, and that was incomplete, still unfolding in the lives of men.

Writing history in the Augustinian mode therefore meant keeping three elements straight: the thing signified, the sign, and the interpreter of the sign. Creating or reading a sign was an exercise in setting forth a likeness in dissimilar things, and, thus, in analogy and mimesis. It was essential, however, that the sign be true, unlike self-deceptive illusions or the false visions cast up by demons.

Interestingly, Hincmar did not perform the exercise in signification when he recorded the events of his time in the *Annales Bertiniani*. They had continuity without significance. There are other instances of this approach, when he recognized the continuity of magical lore from Assyria and Babylon until his own day, when he argued that the heresies of his time repeated those that appeared in the patristic era, when he wrote about pagans, and when he meditated on the instability of kingly power, even among Christians, as kingdoms rose, splintered, and fell.

Hincmar did perform the exercise of signification repeatedly in discussions of events described in Scripture and also in expounding on the lives and texts of exemplary Christians, such as St. Remigius. It was in the atmosphere of holiness that unity existed and grew through signification; for, by understanding the sign, one passed beyond it to the thing signified. To signify was therefore to mediate; to read the sign correctly was to complete the circuit of mediation and thus to become one in action (*operatio*) with the sign and the thing signified. Hincmar paid considerable attention to non-signifying events in the *Annales Bertiniani* and elsewhere, for he recognized in them a didactic and precedential force essential to social order. But he read the unfolding pattern in human experience through signifying events, in which unity expanded as it passed from faith to faith.

Augustine supposed that the course of events reproduced a pattern that was already complete before the eyes of God. We have already referred to two metaphors with which he illustrated this idea. The first is the metaphor of history as a poem in which good and evil were deployed as antitheses for the beauty of the composition. We are now concerned with the other Augustinian metaphor, one emphasizing more explicitly the disequilibrium between image and archetype: that of a garment taking shape on the loom.

Hincmar accepted the tunic of Christ as symbolizing the Church. Its four equal parts, he wrote, represented the dissemination of the Church, in concord, throughout the four quarters of the earth. Its wholeness represented the unanimity produced by the bond of charity; the fact that it was woven from top to bottom, the superiority of charity to knowledge [206]. And yet, the tunic was faith [207], not the clear and unmediated vision of God that heaven afforded. The Pauline and Augustinian dichotomy – faith in this world, sight in the next – operated in Hincmar's statement that the tunic was woven together by the labors of the Fathers [208], including the comparatively recent Bede [209], and perhaps Alcuin and Paulinus of Aquileia[210]. While the unity of faith was preserved, spiritual understanding changed. Charity being superior to knowledge, some doctrines remained as they were laid down, while others shifted over time, or were entirely abolished. Likewise, canons varied according to the needs of the time, although the same Spirit inspired them [211]. The whole Church over the centuries, and regional churches at any particular time, were diverse in customs, while one in faith [212].

As faith, the tunic belonged to a heaven and earth that were both transitory and permanent, to an existence that would pass away in its figural aspects and abide forever in its true essence [213].

Like Augustine, Hincmar attempted to reconcile the ambiguities of permanence and change in history, and

---

(206) *De praedestinatione, diss. post.,* c. 38, *epilogi* c. 1. *P. L.,* CXXV, col. 418 f. *De regis persona,* c. 25. *P. L.,* CXXV, col. 850. YVES MARIE-JOSEPH CONGAR, ' Structures et régime de l'Eglise d'après Hincmar de Reims', *Communio. Commentarii Internationales de Ecclesia et Theologia,* I (1968), p. 7. The reference to the tunic, in *de regis persona,* is taken from Pseudo-Cyprian's *De XII, Abusivis Saeculi,* c. 11, a crucial text for Hincmar in its emphasis on penitential correction, and hence on change. See below, p. 677.

(207) *Ep.* 1. *P. L.,* CXXVI, col. 13.

(208) *De praedestinatione, diss. post.,* c. 22. *P. L.,* CXXV, col. 205.

(209) Ibid., c. 34, coll. 351-353.

(210) *Ep. ad Carolum Calvum de praedestinatione, P. L..,* CXXV, col. 54.

(211) *LV Cap.,* c. 20. *P. L.,* CXXVI, col. 353 f.

(212) *Ep.* 18. *P. L.,* CXXVI, col. 108.

(213) *De divortio, responsio* 6. *P. L.,* CXXV, col. 663 f.

636

found himself caught in the quandaries of predestination and evil. On the one hand, he was convinced that God worked through the ministry of men and angels, disposing events according to the times, and providing what was needful for individual eras, or persons, by hidden inspiration, by more open illumination, or by full revelation [214]. God either determined or permitted everything that took place [215]. This was emphatically true of the Church. Whatever occurred in prayers and in the mysteries of the Church happened by God's predestination, since it was by the preparation of grace, operating through the sacraments, that the elect approached the eternal life predestined for them [216].

Difficult questions arose. If God wished all men to be saved, as Scripture affirmed, why did He not give the same knowledge of truth to the whole world at the same time, and why, over the course of centuries, did perplexing irregularities occur in the vocation of the Jews [217] ? Even within the Church, evil took place, raising the quandary that, while Jesus suffered for all, all were not redeemed by the mystery of His Passion [218], and some, indeed, were spiritually destroyed by the sacraments.

To be sure, Hincmar was not at a loss for answers. Being free of necessity was part of man's image-likeness to God that was not lost in Adam's fall [219]. Therefore, the nature that God had made remained free and good, though man might abuse it. The nature, which came from God, was good; the action (*operatio*), which came

---

(214) *LV Cap.*, c. 11. *P. L.*, CXXXVI, 325.

(215) *De divortio, quaestio 6 responsio. P. L.*, CXXV, col. 758.

(216) *De praedestinatione, diss. post.*, c. 22. *P. L.*, CXXV, col. 197 f.

(217) *Ibid.*, cc. 25, 33. *P. L.*, CXXV, coll. 257 f, 335 f.

(218) *Ibid.*, c. 34. *P. L.*, CXXV, col. 349.

(219) *Ibid.*, c. 38, *epilogi* c. 5. *P. L.*, CXXV, col. 449.

from man, might be evil [220]. Therefore, God was not
responsible for evil, nor did he predestine men to do evil,
for which they would be punished. But He did use evil
to achieve his broad design, and to prove the good by
the increase of heresy [221].

Thus, while Hincmar emphasized the instability,
changefulness, and fragility of this world [222], he also detected a consistently developing pattern beneath the
variable surface; and, while he taught that God knowingly
ordained all things [223], he still left the human will free.

According to the pattern that he saw, history consisted of three ages: before the Law (the patriarchs of
the Old Testament), under the Law (Moses and the prophets), and under grace (from Christ and the apostles
onward) [224]. By these steps, the Church was moving
toward that last phase, when it would be ' as the full
moon forever ' [225]. Within this broad scheme, Hincmar
could regard events widely separated in time as being
one ' by the mystery of action ' [226], and he could also
concede a creative autonomy to the human will.

As he surveyed the long course of Church history,
Hincmar detected many decisive innovations by which
human choice added unanticipated motifs to the deve-

---

(220) *Ibid.*, c. 12. *P. L.*, CXXV, col. 120.   *De divortio, responsio* 16.
P. L., CXXV, 725 f.

(221) Cf. *de una et non trina Deitate*, *P. L.*, CXXV, col. 481 f.

(222) *LV Cap.*, c. 49. *P. L.*, CXXVI, 483.

(223) *P. L.*, CXXVI, 643 f.

(224) *Explanatio in Ferculum Salomonis*. *P. L.*, CXXV, col. 819. *LV
Cap.*, c. 20. *P. L.*, CXXVI, col. 354. The three ages are designated by
the *lex naturae*, the *lex litterae*, and the *lex evangelii*. Cf *LV Cap.*, c. 25. *P. L.*
CXXVI, col. 387, *ante legem, sub lege, sub gratia*. An exposition on Church
history occurs in the letter of the Synod of Touzy (860), *ep.* 21. *P. L.*, CXXVI,
col. 122 ff.

(225) *Ep.* 20, c. 9. *P. L.*, CXXVI, col. 120. Cf *LV Cap.*, c. 25. *P. L.*,
CXXVI, col. 387.

(226) *De divortio, responsio* 6. *P. L.*, CXXV, col. 664.

loping pattern. He thought of the replacement of Old Testament sanctions and practices by those of the New Testament [227]; he recalled the adoption of the Roman administrative hierarchy as a model for Church offices [228]. He recognized that, as spiritual physicians, bishops quite consistently brought forth medicines appropriate to the various diseases that afflicted the Church in different eras. While they always acted under the direction of the same Spirit [229], they had legislated in diverse ways for their own generations. Hincmar could acknowledge no contradictions among them; their ' fixed and changeless ' decrees could not be reconsidered or broken [230]. And yet, it was evident to Hincmar that, in the long corrective process of history, not all canons had the ageless validity of the ' mystic ' Council of Nicaea. Some of their decrees had fallen out of use and others had been altered. In fact, the canons themselves provided the very means by which innovations could be tested to see whether they were presumptuous novelties, or whether, in addressing new perplexities in new ways, they remained true to authentic canonical tradition [231].

The idea of indefinite, amorphous change repelled Hincmar. Such was the vigor of his mind, that he required the greatest possible degree of clarity, certainty, and stability in judgment [232]. But, being part of a work

(227) Ibid., *responsio* 12, col. 706.

(228) *LV Cap.*, c. 25. *P. L.*, CXXVI, 387.

(229) *De praedestinatione, diss. post.*, c. 37. *P. L.*, CXXV, col. 413.

(230) *LV Cap.*, cc. 25, 34, 36. *P. L.*, CXXVI, 385 f, 419, 428.

(231) On variations in ecclesiastical law, *LV Cap.*, cc. 20, 21, 25. *P. L.*, CXXVI, 353 f, 365, 385 f. On the parallel variations in civil law, *LV Cap.*, c. 20. *P. L.*, CXXVI, col. 355. On tests of innovation, *epistola ad Carolum Calvum de praedestinatione*, *M. G. H., Epp.* VIII, *K. A.* VI, no. 131 b, p. 70 f. *P. L.*, CXXVI, 528, 550.

(232) *LV Cap.*, c. 25. *P. L.*, CXXVI, col. 385: ' sed et a consuetudine quam catholica ecclesia habuit, ex quo in sacrum Nicaenum concilium patres nostri convenerunt, qui adhuc, sicut Leo dicit, nobiscum in suis constitutio-

in progress – a song being sung, or a garment taking
shape on a loom – intruded uncertainty upon him.
What he wrote in one crisis could apply to his general
view of history. Amidst the turmoil of events, he found
himself between the hammer and the anvil, he wrote,
and, in such a position, metal was either shattered or
formod. Ho aopirod to bo ohapod, ao woro tho oilvor
trumpets described in the book of *Numbers*, the trumpets
by which the people were summoned to the worship of
God and aroused to battle. How could this be achieved?
' Remember them that had rule over you, who spoke
the word of God to you, and, considering the outcome
of their life, imitate their faith ' (*Hebrews* 13:7). On the
anvil of events, Hincmar would be shaped and not broken if he walked in the footsteps of his predecessors [233].
Doing so, however, required inventiveness; it invited
uncertainty and conflict. As they explored the inner
rocesses of bolicf, the Fathers differed among themselves,
and changed their minds [234]. Among the Fathers, controversy with heretics had been, and, in the ninth century,
it remained, a major impulse for the review and clarification of doctrine. During the process of dispute, solu-
tions to very different questions were discovered, and enduring doctrinos – on tho Trinity, on ponanco, on baptiom,
on the natures of Christ – were perfected [235].

As a controversialist, Hincmar rejoiced in the idea
that truth was like fire; the more it was stirred up, the

nibus vivunt, perniciosissime discedemus, et nihil certi tenentes in sectam
Genethliacianorum, id est mathematicorum, offendemus, qui diffinierunt omnia
in incertum '.

(233) *De fide Carolo servanda*, cc. 8, 13. *P. L.*, CXXV, coll. 965, 967. Hincmar applied this verse to himself again in his controversy with Hincmar of
Laon (*LV Cap.*, *praef.*, *P. L.*, CXXVI, col. 291). Cf. his concept of the Church
' fidei imitatione progenita ' (ibid., c. 15; col. 328).

(234) *De praedestinatione, diss. post.*, c. 3. *P. L.*, CXXV, col. 86 f.

(235) *De una et non trina Deitate*, *P. L.*, CXXV, col. 481 f.

640

more brilliantly it shone [236]. His readiness for battle
sprang from this view of mimetic development through
conflict. The same intricate network of convictions prompted him to write to Popes Nicholas I and Hadrian II,
wishing that God would preserve them ' for the doctrine
and the correction of His holy Church ' [237]. But his pious
wish merely emphasized the discrepancy between the
knowledge accessible to the eyes of faithful men and the
eternal present before the eyes of God, where the things
that were to come had already been created, and there
was no sequence of times [238].

As we said, imitation was the most comprehensive
of the three corrective rationales, it included both healing
and participation. Evidently, imitation of faith transcended the historical ambiguities that flawed all the
rationales. Imitation of holy predecessors in the faith
prompted Hincmar's doctrines about a bishop's corrective functions; but that imitation itself derived
from prior doctrines concerning the object of faith, the
Incarnation of Christ, the supreme paradigm and mediator. To imitate the faith of holy predecessors was,
ultimately, to imitate Christ. This leads us back to the
center of Hincmar's thought about mimetic correction:
the Incarnation.

The Incarnation had two aspects, summed up in the
portrayal of the Virgin as the handmaid of her Son by
virtue of His divinity, and as the mother of the Lord,

(236) *Ep.* 23. *P. L.*, CXXVI, col. 154.
(237) *Epp.* 7, 11. *P. L.*, CXXVI, coll. 64, 89 (to Nicholas I). *Ep.* 27. *P. L.*,
CXXVI, col. 186 (to Hadrian II). Charles the Bald's personal subscription
follows the same formula, but interestingly differs by omitting the reference
' ad doctrinam et correctionem sanctae suae [i. e., Dei] ecclesiae ', replacing
it with ' ad honorem et salvationem atque exaltationem sanctae suae ecclesiae... ' *Epp.* 7, 8, 9. *P. L.*, CXXIV, 881, 896.
(238) *De praedestinatione, diss. post.*, c. 12. *P. L.*, CXXV, col. 116 f.

by virtue of His carnality [239]. The first aspect – the manifestation of God – brought into play an elaborate scheme of mimetic associations, by which Hincmar explained the reformation of man according to the image of God, and thus, also, the historical development of the Church. All this hinged on the second aspect – the carnality of Christ; for, before Christ could mediate the tensions between image and archetype, others had to mediate the carnality of man to Him. It was only in the flesh that He died, and only in the flesh that He rose from the dead [240]; it was through the flesh that believers were in Him and He, in them [241].

Hincmar adhered to a dominant strand in patristic thought when he insisted that mimetic mediation – through the sacraments and the slow, historical development of the Church – did lead to an ultimate unity, but a unity in which (as in compound numbers) individuals retained their integrity. He also taught that, while mimetic mediation (and sacramental unity) was complete in itself, yet, in the experience of individual persons, it varied. Hincmar's doctrine of free will was basic to his concept of gradual unification. It was essential, he argued, that each man choose to imitate Christ or the devil. This vital element of rational choice was at the heart of the motif of correction – and hence of the medical and artistic analogues – that ran so powerfully through all the writings of his long career. Just as it was essential that Christ, as rational victim, be offered for the redemption of man, so it was also essential that man's likeness to God be perfected in his intellectual vision, and in his freedom from necessity. Because of God's grace, the world

(239) *Explanatio in Ferculum Salomonis.* P. L., CXXV, col. 824.
(240) *Loc. cit.*
(241) *Vita Remigii,* c. 31. *M.G.H., SS. Rer. Mer.* III, p. 334.

was to be saved; because of man's free will, the world was to be judged [242]. Medicine and the other arts exemplified how reason, sustained by grace, could be employed to correct the imperfect image, to purge it of its impurities, and to bring it at last into conformity with the Image of the invisible God.

The controversies of the patristic age demonstrated that it was possible to emphasize Christ's mediation of divinity to man so greatly as to discount man's mediation of carnality to Christ. But Hincmar's doctrine of mimesis kept him from so doing. It was in His full humanity that Christ took on the form of a servant – that is, of man –, and thus became the mediator for men, rather than for illusory spiritual beings, such as demons. The efficacy of the sacraments as acts by which the believer was mimetically assimilated to Christ depended upon the veracity of His flesh. Therefore, the mediation of humanity to Christ was central to Hincmar's thinking about the historical life of Christ, about the sacraments, and about the gradual expansion of the Church, the Body of Christ, through time.

We have already indicated that Hincmar identified the Virgin with bishops in their role as propagators of the body of Christ. Like the Virgin, bishops, through the flesh, mediated divinity to men and humanity to God, as they built up the body of Christ through the dynamic of their sacramental functions. Whether at the conception of Christ in the Virgin's womb, or in the continual birth of members of Christ's body through the womb of the Church, procreation of His flesh occurred by maternity. At the Creation, Eve received her flesh from Adam. At the conception, Christ received His flesh from Mary.

(242) *Ep.* 21. *P. L.*, CXXVI, col. 124.

Since Mary was the offspring of Adam, and since the
Church took her existence from Christ, what might appear
to be a reversal of sexual roles at the conception of Christ
actually formed an alternating male/female sequence
(Adam-Eve/Mary-Christ/Church), the *cantus firmus* of
all history. 'The whole body is man and woman, since
woman is part of man' [243]. In a moment of paradox,
Augustine had shifted Paul's delicate balance between
Adam and Christ to Eve and Mary. Thus, he was able to
adapt I. Cor. 15:21, declaring ' by woman came death,
by woman, life ' [244].

As we shall see in detail later on, the idea that the body
of Christ was the flesh of Mary figured prominently in
Hincmar's doctrine of salvation. For the moment, we
need only point out the Archbishop's stress on the doctrine
that to become the ' head, light, and model (*exemplum*)
of all the predestinate ', Christ was ' made of a woman ' [245].
This premise was sufficiently marked for Hincmar to
draw the Mother of God into all of his discussions of
Christ's death and resurrection, the sacraments, and the
progressive unification of the Church. It also pervaded
his conviction that, when their bodies were raised from

(243) *De divortio, responsio* 13. *P. L.*, CXXV, col. 710. On why Christ
is not the mediator of demons, see *de praedestinatione, diss. post.*, c. 26, *P. L.*,
CXXV, col. 278 f.

(244) JOSEPH VOGT, ' Ecce ancilla Domini. Eine Untersuchung zum so-
zialen Motiv des antiken Marienbildes ', *Vigiliae Christianae*, 23 (1969), p. 256.
In general, see BASILE STUDER, ' Consubstantialis Patri, consubstantialis
Matri. Une antithèse christologique chez Léon le Grand ', *Revue des études
Augustiniennes*, 18 (1972), pp. 87-115. On a later period, see CAROLINE W.
BYNUM, ' Jesus as Mother and Abbot as Mother: Some Themes in Twelfth-
Century Cistercian Writing ', *Harvard Theological Review*, LXX (1977), pp. 257-
284, and ' Feminine Names for God in Cistercian Writing: A Case Study in
the Relationship of Literary Language and Community Life ', *Proceedings
of York University Conference on Consciousness and Group Identification in
High Medieval Religion*, in press.

(245) *Ep.* 21. *P. L.*, CXXVI, col. 124.

644

the dead, and they gave account of their acts, as imitators of Christ, the blessed would gain a two-fold reward, a vision of the divine majesty, and the splendor of a glorified humanity [246].

Our three problematic rationales have led us to the theological bedrock on which Hincmar rested his mimetic analogies. His emphasis on wholeness in each of the two aspects of the Incarnation – mediation of divinity to man and of carnality to Christ – underlies his program of correction by the episcopal functions of healing, participation, and, most comprehensively, by imitation. We can now appreciate how intimate and deep-seated were the reasons that led Hincmar to follow a consistent pattern of thought through the major doctrinal controversies of his age, a pattern that led him to oppose Ratramnus of Corbie on every question [247]. Because his doctrine of carnality included assertions of man's inherent rationality and free will, he could not accept the doctrine of double predestination, and, indeed, he gave his opponents grounds for thinking that he exalted nature over grace. Because he insisted that the Trinity was absolute unity, and, consequently, that all persons of the Trinity performed every divine act – and that this was most crucially so when the Trinity 'constructed' the fleshly body of Christ in the Virgin's womb – he ferociously rejected doctrines that appeared to revive the Arian heresy, by preaching a three-fold God. Because Christ's conception was of grace, instead of nature, without the will of the flesh or of a man, and because it happened by virgin semen and blood, it did not deprive Mary of her virginity. Both mother and perpetual Vir-

(246) *Explanatio in Ferculum Salomonis. P. L.*, CXXV, col. 823.
(247) JEAN-PAUL BOUHOT, *Ratramne de Corbie. Histoire littéraire et controverses doctrinales* (Paris 1976), esp. pp. 12 f, 17 f, 44-47.

gin, Hincmar argued [248], she conceived and gave birth
with her flesh intact. Therefore, he opposed doctrines
that appeared to suggest that the birth of Christ was
like that of other men, requiring the ritual purification
of His Mother in the Temple. Because he was convinced
that the participation of Christ's body through the Eucharist must be complete, he repudiated doctrines denying
that Christ's historical body was identical with the Eucharistic elements. It was essential to the work of redemption, he held, that visible and invisible become one in
the Eucharist, both figure and reality.

The rationales of healing, participation, and imitation
first met us in regard to Hincmar's conception of the episcopal office; they then led us from the world of metaphor
to administration and law. Now, we have passed beyond
the rationales to the theological propositions on which
they rested. Recalling the inherent ambiguities of historical progression, we can press the analysis a step further. Read in the light of Hincmar's view of history,
the three problematic rationales give us a clue to his interior life. We are now in a position to consider how they
figured in a work of art that most poignantly expressed
the Archbishop's fragile integration of theory and practice: that is, his tomb.

* * *

Unification came by faith, particularly by imitating
the faith of predecessors in the Church. Hincmar's
tomb was a monument to the community that imitation
gradually formed over time, amidst, and in defiance of,
the transitory world. In the flower of youth, Hincmar

(248) *De divortio, responsio* 12. *P. L.*, CXXV, col. 694.

646

wrote, physical wellbeing and the world's delights could blind one to the brevity of life, and to the stark terror of the Last Judgment [249]. Avoiding this shortsightedness, Hincmar prepared his tomb [250]; but, in designing the tomb, he held fast to his dogmatic ambiguity that the transient and the eternal coincided in the flesh.

Hincmar's sarcophagus was actually one element in an architectural composition. It stood in a mortuary chapel, a crypt built by Hincmar in the monastery of St. Remigius, in Rheims. Early in his pontificate, Hincmar determined to translate the relics of Remigius from their old crypt to a ' larger and more beautiful ' one [251]. By 852, the new crypt had been completed. Eventually, if not from the start, Hincmar arranged for it to contain three sepulchres: those of Remigius, of Hincmar's predecessor Tilpin ' at the feet ' (ad pedes) of the Saint, and of Hincmar himself ' behind the tomb ' of Remigius [252].

By renewing the tomb of St. Remigius, Hincmar proclaimed in a most dramatic fashion the legitimacy of his own title as archbishop of Rheims. When the crypt was dedicated (852), the attempt to eject him and re-instate his predecessor, Ebo, had failed. Ebo himself had just died (851). But a case against Hincmar was

---

(249) *LV Cap.*, c. 54. *P. L.*, CXXVI, col. 493 f.

(250) One of the Archbishop's most frequently-mentioned charges against Hincmar of Laon was that, because of the interdict that he laid on his diocese, infants died without baptism, men died without the Eucharist, and Christian burial was denied them.

(251) *Vita Remigii, translatio*, c. 29. *M.G.H., SS. Rer. Mer.*, III, p. 325 f. The exact date of Hincmar's own tomb is hard to pin down. The tomb relief shows the completed cathedral of Rheims, which might suggest a date around 862, the year the building was consecrated. Hincmar refers in the *Vita Remigii* to his plans to be buried near the Saint (below, n. 339); but, since the general lines of the *Vita* were laid between 868 and 870 and the final redaction came ca. 877, (DEVISSE, *Hincmar, Archevêque*, II, pp. 1006, 1011), those references hardly suggest a precise date. In effect, Hincmar's tomb could have been prepared as early as 851/2, with the rest of the crypt.

(252) Flodoard, II, 17; III, 9, 30. *M. G. H., SS.* XIII, pp. 465, 482, 554.

still pending in the papal court, brought by clerics whom
Ebo had ordained during his brief restoration, and whose orders Hincmar refused to acknowledge. In 853, the
case was decided in Hincmar's favor (though continuing
litigation over this verdict led to its reversal by Pope
Nicholas I, more than a decade later). The Archbishop
had received the pallium in 851, and he may have anticipated a victory as he put the final touches to the crypt.
However, the danger was far from past.

As it took shape, the tomb complex was a study in
analogies. These were grounded, historically, in associations among the three men that both reinforced Hincmar's title and testified to his own achievements. To
justify is to correct. Looked at from the end of Hincmar's
career – say from the moment when he completed the
Vita Sancti Remigii (about 877)[253] – those associations
had so greatly accumulated that the tomb complex took
on the features of an essay in autobiography, dominated
by the theme of correction. Let us identify some of these
historical analogies.

What, bearing on the imitation of faith, did Remigius,
Tilpin, and Hincmar have in common? The obvious fact
was that they, and only they among the archbishops of
Rheims, had received the pallium. Eventually, Hincmar
exceeded his predecessors by receiving from two popes
the privilege of wearing the pallium[254], the sign of authority to share in the ministry of the Roman see itself, enforcing the rules of the Fathers and decrees of synods,

(253) See the very extensive discussion in DEVISSE, *Hincmar, Archevêque*,
II, p. 1008 ff. On the general relation between Carolingian reforms and the
veneration of relics, Geary, *Furta Sacra*, pp. 40 ff.

(254) *LV Cap.*, c. 16. *P. L.*, CXXVI, col. 339. On the question of pri-
matial rights under Remigius and Tilpin, as Hincmar wished to present them,
see DEVISSE, *Hincmar, Archevêque*, II, p. 651 ff, and p. 657 ff on the vexed
issue of whether Hincmar forged the texts that gave his argument historical
weight.

648

settling disputes according to the ' sacred law ', and having authority to call a ' universal council ' on a matter
of religion. This exceptional bond with Rome, ' mother
and mistress of all churches ' [255], most plainly defined our
group of three. Indeed, Hincmar's reception of the pallium early in 851 after such ferocious challenges to the
legitimacy of his title, established a vital association
between Hincmar and his sainted predecessor.

More broadly, of course, the three men shared succession to the see of Rheims, established by a bishop
acting under papal authority, and perhaps under commission from St. Peter himself [256], a see that was adorned,
moreover, by the merits of martyrs, including Bishop
Nicasius, who first built a cathedral dedicated to the
Virgin. To Hincmar under fire, in 852, the exceptionally
long pontificates of Remigius (67 years) and Tilpin (' forty
years and more ', as Hincmar wrote in an epitaph) must
have given some comfort. Looking backward, in 877,
Hincmar could draw a parallel with his own rule, which
eventually ran for almost 38 years.

The point, however, was that all three pontiffs, suc-
ceding after periods of decline, restored the temporal and
spiritual vigor of their see, having been prepared for the
task by education and skill in the literary arts [257]. In

(255) *De praedestinatione*, cc. 24, 38 *epilogi* 3. *P. L.*, CXXV, coll. 211 f,
434. *Vita Remigii*, c. 20. *M. G. H.*, *SS. Rer. Mer.*, III, p. 312, the (alleged)
letter of Pope Hormisdas to Remigius.

(256) Hincmar wrote that Pope Sixtus sent St. Sixtus to the metropolis
of Rheims as its first bishop. *LV Cap.*, c. 16. *P. L.*, CXXVI, col. 334. Flodoard claimed that St. Peter ordained Sixtus as bishop and sent him to Gaul
with two companions. I, 3. *M. G. H.*, *SS.* XIII, p. 414. On a related theme,
see G. H. TAVARD, « Episcopacy and Apostolic Succession according to Hincmar of Rheims », *Theological Studies*, XXXIV (1973), pp. 594-623.

(257) Hincmar mentioned Remigius' literary education in *Vita Remigii*,
c. 2. *M.G.H.*, *SS. Rer. Mer.*, III, p. 262 f. Flodoard refers to codices of the
Scriptures that Tilpin provided, and that were still in use. Hincmar no doubt
was familiar with them monuments to his predecessor's literary taste. Flodoard,
II, 17. *M.G.H.*, *SS.* XIII, p. 464.

doing so, they fought against idolatry, whether the actual
worship of graven images encountered by Remigius, or
the ' abuses ' of sacred art encountered by Tilpin and
Hincmar in the Iconoclastic Dispute, or the yet more
insidious forms of spiritual idolatry to which Hincmar
was so alert.

Not surprisingly, therefore, Hincmar sensed further
analogues between himself and his two predecessors, both
in the exercise of authority on a grand scale, and in the
intimate depths of spirituality. When he crowned Charles the Bald in Metz (869), he took occasion to draw parallels between that event and the anointing of Clovis
by St. Remigius, on the one hand, and, on the other,
the coronation of Louis the Pious at Rheims (816) and
his restoration at St. Denis (834). He did not mention
the ceremony that instituted the Carolingian dynasty –
Pope Stephen III's anointing of Pippin the Short and
his sons at St. Denis (754) – though, as a disciple and collaborator of Hilduin, he undoubtedly knew the description
of this momentous act, and the Pope's blessing on the Carolingian dynasty, both of which are included in Hilduin's
dossier on the Areopagite [258]. Hincmar might have legitimately assumed that, as a former monk of St. Denis and
archbishop of Rheims, Tilpin participated in the ritual.

As to spirituality, one line of analogy ran between
the solitary life in which Remigius first ' served the Lord ',
and the austerities that he continued to practice after
becoming bishop [259], and the monastic discipline under
which both Tilpin and Hincmar had lived at St. Denis,
which Tilpin had instituted at St. Remi, and which he and
Hincmar imposed as abbots of St. Remi. There was, mo-

(258) *M. G. H.*, *SS.* XV, p. 2 f.
(259) *Vita Remigii*, cc. 2, 4. *M.G.H.*, *SS. Rer. Mer.*, III, pp. 263, 265.

650

reover, a common devotion to the Virgin. All three men had grown to adulthood before altars dedicated to the Virgin; they also presided in a cathedral consecrated to her [260]. Hincmar particularly emphasized Remigius' reverence for Mary before the conversion of Clovis, for example [261], and, since the main altar at St. Denis was consecrated to the Virgin, as was his own cathedral, Hincmar could easily have assumed a kindred devotion in Tilpin [262].

And so it was appropriate that the three bishops await the same resurrection in one place; for, while they lived in diverse times, they had been one in faith.

The tomb complex carried a double message. The first applied to the place of Remigius and his successors in the world; for the crypt was certainly a monument to the corrective power that the archbishops had exercised over others. The network of historical analogies taught the moral of obedience to the successors in whom Remigius still presided [263]. Through his miracles, Remigius, indeed, was a living reality in the tomb [264], preaching the lesson that Christ taught to His disciples, ' Who hears you, hears me ', and demonstrating for all to see that Christ could remove the folly of disobedience from the hearts of men as He had commanded that the stone be removed from the tomb of Lazarus [265].

---

(260) Remigius grew up in Laon, where the cathedral was dedicated to the Virgin (*Vita Remigii*, c. 16, *M. G. H.*, *SS. Rer. Mer.*, III, p. 300), and the main altar at the monastery of St. Denis, where Tilpin and Hincmar grew up, had the same dedication (Panofsky, *Suger*, pp. 60, 179).

(261) *Vita Remigii*, cc. 14, 16. *M.G.H.*, *SS. Rer. Mer.*, III, pp. 295, 303.

(262) On Tilpin, see *Gallia Christiana* (n. s.), IX, pp. 28-32, 220 f, 225 f. Devisse, *Hincmar, Archevêque*, II, p. 910, Tilpin began the reconstruction of the basilica of St. Timothy and St. Apollinaris, another point of analogy with Hincmar as builder.

(263) Below, n. 331.

(264) *Vita Remigii*, c. 31, *M. G. H.*, *SS. Rer. Mer.*, III, p. 332.

(265) *De divortio, praef. M. G. H.*, *Epp.* VIII, K. A., VI, no. 134, p. 80.

The Archbishop therefore lavished his treasure on this shrine. He constructed a new sarcophagus of silver, large enough to hold the still intact body of St. Remigius, and rested it upon the marble chest that had earlier held the corpse. In front of the tomb proper, he erected a screen of gold, set with gems and pierced by an aperture through which the sarcophagus could be seen. Nor was this all. Hincmar supplied the tomb with a large cross in gold and jewels, and with books of the greatest magnificence – a Gospel written in letters of gold and bound in gem–encrusted plates of gold, a sacramentary bound in silver, with ivory plaques, and a lectionary similarly adorned, together with other books and ornaments [266]. As a last flourish, Hincmar decorated each of the three tombs with metrical compositions, epitaphs from his own pen.

With regard to the externals of power, therefore, the tomb complex was important to Hincmar because, according to rules of evidence, it might just possibly cut through the mists of analogy, yielding the divine judgments and miraculous signs that human reason accepted as direct proof [267].

But the archbishops' power derived from their faith. Side-by-side with the message of Rheims' dominance there

(266) Flodoard, III, 9, *M. G. H.*, *SS.* XIII, p. 482, Cf. *Vita Wigberti*, c. 25. *M. G. H.*, *SS.* XV, p. 43: « Atque Lullus, annuente Magno Karlo monumentum illius quo more per Gallias Germaniamque ceterorum sanctorum visuntur, auro et argento necnon reliquis congruentibus metallis exornandum curavit et id opus ad Idus Augusti complevit ». The crypt was large enough to accomodate a solemn mass, celebrated by the Archbishop, on the feast of St. Remigius. *Ep.* 15, *P. L.*, CXXVI, 97, Another indication of size is the fact that, under Archbishop Fulco (883-900), the relics of St. Gibrianus were buried, first, beside the tomb of Remigius, and, later, at the right side of the church, near the door of the crypt. A new altar, clad in silver, was erected there as the center of a secondary cluster of burials. Flodoard, IV, 9. *M. G. H.*, *SS.* XIII, p. 574.

(267) *De divortio, responsio* 6, *P. L.*, CXXV, col. 665 f.

runs a second message of high spirituality, of ascetic discipline and steadfastness through conflict, suffering, and death.

We have stressed the role of humility in Hincmar's mimetic doctrines of correction. The tomb complex proclaimed this sovereign virtue, with its imperative self-criticism, as a safeguard of faith.

In the magnificent flash and glitter of the crypt, Hincmar gave visible expression to his belief that the saints would rise from the dead with no taint of sin in their bodies, because, in this life ' they had built precious works upon the foundation, which is Christ – gold, silver, and precious stones: that is, a luminous understanding of the faith and a clear avowal of salvation '. With wholeness of faith, they had kept the precepts of Christ's love, and they would pass unharmed through the flames of judgment [268]. Indeed, while it memorialized the corrective acts of bishops, the tomb crypt also extravagantly proclaimed the ascetic corrective of life through penance, as, with weeping and fear, the heart prepared itself to stand before the eternal Judge [269]. Hincmar remained true to the monastic ethos in affirming penitential exercises as a means to salvation. The motif of tears, which recurs in his writings, stands out especially in his life of St. Remigius. Not only did Remigius wear down his bones with continual fasts [270]; he also set a pattern for others to follow in fasts, vigils, alms-giving, prayers, and tears, and in casting themselves down with lamentation before the Lord who made them [271]. Like the Saint, they should rise before the dawn – that is,

(268) *Vita Remigii*, c. 9. *M. G. H.*, *SS. Rer. Mer.*, **III.** p. 287.
(269) Ibid., c. 9, p. 288.
(270) Ibid., c. 4, p. 265.
(271) Ibid., c. 5, pp. 268, 270.

before the splendor of eternal retribution rose over the earth – and eat the bread of grief in the darkness of this present life, assured that the soul was refreshed by tears [272].

Even the number of verses that Hincmar wrote for the tomb complex testifies to this ascetic motif. They total 60. (The Archbishop wrote an epitaph of 10 verses for Tilpin, another 14 verses for himself, and two compositions for Remigius, the shorter consisting of 4 verses, the longer, of 32, in two stanzas of equal length. The individual compositions are built around the numbers, 2, 3, 4, 5, 7, and 10, representing unities of theology, cosmos, and history, as elucidated in Hincmar's *Explanatio in Ferculum Salomonis*). Hincmar's practice of keying the number of verses in metrical compositions to symbolic meaning provides the clue. The number 60, as Hincmar wrote, includes the number 10, consecrated by the Decalogue. Indeed, 60 completes, with 10, the number 50, which represents the Jubilee year: i. e., the remission of sins, the return to the inheritance of the heavenly country, and eternal rest, prophesised in the Old Testament and preached more clearly in the New. But this was not all. Remembering that 60 was twice 30, Hincmar somehow drew in the metaphor of marriage, which he combined with the parable of the sower. By the marital kiss or the hands of the sower, the seed was scattered. Nourished by good works, it brought forth much fruit, to some thirty, to some sixty, and to some a hundred-fold. And thus, among the redeemed, he who sowed in tears would reap in joy [273].

Why then, did Hincmar not compose a full hundred verses for himself and his predecessors? It was a matter

---

(272) Ibid., c. 23, p. 317.
(273) *Explanatio in Ferculum Salomonis*, *P. L.*, CXXV, col. 825.

of scale; elsewhere, he had devoted 100 verses to the Mother of God [274].

The tomb complex, therefore, proclaimed the virtue of humility. The career of Remigius gave Hincmar proof that humility should be exercised in works of power, in corrective acts of healing, participation, and imitation.

Remigius' corrective work as ' a physician from heaven ' [275] began before his birth. Like Isaac and John the Baptist, he was conceived by a long-sterile couple, a woman past child-bearing and a man, ' frigid in his aging body ' and entirely lacking in impulses of passion [276]. Afterwards, the venerable monk, Montanus, who had foretold his birth, was healed of blindness when his eyes were wiped with milk from Remigius' mother's breast [277]. Hincmar recorded with obvious satisfaction the miraculous cures, and the one resuscitation from the dead, that punctuated the Saint's life. His account also included posthumous cures, notably a spectacular end to chronic toothache that took place on the very day when Hincmar solemnly translated Remigius' body to the new crypt [278], to the tomb where Remigius still lived in miracles, restoring sight to the blind, and freeing the possessed from demons [279].

Proofs of the two rationales – healing and participation – coincided. As a spiritual physician, Remigius addressed himself to blindness of mind; and, in this task of mediation, his own direct participation in the uncircumscribed light of God was vital. As we said, the theory that sight occurred by intromission made it possible to

(274) *M.G.H.*, *SS. Poet. Lat.*, III, pp. 410-412.
(275) *Vita Remigii*, c. 4. *M.G.H.*, *SS. Rer. Mer.*, III, p. 265.
(276) Ibid., c. 1, p. 260.
(277) Ibid., c. 1, p. 260 f.
(278) Ibid., c. 9, p. 286.
(279) Ibid., cc. 29, 31, pp. 326, 332.

argue that, in some fashion, one became the light that one saw.

Hincmar's own fascination with light betrays itself in many ways – in his partiality to various hymns of St. Ambrose, in the provision of glass windows for his new cathedral, in the lavish use of gold and silver, with their highly reflective surfaces. It was quite natural that he found additional proof of his corrective rationales, by way of light, in Remigius' career.

When the Saint was elected as bishop, a beam of light suddenly struck his head, as bright as though the sun itself had fallen upon him. Thus, Hincmar remarked, it was understood that, inwardly anointed by the Holy Spirit, Remigius was the lamp that would give light to future Christians [280]. Again, at the conversion of Clovis, the entire church was irradiated, as though with the light of the sun. As Remigius instructed the king and others, a great splendor issued from the Saint himself, striking the onlookers with fear, and yet illuminating their hearts to receive from him the grace of the Gospel [281].

Finally, Remigius' career vindicated the corrective rationale of imitation. Evidence of his power as the ' express image of holiness ' came in his mercy toward the good and in his severity toward the wayward [282]. The most convincing evidence of all was the conversion of the

(280) Ibid., c. 3, p. 263 f. Cf. *LV Cap.*, c. 53, *P. L.*, CXXVI, col. 492, bishops are seen to be the light of the world, lamps placed upon a stand to enlighten all who are in the house of the Lord. As exemplars, kings are like lamps set on a stand. Synod of Quierzy to Louis the German (858). *M. G. H.*, *Cap. Reg. Fr.*, II, no. 297, c. 11, p. 435.

(281) *Vita Remigii*, c. 14. *M.G.H.*, *SS. Rer. Mer.*, III, p. 295 f. Cf ibid., c. 11, p. 292. Even the blindness that afflicted Remigius in his extreme old age proved to be a sign of grace. Having lost the light of his bodily eyes, Remigius was able to contemplate heavenly things all the more intently with the eyes of his mind. God restored his physical vision shortly before he died, as a pledge of eternal light. Ibid., c. 23, p. 318 f.

(282) Ibid., c. 3, p. 264.

Franks, and the submission of their king to anointing by the Saint. Hincmar was able to regard the baptismal unction as somehow a blessing on Clovis' reign, and, thus, an analogue, or even a precedent, of the coronation ritual [283]. At any rate, through the mimetic act of baptism, Clovis was ' reborn from the immaculate womb ' of the ' Mother Church ', just as ' the Lord, our God, was born of the glorious, ever virgin, Mary, our Lady '. So reborn, he was incorporated in Christ [284]. Remigius imitated the Lord, and, in imitating Remigius, his spiritual sons imitated Christ [285], whose members they thereby became.

The fate of the disobedient gave Hincmar further proof, evidence that also expressed the affinity of imitation and procreation. There was an area, he wrote, a village (Sault-les-Rethel) whose peasants defiantly burned their harvest, rather than giving St. Remigius his rightful share. Remigius cursed them. The men were to be afflicted with hernias. Since the woman lacked genitals that could be visibly afflicted, they would be plagued with goiters. These maladies were to be congenital, and Hincmar recorded that, even though the village had been dispersed under Charlemagne, some of its residents had returned to the site and, as anyone could see, their descendants still carried the burden of Remigius' curse [286].

The cursed village brings us to another level of proof. Remigius exercised his corrective functions against opposition. Apart from disobedient peasants, he struggled against the idolatry of the Franks; he brought a culpable bishop of Laon to heel; he struck an Arian heretic dumb

---

(283) See the verse in the epitaph that Hincmar wrote for Remigius, "Sicambrae gentis regia sceptra sacrans ", in *M.G.H.*, *Poet. Lat.*, III, p. 413, 1. 12.
(284) *Vita Remigii*, c. 5. *M.G.H.*, *SS. Rer. Mer.*, III, p. 267.
(285) Ibid., c. 9, p. 289 f.
(286) Ibid., c. 22, p. 315.

in the midst of a synod (and later restored his speech).
Even the pallium that he received from Pope Hormisdas
did not free him from the torments that he suffered from
the flesh, the devil, and wicked men. Patiently bearing
them, Hincmar wrote, he won the palm of martyrdom
through inner sufferings, although death under persecution was not vouchsafed to him [287]. The cause, not the
manner of death, made a martyr [288]. He had triumphed
over his persecutors, but his conflicts had not ended.
Hincmar recounted a number of miracles in which Remigius struck back at those who sought to impair the dignity and holdings of his see [289]. Though so often victo-
rious, he continued to be persecuted in the afflictions visited upon his successors [290].

In addition to the proofs drawn from the career of
St. Remigius, Hincmar invoked two other saintly paradigms, justifying his mimetic strategy of correction
through strife; Dionysius the Areopagite and the Virgin.
Hincmar associated both with Remigius, mentioning
them in his own epitaph and representing them on his
tomb relief.

Despite his long, and cherished, association with the
monastery of St. Denis, the exact contours of Hincmar's
devotion to the Areopagite are indistinct. We can, however, trace some lines of analogy with St. Remigius.
As a young associate of Abbot Hilduin, of St. Denis,
Hincmar had shared in the thrilling ' discovery ' that the
saint revered in their monastery was indeed the disciple
of St. Paul, the archbishop of Athens, and, under papal

---

(287) Ibid., c. 23, p. 319.
(288) *P. L.*, CXXVI, col. 551.
(289) *Vita Remigii*, c. 4, p. 265, Remigius triumphed, in martyrdom, over
persecutors by continual fasts. For miracles regarding property, see ibid.,
cc. 24-28, pp. 319-325.
(290) *LV Cap.* c. 16. *P. L.*, CXXVI, 337. Also *P. L.* CXXVI, coll. 510, 548.

commission, ' the apostle of all Gaul ' [291]. Unlike Remigius, Dionysius had not anointed a king, but the defect had surely been remedied – and a linkage between their shrines forged – in the fact that Louis the Pious had been crowned as emperor by Pope Stephen IV before the altar of St. Mary, in Rheims, and, after his disgrace, restored to the throne before the tomb of St. Denis [292]. It was the treatises of (Pseudo-) Dionysius that revealed to Hincmar the angelic hierarchies in which he imagined St. Remigius's soul to be moving, and according to which he argued administrative orders in ecclesiastical and secular government should be modelled [293]. Finally, Hincmar found St. Denis, like St. Remigius, an exemplar of learning, who, even in extreme old age, pursued his apostolic mission in Gaul, attacked idolatry, and suffered martyrdom. With these connections in mind, as a former ' monk of the holy martyrs, Dionysius and his companions ', Hincmar commemorated St. Denis in his actual tomb, and gave the monks of St. Denis the large sum of 200 *solidi*, in pure coin silver, to pay for services in the event of his death [294].

We can define the Virgin's place in Hincmar's thinking a bit more fully. The assumption of the Virgin was

(291) Hilduin to Louis the Pious, *M.G.H.*, *Epp. V, K. A.*, III, no. 20, p. 332. Hilduin, *Passio Sanctissimi Dionysii*, *P. L.*, CVI, col. 23. On Hincmar's use of the Pseudo-Dionysian treatises, see DEVISSE, *Hincmar Archevêque*, II, pp. 801, 1007. Cf. *P. L.*, CXXV, 225 f, 287, 315, 353, 443, 588. *P. L.*, CXXVI, 325. A decisive point to bear in mind is that Pseudo-Dionysius did not describe the Eucharist as actual participation in the body and blood of Christ, a position held by John Scotus, whereas Hincmar undeviatingly held to the opposite position.

(292) Louis the Pious to Hilduin, *M.G.H.*, *Epp. K. A.*, III, p. 326. *Annales Bertiniani* (869), ed. cit., p. 162 f. The restoration occurred at the altar of St. Stephen, " cuius nomen interpretatum resonat coronatus... ".

(293) *LV Cap.*, cc. 12, 14. *P. L.*, CXXVI, 325 f, 327 f.

(294) Flodoard, III, 25. *M.G.H.*, *SS.*, p. 538. For the reference to Hincmar as a monk of St. Denis, *P. L.*, CXXV, col. 392.

a major feast at Rheims. Hincmar had a sermon on that subject, (falsely) ascribed to St. Jerome, copied out and bound with ivory plaques encased in gold for the altar; and he had occasion vigorously to defend the authenticity of the sermon against charges of forgery [295]. We can therefore assume that the treatise reflects Hincmar's own thinking.

The author of the sermon refused to decide the burning issue of whether the Virgin had been assumed bodily into heaven. All things were possible with God, he wrote, and the Virgin – and St. John the Evangelist – might well have been taken up, body and soul, as some asserted. But no one knew the facts of the matter [296]. It was clear, however, that, having been overshadowed by the power (*virtus*) of God and filled with grace, she had been pervaded with all virtues. Having within herself the grace that Christ had in its fulness, she became a ' pattern of human life ' (*exemplum humanae vitae*) [297]. The author repeatedly admonished his readers to imitate the Virgin, to reform themselves in the image of her integrity, to impress her face on the statue into which the Holy Spirit was shaping their souls [298].

One striking aspect of the sermon is the author's insistence that the Virgin exemplified Christ's own saving humility. The Virgin adored Christ as her Lord and King [299], but, from her royal Son, she learned to be hum-

---

(295) CYRILLE LAMBOT, " L'homélie du pseudo-Jérôme sur l'assumption et l'évangile de la nativité de Marie d'après une lettre inédite d'Hincmar ', *Revue bénédictine*, XLVI (1934), pp. 265-282. ALBERT RIPBERGER, *Der Pseudo-Hieronymus-Brief IX ' Cogitis me '. Ein erster marianischer Traktat des Mittelalters von Paschasius Radbert (Spicilegium Friburgense, 9.)* Freiburg 1962. Cf. Hincmar's reference to the assumption of the Virgin in *de cavendis vitiis*, c. 8. *P. L.*, CXXV, col. 913. Flodoard, III, 5. *M.G.H.*, *SS.* XIII, p. 479.

(296) Ripberger, *Brief*, c. 10, p. 61.

(297) Ibid., cc. 19, 32, 40, 42; pp. 66, 72, 75 f.

(298) Ibid., cc. 105, 107; pp. 108, 109.

(299) Ibid., c. 87, p. 99.

660

ble and to preserve the other virtues under the shelter of humility. She did not learn from Him how to construct the heavens, or to create angels, or to perform the signal wonders of divinity. But she did learn the lesson that He taught, saying, ' Learn of me, for I am meek and lowly of heart ' (Matt. 11:27), and that He enacted when He performed the work of redemption, becoming obedient to the death of the cross [300]. This virtue above all she herself taught to those who imitated her.

The Virgin's blessing reversed Eve's curse. Her flesh was exalted in Christ; and the author delighted in the vision of her as ' queen of the world ' (*regina mundi*) [301], enthroned by Christ with Himself [302] and reigning forever with Him [303]. She was the ' garden of delights ', the very type of paradise [304], in whom the King had set His own throne, because He desired her beauty and comeliness [305].

(300) Ibid., c. 104, p. 108. Cf. Hincmar, ep. 45. *P. L.*, CXXVI, col. 266, ' ... cum charitatis concordia, quae est omnium virtutum mater et cum humilitate quae est custos ipsarum virtutum, atque cum vera obedientia, quae scala est qua ad caelum pertingitur '. *LV Cap.*, c. 13. *P. L.*, CXXVI, col. 327: Christ was obedient to the Father, even to the death of the cross. Thus, ' Christus humilis hominem obedientem reduxit ad vitam '.

(301) Ripberger, *Brief*, c. 23, p. 68.

(302) Ibid., c. 51, p. 80.

(303) Ibid., c. 44, p. 77.

(304) Ibid., c. 59, p. 85.

(305) Ibid., c. 91, p. 102. This idea, and Hincmar's concept that the entire Trinity made the flesh of Christ in the Virgin's womb, received iconographic expression in the late Middle Ages. An example is the Schutzmantelmadonna in the Erzbischöfliches Dom- und Diözesan Museum, in Vienna (catalogue nr 64, plates 12 and 13). This polychromed wood carving (ca. 1430) represents a Madonna enthroned. If she were depicted originally holding the infant Jesus, all traces of the child have been lost. The distinctive aspect of the figure is that the lower part, below the Virgin's neck, opens into two wings, with women venerating on the right side of her cloak and men, on the left. At the center, where the Virgin's body should be, there is a characteristic Gothic representation of God the Father holding the Crucified. Although the original cross has been lost, its replacement adheres to a standard pattern that the original probably followed, displaying both the body of the Crucified and the dove, representing the Holy Spirit. Other examples of this complex representation are known, especially from lands governed by the Teutonic Order.

Among the feasts of all the saints, the feast of the
assumption, then, was incomparably great because, in
the Virgin, it revealed the life of heaven [306]. It revealed,
in her, the truth of the Incarnation and, thus, the entire
refutation of every heretical depravity [307]. It revealed,
finally, the supreme glory of martyrdom. Other martyrs
suffered in body; their souls, being immortal could not
feel pain. And yet, such was the miracle of the Incarnation that, at Christ's crucifixion, the Virgin's immortal
soul was pierced with grief. So vast was her love that she
made Christ's death her own, being more than a martyr
because of what she suffered in her mind [308].

Four metrical compositions by Hincmar about the
Virgin survive; none of them provides a counterpart for
the richness of thought expressed in the sermon. What
does stand out plainly is an identification of the Eucharistic body with the body that Christ took from the Virgin's flesh, the incorruptibility of Christ's body and the
Virgin's in the tomb, and a portrayal of the Virgin, co-
reigning with Christ in heaven, and extending to the dead
her work of compassion [309]. To these verses, we can add
our last datum concerning Hincmar's tomb; the stone
relief.

Much of what we have said concerning Remigius, Dionysius the Areopagite, and the Virgin is summed up in
this carving (fig. 1). Let us briefly identify the figures.
Hincmar's epitaph mentions Christ, the Virgin, Remigius
and Dionysius, and their figures are easily recognizable.
Outside his own diocese, St. Denis stands, without episcopal staff or abbot's cap, at the far right. St. Remigius,

(306) Ripberger, *Brief*, cc. 45, 98, pp. 77, 105.
(307) Ibid., c. 13, p. 63 f.
(308) Ibid., c. 90, p. 101.
(309) *M. G. H.*, *Poet. Lat.*, III, p. 409-12.

II

Relief from the tomb of Hincmar. BERNARD DE MONTFAUCON, *Les monuments de la monarchie française*, vol. I, pl. 28. Photograph courtesy of the Department of Special Collections, Joseph Regenstein Library, University of Chicago.

with both symbols, is represented next to Hincmar, who
kneels before the Virgin. The figures at the extreme
left of the slab clearly represent the anointing of Clovis
by St. Remigius. By contrast with the figures on the
opposite side, they are crowded, and this may indicate
that the relief continued around the foot of the sarcophagus, perhaps with other miracles of St. Remigius,
such as the raising of the dead girl and the filling of
empty cruses with oil, which are represented, together with
the baptism of Clovis, on a celebrated ivory plaque in
Amiens [310]. The remaining two figures – between the
child Christ and Clovis – are uncertain. However, the pro-
mince given the church in the Virgin's left hand, and the
general theme of martydrom defined in our previous
discussion, may suggest that the nearer figure represents
St. Nicasius, the bishop of Rheims who originally built
and dedicated Rheims cathedral to the Virgin. Hincmar
recalled that Nicasius ' did not desert his city during a
general persecution by the Vandals, but was worthy to
be crowned with martyrdom inside the walls of the
church [311] '; and he appears to have represented Nicasius
next to the Virgin, as here, but at her right, on the main
altar of the new cathedral [312]. The second doubtful figure,
wearing abbot's cap and bearing a crozier (like Remigius),
may represent Tilpin, whom Hincmar obviously regarded

(310) ADOLPH GOLDSCHMIDT, *Die Elfenbeinskulpturen aus der Zeit der
karolingischen und sächsischen Kaiser*, Bd. I (Berlin 1914), no. 57, p. 31, Ta-
fel XXIII.

(311) *De fide Carolo servanda*, c. 17. *P. L.*, CXXV, col. 970 f. Hincmar
also refers to Remigius' devotion to St. Nicasius, *Vita Remigii*, c. 8, *M. G. H.*,
SS. Rer. Mer., III, p. 279. Cf. Flodoard, I. 6. *M. G. H.*, *SS.* XIII, p. 417,
419 f.

(312) DEVISSE, *Hincmar, Archevêque*, II, p. 914. ARTHUR KINGSLEY POR-
TER, '' The Tomb of Hincmar and Carolingian Sculpture in France ', *The Bur-
lington Magazine*, CCLXXXVII (1927), pp. 75-91 follows the interpretation
of Montfaucon, which would make Charles the Bald the central figure, instead
of the Virgin. See esp. p. 83.

as a great rebuilder of the see, and who secured properties for St. Remigius and the Virgin [313].

The exceptional feature of the relief, is the central group, which visually portrays doctrines set forth in the pseudo-Jerome's sermon on the assumption of the Virgin. Bearing that treatise in mind, we can understand the unusual representation of the Virgin and child on separate thrones, with the child, deferring to his mother. As at the time of her assumption, the ' Queen of the world ', the ' mother of the Lord and our *dominatrix* ' [314], sits on a royal throne, which is also a *cathedra doctrinalis* [315], exemplifying to the viewer the royal humility that her Son exemplifies yet more completely, taking a subordinate position in the relief and yet holding a scroll, a symbolic Logos, in His hand. The Virgin holds Hincmar's basilica in her left hand, representing the present life and the sacraments of the Incarnation, and she bestows upon the Archbishop the banner of victory with her right hand, which represents the future life, and the rewards of the blessed, ' among which is not only the vision of divine majesty, but also the splendor of the glorified humanity of one and the same Mediator of God and men ' [316].

Many themes converge in this representation, but two addressed Hincmar's concept of the episcopal office

(313) *De Villa Novilliaco, P. L.*, CXXV, col. 1122; *Vita Remigii, praef.,* M. G. H., SS. Rer. Mer., III, p. 252.

(314) *Explanatio in Ferculum Salomonis. P. L.*, CXXV, col. 817.

(315) Applied to the Roman church, the phrase occurs in *de praedestinatione, diss. post.*, c. 6, *P. L.*, CXXV, col. 88; and *ep. ad Carolum Calvum de praedestinatione, P. L.*, CXXV, col. 54. For a vivid characterization of Rome's maternity, cf. *de praedestinatione, diss. post.*, c. 23, *P. L.*, CXXV, col. 214.

(316) On the significance of the right and left hands, see *Explanatio in Ferculum Salomonis, P. L.*, CXXV, coll. 822 f, Cf. *Vita Remigii*, c. 4, M. G. H., SS. Rer. Mer., III, p. 266, the right hand represents the life above, the left, the life in this world. On the equivalence of the banner (*vexillum*) and cross, see Hilduin, *Passio Sanctissimi Dionysii*, c. 28 P. L., CVI, col. 45, " vexillo sanctae crucis armatus... '. HAENDLER, *Epochen*, p. 89.

most directly. The first was apostolicity. We have already mentioned Hincmar's belief that the Virgin received the gifts of the Holy Spirit at Pentecost, together with the apostles. This association therefore relates her to St. Denis and St. Remigius, whose apostolic missions of conversion in Gaul Hincmar so revered, and, more widely, to all bishops, including Hincmar himself, as successors of the apostles. The relief thus displays the theme of apostolicity with its motifs of heavenly unction, and of the Holy Spirit's continual inspiration of apostles and bishops in the Church from Pentecost onward.

A second, related theme is that of martyrdom, which united the figures of the Virgin, Dionysius, Remigius, and Nicasius, and which, as we shall see, Hincmar also applied to himself. But martyrdom is only the most obvious part of a wider message.

Let us underscore the ascetic spirituality summed up in this visualization of the *Magnificat*. We have mentioned the vital importance that humility and obedience had in Hincmar's concept of unification. In the post-apostolic and patristic eras, the Virgin had been portrayed as the supreme example of humility, a virtue that was thought to be most completely realized in the poverty, chastity and obedience of the monastic life [317]. Hincmar drew on this perception when planning his tomb relief as surely as he drew on the decrees of Christian emperors in the same era for juristic axioms and for exempla to set before his contemporary kings [318].

The humility of the Virgin was the nodal point at which history became one; for there, the Old Testament

(317) VOGT, ' Ancilla Domini ', p. 262.
(318) Ibid., p. 254, concerning the fourth century: '' Für das Marienbild... ist es charakteristisch, dass die Mutter des Herrn hier von allem Anfang an vor Gott und den Menschen erhöht erscheint, dass die Erinnerung an ihre Armut verklärt wird '.

666

fused with the New. There, the prophetic insistence that the poor and oppressed were especially dear to God, combined with the self-emptying of the Word when He took on the form of a servant and became obedient unto death. At that intersection, the Virgin, in her submission and obedience, became the ' cause of salvation ', and, thereby, revealed how profoundly ' the wisdom of this world is foolishness with God ' (I. Cor. 3:19). Through her mediation, the fundamental paradoxes of Christianity became apparent – those non-logical inversions of rational and secular values that already stood complete before God's eyes, and that were gradually unfolding before the eyes of men. Thus, in his tomb relief, Hincmar commemorated the Creator born of a creature, the Virgin birth, the Word made flesh, the triumph of martyrdom, the exaltation of humility and obedience, the superabudance of poverty, a love that conquers death. To the Virgin, the apocalyptic promises of God had already been fulfilled: ' He hath put down the mighty from their seat, and hath exalted the humble and meek. He hath filled the hungry with good things: and the rich he hath sent empty away ' (Luke 1:52-53). Such were the lessons that Hincmar expressed in marble, gold, and precious stones.

As he heard reports of Charles the Bald's fetid carcass [319], and contemplated the moment when worms would devour his own body [320], it may have comforted Hincmar to look at this ascetic, world-defying representation, and to recall that for three centuries, God had kept intact the flesh of St. Remigius, who was his model and patron and who would be his near neighbor at the resurrection [321].

(319) *Annales Bertiniani* (877), ed. cit., p. 217.
(320) *M. G. H.*, *Poet. Lat.*, III, p. 420.
(321) Flodoard, III, 9. *M. G. H.*, *SS.* XIII, p. 482. Hincmar declined to

We have emphasized mimesis of faith as a strategy
of historical progression in Hincmar's thought, and we
have found it expressed in rationales of correction by
healing, participation, and imitation. Our discussion of
Hincmar's tomb complex has emphasized the acceptance
of strife for the sake of correction, the price of movement
from an imperfect toward a perfect state. Therefore to
find the mimetic rationales justified – as Hincmar did
in the paradigms of Remigius, Dionysius the Areopagite,
and the Virgin – was also to embrace conflict, suffering,
and martyrdom.

Of course, Hincmar wished particularly to emphasize
similarities in the faith between himself and Remigius.
He could easily feel at one with a great prelate who practi-
sed severe asceticism, a man imbued with letters as a
child [322], ' wise and most holy, an excellent rhetorician,
outstanding in virtues ', a man who was renowned as most
learned in the Holy Scriptures and most experienced in
Church doctrines [323], who wrote metrical verses engraved
on a chalice [324], who urged his King to send a crown of
gold encrusted with gems to St. Peter [325], and in whose
career the vase of Soissons played such a dramatic part [326].
As he wrote the life of his predecessor the present intruded
itself on his mind. He inserted analogues of his own
conflicts and, from other treatises that he had written,

---

send relics to Louis the German: ' Sed hic pontifex pro maxima praesumptione
asserit se duxisse corpus eius, quod Dominus per tanta tempora integrum
conservaverat, disrumpere '.

(322) *Vita Remigii*, cc. 2, 11. *M. G. H., SS. Rer. Mer*, III, pp. 262 f, 292.
(323) Ibid., c. 21, p. 313.
(324) Ibid., c. 2, p. 262.
(325) Ibid., c. 20, p. 312 f.
(326) Ibid., c. 11, p. 292 f. Cf. Remigius' testament, bequeathing to the
church of Rheims a silver vase, which Clovis had given to the Bishop. The
testament specifies that it be made into a thurible and a figured chalice. Ibid.,
c. 32, p. 337.

he borrowed excerpts on predestination [327], the resurrection [328], the Incarnation and the Eucharist [329]. Pope Hormisdas' designation of Remigius as papal representative, with the right to wear the pallium, bore directly on Hincmar's assertions of his own authority as metropolitan, and particularly late in his career on his protest against the papal vicariate conferred on Ansegisus of Sens (876). Remigius's posthumous thrashing of Pippin the Short balanced Hincmar's disputes over property with Charles the Bald; and Bishop Genebaud of Laon's submissiveness to seven years' strict confinement, pending Remigius' pleasure, set an ideal hardly to be reached in Hincmar's conflict with Hincmar of Laon [330]. It was this last dispute that held out the glory of martyrdom to the Archbishop, for surely under the abuse and persecution that his nephew heaped upon him he was dying for Christ, as John the Baptist had done. The blows were carried, not only by St. Remigius, but by Christ [331]. Sustained though he might be by the prayers of the Virgin and Remigius [332], he realized with grim, circuitous irony that he was imitating Christ, ' who came to die even for His enemies, and yet said that he was going to lay down His life for friends, so as to demonstrate to us that when,

(327) Ibid., c. 8. p. 281; also *de praedestinatione*, c. 21. *P. L.*, CXXV, col. 190.

(328) *Vita Remigii*, c. 9, p. 286; also *Explanatio in Ferculum Salomonis. P. L.*, CXXV, col. 829.

(329) *Vita Remigii*, c. 15, p. 229; also *de cavendis vitiis*, c. 6. *P. L.*, CXXV, col. 903. Hincmar's view that Gottschalk was an Arian struck a connection with *Vita Remigii*, c. 21, p. 313 f.

(330) *LV Cap.*, c. 16. *P. L.*, CXXVI, col. 337 f.

(331) *P. L.*, CXXVI, col. 548 f. On the Archbishop's view that Hincmar of Laon's decrees against his own diocese were worse that the persecutions visited upon the Church by pagan emperors, DEVISSE, *Hincmar, Archevêque*, II, p. 743 f. Earlier, Hincmar of Rheims had considered himself ' persecuted ' by the clerics ordained by Ebo in 840. SCHRÖRS, *Hinkmar*, p. 61.

(332) *P. L.*, CXXVI, coll. 510, 559. *Vita Remigii, translatio*, c. 31, *M.G.H., SS. Rer. Mer.*, III, p. 335.

by loving, we can gain advantage from our enemies, even those who persecute [us] are friends '[333].

Thus, he alluded to the stole of priesthood, the pallium betowed upon them both by Rome, and the two stoles of the resurrection – eternal beatitude of soul and the blessed immortality of the glorified body[334]. Hincmar delicately touched the analogue of Elijah and Elisha, on whom the elder prophet's mantle fell when Elijah, having crossed through the waters of mortality, was taken up bodily into heaven[335].

Clearly, Hincmar's enemies were not convinced, and, in terms of his own theology, Hincmar too recognized a basic uncertainty in his elaborate historical analogies.

Even while he mustered his evidence during the decade and more when he was writing the *Vita Sancti Remigii*, Hincmar knew all too well how inconclusive proof was when it rested on the imitation of faith. Drawn though it might be from divine judgments and miraculous signs[336], it would be read diffcrently by the eyes of the body, the eyes of the mind, and the eyes of God. The righteous would always be at odds with carnal men[337].

---

(333) *LV Cap.*, c. 39. *P. L.*, CXXVI, col. 437 f. Cf. *ep*. 19, *P. L.*, CXXVI, col. 113, "demonstrans quoniam in membris suis Christus persequitur et scandalizatur, et in membris suis suscipitur...'. The idea that bishops were successors to tho apostles also had connotations of martyrdom. *Ep.* 31, c. 4. *P. L.*, CXXVI, col. 212: ' Electos vero apostolos Dominus non ad mundi gaudia, sed sicut ipse missus est ad passiones in mundum mittit '.

(334) *Vita Remigii*, c. 23, *M. G. H.*, *SS. Rer. Mer.*, III, p. 318.

(335) Ibid., c. 31, p. 335. *De divortio, responsio* 6. *P. L.*, CXXV, col. 668. In view of Hincmar's theological concern with the carnality of Christ, it may be worth noticing that he wore the pallium only on Christmas and at Easter. *Ep.* 11. *P. L.*, CXXVI, 88. To round out our review of analogues between Remigius and Hincmar, we should observe that Hincmar considered two of Remigius's characteristics – the angelic and the apostolic – to be common to bishops. The prophet Malachi called the bishop the angel of the Lord (*Vita Remigii*, c. 31, *M. G. H.*, *SS. Rer. Mer.*, III, p. 328), and bishops held the place of the apostles in the Church (*epp*. 17, 32. *P. L.*, CXXVI, 101, 210 f).

(336) *De divortio, responsio* 6. *P. L.*, CXXV, col. 665 f.

(337) Cf. *epp*. 11, 15. *P. L.*, CXXVI, coll. 88, 97 f.

670

Even those minds that had been enlightened by grace saw
' through a mirror, in an enigma ' in this world. Rome
had overturned his rulings against the clerics ordained by
Ebo and against Bishop Rothad of Soissons. Wise and
influential men doubted the soundness of some theological
doctrines that he taught. Hincmar of Laon's deposition was
widely deplored. If God's acts could be comprehended by
the reason (ratio), they would cause no amazement; nor
was there any use for faith, wherever the human reason
could provide self-evident proofs [238]. As he fled to the
tomb of Remigius for shelter in the day of Judgment [339],
Hincmar recognized the limits of his evidence both here,
before men, and hereafter. For he heard the dire voice
of Wisdom exhorting every man: ' Whatsoever thy hand
findeth to do, do it with thy might; for there is no work,
nor reason (ratio), nor knowledge, nor wisdom in hell,
whither thou art hastening ' [340].

The historical ambiguities inherent in the three corrective rationales had been transcended by faith, but in
no way dispelled by objective proof. Essential issues of
authority in the Church remained open to dispute.

We are about to consider the place of mimesis in Hincmar's thought about relations between the royal and
episcopal offices. A word might therefore be in order
about secular rulers as they figure in ideas that the
tomb expressed.

In considering Hincmar's concept of human events,
we were able to distinguish between signifying events,
which took place through the sacramental dynamics of
the faith, and non-signifying events of the secular world.
The former mediated from one stage to the next in the

(338) *Vita Remigii*, c. 15. *M. G. H.*, *SS. Rer. Mer.*, III, p. 297.
(339) Ibid., cc. 9, 31; pp. 288, 332 f.
(340) *LV Cap.*, c. 49. *P. L.*, CXXVI, col. 494. Ecclesiastes 9:10.

historical formation of the body of Christ; the latter,
signifying nothing beyond themselves, could follow one
upon the other, but there was no great historical pattern
for them to mediate, as parts, to the whole. This division
between sacramental unity and secular multiplicity carried over into texts that cast light on the concepts informing the tomb.

The powerful ascetic element of martyrdom evokes
an intrinsic division, and a historical antipathy, between
temporal and spiritual powers. Sharing vicariously in
Christ's death, the Virgin endured the process that began
when her Son stood before Pontius Pilate, that ' member
of the Devil ' [341]. Dionysius the Areopagite also was slain
after a legal process before the Roman authorities, which
Hilduin described in detail; and the fact that the Emperor
Domitian lost his principate and his life after the Saint's
execution – as had Nero after Sts. Peter and Paul were
slain – did not reverse the martyrdom [342]. Though not
subjected to judicial process, Bishop Nicasius too witnessed by his death to a fundamental opposition between
Church and world.

The great exception would appear to come in Remigius'
dealings with Clovis. Hincmar indeed presents a glo-
wingly idealized portrait of Clovis, converted by Remigius
and bringing all his people to baptism with him, fighting
the Arians with the Bishop's blessing, and enriching the
see of Rheims. Hincmar described Remigius, teaching
the Gospel to Clovis, conveying him to the baptismal
font, and there addressing the King ' as though he were
a slave, subject to him ', with an epigram that summed
up the *volteface* of conversion: ' Bow your head humbly,

(341) *Vita Remigii*, c. 8. *M. G. H.*, *SS. Rer. Mer.*, III, p. 280.
(342) *Passio Sanctissimi Dionysii*, cc. 24-32, 36. *P. L.*, CVI, coll. 42-47, 50

Sicamber. Burn what you have adored; adore what you have burned ' [343]. Because he predicted to Clovis what would befall his family, Remigius was like Isaiah, Hincmar wrote, and, in knowing of the King's death without a human messenger, he was like Elisha. But, instructing Clovis, addressing him with power, and baptising him, Remigius was more. He thereby participated in the fifth degree of angelic hosts, the principalities [344].

Whatever else he may have intended when he transcribed Remigius's powerful words to Clovis, Hincmar certainly had the ritual of baptism in mind. There, the priest, having commanded demons in the exorcisms of water and salt, and administering the healing powers of the sacrament, demanded from the baptizand a threefold renunciation of the devil, his works, and all the vices issuing from pride. Among the latter, Hincmar mentioned especially ambition, which ' in Greek is called *phantasia*. By that name is designated the manifold splendor and pomp of the regal office ' [345].

Remigius' strong words to Clovis can therefore be read in the light of the normal order of baptism. And, as Hincmar went on, identifying Remigius with angelic orders, he passed from principalities to thrones, Cherubim, and finally to Seraphim. These last Remigius resembled because he burned in love for the eternal, and, kindling others with his words, he converted the entire nation of the Franks with their king. By his consuming

---

(343) *Vita Remigii*, c. 31, *M. G. H.*, *SS. Rer. Mer.*, III, p. 329: ' ut servo sibi subjecto '. Cf ibid., c. 15, p. 296 f.

(344) Ibid., cc. 30, 31; pp. 327, 329. In this regard, Hincmar also mentioned the installation of other bishops by Remigius and the thrashing that (posthumously) he administered to Pippin the Short. Ibid., c. 25, p. 321 f.

(345) Ep. 18. *P. L.*, CXXVI, col. 109. Cf. the charge against Hincmar of Laon: ' pompas et illecebras saeculi coepit sequi... '. *P. L.*, CXXVI, col. 642.

love, he transcended earthly things in ardent desire, according to the Psalmist: ' My tears were my bread day and night. My soul hungers for the living God ' [346].

What does this portrayal suggest about relations between the royal and episcopal offices? Though, at the baptism of Clovis, Remigius ' consecrated ' the royal sceptre [347], Clovis had been king long before his conversion, and, indeed, his armies had then despoiled many churches [348]. The description of Clovis after his conversion portrays close cooperation between a ruler and a bishop whom he venerated, but it does not suggest a departure from the intrinsic separation of kingship and episcopate that persecution had exemplified. This conclusion is strengthened by Hincmar's references to Clovis' alleged descendents [349].

He wrote that the Christian religion had almost been abolished under Charles Martel, who permitted dissipation of episcopal properties, and whose eternal damnation had been revealed in a vision. Though suitably edified by that vision, Pippin the Short too encroached on the property of St. Remigius, only to be beaten black and blue by an apparition of the Saint. On his own tomb, Hincmar represented Remigius in the act of speaking to Clovis ' as though he were a slave subject to him '. But the meaning of that act, as we have described it, and the other associations with secular rulers that converged in Hincmar's thinking about the tomb, emphasized the distance between the royal and the episcopal offices. Kingdoms were transitory, liable to be subverted and tran-

---

(346) *Vita Remigii*, cc. 4, 23, 31. *M. G. H.*, *SS. Rer. Mer.*, III, pp. 265, 317, 330.

(347) *M. G. H.*, *Poet. Lat.*, III, p. 413, 1. 12.

(348) *Vita Remigii*, c. 11. *M. G. H.*, *SS. Rer. Mer.*, III, p. 292.

(349) Cf. *Annales Bertiniani* (869), ed. cit., p. 163.

674

sferred from nation to nation [350]. They were divisible
and perishable, while the Church endured in its unity.
Clovis gained his royal title by inheritance and war, and
his further title, ' *consul* and *augustus* ', from the Emperor
Anastasius [351]. Remigius gained his episcopal consecration
by a two-fold action of the Holy Spirit, both direct and
mediated through bishops, and his pallium from the successor of St. Peter [352]. Surely there was little ground for
analogy between their offices. Had not Christ Himself
set a pattern for Christians to imitate in faith when He
rejected, and fled from, an earthly kingship [353] ?

III. *Mimetic Rationales and the Rejection of Political
Synthesis*

Hincmar's mimetic rationales for unification have
served us as symbolic keys to his inner life. Can they also
open perspectives on his political thought? The Church,
the company of the elect, was gradually moving toward
its perfect form, a destiny that, though incomplete, was
already present through the sacraments. The sacramental
bond was entirely separate from secular government.
The division between sacramental and non-sacramental
areas of life reached beyond the functional distinction
between priests and laity. Events and lives grounded
in the sacramental dynamic of the Church shared in an
unfolding unity because they signified and mediated

---

(350) *Vita Remigii*, c. 14, p. 296. On Charles Martel and Pippin, ibid.,
praef., cc. 25, 31; pp. 252, 321 f, 329. The account of Charles Martel's damnation also occurs in the letter of the Synod of Quierzy to Louis the German
(858), *M. G. H.*, *Cap. Reg. Fr.*, II, no. 297, c. 7, p. 432 f.

(351) Ibid., cc. 11, 20, pp. 291, 311.

(352) Ibid., cc. 3, 20; pp. 263 f, 311 f.

(353) *De praedestinatione, post. diss.*, c. 33. *P. L.*, CXXV, col. 346.

enduring realities from faith to faith, while secular events signified nothing other than themselves, and thus could not mediate. Persecution, martyrdom, and the ascetic inversion of secular values, all of which Hincmar commemorated on his tomb, merely emphasized the distance between the world and the Church, in which visible things became one with the invisible things of God. Was any political synthesis possible between the two orders?

The mimetic rationales will enter into the answer. But, while we have been discussing them mainly in regard to acts by individual bishops, we shall now have to consider them from a different point of view. We shall need to think of mimesis as a collective act. It is obvious that the Church's movement toward perfection involved a double reflex: that of the individual upon the whole and the other of the whole upon the individual. Hincmar was convinced that individuals were united to Christ through the flesh [354], but that martyrdom and other acts that built up the body of Christ issued from reason (as spiritual power), enlarged by faith. Again: Could a political synthesis of kingship and episcopacy occur in this mystical union, that took shape in time, even while it transcended time?

Our position is that Hincmar's theology led him to pose antitheses that could be mediated intellectually, but not resolved institutionally. We maintain therefore that the crucial fact about his political thought consisted in the questions that he raised, questions that remained unanswerable in large measure, not only for Hincmar, but also for religious and secular thinkers well into modern times. The disjunction between Hincmar's metaphysical and his institutional doctrines needs to be stres-

---

(354) *Vita Remigii*, c. 31. *M. G. H.*, *SS. Rer. Mer.*, III, p. 334.

676

sed. The unanswerable questions concerning institutional powers arose from metaphysical – we may add, mimetic – ideas of transformation that we have already discussed. Collectively, as well as individually, historical transformations were states of mind for Hincmar, rather than states of temporal existence.

One major adjustment had to be made in Hincmar's mimetic apparatus, then, if it were to be applied to all humanity – the ' one man ' that he thought was forming in Christian society [355]. A new faculty, a collective reason (*ratio*), was needed, one by which the whole could perform the critical functions of reason on a universal scale, and thereby react upon its individual members as they did on it. To Hincmar's mind, consensus was that faculty. But we must remember that reason was equivalent with spiritual power, or virtue, and that the soul moved toward it by stages of perfection, ' from virtue to virtue '. Consensus was a compound, made up of individual minds. Like its components, it moved through stages of incompleteness toward an archetype that was both present in part and absent in its completeness. Like its components', its virtue was perfected in weakness: that is, in faith.

We have already suggested how doctrines of mimetic correction figured in Hincmar's theories about the episcopal office. We can now take up the wider subject of how they informed his ideas about correlations between secular and ecclesiastical government, particularly with regard to consensus. We shall encounter the historical ambiguities of corrective mimesis again, this time at the heart of Hincmar's canonistic reasoning.

(355) *De praedestinatione, diss. post.*, c. 29. *P. L.*, CXXXV, col. 289.

Throughout his life, Hincmar never ceased to insist that correction was a primary duty, and that it should be a joint effort, of kings as well as of bishops. Though the Archbishop drew on other texts as well, he found a most congenial statement of his view in the treatise, *De XII. Abusivis Saeculi*. The author, known as Pseudo-Cyprian, declared that the king should correct his own habits, even as he corrected other men, so that justice might be exalted in his throne, justice that would defend the innocent and helpless and destroy the impious from the earth [356]. What if the king were delinquent? God was above him, as he was above other men. If the king acted wickedly and failed to correct his own misdeeds and those of others, his negligence and evil works would be judged by God Himself. The severity of His judgment would correspond with the degree to which a given man had been exalted as king above all. *Mutatis mutandis*, as we have seen, Hincmar applied this same principle to bishops [357], likewise drawing a test passage from Pseudo-Cyprian [358]. Humility was as great a virtue for kings as for bishops, and as sure a defence of other virtues for them as for monks or nuns [359].

(356) Pseudo-Cyprian, Siegmund Hellmann ed., *De XII. Abusivis Saeculi*, (Texte und Untersuchungen zur Geschichte der altchristlichen Literatur, 3. Reihe, Bd. IV, Heft 1. Leipzig 1909), pp. 51 ff. Hincmar refers to this treatise in *de divortio, quaestio 7 responsio ; de regis persona*, cc. 2, 25. *P. L.*, CXXV, coll. 770, 835, 850. *Ep.* 24. *P. L.*, CXXVI, col. 157 f. *De ordine palatii*, cc. 5-6. *M. G. H.*, *Cap. Reg. Fr.*, II, p. 519 f. Cf. *ep. ad Carolum Calvum*, *M. G. H.*, *Epp.* VIII, *K. A.* VI, no. 126, p. 65. On the moral emphasis in Hincmar's mind to which Pseudo-Cyprian appealed, see Anton, *Fürstenspiegel*, pp. 286 f, 329.

(357) *De divortio, responsio* 12. *P. L.*, CXXV, col. 701 f.

(358) *De divortio, quaestio 7 responsio*. *P. L.* CXXV, col. 771. Hellmann ed., p. 53 ff. See the emphatic statement in *LV Cap.*, c. 43. *P. L.*, CXXVI, col. 451 ' ... vae mihi est, si non docendo, custodiendo, suadendo, increpando, mulcendo, terrendo, aliquando leniter aliquando vero severius agendo, pro viribus et captu meo evangelizavero tibi [Hincmar of Laon] cum aliis, quae ad fidem rectam et bonos mores atque ad bonas actiones pertinent.... '.

(359) Anton, *Fürstenspiegel*, p. 304. Cf. *ep.* 45. *P. L.*, CXXVI, col. 266.

678

Since the corrective functions of kings and bishops were supposed to build up the body of Christ, Hincmar applied his rationales of healing, participation, and imitation to both offices. Through his legislative functions, the king was party to the relentless search for new medicines to counteract new diseases [360]. The king's sword and the bishop's surgical knife should move with the same gesture to cut the putrid member off from the healthy, and to destroy the impious [361].

Properly ordered, their efforts must be coordinate. For, having been regenerated from the same immaculate womb of the Church, and become incorporate in Christ as His members, they lived together ' in the unity of Mother Church ' [362]. Through their carnality, ' according to the participation of nature ', they shared the carnality of the true King and Pontiff [363]. Anointed as Christians, they participated in the name of Christ [364]. Anointed according to their discrete offices, they participated in His names (or titles), kings in His kingship, bishops in His high priesthood [365].

Participating in His nature, name, and offices, rulers – kings as well as bishops – were obliged to imitate Christ, if they wished to rule with Him [366]. In any case, as rulers,

(360) Charles the Bald to Pope John VIII. *Ep.* 32, c. 3. *P. L.*, CXXVI, col. 231.

(361) *De divortio, quaestio* 7 *responsio. De regis persona*, c. 19, a citation also applied to bishops (see above, n. 50). *Ad episcopos reqni admonitio altera*, c. 1. *P. L.*, CXXV, 772, 846, 1008. Cf. Charles the Bald to Hadrian II, *P. L.*, CXXIV, col. 891.

(362) *De divortio, responsio* 12. *P. L.*, CXXV, col. 699.

(363) *Ad episcopos regni admonitio altera*, c. 1. *P. L.*, CXXV, col. 1007 f.

(364) *Cap. Pistensia* (862), c. 4. *M. G. H..*, *Cap. Reg. Fr.*, II, no. 272, p. 310.

(365) Synod of Quierzy to Louis the German (858), *M. G. H.*, *Cap. Reg. Fr.*, II, no. 297, c. 15, p. 439 ' dominus christorum Christus '. *De divortio, responsio* 12. *P. L.*, CXXV, col. 700.

(366) Synod of Quierzy to Louis the German (858), *M. G. H.*, *Cap. Reg. Fr.*, II, no. 297, c. 11, p. 435. *De coercendo et exstirpando raptu viduarum*,

kings and bishops were set up as examples – as though in a mirror – for their subjects to imitate [367]. By virtuous action, they would propagate virtuous subjects, but, by wickedness, they would propagate evil ones, for whose spiritual deaths God would hold them accountable in this world and, later, in ' the fires of hell ' [368].

The treatises of Dionysius the Areopagite suggested another kind of imitation to Hincmar's mind. He asserted that the hierarchies in secular and ecclesiastical government replicated the celestial orders, those powers that descended by procreative imitation, and that Hincmar called ' paternities '. According to the Prophet Malachi, the Archbishop held, bishops could be thought of as angels [369]. The teachings of Dionysius opened to him the prospect that kings, too, even those of the Gentiles, were counterparts and analogues of angels in the generative order that God had established on earth [370].

On balance, however, the functional paradigms that Hincmar set for the royal and episcopal offices emphasize their separateness. To be sure, the moral exemplarism of some transcended distinctions of office. Like all Chri-

---

c. 4. *P. L.*, CXXV, col. 1019. ANTON, *Fürstenspiegel*, p. 304 n. 809. On bishops, see above, pp. 597 ff, 668.

(367) On the king, *de divortio, praef. M. G. H., Epp.* VIII, *K. A.* VI, no. 134, p. 78. On the bishop, *ep.* 32 to John VIII. *P. L.*, CXXVI, col. 233. A very different application of the metaphor is in *LV Cap.*, c. 52, *P. L.*, CXXVI, col. 489.

(368) Synod of Quierzy to Louis the German (858), *M. G. H., Cap. Reg. Fr.*, II, no. 297, c. 14, p. 437 f. *De divortio, quaestio* 6 *responsio. P. L.*, CXXV, coll. 758-760. Hincmar is presenting, in Christian costume, the classical notion that Claudian set down in his panegyric on the Emperor Honorius' fourth consulate (11.299-302), ' ... componitur orbis/regis ad exemplum, nec sic inflectere sensus/humanos edicta valent quam vita regentis: / mobile mutatur semper cum principe vulgus '. (Loeb ed., I, p. 308). Claudian omitted the fires of hell. See ANTON, *Fürstenspiegel*, pp. 310, 317. On bishops, see *LV Cap.*, c. 43. *P. L.*, CXXVI, 451 f. On the bishop as *forma vivendi, ep.* 39, *P. L.* CXXVI, col. 260, and above, n. 185.

(369) Above, n. 335.

(370) *LV Cap.*, cc. 12, 14-15. *P. L.*, CXXVI, coll. 325-328.

stians, kings and bishops should imitate the virtues of
Christ, David, and Job, But, when he thought of paradigms for official action, Hincmar's mind ran to models
that were not interchangeable between the royal and
episcopal orders – to David in his secular functions, and
to Christian emperors of the fourth century, for kings,
and to priests and prophets of the Old Testament, for
bishops – and it is also striking how meagre the royal
paradigms are, by comparison with the ornate array of
Scriptural types with which he identified St. Remigius,
whom he had taken for a model himself [371].

Given the distinction between the royal and the episcopal offices, any political synthesis between them would
seem improbable. Hincmar recalled St. Ambrose's refusal
to surrender his basilica to the Arian court: ' Palaces
belong to the emperor; the church, to the bishop '. Coin
of the realm carried Caesar's image and inscription; the
Church could pay it to him in tribute. The Church herself carried the image of the invisible God, the brightness
of His glory and the image of His substance. Ambrose
contended that to cede the basilica to the Emperor would
be tantamount to separating the image – Christ – from
the Father [372]. Throughout his writings, Hincmar insisted on this division between the juridical competence
of royal courts and that of episcopal [373]. Even on the day

(371) See the discussion of Biblical and Imperial types applied to Carolingian kings in ANTON, Fürstenspiegel, pp. 419-446. The impact of Old Testa-
mental models on Carolingian political thought is fully discussed by WALTER
MOHR, Die karolingische Reichsidee. Aevum Christianum, Bd 5. Münster 1962.
(372) De fide Carolo regi servanda, c. 38. P. L., CXXV, col. 981 f.
(373) Synod of Quierzy to Louis the German (858), M. G. H., Cap. Reg.
Fr., II, no. 297, c. 15, p. 439 f. Ep. 22, P. L., CXXVI, 135, and col. 507.
Pro ecclesiae libertatum defensione, P. L., CXXV, col. 1064. Cf. Hincmar's
objections against bishops who act and fight as though they were laymen.
E. g., LV Cap., c. 52. P. L. CXXVI, col. 491 f. LÖWE, ' Apocrisiar ', p. 220
n. 82. P. L. CXXVI, col. 504: ' sit etiam rex portans gladium ad vindictam
malefactorum, sint episcopi ad canones ad judicanda crimina sacrilegorum... '.

of judgment, kings and bishops would appear in separate cohorts before Christ, King of kings and Bishop of bishops [374].

The mimetic theme of correction and its rationales gave Hincmar a theory of what actual government should be and do; but the functional distinction between kings and bishops posed difficulties. Of course, imitation, whether of an imperfectly seen divine archetype, or of ' the wisdom of earlier men ' [375] – was an easily recognizable, and quite essential, principle of government: that is, precedent. Hincmar explicitly took up imitation of predecessors in this sense, and tried to institutionalize it by formal oaths in which contemporary kings guaranteed established rights and privileges [376]. He ritualized the imitation of predecessors, of Christ, and of the celestial hierarchy in the coronation orders, to which modern scholars have justly applied the term, ' Christomimesis '. But, in the give-and-take of actual government, his mimetic doctrines presented insoluble quandaries.

The duty of correction could not be performed in a stable equilibrium. Except in a limited sense, Hincmar could not accept royal jurisdiction over bishops. Could bishops judge kings? Midway in his career, he argued that it was blasphemous and full of the spirit of the devil, to say that a king could not be judged by bishops, whether by those of his own lands, or by others. [377]. Surely, he pointed out, Nathan rebuked David, the king and prophet, and later prophets also called their errant kings to account. Ambrose had excluded the Emperor Theodosius

---

(374) *Ep.* 44. *P. L.* CXXVI, col. 265 f.

(375 *De ordine palatii*, c. 33. *M. G. H.*, *Cap. Reg. Fr.*, II, p. 528. The entire purpose of this treatise is to record an old model by which degenerate times might be made good. Cc. 1, 37, pp. 518, 530.

(376) *Pro ecclesiae libertatum defensione*. *P. L.* CXXV, coll. 1039 f, 1042.

(377) *De divortio, quaestio* 6 *responsio*, *P. L.* CXXV, col. 756.

from the Church for grievous crimes, and, by penance, recalled him. Latterly, ' episcopal unanimity ' – with the consensus of the people – restored Louis the Pious to Church and kingdom, after he had given satisfaction. And yet, Hincmar found himself confronted by wise bishops who argued that the king was subject to no laws or judges, except God, having been established by God in the kingship, and ruling as he did by divine assent, as the Scriptures said: ' the heart of the king is in the hand of God.... He turneth it whithersoever He will ' [378]. Toward the end of his life, Hincmar attempted to clarify the issue by teaching that the episcopal office was greater than the royal because bishops consecrated kings [379], and more perilous than the royal because bishops would be held responsible for kings at the Last Judgment [380]. But he deduced no juristic principles from these propositions. As we shall see, he never framed a systematic rebuttal to the doctrine of royal unaccountability.

Thus far, we have said that, in a Christian society, kings and bishops could be expected to function in harmony. The analogues for their acts, however, did not run laterally between their offices; instead, they ran vertically between the ruler and Christ as King, and between the bishop and Christ as Pontiff. We have therefore described two parallel subsystems, according to the Gelasian pattern.

---

(378) Loc. cit, *quaestio*, Proverbs 21:1.

(379) Synod of St. Macra, c. 1. *P. L.*, CXXV, col. 1071.

(380) *De divortio, praef. P. L.* CXXV, col. 627. As will become apparent in the following remarks, I agree substantially with Devisse that Hincmar remained faithful to the Gelasian concept that kingship and episcopacy were two parallel offices within the Christian community. They were interdependent. Each was superior in its own proper sphere of action; but they operated in " un équilibre réel '. The coronation anointing established no right of resistance. DEVISSE, *Hincmar, Archevêque*, II, pp. 677, 695 f, 703 ff.

The dense symbolism of coronation, however, has opened the possibility that parallelism and interdependence gave way to synthesis. To scholars exploring this possibility, the crucial event is Charles the Bald's coronation as King of Lotharingia, in 869. The coronation was the first in a series of consecrations by which Charles attempted to establish territorial bridgeheads against Louis the German in the kingdom suddenly left vacant by the death of Lothar II. Within a few months after he himself had been anointed and crowned, Charles advanced men favorable to himself to the sees of Trier, Cologne, and Verdun. The attempts to fill the sees of Trier and Cologne required serious infringements of the canons, with which Hincmar himself connived. Even had their titles been impeccable, the new bishops would have found, when they arrived in their dioceses, that Louis the German had already installed appointees of his own. The kings used episcopal consecration as a tool in their territorial rivalry, and, when the time for compromise arrived, both of them demonstrated that they could give up episcopal pawns as well as they could move them. And still, Louis had not had himself consecrated as king. The question before us is whether, in the minds of Hincmar and his contemporaries, the ritual consecration of Charles altered the parallelism that we have described by subordinating one subsystem to another.

Our position is that the coronation ritual was an anomaly that casts little light on Hincmar's general theme of correction. There are reasons to think that the coronation in 869 was a precipitate manoeuver devised by Charles, rather than a considered ritualization of Hincmar's political theories. How could so crucial an event have been anomalous, and possibly unrepresentative of Hincmar's settled convictions? Let us examine views on the other side. On balance, scholars who hold that the ritual did alter the Gelasian parallelism have followed two, quite different, lines of reasoning, both of which involve dilemmas.

It has been argued that coronation hallowed the person of the ruler, elevating him as a ' theocratic king ' endowed with quasi-episcopal dignity [381]. In another connection, I have specified some difficulties in this viewpoint [382]. They center on a comparison of the *ordo* for episcopal ordination with that for regal coronation. The essential act of the episcopal ceremony – the transmission of the seven-fold gifts of the Spirit by the imposition of hands – has no place in the royal *ordo*. To be sure, the king was ' consecrated to the Lord ', but, as in so many other rituals of blessing, no mediation of spiritual powers from consecrator to consecrand was thought to occur. Thus, the ring and the crozier, the episcopal symbols, were not bestowed; and it is unlikely that the fraternal kiss had any part in the royal ceremony. The coronation *ordo*, therefore, yields little in the way of evidence that Hincmar brushed functional parallelism aside in favor of theocratic kingship.

God struck the Old Testament king, Ozias, with leprosy when he dared to perform a priestly function. The immense relish that Hincmar took in Ozias' dreadful fate would appear to caution against attributing any

(381) The most compelling statement of this interpretation is in WALTER ULLMANN, *The Carolingian Renaissance and the Idea of Kingship* (The Birkbeck Lectures 1968-9). London 1969, though it had previously been developed in his books, *Principles of Government and Politics in the Middle Ages* and *The Growth of Papal Government in the Middle Ages.*

(382) *The Two Kingdoms. Ecclesiology in Carolingian Political Thought* (Princeton 1964), p. 178 ff. and passim. For a penetrating account of the event, see W. SCHLESINGER, « Zur Erhebung Karls des Kahlen zum König von Lothringen 869 in Metz », *Landschaft und Geschichte. Festschrift Franz Petri* (Bonn 1970), pp. 454-476.

notions of theocratic kingship to him [383]. There is certainly much to suggest that the idea of consecrating Charles the Bald to any sort of quasi-episcopal dignity would have repelled him. There is no need to recount the many harsh passages of arms between the two men that culminated in Charles' deliberate humiliation of the Archbishop in 877 [384]. We should, however, bear in mind that, during the three years before the coronation in Metz, Charles had followed policies inimical to Hincmar, in a case that brought into question the legitimacy both of his judgment and of his very accession to the see of Rheims.

The clerics ordained by Ebo during his brief restoration as archbishop in Rheims (840) had not faded away, though Hincmar had secured a papal judgment against them and persisted in denying the legitimacy of their orders. In 865, Pope Nicholas I reopened their case probably at the behest of Charles, who could not wait until this stage of the protracted litigation had been concluded to name Hincmar's archenemy among the clerics, Wulfhad, as archbishop of Bourges. Reinforced by a decree in which the Pope heavily censured Hincmar on grounds that (Hincmar alleged) ' by plain proof (*ratio*) were untrue ', Charles had sided with bishops who conspired against him ' contrary to truth and the holy authority of the canons '. He broke open the decrees of the Synod of Troyes, sealed for transmission to the Pope, and, finding that Hincmar had not been repudiated, he composed a hostile letter in his own name to Nicholas.

---

(383) E. g., *P. L.* CXXV, col. 1058 f. Anton, *Fürstenspiegel*, p. 435. Hincmar described in detail the *ordo* followed in his own episcopal ordination, and by him in those ordinations over which he presided (*ep.* 29. *P. L.*, CXXVI, col. 187 f), and he repeatedly emphasized the imposition of hands as the decisive act (e. g., *P. L.*, CXXVI, coll. 534, 559)..

(384) DEVISSE, *Hincmar, Archevêque*, II, p. 814 ff.

686

Another sphere of conflict had opened. In his own dispute with Bishop Hincmar of Laon, Charles had repeatedly attempted to violate the canons in order to bring the Bishop before secular judges, and even to drag him to the royal court by force of arms. As of 869, the King's efforts had been frustrated. They had even been momentarily laid aside; the Bishop served as one of his consecrators at Metz. On balance, however, there was nothing in Charles' conduct that might have induced Hincmar to devise a theocratic kingship, much less to confer it upon him. For Hincmar, the words were far from empty when he prayed, in the coronation *ordo*, that God would remit (*indulgeat*) all Charles' evil deeds [385].

A second interpretation holds that the coronation upset the equilibrium between kingship and episcopacy, not by exalting the king, but by subordinating him, at least implicitly, to episcopal judgment. According to this view, the ritual for consecrating bishops suggested to Hincmar that the coronation might be employed as a juristic act that would warrant episcopal censure, or even deposition, of a king who flagrantly and incorrigibly violated his coronation oaths [386]. Bishops could depose

---

(385) *M. G. H., Cap. Reg. Fr.*, II, no. 302, p. 456. The account given above follows Hincmar's own views as set down in the *Annales Bertiniani* (866-869), ed. cit., pp. 129, 134-138, 150-152. Cf. *ep.* 27, *P. L.* CXXVI, col. 186, an instance of collusion between Hincmar of Laon and Charles against the Archbishop. It should be added, however, that the facts of the matter do not agree in every instance with Hincmar's recorded perceptions. See DEVISSE, *Hincmar, Archevêque*, II, p. 627.

(386) This case is stated forcefully by NELSON, ' Political Thought ', esp. pp. 245 f, 250. It rests on an analogue with the position that Hincmar stated when asserting his authority over Hincmar of Laon: ' sicut enim secundum Scripturam, minor a majore benedicitur; ita prorsus minor a majore, et non major a minore judicatur, ligatur, et solvitur '. *Libellus expostulationis*, c. 33. *P. L.*, CXXVI, col. 625. As indicated below, I believe that this interpretation mistakes analogy for identity. WALLACE-HADRILL, I think, struck the right note when he concluded, ' What we actually find in the Carolingian age is practical resistance to kings and emperors without intention to limit the power

bad bishops. Why not bad kings, if they, like bishops had taken oaths of office before they were instated by ritual anointing?

One cardinal fact should not be minimized. The validity of Hincmar's own title as archbishop of Rheims hinged on the legality of Ebo's deposition for his proceedings against Louis the Pious. Hincmar firmly and repeatedly argued that his predecessor had been canonically deposed. By contrast, Louis had been deposed, he wrote, ' by a faction of certain men ', who then proceeded to fabricate charges that would retroactively justify what they had done [386a]. It is quite apparent that, in Hincmar's eyes, the deposition of Louis the Pious was a blatant miscarriage of justice that rebounded against Ebo, and thus a dubious precedent.

We can not now recover the impact of this event on Hincmar's general thinking about the royal office, but it does illuminate difficulties in the second interpretation that we are to discuss. In the first place, as Hincmar wrote, kings came to the throne in many ways, other than by sacramental action, while episcopal faculties were conferred only by consecration. When Charles appeared at Metz, Bishop Adventius presented him as already ' our present lord, king, and prince ', by inheritance, before the coronation [387].

---

of Christian kingship. There was a real problem here and no mere debating point; sooner or later, someone would want to limit kingship itself: Hincmar nearly did '. *Early Medieval History*, p. 197.

(386a) *Annales Bertiniani* (869) ed., cit., p. 163. Synod of Troyes (867), *Mansi* XV, col. 792. Cf. a letter of Charles the Bald to Pope Nicholas I (*ep.* 5, *P. L.*, CXXIV, col. 872: ' ... quem [Louis the Pious] in monasterio beatissimorum martyrum Dionysii, Rustici et Eleutherii, a custodia reducentes archiepiscopi et episcopi, ut dignum erat, se in eum humiliter deliquisse confitentes, veniam ab eo suppliciter postulaverunt '. Hincmar actually witnessed the restitution of Louis the Pious, *Annales Bertiniani* (869), loc. cit. ' sicut vidimus qui adfuimus '. See below, n. 404.

(387) *M. G. H., Cap. Reg. Fr.*, II, no. 276 (A), p. 339.

Secondly, the oath which Charles rendered before his sacring was markedly different from oaths submitted by episcopal consecrands. There was no promise of obedience to correspond with the oath that, Hincmar of Rheims insisted, bound suffragans to their metropolitan; and no submission to a fixed body of law, corresponding with the canons. Furthermore, the king's oath was conditional. He promised to defend the Church and to preserve ecclesiastical and temporal laws, on the condition that his subjects yield him royal honor and power, and due obedience for preserving and defending the kingdom given him by God [388]. (On Charles the Bald's death, Louis III similarly acceded to the kingship before giving oaths and before being crowned. The Empress Richildis invested him with the royal office, using the dead King's ' sword of St. Peter ') [389].

Thirdly, Hincmar's subsequent words and actions militate against the view of the coronation as a mechanism of juristic control. In this regard, his celebrated letter to Pope Hadrian II, written some months after the coronation, is hard to discount. To be sure, the letter tendentiously defends the event, which had outraged the Pope, and we may suspect Hincmar's statement that he, alone, had derived no benefit, but only burdens and expenses, from the attempted annexation of Lotharingia.

One can not overlook the fact, however, that the Archbishop presented a cogent argument against withdrawing from Charles' communion, much less excommunicating the King, as Hadrian had ordered. Hincmar must have enjoyed the irony of his position. Two decades earlier, he had threatened to anathematize the Emperor Lothar I,

(388) Ibid., no. 276 (B), p. 339.
(389) *Annales Bertiniani* (877), ed. cit., p. 218 f.

together with Charles the Bald and his family. Incensed, especially, by the affront to Lothar, whom Pope Paschal I had anointed as emperor, Pope Leo IV denounced Hincmar to all the bishops of Gaul, and excoriated him for the swollen pride of his act. In 870, the shoe was on the other foot.

Recalling the chequered religious history of the fourth century, Hincmar alleged that what Hadrian commanded had never been ordered by popes, or by other authoritative and holy bishops, even when there were grounds for doing so against heretical, schismatic, or tyrannical emperors [390].

The Pope's case against Charles was ill-founded, Hincmar argued. But there were also weighty practical objections to his orders. How could Hincmar avoid the presence, communion, and company of the King, when Charles and his entourage were so frequently in the diocese and city of Rheims, where Hincmar was obliged, by long usage, to receive him with royal state, and to maintain him from ecclesiastical resources as he commanded and for as long as he commanded [391]? Since property was held by the jurisdiction of kings (*per iura regum*), he could not deny to Charles this service, which his predecessors had rendered to the King's [392]. Ecclesiastical sanctions did not apply.

Indeed, Hincmar recalled how the bishops and people of Lotharingia, suffering, without a king, from pagans and seditious men, invited Charles to enter into Lothar's

---

(390) On his threat to excommunicate Lothar I, SCHRÖRS, *Hinkmar*, p. 59 f. DEVISSE, *Hincmar, Archevêque*, I, p. 40 f. Pope Leo IV had used epithets of Satan to denounce Hincmar as ' the father of pride and the first-born of presumption '. *M. G. H.*, *Epp.* V, *K. A.* III, no. 37, p. 605. *Ep.* 27, to Hadrian II. *P. L.*, CXXVI, col. 179.

(391) *Ep.* 27, col. 183.

(392) Ibid., col. 184.

realm. They had invoked a secular text that affirmed that every kingdom in this world was gotten by wars and extended by victories – and not obtained by any excommunications that popes or bishops could launch. For, as the Scriptures proclaimed, ' the kingdom is the Lord's, through whom kings reign; and He gives it to whomever He wishes ' [393]. They now complained against Hadrian. He had forgotten, they said, that he could not be both king and bishop. He should content himself with the ecclesiastical order, and stop trying to settle the civil (*respublica*), which belonged to kings. By attempting to confer upon them a king (the Emperor Louis II) who, living in distant parts, could not defend them, he foisted a yoke on them that his predecessors had never attempted to impose. They would not bear it; they would fight to death for their freedom and their inheritance [394].

There is some evidence that this letter expresses Hincmar's own position. A major difficulty in thinking of the coronation order as a juridical check on the king is that Hincmar never invoked it to impose sanctions against rulers. From 870 on, Charles the Bald gave him many occasions to do so, and none was more apparent than when – in 875 – he marched into Italy to grasp the Empire, leaving his own lands open to invasion by Louis the German. With all the contempt built up through more than a decade of ill-will, Hincmar denounced this excursion into Italy as a desertion, a flagrant neglect of the royal office. But, far from censuring or abandoning Charles, or going over to the invader, Hincmar admonished his people to remember that they must not raise their

---

(393) Ibid., col. 180.

(394) Ibid., col. 180 f. DEVISSE insists throughout on ' la rigoureuse séparation établie par [Hincmar] entre rex et sacerdos ' (*Hincmar, Archevêque,* II, p. 703, n. 190), an attitude running through this letter to Hadrian.

hands against the Lord's anointed, and that, though betrayed by their lord, they were bound to observe their
oaths of fidelity, even if so doing meant death. As to
Charles, God would preserve him or not [395].

As a young man, Hincmar had lived through the di-
sintegrative results of the public humiliation of a king,
whether it took place by the king's own choice, as at
Louis the Pious' so-called Penance of Attigny (822), or
under duress as in Louis' humiliation at Soissons (833).
The consequences blighted order, peace, and justice, all
of which he cherished. And yet, the fact that Hincmar
imposed no juristic sanctions against Charles the Bald,
after his coronation in 869, or against Louis III, after
his in 877, can not be satisfactorily elucidated on grounds
of practical expedience. Such a consistent pattern of
behavior does correspond with the principle of parallelism which we have described. We can grasp the coronation as a covenant between a king and his subjects,
especially his bishops. The lack of effective sanctions
rendered the covenant unenforceable, however, and this
juristic void can only have been obvious to Hincmar.
It did, however, leave open the path exemplified by his
patrons, the Virgin, Dionysius the Areopagite, and Remigius: the path of martyrdom.

Writing to Hincmar of Laon, the Archbishop denounced acts that his nephew had taken against Charles.
He should bear in mind Christ, who prayed, on the cross,
for those who persecuted and killed him; Peter, shut in
prison and bound in double chains, yet praying for the
Church; Paul, while in prisons and in chains, always
praying for the Church; James, kneeling in prayer for
his executioners before they cast him down from the Tem-

(395) DEVISSE, *Hincmar, Archevêque*, II, pp. 806-09.

ple; and Stephen, the protomartyr, praying for those who were stoning him [396]. Had the Bishop sustained losses, or the threat of loss? He should follow the examples of Peter, and of popes, and of many holy bishops who had been imprisoned, or sent into exile, unresisting. He should think of St. Ambrose, shut up in his church by command of the Arian Empress Justina, surrounded by armed soldiers with a cart at the door waiting to take him into exile. Bishop Rigobert of Rheims, and other prelates, even in Hincmar's own day, had been expelled from their sees, some irrevocably, and yet none had imposed excommunications or curses [397]. For any just person who patiently bore his sufferings imitated Christ [398].

Hincmar's consistent behaviour towards Charles the Bald through their many hostile encounters between 869 and 877 certifies that he applied these models to himself. In the same spirit, he defied Louis III's command that he ordain a certain Odacre as bishop of Beauvais. He and others had elected Louis as king on condition that he preserve the laws, as specified in his coronation oath, a condition which Louis has now outrageously violated [399]. Despite his intense fury, Hincmar invoked no sanctions against the King, other than those which God might impose: early death, and condemnation in the hereafter. For himself, Hincmar was prepared to suffer Louis' wrath, rather than offend God. He fervently wished that God would send Louis, or anyone else, to deliver him from the prison of his body [400].

We can conclude that, at least in Hincmar's mind, the coronation ritual re-inforced the analogue between the

(396) *P. L.*, CXXVI, col. 528.
(397) *P. L.*, CXXVI, col. 516.
(398) *P. L.*, CXXVI, col. 552.
(399) *Ep.* 20, c. 7. *P, L.*, CXXVI, col. 119.
(400) Ibid., col. 120 f.

king and Christ, as King, without establishing an analogue
between the royal and the episcopal offices. The crucial
event – Charles the Bald's coronation at Metz – was
hardly the stage for a meticulously planned ritualization
of any ideological program. Lothar II died on 8 August;
by 23 August, Charles had ordered Hincmar to join him.
On 5 September, receiving homages along the way, the
King and his entourage arrived in Metz. The coronation
occurred on 9 September. The brevity of time, the haste
and confusion of these few summer days, and – it would
appear – the shadow of a charge that, by officiating at
the coronation, he would violate the canons [401], militated
against Hincmar's composition of a tightly reasoned pro-
grammatic ritual, much less an innovative one.

Anomalies resulted. To put the coronation in the
form of a covenant was to lean on a bruised reed. As he
cast his mind's eye over the years since Charlemagne's
death, Hincmar could see that oaths, and compacts, merely gave breathing space between wars. The ceremony
that he performed in Metz violated an agreement that
Charles and Louis the German had consecrated by oaths.
Better than most, he had reason to know that the contract
had been drained of value, and that, using the coronation
covenant to void an earlier compact, as he had done,
might very well disrupt political order. Indeed, there
was every reason to think that disruption would follow.
Even without knowing that, on 5 September, Pope Hadrian had issued severe letters forbidding Charles to seize
Lotharingia and threatening to excommunicate and depose bishops who failed to resist any such effort, and
even without foreseeing that Louis the German would

(401) Hincmar's first words, in his coronation address, concerned the ca-
nonicity of his action. *Annales Bertiniani* (869) ed. cit., p. 160 f.

recover from what promised to be a fatal illness and demand his share of the spoils, Hincmar could still see resistence to Charles flaring up on every hand. After almost
a year of controversy, Charles divided with Louis the
German the kingdom that he had tried to appropriate
for himself in 869, and, with it, the diocese of Metz, in
which he had been crowned. His coronation in Orléans
(848) had assisted him in consolidating his appropria-
tion of Aquitaine, a realm for which he had to fight throughout the rest of his life. Likewise, when he laid hands on
Lotharingia, another realm that would clearly cost him
a struggle, he drew as close as he could to God. Together
with the uncanonical accessions to the sees of Trier and
Cologne, and the canonical one to Verdun, the coronation
of 869 was a precipitate early thrust in Charles' play for
power, rather than a considered enactment of Hincmar's
abstract ecclesiological, or juristic, doctrines.

Given his experience of Charles' hostility, Hincmar
may well have wondered whether the ceremony were an
empty charade, like baptisms, or weddings, from which
the Holy Spirit withheld sanctification, or a curse, like
uncanonical ordinations of bishops or sacraments received by wicked men. At any rate, the impending ha-
zards of the King's venture meant that the enterprise
could have no foregone conclusion.

However, the coronation was not all anomaly. For,
over and beyond it, Hincmar could see the force of consensus at work in the discontent festering against Charles.
In his letter to Pope Hadrian, Hincmar referred to consensus as calling Charles to Lotharingia – and thus to
his coronation – and as sustaining him, though Hincmar knew that support was not so uniform as he described it. Likewise, ' by the consensus and will of the people ', Charles had been anointed and crowned as king of

Aquitaine, twenty years earlier [402], even while political divisions widened on every hand. One might say that consensus created kings.

For our purposes, it is important to notice that consensus was corrective, as well as creative. After promulgating a law, Charlemagne had to amend it, when the Church and the civil community (respublica) withheld consent [403]. While he may not have doubted that the deposition of Louis the Pious was licit, Hincmar certainly impugned its rightfulness, as we have seen. He knew that Hilduin, his patron and abbot, refused to withdraw allegiance from the Emperor; he considered the charges against Louis to be self-justifying fabrications concocted by a clique ' of certain men '. Thus, he could view it as a corrective when, with ' the consensus of the people ', bishops had restored Louis the Pious to his throne [404]. And the vicariate of Bishop Drogo of Metz – set up with all panoply by Pope Sergius IV and the Emperor Lothar I – had become moot, when it failed to receive the consent of those among whom it was to be exercised [405].

There was then, a point at which consensus performed the corrective functions of mimesis, adjusting the three orders of knowledge – represented by the eyes of the body, mind and faith – as they moved through history toward a final equilibrium with the wisdom of God. But it certainly did not remove disjunctions among the three

(402) Synod of Quierzy to Louis the German (858), *M. G. H.*, *Cap. Reg. Fr.*, no. 297, c. 15, p. 439. Cf. *Libellus proclamationis adversus Wenilonem* (859), ibid., no. 300, c. 3, p. 451.

(403) *Ep.* 15. *P. L.*, CXXVI, col. 96. Cf. *LV Cap.*, c. 24. *P. L.*, CXXVI, col. 375, on the acceptance and rejection of conciliar decrees by Pope Gregory I.

(404) DEVISSE, *Hincmar, Archevêque*, II, p. 1093 f. *De divortio, quaestio* 6 *responsio. P. L.*, CXXV, col. 757: ' Nostra aetate pium Augustum Ludovicum a regno dejectum, post satisfactionem episcopalis unanimitas, *saniore consilio*, cum populi consensu, et ecclesiae et regno restituit '.

(405) *Ep.* 30, c. 31. *P. L.*, CXXVI, col. 206. LÖWE, ' Aposcrisiar ', p. 218.

human orders that eluded other correctives. In the very treatise where he asserted most vehemently the duty of bishops to correct and judge sinful kings, he also recognized that churches, Christ's poor, and men of humble rank might be oppressed and destroyed, and just sentences, blocked, and that, in the eyes of men, the kings who fostered these wrongs might continue to wield the unstable power of this world, while, in God's eyes, they had been deprived of their kingly title and office [406].

With all the machinery of canonical deposition ready to hand, it was also true that bishops fell into schism, or even apostasized. Hincmar was pleased to remember those who, repenting, were worthy to retain their orders and to enter into the fellowship of holy bishops [407]; but he was also painfully aware of bishops who, in the eyes of God, had deposed themselves by disregard of the canons, and who yet remained in full possession of their sees, attending synods and councils, conferring holy orders, and sometimes leading their people with them into schism [408]. There was every reason to think that the silent judgment of God might differ from the spoken judg-

---

(406) *De divortio, responsio* 12. *P. L.*, CXXV, coll. 698-700.

(407) *Vita Remigii*, c. 16. *M. G. H.*, *SS. Rer. Mer.*, III, p. 302.

(408) Hincmar, of course, could think of his nephew's administration of Laon. His attitude toward Wulfhad of Bourges was much more sharply focused. Wulfhad, a leader of the clerics ordained by Ebo in 840, was advanced to the see of Bourges in 866 by Charles the Bald. Hincmar commented mordantly, ' statim in mense septembrio a quibusdam episcopis legibus ecclesiasticis minus necessario peritis, factione praedicti Vulfadi emendicatis et minis a Karlomanno ex auctoritate patris sui flexis, contra omnes leges ecclesiasticas sepefatus Vulfadus pro ordinatione episcopali maledictione indutus est sicut vestimento. Cuius exordinator potius quam ordinator Aldo Lemovicensis episcopus in ipsa ordinatione febre correptus in brevi moritur '. *Annales Bertiniani* (866), ed. cit., p. 130. Cf. his comment (in 881), that, if any bishop were consecrated contrary to the canons, both he and his ordainers became heretics, the latter as ' non ordinationis sed exordinationis mediatores '. *Ep.* 19, c. 10. *P. L.*, CXXVI, col. 116. All the same, Wulfhad enjoyed a pontificate of ten years (866-876).

ments of individual kings and bishops[409], and, indeed, from the broad human judgment of consensus itself. As a theological conception, consensus therefore labored under the ascetic, self-critical humility that we have found to be generally characteristic of Hincmar's attitude toward human knowledge.

Our task is to locate consensus in Hincmar's general doctrine of mimetic correction, and, furthermore, to relate it to the theological center of his thought. Let us therefore set down a few general points of reference.

The Archbishop recognized consensus as a formative act in secular government as well as in ecclesiastical. It was by the consensus of the faithful that kings promulgated laws[410] and issued judgments[411]. Hincmar was also aware of what, in antiquity, had been called the *consensus gentium*, invariable demands of human nature as manifested in universal human practices[412]. But he devoted his primary concern to consensus in the Church. This emphasis was laden with importance for secular rulers, as well as for ecclesiastical; for, Hincmar argued, the king, as a Christian, was personally subject to Church discipline and, as a ruler, was officially advised by bishops acting as custodians and interpreters of divine law[413].

What general contours did Hincmar give the notion of consensus? One might be tempted to regard consensus

---

(409) *De una et non trina Deitate. P. L.*, CXXV, col. 506.

(410) *De ordine palatii*, cc. 8, 23. *M. G. H., Cap. Reg. Fr.*, II, pp. 520, 525.

(411) *De divortio, responsio* 6. *P. L.*, CXXV, col. 672.

(412) Cf. *de divortio, responsiones* 21, 22. *P. L.*, CXXV, 736-738.

(413) Cf. his dread that all men, ' even Jews, the enemies of Christian law ', would be permitted the use of their own laws, and that the norms of jurisprudence established under the Christian Roman emperors would thereby be lost. *Pro ecclesiae libertatum defensione, P. L.*, CXXV, col. 1055. The argument resembles that more fully developed by Agobard in his treatise *Adversus Legem Gundobadi, P. L.*, CIV, coll. 114-126.

as a structured body of opinion; but Hincmar consistently thought of it as an act that imparted structure. Consensus was one of the three modes of action that constituted original sin, the others being choice and deed [414]. It was not the Eucharistic communion with evil men that made one a participant in evil, but rather the individual act of consenting to their deeds, explicitly or tacitly [415]. Thus, when Hincmar thought about consensus in a marriage settlement [416], or in the separation of man and wife [417], he considered, not a body of general assumptions, but a specific act of assent. The same sense applied when he discussed the consensus of participants in episcopal elections [418], the consensus of bishops to the consecration of a new confrère by their metropolitan [419], or to aspects of diocesan administration, the consensus that operated in ecclesiastical trials, and the consensus that regulated jurisdictional matters concerning more than one diocese [420].

Such was also the meaning that Hincmar employed when he wrote of the entire Church, bound together by one dogma, one charity, and one assent, the many faithful consenting in one communion [421]. The canons embodied

(414) *De una et non trina Deitate, P. L.,* CXXV, col. 555 f.

(415) *LV Cap.,* c. 48. *P. L.,* CXXVI, col. 479. *De praedestinatione, diss. post.,* c. 38 *epilogi* c. 1; *De una et non trina Deitate* ; *De divortio, responsio* 7; *De cavendis vitiis,* c. 10. *P. L.,* CXXV, coll. 419, 483, 674, 928. CONGAR, 'Structures', p. 9.

(416) *Ep.* 22. *P. L.* CXXVI, col. 133, 'una cum consensu parentum et amicorum meorum... '.

(417) E. g., *de divortio, responsio* 23. *P. L.,* CXXV, col. 744.

(418) E. g., *ep.* 29. *P. L.,* CXXVI, col. 186 ff. *Ad episcopos regni, admonitio altera,* c. 5. *P. L.,* CXXV, col. 1010.

(419) *LV Cap.,* c. 16. *P. L.,* CXXVI, col. 340. *Libellus expostulationis,* c. 3. *P. L.,* CXXVI, col. 569.

(420) E. g., *LV Cap.,* c. 2, 15, 28, 29. *P. L.,* CXXVI, 296 f, 300, 397, 403 f.

(421) *De praedestinatione, diss. post.,* c. 38, *epilogi* 1. *P. L.,* CXXV, col. 418. *LV Cap.,* c. 48. *P. L.,* CXXVI, col. 477.

this agglomerate consensus, establishing the norms by which the Body of Christ must be shaped toward its final perfection [422]. At his consecration, every bishop signed a formal declaration of obedience to the canons [423]. And rightly so; for they had been dictated by the Holy Spirit, and confirmed by the blood of Christ [424]. By flagrantly refusing to submit to canonical correction, Hincmar of Laon fell into schism [425].

All Christian laws, including those of kings and emperors, were established by divine inspiration [426], but the canons supremely expressed the will of the Holy Spirit, or of Christ, ' the celestial legislator ' [427]. God expressed that universal will particularly through the consensus of episcopal assemblies; for He had promised always to be present whenever two or three were gathered together in His name [428], and He had affirmed that the Spirit of the Father, which filled the world, spoke through them [429].

Hincmar argued, yet more broadly, that the divine power to express the consensus of the Church in canons resided in the episcopal order as a whole. All bishops, he held, received the same power to bind and to loose; all received the same faculties at their consecrations. Therefore, it fell to bishops generally to express the Church's

(422) Cf. *LV Cap.*, cc. 6, 32. *P. L.*, CXXVI, coll. 312 f, 413 f.
(423) *Quae exsequi debeat episcopus*, *P. L.*, CXXV, col. 1093.
(424) Synod of Quierzy to Louis the German (858), c. 15. *M. G. H., Cap. Reg. Fr.*, II, no. 297, p. 440.
(425) E. g., *Libellus expostulationis*, cc. 21, 22. *P. L.*, CXXVI, coll. 596 f, 601. The motive of correction appears, also, in Hincmar's comment to Hadrian II: ' cui [Hincmar of Laon] multa et multipliciter ut se corrigeret, scripsi, quae si in unum corpus fuerint congregata non puto minoris fore voluminis quam quinque sunt libri Moysi '. *P. L.*, CXXVI, 644.
(426) *De divortio, responsiones* 11, 21. *P. L.*, CXXV, coll. 688, 738.
(427) *De divortio, responsio* 23. *P. L.*, CXXV, col. 744. *Ep.* 31, c. 4. *P. L.*, CXXVI, col. 211 f.
(428) *Ep.* 33. *P. L.*, CXXVI, col. 251.
(429) *Ep.* 41. *P. L.*, CXXVI, col. 262.

divinely inspired consensus and, what is more, to censure or depose such bishops as acted contrary to the rules promulgated by the Spirit of God [430].

So great was the force of consensus that even St. Peter submitted to it. Despite the powers committed to him by Christ, he had denied Christ three times, and, being penitent, received forgiveness [431]. Subsequently, the Pastor of the Church and Prince of the Apostles was rebuked for consorting with Gentiles and receiving them in baptism. Although empowered to work signs and miracles, Peter defended himself before the Church; and, later still, he submitted to rebuke by St. Paul [432]. Such was the '*forma Petri*' imposed on all bishops [433], even on the pope, patriarch of patriarchs and primate of all primates as he was [434]. History had demonstrated the wisdom of this submission to a common discipline of faith; for Pope Vigilius had ceased to be 'apostolic' when he lapsed into heresy [435], and Pope Honorius I had been anathematized after his death for heresy [436]. Recognizing that the Church was a body with many members, Pope Gregory the Great denounced and repudiated titles such as 'universal patriarch' and 'universal pope' [437]. And, when in error, he – and Hincmar followed his

(430) *M. G. H.*, *Epp.* VIII, *K. A.* VI, no. 160 a, c. 25, p. 132 f.

(431) *De divortio, responsio* 6. *P. L.*, CXXV, col. 669.

(432) *De divortio, interrogatio* 3; *quaestio* 3 *responsio* ; *de praedestinatione*, c. 36. *P. L.*, CXXV, coll. 645, 749 f, 393. *LV Cap.*, c. 43. *P. L.*, CXXVI, col. 443. Charles the Bald to Hadrian II, ep. 8. *P. L.*, CXXIV, col. 885.

(433) *Libellus expostulationis*, c. 26. *P. L.*, CXXVI, col. 609.

(434) Loc. cit.

(435) *LV Cap.*, c. 48. *P. L.*, CXXVI, col. 477.

(436) *De una et non trina Deitate*, *P. L.* CXXV, col. 508.

(437) *LV Cap.*, c. 17. *P. L.* CXXVI, col. 346 ff. But Charles the Bald addressed Pope Nicholas I as ' catholicae et apostolicae sedis summus pontifex et universalis papa '. *Ep.* 5. *P. L.*, CXXIV, col. 870 f.

example – submitted to correction by the better judgment of lesser men [438].

Determining the act of consensus was an endless task; it required continual application, as well as divine enlightenment. The entire stock of philological techniques – collation of manuscripts [439], comparison and evaluation of authorities [440], verification of quotations [441], argument from context and from the intent of the author [442], and the tools of rhetoric and grammar [443] – was brought to bear. To these techniques, Hincmar added a comprehensive and rigorous knowledge of the Scriptures themselves, of the Fathers, and of ecclesiastical history. With such tools, bishops, individually and collectively, could prepare new canonistic medicines for the new spiritual diseases of their generations.

Thus, while the faith remained one and inviolable, consensus was susceptible to change. In this world, the canons belonged among the works of knowledge, which were inferior to charity in weaving the tunic of Christ. They were made by human minds, individually and collectively, using the critical arts of philology and exegesis. They expressed consensus that, while divinely inspired, was empirically determined, and therefore bound to specific times and situations. Hincmar asserted unity in faith, charity, and ' true understanding ' that transcended particular circumstances.

(438) On Gregory, above, n. 185. On Hincmar, *LV Cap.*, c. 4. *P. L.*, CXXIV col. 302. Cf. Hincmar's objection that bishops who disapproved his doctrines on predestination published synodal condemnations, instead of seeking to correct him. *Ep. ad Carolum Calvum de praedestinatione*, *P. L.*, CXXV, col. 51 f.

(439) *De una et non trina Deitate*, *P. L.* CXXV, coll. 512 f, 527. DEVISSE, *Hincmar, Archevêque*, I, p. 175 ff.

(440) *De praedestinatione, diss. post.*, c. 35. *P. L.*, CXXV, col. 381.

(441) Ibid., cc. 28, 34; coll. 295, 368.

(442) Ibid., c. 23, col. 218.

(443) Above, nn. 58-67.

Imitation established that unity. Later generations imitated the wisdom of earlier, but, even more, they imitated their faith. Mimesis operated particularly in the area of faith, where human reason could provide no self – sufficient proofs. For, by informing their doctrines and canons with the faith of ' imitable ' bishops, such as Gregory the Great, modern prelates became their heirs, born to them as sons to fathers and, like them, imitators of Christ [444].

Fideistic unity forged a bond that was impervious to time. And yet, that unity expanded. Like each person, each generation was ambiguously end and means in the mediation of form. At the end of time, when mediation ceased, the Church would shine as the full moon forever. Until then, it had to go through phases of mediation, just as it had passed through stages before the law and under the law. Even now, under grace, mimetic mediation continued, between time and eternity, through the sacraments and, across time, through the canons. Excepting the ' fixed and immovable ' canons of Nicaea, the decrees of synods and councils were liable to reinterpretation or obsolescence over the years, being replaced by canons that addressed new contingencies. Therefore, consensus, the collective *ratio*, also labored under ambiguities, as it advanced by analogical inference, applying its mimetic strategies of adaptation, self-criticism, and correction.

Canon law was not perfect, and Hincmar's own experience of consensus as criticism of criticism provided many examples of how retrogarde its actual movement could

---

(444) Above, nn. 185 (imitable bishops), 233 (imitation of faith), 338 (insufficiency of rational proofs), 375 (imitating the wisdom of earlier men). Psalm 44: 17 (pro patribus tuis nati sunt tibi filii) was one of Hincmar's favorite passages with regard to the apostolic succession of bishops. E. g., Synod of Quierzy to Louis the German (858), *M. G. H., Cap. Reg. Fr.*, II, no. 297, c. 15, p. 441.

be. Learned bishops at the synods of Valence and Lan-
gres, had embraced doctrines about predestination that
Hincmar condemned; bishops had consented to the restoration of the deposed Ebo to Rheims; bishops in synod
had approved the divorce of Lothar II. Not stopping
at what Hincmar considered misapplication of the canons, the bishops of Gaul had strained themselves to
write new canons approving the ' spiritual adultery '
by which a prelate might hold two sees [445]. Such things
were not unexpected, Hincmar wrote, in his ' most pestilential time ' [446], when everyone did what was right in
his own eyes. By the Flood, God had destroyed the entire
world for its wicked consensus, and it was possible that,
in the events of recent years, there might lie hidden another terrible judgment upon the sons of men [447]. In these
apocalyptic tones, Hincmar's doctrine of consensus retained the ascetic, self-critical element of humility that
we have noticed in his aesthetic and spiritual thought.

Quite obviously, consensus was a fundamental juristic concept in Hincmar's picture of Church government.
It was an act of will that enabled licit marriages to be
performed, bishops to be elected and consecrated, and
every sort of administrative act to be executed. The motif of correction, however, has carried us beyond formal
jurisprudence to the inmost, nonrational dimension of

(445) *Ep.* 31, c. 16. *P. L.,* CXXXVI, col. 226. This was an instance in
which Hincmar changed his mind abruptly, and perhaps ' avec beaucoup
d'hypocrisie '. Devisse, *Hincmar, Archevêque,* II, p. 790 n. 514.

(446) *De divortio, quaestio* 1, *responsio. P. L.,* CXXV, col. 746.

(447) *P. L.,* CXXVI, coll. 52, 115, 244, 249, 433, 537, 630 f, quoting Innocent I, decr. 56. Hincmar apparently did not realize that, by invoking this
principle, he negated the principle of catholicity, which he had invoked against
the ' new predestinarians '. *P. L.,* CXXV, coll. 350-52. The principle of catholicity – i.e., that universality is a sign of authentic faith and practice –
was also used against the Byzantine iconodules by the *Libri Carolini* (IV, 28),
in a passage known to Hincmar. Above, n. 7. *LV Cap.,* c. 20. *P. L.,* CXXVI,
col. 360 f.

faith. When Hincmar taught that universal consensus could deceive, he plainly indicated that, as a means of correction, consensus was a theological notion with legal consequences, rather than being, first and foremost, a legal concept. Its detachment from juristic formalism becomes yet more obvious in regard to enforcement.

To be sure, Hincmar's ecclesiology gave him a magnificent order of adjudication, in which the greater blessed and judged the less. Beginning with the diocesan court, he passed upward to the provincial synod over which a metropolitan presided, and thence to a general synod, combining several provinces, and, finally, to the apostolic see, which had the power to reconsider and to sustain or annul judgments of provincial and general synods. Beyond the pope, there was the wider community. The Holy Spirit had descended upon the apostles, the faithful, and the Virgin, at Pentecost, bestowing its gifts on over 120 followers of Christ. Consequently, St. Peter, the prince of the Apostles, rightly submitted to cross-examination by the brethren, and, following his example, prelates should humbly answer accusations against them before those who held inferior authority [448]. The theological principle of general inspiration pervades this structure. But, as in the case of coronation, it leaves juristic questions unresolved.

In fact, Hincmar's juristic notions are elegantly clear with regard to diocesan and provincial adjudication, but prodigiously vague with regard to higher levels. At the highest, the pope may review decrees of synods and councils. But are there circumstances in which, betraying his sacred ministry by violence, neglect of the canons, or heresy, he, like any other bishop, could come under

(448) *De divortio, quaestiones* 1-3 *responsiones. P. L.,* CXXXV, coll. 746-51.

judgment of a synod? What juristic recourse was there when a self-proclaimed universal council issued canons contrary to the teachings of orthodox doctors, and a pope assented to its decrees?

Neither was an abstract query. 'Not by the rules, but by force ', Pope Nicholas I had commanded that Rothad be re-instated as bishop of Soissons, though he ' had been canonically deposed by bishops of five provinces '. Casting aside canonical order, Nicholas ' restored him by his own power ', without the ' advice or consent of the bishops who had deposed him '. Pope Hadrian II had given another lamentable example of malfeasance when he assented to the decrees issued by the Council of Constantinople (869-70) on the veneration of sacred images [449].

And yet, neither in these instances, nor in any other of his many serious disputes with popes, did Hincmar invoke juristic sanctions. Hincmar the theologian insisted that popes were subject to correction by the force of consensus; but Hincmar the canonist supplied no mechanism by which that could be done, even in cases of heresy. When the Council in Trullo (681) condemned Pope Honorius I's Christological doctrines, it could impose no punitive action against the long-dead man himself. Perhaps the condemnation of Pope Vigilius I, at the Council of Constantinople (553), might have served as a precedent, always remembering that the sentence passed against him did not include deposition. Certainly, consensus against popes had found no juridical channel in Hincmar's own day. There was, of course, the instance of Pope Gregory IV, who while in Gaul, connived in the

(449) *Annales Bertiniani* (865, 872), ed. cit., pp. 118 f, 187.

humiliation of Louis the Pious. While they had threatened to depose the Pope, bishops friendly to the Emperor simply made sure that he went home without the honors that his predecessors had received. And there was the further instance in which the vicariate that Pope Leo IV committed to Drogo of Metz had lapsed, as we mentioned earlier, for lack of consensual ratification.

When he turned to the problems of synodal judgments, Hincmar likewise encountered questions that could be answered in terms of faith, but not in those of law. The descent of the Holy Spirit on the Apostles, collectively and individually, imparted a wisdom to the episcopal as a whole that was superior to the wisdom of any single bishop. And yet, assemblies of bishops erred; their acts required emendation by other synods. How could any synod know that it had spoken by the Holy Spirit, and not by its own imperfect wisdom? Hincmar answered that it would do so if it built with the living stones of orthodox judgments, conforming its decrees with the meaning, doctrine, and very words of the Fathers. Even so, he was aware of a wide discrepancy between the mediated knowledge that men could transmit from one to another, and the immediate perception of truth, open to the eyes of God and to those, like Paul and Dionysius the Areopagite, who had been rapt up to the third heaven. Even in synods, consensus was bound to the changefulness of this world.

As a juristic concept, consensus required closure. As a theological concept, it shared in the open spaces through which the body of Christ was built up. This was true of the episcopal order, consecrated with the sevenfold gifts of the Holy Spirit, and armed with the full apparatus of ecclesiastical laws and institutions, and even more so with regard to the secular order.

A salient feature of Hincmar's political thought was precisely that it raised questions that were institutionally unanswerable, questions that arose because of the disparity between metaphysical and political orders. As a specific result of that imbalance, we have considered the disjuncture between the theological doctrine of consensus and Hincmar's canonistic doctrines. Until recent times, the appeal to consensus has been a metaphysical one, without legal sanctions, and the problem of enforcement continually plagued secular philosophers as well as theologians. Hincmar was far from the last to encounter it. Even after centuries of learned discourse on the subject, and the experience of national revolution, John Locke ran athwart this generic perplexity. Government, he insisted, was formed by the consent of the people, and dissolved when rulers violated the offices committed to them. How was the breach of the social contract to be punished? 'Who shall be judge, whether the prince or legislative act contrary to their trust?' Locke's resounding answer – 'The people shall be judge' – grows fainter, as he searches for some mechanism of enforcement. In the end, Locke adds, God will judge. Yet, 'every man is judge for himself, as in all other cases, so in this, whether another hath put himself into a state of war with him, and whether he should appeal to the Supreme Judge, as Jeptha did'. (*Second Treatise on Civil Government*, ss. 240, 241).

Without being a prophet of popular revolution, Hincmar did advance a doctrine of consensus that displayed some of the same characteristics as Locke's. Let us summarize.

1. Social unity is a composite association, in which individual members retain their integrity, as in the Body of Christ.

2. The object of the association is the welfare of its members. Thus, each member enters into a union by a personal act of submission, which is both rational and free. To add a voice to the agglomerate consensus was to receive communicated knowledge and to become a willing cooperator in that act of mediation, as one did in duly receiving the sacraments.

3. If the social union is to persist, a deep and abiding consensus must prevail. But the balance between indidual and agglomerate consensus is difficult to maintain, and never universal at any moment. Who is to judge whether the majority consensus is badly in error, and whether the rulers who impose it have violated their ministries? Who is to say whether adaptation, or rejection, or discreet silence is called for? Judgment devolves upon the individual. Hincmar saw the result in heresy and schism, and in the varying judgments of orthodox men as they moved through the dialectic between old canons and new contingencies, as they conflicted with and denounced him. Consensus adapted itself through the criticism of criticism; but, in the end, God would judge.

** *

Like Locke's doctrine of consensus, Hincmar's was metaphysically powerful, but juristically toothless. Unlike Locke's political world, however, Hincmar's was double, as is any idealist order. The Archbishop was convinced that secular and ecclesiastical government replicated the celestial hierarchies, and that history itself was a modelling process through which the Church moved toward its supreme archetype, the heavenly taber-

nacle, not made by hands. The tensions of mimetic mediation therefore operated in his doctrines, as they could
not in Locke's. It had also been characteristic of idealist
thought since Plato, that those tensions, or ambiguities
were clarified in non-rational states, such as madness
and love. Hincmar elucidated them through analogues
of faith. Thus, by resorting to consensus without any
apparatus of referendum or adjudication, the Archbishop
did nothing to create a political synthesis between kingship and episcopate, but much to justify thinking of the
Church, and society, as a dynamic structure of oppositions, moving through strife and self-criticism toward
some future equilibrium. Hincmar taught a chiaroscuro
doctrine in which disunity was the necessary aesthetic
contrast of unity.

*   *   *

There is no need to restate here the view, which seems
so plausible to us, that Hincmar embraced a ' conciliar '
doctrine of authority in the Church [450].

Let me therefore conclude, directly addressing the
theme of this conference.

Hincmar's legal and political thought has generally
been detached from his ascetic spirituality; and the
bearing of his aesthetic doctrines on his general concept

(450) I have outlined an argument for ' conciliarism ' in Hincmar's thought
in *The Two Kingdoms*, pp. 76 ff. See also CONGAR, ' Structures ', p. 10, on
Hincmar's ' théologie conciliaire '. On the intimately related issue of the
Archbishop's knowledge, and use, of the Pseudo-Isidorian decretals, see HORST
FUHRMANN, *Einfluss und Verbreitung der pseudoisidorischen Fälschungen von
ihrem Auftauchen bis in die neuere Zeit*, I (Schriften der Monumenta Germaniae
historica, Bd. 24/I. Stuttgart 1972), pp. 200-10, 219 ff, ibid., III (Stuttgart
1974), pp. 627 f, 651 ff. DEVISSE, *Hincmar, Archevêque*, II, p. 58 f and *passim*.

of unity has gone largely unnoticed. I hope to have suggested that these various areas of thought and feeling actually reflected upon one another, and in decisive ways. Therefore, while some historical writers have quite simple concepts of change, this was not true of Hincmar. Faithful to patristic doctrines and to the monastic ethos of his day, his mental world was a sacramental dynamic, a structure of mediated oppositions, rather than one of stable forms. The mimetic theories that made up that dynamic integrated the most diverse areas of Hincmar's thought and action.

Throughout his life, he continued to preach the message of correction that, in his youth, he had learned at St. Denis and at the court of Louis the Pious. Therefore, he represents a mentality, institutionalized by monastic life, that persisted in his homeland, and that passed with many changes into the movements associated with the names of Gorze and Cluny. Given his opposition to papal centralization, Hincmar can certainly not be claimed as a forefather of the Gregorian reform. But, as Marx recognized when he denied that he was a Marxist, great ideas may be applied in many ways. A Lotharingian, Pope Leo IX, inaugurated the Gregorian program before Hincmar's altar to the Virgin in the cathedral of Rheims, lifting the relics of St. Remigius to his shoulders; and an interlacing of theology and canon law, resembling Hincmar's, played in his mind.

There was, however, one great difference between the idea of correction, represented by Hincmar, and the various programs of ecclesiastical reform that followed it. Later advocates of reform deplored the corruption of recent times, and aimed to recover an ancient purity. This pattern of loss and recovery is absent from Hincmar, and it is perhaps a telling difference between reform – or renewal – and correction, understood as a permanent and continuing state of life.

The idea of continual correction relates Hincmar's mentality to a wider spectrum in European intellectual history, one that transcends the monastic doctrine of reform. Hincmar had no extraordinary gifts in speculative thought; he lacked the instinct for paradox. And yet, his vision of transformation was both speculative and paradoxical. Enough has been said to suggest that these traits of idealist philosophy were conveyed to him through the teachings of the Fathers. We must resist the temptation to pretend a foreshadowing of Goethe's *Ewig-Weibliche* in Hincmar's veneration of the Virgin, as epitomizing the procreative force of mimesis in history. But, in the remote and general sense permitted by tradition, we might be able to number him among the precursors of modern idealists, including Goethe and Hegel. From the fourteenth century on, some idealists were fascinated by the thought – so foreign to Hincmar – that the archetypes themselves unfolded from a primal formlessness, and, consequently, that even the hypostases of the divine might be subject to change. Hegel, of course, shared this fascination. But, surely there are unmistakable resonances between such later idealisms and Hincmar's in the interlacing of aesthetics, theology and politics, in the concept of mimetic transformation (understood as dialectical process), in a distinction between historically significant events (informed by one Spirit throughout time) and non-signifying ones, and in the ascetic self-negation of the mediator, leading to ever higher states of mind.

The contribution of Hincmar and of others in his age to the intellectual formation of Europe was not simply that they forged some links among many in the long chain of tradition. They applied mimetic principles to an actually existing and vital social order, and not to an imaginary one, as Plato had done, or to a perishing society, as had Cicero. The Carolingians also differed from the Fathers, who had fully developed conceptions of mimetic mediation in the Church, but who applied them in a very tentative and fragmentary way to society as a whole, which they still regarded as alien and potentially hostile.

From their predecessors in the Merovingian age, and under the first Carolingians, Hincmar and his contemporaries – bishop and abbots – inherited secular functions that were quite unprecedented as territorial princes, as captains of men, as dominant members of a military, landed aristocracy. Trying to elucidate their own novel position, they began weaving the idealist structure of self-criticism and mediated oppositions into a program for transforming the entire social world. Their major legacy lay in the questions that they opened, and left unresolved. Providing adequate answers was the work of centuries; and the practical results of the doctrine of corrective process that we have described are still to be read on the map of Europe and, indeed, throughout the world in the diaspora of Europeans and their culture.

III

THE CHURCH, REFORM, AND RENAISSANCE
IN THE EARLY MIDDLE AGES

EARLY in the fourteenth century, Petrarch, a noted antiquary and a poet of sorts, wrote patronizingly of medieval scholars. Theirs had been a world of darkness, he said, in which only a few men of genius had prevailed over contemporary error to glimpse the truth; and even these men had seen through a glass darkly.[1] Petrarch wrote with the easy disdain of the classicist toward those who are not conversant with the languages and the literatures of Greece and Rome, and with the pride of a man who felt that the revival of classical studies to which he himself contributed had exalted his day over more benighted ages. This condescending spirit has persisted. For all his elegance and wit, Professor Highet does nothing but repeat opinions more than half a millennium old when he writes: "The sense of beauty always exists in mankind. During the Dark Ages it was almost drowned in blood and storms; it reappeared in the Middle Ages, although hampered and misdirected. Its revivification as a critical and creative faculty in the Renaissance was one of the greatest achievements of the spirit of Greece

[1] See T. E. Mommsen, "Petrarch's Conception of the 'Dark Ages,'" in E. F. Rice, Jr., ed., *Medieval and Renaissance Studies* (Ithaca, N.Y., 1959), p. 106.

and Rome." [2] And again: "The Dark Ages in western Europe were scarcely civilized at all. Here and there, there were great men, noble institutions, beautiful and learned works; but the mass of people were helpless both against nature and against their oppressors. . . . The very physical aspect of Europe was repellent . . . the land and natives were nearly as savage as in central Africa. In contrast to that gloomy and almost static barbarism, the Middle Ages represent the gradual, steady, laborious progress of civilization; and the Renaissance a sudden explosive expansion, in which the frontiers of space and time and thought were broken down or pushed outwards with bewildering and intoxicating speed." [3]

Stung by this sort of judgment, medievalists have laboriously tallied references to Cicero and Virgil, reconstructed curricula of instruction, and registered any outbursts of what Highet calls the "sense of beauty," seeking to establish as fact that the humane spirit, the knowledge and admiration of the classics, and the secularism of the Renaissance were present in the early Middle Ages. This has led to a confusing proliferation of renaissances. Almost every century can now boast a classical revival. Even in sixth-century Gaul, where books were few and readers fewer, one king (Chilperic, the grandson of Clovis) attempted to facilitate writing by adding four letters to the alphabet, encouraged the purification of texts, and expressed his own cultural pretensions by having a statue carved representing himself as the sun-god Apollo bearing his lyre before him. [4]

These studies have served a useful purpose in showing clearly that classical authors were read and appreciated throughout the early Middle Ages. But the term "renaissance" has become virtually meaningless through very frequent and general usage. Indeed, its indiscriminate application to cultural movements in that period was never well advised or appropriate for one critical reason. That is, it leaves out of consideration the goals of the movements, the purposes for which study of the classics was cultivated. Pe-

[2] G. Highet, *The Classical Tradition* (New York, 1957), p. 21.
[3] *Ibid.*, p. 11.
[4] H. Waddell, *The Wandering Scholars* (New York, 1955), p. 25.

Church, Reform, and Renaissance

trarch and the other leaders of the Italian Renaissance cultivated classical learning for its own sake. A pride in the achievements of their ancestors and a desire to revive the spirit of past greatness in their own time led them to study the known literary and artistic works of antiquity and to ransack libraries and to excavate ancient sites in search of hidden works. Every ancient artifact, every ancient poem or history, was an expression of the spirit of the past; through possession of the artifact and study of the literary work, the fourteenth-century Italian humanists sought to capture and to share in the spirit of Imperial Rome.

Leaders in the earlier "renaissances" were not Italians, and consequently they were not impelled by the strong Roman or Italic patriotism which motivated Petrarch and his contemporaries. They did not cultivate classical studies because the works read had some intrinsic value, but rather because study of ancient authorities was thought likely to serve some specific and predetermined ends. The revival of classical learning was not an end in itself; instead, it was merely a part of a broader program. Finally, even though they read Horace and Virgil with pleasure, the earlier scholars sought their inspiration, not in pagan antiquity, but in Christian Rome.

The focus of the Carolingian and Ottonian renaissances was theological, and the learned apparatus of the seven liberal arts and classical scholarship was subordinated to the understanding of the Scriptures. The greatest works of the Carolingian movement — the Alcuinian Rescension of the Scriptures, the revised order of liturgical service, and the learned treatises of John Scotus Erigena and Hincmar of Rheims — all treat of strictly theological or, more broadly, ecclesiastical problems. Alcuin himself, whom Einhard calls "the most learned man of his time," the presiding genius of the Carolingian Renaissance, described this characteristic explicitly when he compared the learning of antiquity with the learning of his own day. He congratulates Charlemagne for encouraging intellectual activity: "Your intentions have so far prevailed that a new Athens is taking shape in Francia, or, so to speak, an Athens more lovely than the ancient one. For ennobled by the teaching of Christ, our wisdom surpasses all the wisdom of the Academy. The ancient Athens had only the disciples of Plato to instruct her; but still, formed by the seven liberal arts, her glory has not ceased to shine. Our wisdom, however, is endowed beyond this with the seven-fold fullness of the Spirit, and exceeds all the dignity of worldly wisdom."[5] A century and one-half later, when Otto I undertook the encouragement of learning, he patterned his own patronage on that of Charlemagne and adopted the theological stamp of the earlier movement. In Ottonian Germany as in Caroline Gaul, the royal court and the greater ecclesiastical and secular princes maintained schools where the ancient Roman curriculum of the arts was taught, and in some of these foundations, Greek — a language which even Petrarch never mastered — was taught. But these schools existed, in the main, for the training of clergy, and, as the biographies of numerous bishops of the Ottonian period show, the seven liberal arts were taught to prepare the future clergy, especially the higher clergy, for interpreting the Scriptures and administering Church property. (Toward the middle of the eleventh century, Wipo complained vigorously that in Germany no one received instruction unless he were a cleric.[6]) Finally, on the eve of the renaissance of the twelfth century, a distinguished ecclesiastic gave his judgment on the relative values of the classics and Holy Writ: "Once was Cicero music in my ears, the songs of the poets beguiled me, the philosophers shone upon me with golden phrases, the sirens enchanted my soul nigh unto death. The Law and the Prophets, Gospel and Epistle, the whole glorious speech of Christ and His servants, seemed to me a poor thing and empty. I know not what the son of Jesse whispered in my ear, so gracious in its consonance of speech and thought, that all these others whom I once had loved fell inarticulate and silent."[7]

The leaders of the cultural revivals in the ninth, tenth, and late

[5] Ep. 170, MGH Epp. K. A. II, p. 270.

[6] *Tetralogus*, v. 197ff, in H. Bresslau, ed., *Die Werke Wipos*, 3rd ed. (Hanover, 1919), p. 81.

[7] Peter Damian, Sermo LXII, Migne PL. 144, 852. The translation is Miss Waddell's in *The Wandering Scholars*, p. 91.

Church, Reform, and Renaissance

eleventh centuries reiterate the thought that they are engaged in a work of restoration, a work in which the remains of antiquity are useful instruments. But when Charlemagne built his new capital at Aachen and called it "the second Rome," he referred not to the pagan Rome of Julius Caesar or Augustus, but to the Christian Rome of Constantine or Theodosius the Great.[8] Students labored in the liberal arts, not to capture the spirit of a glorious past, but to acquire administrative skills useful to the Church and to the king. In temper and in goals, the so-called "renaissances" of the early Middle Ages were quite alien to the Italian Renaissance of the fourteenth century, so alien in fact that the term "renaissance" should not be applied to them at all.

Recently, scholars have given some attention to this problem of nomenclature. Some of them have washed their hands of the whole business by asserting that there were no renaissances in the early Middle Ages. They leave the matter there, without telling us what we should properly call the unnamed movements. Others have proposed the terms "renascence" or "proto-renaissance," [9] but these terms preserve the classics-centered connotations which must be avoided. Like the word "renaissance," they cast the nature of the movements in question and their contributions to cultural development into false perspective, for they emphasize the revival of classical studies, an important ancillary aspect of those movements, but not their principal goal.

These early cultural revivals were only parts of greater movements which had as their first purpose the encouragement of Scriptural study and the purging of error from theological doctrines and of corruption from the administration of the Church. Charlemagne encouraged the study of Latin, and consequently the study of

[8] See especially R. Krautheimer, "The Carolingian Revival of Early Christian Architecture," *Art Bulletin*, XXIV (1942), 1–38.

[9] See the fine essay by E. Panofsky, "Renaissance and Renascences," *Kenyon Review*, VI (1944), 201–236, fully developed in his *Renaissance and Renascences in Western Art*, 2 vols. (Stockholm, 1960), and the comments upon the article by U. T. Holmes, Jr., "The Idea of a Twelfth-Century Renaissance," *Speculum*, XXVI (1951), 642–651, W. A. Nitze, "The So-Called Twelfth Century Renaissance," *Speculum*, XXIII (1948), 464–471, and E. M. Sanford, "The Twelfth Century — Renaissance or Proto-Renaissance?" *Speculum*, XXVI (1951), 635–642.

classical authors, expressly because, as he himself wrote, "we have begun to fear lest, just as the monks appear to have lost the art of writing, so also they may have lost the ability to understand the Holy Scriptures; and we all know that, though mistakes in words are dangerous, mistakes in understanding are still more so. Therefore, we urge you to be diligent in the pursuit of learning and to strive with humble and devout minds to understand more fully the mysteries of the Holy Scriptures." [10] Facility in Latin, acquired through the study of classical authors, was merely the key which opened the understanding of the Scriptures, which led to close scrutiny of the writings of the Fathers and to exact knowledge of the laws of the early Church. The so-called "renaissances" of the early Middle Ages are more properly called "reforms," or aspects of "reforms," not because they were lacking in humane disciplines, nor because the classical authors were unknown or unappreciated, but because of the purposes they served. "Renaissance" is a basically secular concept; "reform" is its ecclesiastical counterpart. Both reject the immediate past as being corrupt, and attempt to improve or overturn deficient institutions, practices, and opinions by returning to the standards of older and better ages. Consequently, both encourage learning; for since the standards of the past lie in the writings of the past, they can be discovered only by research and study. If, as in the case of the fourteenth century and of the earlier movements, the standards are sought in antiquity, such work involves mastery of the classical languages. Both are, in short, intellectual revolutions. When he wrote disparagingly of medieval scholars, Petrarch spoke for the revolutionaries of the Renaissance. The revolutionaries of all the early reforms had their spokesman in a pope of the eleventh century, Gregory VII, when he wrote that he would not allow the reform which he led to be obstructed by custom, "for it must be observed that the Lord says, 'I am the Truth and the Life' [cf. John 14: 6]. He does not say, 'I am custom,' but rather, 'I am the Truth.' And surely, to use the statement of St. Cyprian, any custom — however old, however

[10] MGH Cap. Reg. Fr. I, no. 29, p. 79.

Church, Reform, and Renaissance

common — must be entirely subordinated to Truth, and the practice which is contrary to Truth must be abolished." [11]

Judged by the criteria of classical scholarship, the cultural movements, the reforms of the early Middle Ages, deserve the strictures which classicists have issued against them since the time of Petrarch. The sense of truth to which Gregory VII referred — the search for theological verities and the attempt to implement those verities in the administration of the Church — is very different from the "sense of beauty" which Professor Highet seeks and which he finds deficient in medieval Europe. And yet it is harsh to censure an age distinguished for its advances in legal thought and institutional development and for its artistic productions as a period of "gloomy and almost static barbarism" simply because it does not meet standards arbitrarily imposed upon it by later critics. Every age must be judged according to its own standards, and according to the positive contributions it makes to the progress of civilization. By the standards of the early Middle Ages, revivals of classical learning accompanied and were later encompassed by reform of the Church; in serving these standards, the age made distinctive and important contributions to European culture in the revival of law and theology, and in the development of political theory. Its greatest direct achievement was in ecclesiology.

The scrutiny of Christian antiquity, of which the classical revivals were a part, posed two questions: "What is the Church?" and "How is the Church rightly to be governed?" In answering these questions, medieval scholars dramatically changed the concept of the Church as an institution in this world: they formulated doctrines which could be called "juristic ecclesiology." Because the questions which they were trying to answer required a definition of what could be accepted as authentic law in the Church, scholars were at great pains to study the canons of councils, the letters of bishops, the writings of the Fathers, papal decretals, and

[11] G. B. Ladner, "Two Gregorian Letters on the Sources and Nature of Gregory VII's Reform Ideology," *Studi Gregoriani*, V (1956), 225ff, and H. G. Krause, *Das Papstwahldekret von 1059 und seine Rolle im Investiturstreit* (published as *Studi Gregoriani*, VII [1960]), p. 39.

secular laws to decide which were the most authoritative. Because their questions required specification of the lines of authority in the Church, they had to define more precisely than earlier thinkers the relative powers of bishops, archbishops, and popes; and, most important, they had to establish where supreme authority in the Church rested. There was no unanimity in the legal and administrative theories which this work produced. Two answers predominated. The first was the conciliar theory, which held that supreme authority rested in general councils, and that only such councils could establish law in the Church and judge all bishops. The second was the doctrine of Petrine primacy, according to which the bishop of Rome held final authority in the Church, establishing laws and exercising disciplinary powers over all clergy and even over general councils. Out of the conflicts between these two theories came doctrines which were of the greatest importance to later political thought outside the ecclesiastical context: the conflicting doctrines of monarchy, popular sovereignty, and representative government.

There is very little juristic ecclesiology in the Fathers. Christian antiquity, to which medieval authors looked for inspiration, was rich in theology, but poor in the precise legal definitions which they sought. It is true that St. Jerome affirms very strongly the supremacy of the bishop of Rome in matters of faith,[12] and that St. Augustine maintains just as strongly that supreme authority rests in the episcopacy as a whole and, therefore, in general councils.[13] These Fathers, who, at one time, entertained as cordial a distaste for each other as they could within the limits of Christian charity, did not elaborate upon their contradictory theses. They never discussed in detail the bases and nature of authority, and the limits of rightful government in the Church. Indeed, they neglected the primary questions which would have led to a discussion of these problems: nowhere do the Fathers distinguish the clergy as an order subject to a law other than the one to which laymen

[12] Ep. 15, 1, 2; ep. 16, 2. See E. Caspar, *Geschichte des Papsttums*, I (Tübingen, 1930), 246.
[13] Ep. 53, 2; Retractationes I, 21, 1. See Caspar, *Geschichte des Papsttums*, I, 338–339.

Church, Reform, and Renaissance

were subject, and nowhere do they give a clear formulation of what constituted ecclesiastical law. Despite these major deficiencies, the patristic age made two contributions to later juristic thought concerning the Church. The first was the practice of taking important matters, such as questions of faith and the trials of bishops, before synods and councils. And the second was the image of the Church as the body of Christ, a spiritual community living in the world, but being independent of the governments and laws of the world. These points of synodal or conciliar procedure and the independence of the Church were central to the development of more sophisticated legal doctrines; but, in the age of the Fathers, the Church was not yet considered a predominantly legal institution, and St. Augustine's statement that the "Church is the congregation of the faithful" had only mystical or theological connotations.

The theological concept of the Church as formulated by the Fathers became a permanent and basic part of ecclesiological thought. But the structure of that thought was incomplete as it stood without reference to the administrative side of the Church. Scholars are agreed — from Mirbt to Merzbacher[14] — that the first major step in supplying this deficiency came in the eleventh century.

As in many cases of scholarly agreement, this consensus is inadequate. Two hundred years earlier, the Frankish clergy formulated juristic ecclesiology of remarkable sophistication. In attempting to revive the spirit of Christian antiquity, the Carolingian reform purified Scriptural texts, reformed the liturgy, received for the first time the complete body of the canons of early Church councils, recovered some elements of Roman law, and collected papal decretals in a convenient and systematic form. Fed by all

---

[14] R. Seeberg, *Der Begriff der christlichen Kirche, I. Teil: Studien zur Geschichte des Begriffes der Kirche* (Erlangen, 1885), p. 59. A. L. Mayer, "Das Kirchenbild des späten Mittelalters und seine Beziehungen zur Liturgiegeschichte," in A. Mayer, ed., *Vom christlichen Mysterium: Gesammelte Arbeiten zum Gedächtnis von Odo Casel, O.S.B.* (Düsseldorf, 1951), p. 277. F. Merzbacher, "Wandlungen des Kirchenbegriffes im Spätmittelalter: Grundzüge der Ekklesiologie des ausgehenden 13., des 14. und 15. Jahrhunderts," *Zeitschrift fuer Rechtsgeschichte, K. A.,* LXX (1953), 275. C. Mirbt, *Die Publizistik im Zeitalter Gregors VII.* (Leipzig, 1894), p. 551.

this, the Carolingian clergy went beyond the largely theological ecclesiology of the age they sought to imitate. Approaching the very questions which the Fathers neglected, they attempted to set the clergy apart from laymen as being under a law of their own, and to define precisely the components of ecclesiastical law.[15]

For the first time in the history of the western Church, the doctrines of papal supremacy and conciliarism were juxtaposed in terms of law. The advocates of the papal monarchy argued that, since Christ had said to St. Peter, "Thou art Peter, and upon this rock I will build my Church, and the gates of Hell shall not prevail against it" (Matthew 16:18), St. Peter had become the principal representative of Christ in the Church, and that, just as St. Peter was set above the other Apostles, so was his successor, the bishop of Rome, set above all other bishops. They held that only the bishop of Rome could establish law in the Church, and that his decretals were consequently "canons." They argued that no conciliar or synodal decrees had legal validity without the approval of the pope, and further that no synods or councils could meet without being called by him. Those who questioned these doctrines they condemned as "blasphemers against the Holy Spirit."[16]

The thinkers who upheld the supremacy of the General Council protested that Christ had spoken to St. Peter merely as the representative of the other Apostles, and that whatever powers had been given to St. Peter had been given to the other Apostles as well. All the Apostles alike had been given the gift of the Holy Spirit; and all their successors, the bishops, had likewise received it in the episcopal consecration. All bishops held the same powers; therefore, no bishop was superior in authority to any other. Consequently, the conciliarists argued, supreme authority in the Church did not belong to one bishop, but rather to all bishops; and it was exercised through assemblies of bishops, or councils. Their argument is the reverse of the papal supremist position, for they

---

[15] For a fuller exposition of this argument, see my study, *The Two Kingdoms: Ecclesiology in Carolingian Political Thought* (Princeton, N.J., 1964).

[16] F. Maassen, "Eine Rede des Papstes Hadrian II. vom Jahr 869," *Sitzungsberichte der AK. der Wiss. zu Wien*, phil.-hist. Kl., LXXII (1872), 541.

Church, Reform, and Renaissance

maintained that only conciliar decrees were true law, and that papal decretals had the force of law only when they had been approved by councils.

Both schools accepted the theological implications of St. Augustine's statement that "the Church is the congregation of the faithful," but they had, in their quite different ways, defined the Church in law as well as in theology. Charlemagne's "new Athens," which Alcuin saw marked by wisdom endowed "with the sevenfold fullness of the Spirit, and exceeding all the dignity of worldly wisdom," had sought to recover the spirit and institutions of the early Church; but it had gone far beyond its patristic prototype. Its recovery of Roman and canon law, and its revival of patristic studies, had brought about two new images of the Church, two images of the Church as an institution in this world as well as an eternal City.

The conflict between the monarchical doctrine of papal supremacy and the representative doctrine of conciliarism continued through the Ottonian period and reached its climax in the early Middle Ages in the great reform movement of the eleventh century.

Despite the efforts of reformers in the ninth and tenth centuries, corruption within the Church increased to an appalling degree in the tenth and eleventh centuries. But, from 1046 onwards for nearly a century, the papacy was held by ardent reformers, who were dominated by the desire to purify the doctrine and the administration of the Church, and by the conviction that this could be accomplished only if the reform were led by the Roman Church. Earlier reforms had been led by secular rulers — by Charlemagne and by the Ottos — and the eleventh-century reform itself began with the support of Emperor Henry III. But the reform popes soon separated themselves from imperial control; the earlier reforms had been limited to the territories under the direct control of royal patrons (e.g., Charlemagne could not reform the churches in Mercia), but the papacy, with its claims to universal competence within the Church, extended the reform to every Christian land in the West. This made reform a matter of general concern, and it made the ecclesiological and political doctrines of the reformers the common property of all Christendom.

The greatest of the reform popes, and the one about whom centered the principal controversies of the eleventh-century movement, was Gregory VII. Like his predecessors, Gregory acted according to the lofty claims of papal supremacy. He held that papal decretals were laws in themselves, and that the bishop of Rome, superior to all councils, could overturn the decrees of councils and modify their canons. He was the ruler over all Christians, even over kings. For, as Gregory wrote: "Who does not remember the words of our Lord and Savior Jesus Christ, 'Thou art Peter and on this rock I will build my Church, and the gates of hell shall not prevail against it. And I will give thee the keys of the kingdom of heaven and whatsoever thou shalt bind on earth shall be bound in heaven, and whatsoever thou shalt loose on earth shall be loosed in heaven.' Are kings excepted here? Or are they not of the sheep which the Son of God committed to St. Peter? Who, I ask, thinks himself excluded from this universal grant of the power of binding and loosing to St. Peter unless, perchance, that unhappy man who, being unwilling to bear the yoke of the Lord, subjects himself to the burden of the Devil and refuses to be numbered in the flock of Christ? His wretched liberty shall profit him nothing; for if he shakes off from his proud neck the power divinely granted to Peter, so much the heavier shall it be upon him in the day of judgment." [17]

Gregory's strong implementation of this doctrine aroused resistance and, in some instances, open rebellion among the clergy. Out of this rebellion came three doctrines which undercut the doctrine of Petrine primacy: two of them were, from the first, counter-theories — the doctrines of parties opposed to Gregory — but the third Gregory himself encouraged. All were landmarks in the development of doctrines of representative government. The earliest resistance to Gregory's reforms came from the lesser clergy and

[17] Reg. VIII, 21, ed. E. Caspar, *Das Register Gregors VII.* (Berlin, 1920, 1922), p. 547, tr. E. Emerton, *The Correspondence of Pope Gregory VII* (New York, 1932), p. 167.

Church, Reform, and Renaissance

from the episcopacy in northern Italy, Spain, France, and Germany. His edicts against simony, clerical marriage, and finally lay investiture were calls to battle. In several cities, prelates who read these edicts to their clergy were publicly ridiculed, some were stoned, and others, like the bishop of Brixen, were beaten almost to death. Many bishops refused to enforce the decrees, arguing that Gregory had usurped powers of legislation and powers to determine doctrine which rightly belonged only to general councils, that he had, in fact, contravened the decrees of the Church stated by such councils, and that he had consequently lapsed into heresy and could no longer be considered the true pope. Finally, the German episcopacy, urged on by its king, attempted to enforce the conciliar doctrine: they gathered in council, declared Gregory deposed, and elected another pope. In this deposition, the German bishops had the support of Hugh Candidus, cardinal priest of S. Clemente in Rome, who subscribed the decree of the synod of Brixen (1080) "in the name of all the Roman cardinals."

It was among the cardinals that the second doctrine of resistance developed. The College of Cardinals had come to prominence in the Roman Church only after the reform papacy began its work in the mid-eleventh century, but its powers became very great in a short time. According to the Papal Election Decree of 1059, the cardinals were charged with nominating to the papacy, and it was soon asserted that the cardinal clergy could judge all bishops in the Roman Empire. They were, Peter Damian wrote, "the spiritual senators of the universal Church." [18] In his major decisions, as for example in his decrees against lay investiture and in his excommunications and depositions of Henry IV, Gregory did not consult the lesser cardinal clergy (the cardinal priests and deacons), and in other ways he excluded them from the government of the Church. The reaction of the slighted clergy was strong. Hugh Can-

[18] See especially H. W. Klewitz, "Die Entstehung des Kardinalkollegiums," *Zeitschrift fuer Rechtsgeschichte, K. A.*, XXV (1936), 115–221; S. Kuttner, "Cardinalis: The History of a Canonical Concept," *Traditio*, III (1945), 129–214; and J. Sydow, "Untersuchungen zur kurialen Verwaltungsgeschichte im Zeitalter des Reformpapsttums," *Deutsches Archiv*, XI (1954/5), 18–73.

didus was the first to desert Gregory; in 1084, a year of bitter reversal for the pope, half the College of Cardinals abandoned him, formulating a new doctrine of Church government which gave supreme importance to their own body. For, they argued, the cardinals were the true representatives of the Roman Church, the head of Christendom, and the bishop of Rome was the true pope only so long as the cardinals recognized him as such. Supreme authority rested, according to their position, neither in the general councils nor in the pope alone, but rather in the pope together with the College of Cardinals.

Different as their positions were, the conciliarists and the cardinals could make common cause in opposition to the third doctrine which ultimately subverted the doctrine of Petrine primacy: the doctrine of popular sovereignty in the Church. This position was not clearly formulated, and it is only implied in the letters and actions of Gregory VII himself, the strong defender of papal monarchy. When Gregory discovered that the German bishops had left his decrees against clerical marriage unenforced, he appealed to the laity to abandon the corrupt priests, and laymen responded to this appeal, accusing married clergy and inflicting gross public humiliation upon them. He urged the count of Flanders to expel married priests, and, in case after case, he admonished the laity to withdraw from bishops and lower clergy whom he had judged unworthy of ecclesiastical office. Gregory himself no doubt considered these measures aspects of the pope's immediate government over every Christian. His enemies, however, saw a wider implication, and they argued that, through these measures, the pope had so far dishonored the clergy that laymen no longer obeyed their priests and that they neglected the sacraments. As the German episcopacy wrote in one edict of deposition against him: "The flame of discord which you stirred up through terrible factions in the Roman Church, you spread with raging madness through all the churches of Italy, Germany, Gaul, and Spain. For you have taken from the bishops, so far as you could, all that power which is known to have been divinely conferred upon them through the grace of the Holy Spirit, which works mightily in ordinations.

Church, Reform, and Renaissance

Through you, all administration of ecclesiastical affairs has been handed over to the madness of the people." [19]

These four doctrines were the results of the attempt to recapture the spirit of Christian antiquity, to revive the Church of the Fathers. Gregory VII himself repeatedly says that he is trying to do nothing other than to restore the ancient canons of the Church to their full vigor, and his enemies affirm just as strongly that they are trying to do the same thing. St. Augustine's image of the Church as the "congregation of the faithful," however, took on a completely new dimension as a result of the reforms of the ninth, tenth, and eleventh centuries. It appeared not simply as a mystical, or sacramental, communion, but equally as a legal body, a corporation, having a specific body of law and precise lines of authority. The "congregation of the faithful" had become a state as well as a church.

And yet, these doctrines had significance far beyond the scope of ecclesiology. It is true that they represent a revolution in the concept of the Church; but the theory of the papal monarchy, the representational theories of the conciliarists and the cardinals, and the nascent doctrine of popular sovereignty continued to develop, and they were later incorporated into doctrines concerning civil government. The papal monarchy corresponded to the later medieval monarchy with its claims to ultimate authority, and many of the same arguments from Roman law which the papalists used in their own defense were used to support the thesis of irresponsible government in temporal kingdoms. The medieval concept of the state as a hierarchy of corporations, each with its own inviolable privileges, derived from the knowledge of Roman law recovered in the eleventh and twelfth centuries; it is closely related to the doctrine of the schismatic cardinals in the time of Gregory VII that the pope, the cardinals, the bishops, the lesser clergy, and the laity, each as a class, had rights which none of the others could infringe. The early Renaissance, or late medieval, theorists Marsilio

[19] C. Erdmann, ed., *Die Briefe Heinrichs IV.* (Leipzig, 1937), p. 66, tr. T. E. Mommsen and K. F. Morrison, *Imperial Lives and Letters of the Eleventh Century* (New York, 1962), p. 148.

of Padua and William of Ockham, with their theories that full sovereignty in State and in Church lay with the commons, were foreshadowed in Gregory's appeal beyond the established organs of Church government to the laity for the execution of his decrees. Parliaments and other representative assemblies of civil states corresponded to Church councils, and the theorists who advocated their supremacy in civil matters found much to support this position in the earlier arguments of the conciliarists.

If the early Middle Ages seem dark, or a period of "gloomy and almost static barbarism" to students of classical learning, it is because they are applying to that age goals and standards which the age itself did not acknowledge or strive after. It is not in the idea of the "Renaissance" that we shall find the proper standards of that period, but rather in the idea of reform; not in the attempt to recover the spirit of pagan antiquity, but rather in the attempt to revive the vigor and the promise of Christian Rome. In this dimension, the early Middle Ages made remarkable contributions to Western civilization, contributions which are present whenever we use the terms "monarchy," "representative government," and "popular sovereignty."

Petrarch did not appreciate the cultural values of the "Dark Ages"; the religious ethos of the period was foreign to him, and he acknowledged judgment under the aspect of time, rather than under the aspect of eternity, as supreme. His older contemporary, Dante, still partook of the earlier spirit. Like men of the early Middle Ages, he honored classical antiquity, but, in his eyes, it did not hold ultimate truth. In the eighth century, Alcuin had written that the learning of Athens was glorious, but that Christian wisdom was yet more glorious, "endowed by the seven-fold fullness of the Spirit." Likewise, in the fourteenth century, Dante received the pagan poet Virgil as his guide through the Inferno and Purgatory on his journey toward divine truth. But Virgil must leave Dante on the threshold of Paradise, the eternal Kingdom, from which he was barred because he had been a pagan. The man whom Dante honored as the greatest poet of classical antiquity could not glimpse the vision of God's eternal glory because he had not been

Church, Reform, and Renaissance

a Christian. Without Virgil, Dante himself continues on his journey into the Heavenly City, and at length he beholds the splendor of Christ enthroned. Rejecting the values of the "renaissance" for those of "reform," he wrote: "O triple Light, which in a single star shining on them their joy can so expand, look down upon this storm wherein we are. If the barbarian . . . seeing Rome and her stupendous works — if he was dazed . . . how dazed past measure must I needs be, I who was come to the divine from man, to the eternal out of time, and from Florence unto a people just and sane."[20]

[20] *Divine Comedy*, tr. L. Binyon, Paradiso XXXI, vv. 28–40.

IV

CANOSSA: A REVISION

By their exchange of articles in the *Studi Gregoriani*,[1] M. Fliche and the Canon Arquillière have reopened the question of what actually happened when Pope Gregory VII received Henry IV at Canossa. Both scholars assume that Henry approached the Pope, excommunicate and stripped of the royal office; but they differ widely in interpreting Gregory's reception of the penitent King. Taking issue with views Arquillière had expressed in his work *Saint-Grégoire VII*, Fliche maintained that when Gregory released Henry from excommunication he also reinstated him in the royal office. In response, Arquillière reaffirmed his earlier position that only the ban, and not the sentence of deposition, was lifted.

Disproving one another as they do, the two arguments offer a curious paradox. It is true, as Arquillière points out, that Gregory explicitly denied having restored Henry to the royal office.[2] And yet, Fliche observes just as accurately that Henry was openly acknowledged as king in the documents issuing from the Canossa interview; moreover, it is difficult to believe that that acknowledgment, coming after a year of bitter struggle and intricate negotiation, was merely 'une incohérence de forme,' as Arquillière suggests.[3] It would appear, then, that the testimony of Gregory himself leads one invariably to a confused judgment of the reception. For the records clearly indicate that Henry, whom Gregory had declared deposed and excommunicate, came to Canossa in full possession of his royal title and that, without rescinding his decision, the Pope himself recognised that title. It is the apparent equivocation epitomised in Gregory's reference to the excommunicate Henry, guilty of 'unheard of depravities and various iniquities,' as still king, though neither Christian nor ruler over Christians,[3a] a reference which recalls by analogy the indelible character of holy orders.

This ambivalence generally characterized Gregory's conduct throughout the dispute with Henry; and before attempting to solve the riddle of Canossa we shall have to establish the principles which the Pope maintained for the whole period.

---

[1] H. X. Arquillière, 'Grégoire VII, à Canossa, a-t-il réintégré Henri IV dans sa fonction royale?' *Studi Gregoriani* 4 (1952) 1-26. A. Fliche, 'Grégoire VII, à Canossa, a-t-il réintégré Henri IV dans sa fonction royale?' *Studi Gregoriani* 1 (1947) 373-386. I should like to thank Professors B. Tierney and F. Cheyette and Mr. E. Karafiol for reading and commenting upon this essay.

[2] *Art. cit.* 1, 6f.   [3] *Ibid.* 19.   [3a] See note 68 (*infra*).

I

To reconcile the stated contradictions, one must examine Gregory's thought and actions in a dimension other than the purely constitutional, in which they have generally been set. Gregory was not primarily a legist. However great the work of canonists in his day, however great his encouragement of their work, Gregory cannot be named among the lawyer-popes. In his decrees and letters, there are no such citations of Roman or barbarian law, no such explicit citations of canons from the synods and councils of the early Church, as there are in the declarations of Nicholas I and John VIII or of the popes in the High Middle Ages. His pronouncements are tissues, not of legal sanctions, but rather of moral and ethical assertions.

Gregory's relations to temporal princes are therefore to be seen in a framework of moral instead of juristic thought. One must acknowledge that his claims to supreme authority in temporal affairs were primarily claims over Christian men, not over their offices; and moreover one must attempt to see those claims in the light of Gregory's own metaphysical orientation as parts of the ceaseless warfare between the Church and the world. An examination of Gregory's dealings with Henry IV from that point of view indicates that the recent construction of his hierocratic concept of relations between the spiritual and the temporal power must be modified:[4] it suggests that Gregory's claims that the Pope could judge of candidates for the royal office and depose unworthy kings were relative and not absolute. In establishing the scope of those assertions, one must observe three major limitations: Gregory never claimed for the Papacy the power to grant the kingship, but rather he consistently attributed it to God alone. He never claimed or, as we shall show, attempted to exercise the power of final deposition over kings, for that also fell to heavenly judgment. Finally, and most important, his assertion of headship over temporal government extended only to Christian rulers in communion with the Roman church; outside that communion were pagan or heretical princes, whose titles to the royal office Gregory himself acknowledged. For him, the kingship was an office existing independently of the Church, employed for the good of the Church if the king were a true believer, but removed from that service or even turned against the faithful if he were not. Consequently, Gregory did not assert that the Pope could bestow the kingship

---

[4] Among the most distinguished analyses of Gregory's thought as illustrative of hierocratic doctrine are those by G. Tellenbach (trans. R. F. Bennett), *Church, State and Christian Society at the Time of the Investiture Contest* (Oxford 1948) esp. 153, 158; M. Pacaut, *La théocratie* (Paris 1957) esp. 79ff, 87; and W. Ullmann, *The Growth of Papal Government* (Oxford 1956) 277ff.

but rather that he could sanction the use of the kingly power; he maintained, not that he could withdraw the royal office, but that he could withdraw ecclesiastical sanctions from its exercise. To use the terminology of a later age, Gregory saw papal relations to temporal government in terms of indirect power.[5]

These views brought Gregory into conflict with his own contemporaries who, like some recent scholars, believed his claims to be absolute. Henry IV vehemently protested that Gregory had snatched from him the office due him by hereditary right, as though kingship and empire were in the Pope's hands instead of in the hands of God.[6] Furthermore, he wrote, Gregory had ordained Rudolf of Rheinfelden as king over him.[7] The imperial construction of Henry's deposition and excommunication was patently that 'that Sarabite had said he had the power to advance to the Empire whomever he wished [to govern] and to remove whomever he did not.'[8]

Understandably enough, Gregory did not answer these charges when they were made by his declared enemies; but his refusal to answer when the reverse charges were made by the Saxons, his alleged allies, is less readily understood. In the early years of the Investiture Conflict (1077-1080), Gregory antagonised the Saxons by continuing to negotiate with Henry and to acknowledge him as king, even after he himself had declared him excommunicate and deposed, and further by refusing for three years to acknowledge Rudolf of Rheinfelden whom the Saxons elected as king on the warrant of that excommunication and deposition. In his history of the Saxon war, Bruno records that when the first excommunication and deposition of Henry became known many persons immediately obeyed Gregory's sentence and acknowledged that 'they owed him no fidelity or subjection, now that he was not king.'[9] He continues to

---

[5] See E. Voosen, *Papauté et pouvoir civil à l'époque de Grégoire VII* (Gembloux 1927) 313f. Gregory's thought was, however, by no means so fully developed as that of later canonistic advocates of the *potestas indirecta*. Indeed, by admitting that legitimate rulers might govern outside the Church, he differed markedly from some of them. See M. Maccarrone, '"Potestas directa" e "potestas indirecta" nei teologi del xii e xiii secolo,' *Sacerdozio e Regno da Gregorio VII a Bonifacio VIII* (Miscellanea historiae pontificiae 18; Rome 1954) esp. 44ff. Cf., in the same volume, A. Stickler, 'Sacerdozio e Regno nelle nuove ricerche attorno ai secoli xii e xiii nei Decretisti e Decretalisti fino alle Decretali di Gregorio IX,' esp. 5f, 21ff.

[6] *Die Briefe Heinrichs IV*. ed. C. Erdmann (Leipzig 1937) nos. 11, 12, pp. 14, 16.

[7] *Ibid*. no. 17, p. 25.

[8] MGH *SS*. 11.670. Dr. Ullmann has accepted this statement as representative of Gregorian thought and attempted to set it in the developing context of papal political doctrine. W. Ullmann, 'Cardinal Roland and Besançon,' *Sacerdozio e Regno* (note 5 *supra*) 115.

[9] *Brunos Buch vom Sachsenkrieg*, ed. H. E. Lohmann (Leipzig 1937) c. 82, p. 78: 'quia nullam apud regem misericordiam, dum rex erat, invenire poterant et ei nullam modo, cum rex non esset, fidem vel subiectionem debebant ....'

mention other rationales the Saxons offered for renouncing their allegiance to Henry, the tenor of which was that by wrongful government he had ceased ipso facto to be king.[10] However, it is clear throughout that Henry's enemies did not consider their own complaints sufficient grounds for deposition until they were ratified by the papal action. The renewed excommunication of Henry imposed at Goslar by the papal legate Cardinal Bernard (November 12, 1077),[11] and the election of Rudolf 'accepta licentia a legatis'[12] were for the Saxons corroborative of Gregory's own decree of excommunication and deposition. Thenceforth, they denied that Henry had any claim to the royal title; Rudolf had acceded to his office.

It has been maintained that Gregory considered temporal princes as his vicars, much as he considered bishops vicars of the See of Peter.[13] Had that been true, he, like the Saxons, would necessarily have considered Henry's removal an absolute juristic act. To be sure, Gregory denied Henry's office to him; he absolved his subjects of their allegiance; he cut Henry himself off from the body of the faithful. The terms of the papal decree are explicit and they are supported by related documents in Gregory's correspondence: Henry was deposed from office, not merely suspended from it.[14] Further, Gregory wrote that it was he who had withdrawn the kingship from Henry, he who had denied the powers of government to him. And remarks in his other letters might lead one to imagine that Gregory conceived of the power to create and to depose kings definitively as the historical right of the Papacy.

And still, Gregory did not conduct himself as though he had taken Henry's position from him. Shortly after issuing his edict, Gregory wrote to the knight, Wifred of Milan, stating his willingness to come to a peaceful settlement 'with the King of Germany,'[15] and in subsequent correspondence, Gregory con-

---

[10] *Ibid.* cc. 25, 127, pp. 29f, 120f.

[11] On the history of the entire process, the most ample account is still that of G. Meyer von Knonau, *Jahrbücher des deutschen Reiches unter Heinrich IV. und Heinrich V.* vols. II, III (Leipzig 1874, 1900).

[12] Paul of Bernried, *Vita Gregorii VII* c. 84 (PL 148.84). Paul also recorded that the legates were present at Rudolf's subsequent coronation (*ibid.* 85).

[13] See A. Fliche, *La réforme grégorienne* II (Paris 1925) 413. For the contrary view, see Voosen, *op. cit.* 248f. There can be no doubt that Gregory considered other episcopal churches and even monasteries as subject members of the Roman church. See JL 5094: J. von Pflugk-Harttung, *Acta Pontificum Romanorum inedita* I (Tübingen 1880) no. 52, p. 51, and further the letter of Liemar of Hamburg in H. Sudendorf, *Registrum merkwürdiger Urkunden* I (Jena 1849) no. 5, p. 9.

[14] For the opposite view among Gregory's contemporaries, see, in addition, Paul of Bernried, *Vita Gregorii VII* c. 86 (PL 148. 85f.) and Bruno, *ed. cit.* c. 104, p. 93. On the history of the juristic process, see V. Domier, *Päbste als Richter über die deutschen Könige* (Bresslau 1897) 14f, 18f, 23ff.

[15] *Das Registrum Gregors VII.* ed. E. Caspar (MGH *Epp. sel.* 2; Berlin 1920-22) 3.15 (p. 277).

sistently allows Henry the royal title.[16] Even in his well-known letter to Herman of Metz (August, 1076), Gregory did not refer to Henry's deposition but rather concerned himself to defend his power to excommunicate kings,[17] making provision at the same time for the possible reconciliation of the 'King' with the Roman church.[18] Finally, two important letters to the German faithful urge that every measure to secure Henry's repentance and release from excommunication be made. Should all efforts fail, then and only then, the Germans were to proceed in concert with the Pope to elect a new king.[19]

This inconsistency is most significant: occurring in the very period when the formalism of the papal chancery was greatly increasing,[20] it indicates a considerable ambivalence in Gregory's own mind. When Gregory wrote to the German faithful that Henry was a king, but that he was not a Christian ruler or their king,[21] he expressed the distinction between the lawful ruler and the lawful and righteous ruler which lay behind that apparent confusion. In Gregory's eyes, Henry was set outside the Christian community and removed from government over true believers; he was not absolutely removed from his royal office, which he continued to exercise lawfully, but not righteously. We shall return to this distinction below. But it should be observed that were the edicts against Henry to be considered constitutionally definitive, the stated inconsistency would imply not merely a legistic imperceptiveness on Gregory's part but, even more, a disregard for simple logic. The Pope's correspondence sustains the first implication, as we have observed, but it strongly contradicts the second.

The serious difficulties in Gregory's relations with his German partisans emphasize this ambivalence. The crisis in papal relations with the Saxons occurred after Canossa, when the Saxons, taking no notice of Henry's restoration to ecclesiastical communion, elected and crowned Rudolf as their king with the apparent approval of the papal legates. To secure final settlement of the dispute, Gregory had commissioned two legates, Bernard, a cardinal priest of the Roman church, and Abbot Bernard of St. Victor's in Marseilles, to go to Germany, directing them to excommunicate and deny the royal office to whichever of the two kings should prove disobedient and to confirm the obedient in the royal office.[22] According to the account of a hostile chronicler, Henry answered the advances of the legates by threatening them with im-

---

[16] See H. Sielaff, *Studien über Gregors VII. Gesinnung und Verhalten gegen König Heinrich IV. in den Jahren 1073-1080* (Greifswald Diss. 1910) 77.

[17] *Reg.* 4.2 (293ff.). In this letter, Gregory did not mention deposition.

[18] *Ibid.* 296.　　　　　　　　　　[19] *Reg.* 4.1, 3 (289ff, 297ff.).

[20] Ullmann, *Growth* 326ff.

[21] See *infra*, note 68.

[22] *Reg.* 4.23, 24 (334ff.).

126

prisonment, while Rudolf promised willing obedience. When Abbot Bernard was indeed captured and imprisoned by a vassal of Henry's, the Cardinal proceeded to renew the excommunication of the King and to forbid all government to him, since he had disobeyed the Pope, acted contrary to the sentence of a Roman synod, and actively worked against the personal welfare of the Pope. Bernard then confirmed Rudolf's accession.

These new complications did not appreciably change Gregory's policy. Even the biographer of Henry IV, who cherished no love for the Pope, reports that he regarded Rudolf's election with silence,[23] and Gregory's own letters indicate that he continued to acknowledge Henry's royal title pending the settlement of charges against him. Indeed, Henry entered into negotiations with the Pope immediately after Forchheim,and Gregory agreed to arbitrate between the King and his enemies;[24] according to one account, he even enjoined the Germans to obey Henry as king.[25] Though Henry neglected to observe the promises he had made at Canossa, Gregory appears to have contented himself with diplomatic expressions of concern, and he did not renew his excommunication of the King at the Lenten Synod of 1078.[26] It became clear at that Synod that Gregory meant to follow the same course he had taken in the past: the German dispute had advanced to a new level, for there were now two kings; but the role of the Papacy was not to be more unilateral than before. Gregory intended to continue his efforts to arbitrate between the contesting parties and by due judicial enquiry, counsel, and judgment to declare which of them held the just cause. As both parties had appealed to papal judgment, the process would occur under papal patronage, but it was to be conducted by representatives of both kings and the princes together with papal legates. Henry's title was still acknowledged, and his supporter, Archbishop Udo of Trier, was charged with special responsibility in the proceedings.[27]

The Saxons were taken aback by this decision and considered it a dangerous and unwarranted reversal of the sentences of excommunication and deposition issued against Henry; it seemed, wrote Bruno, that the throne of Peter had lost the constancy of Peter.[28] In the nine months which followed, they entered

---

[23] *Vita Heinrici IV*, ed. W. Wattenbach - W. Eberhard (3d ed. Hanover 1899) 18, c. 4.
[24] *Reg.* 7.142 (484f.).
[25] Berthold, *Annales an.* 1077 (MGH *SS.* 5.297; JL 5032).
[26] Meyer von Knonau, *op. cit.* III 54ff.
[27] *Reg.* 5.15, 16 (374ff.).
[28] Bruno. *op. cit.* (note 9, *supra*) c. 107, p. 96: 'At nostrates cum ipsas litteras accepissent a magna spe, quam in apostolica petra exciderunt, quia prius coelum stare vel terram crediderant coeli modo moveri, quam cathedram Petri amittere constantiam Petri.' In the light of subsequent events, the attribution of sweeping powers to the Pope by Rudolf in 1073 is in enlightening contrast with Gregory's own statements. Sudendorf, *Registrum* II no. 19, p. 22f.

five vigorous and even threatening protests against Gregory's policy. In the earliest protest, they wrote that Gregory had deposed Henry unconditionally for injuries he did to the Apostolic See, not for wrongs done his subjects. At great cost and peril to themselves, they obeyed the papal injunctions and withdrew their allegiance from Henry and elected a new king, whose title Cardinal Bernard had confirmed 'apostolica auctoritate.' They complain that they now found Henry's title acknowledged beside Rudolf's, and that in view of his previous actions Gregory's acceptance of both men as legitimate rulers is not readily understood; and they admonish him not to contravene his own actions and those of his Synod and legate.[29] The second letter, written in August, four months after the first, restates this position. Gregory's deposition of Henry, corroborated by that of Cardinal Bernard, is held as final, and in the most open terms, the Saxons maintain that Gregory has been duped into accepting Henry's title and adjure him to avoid making himself ludicrous by continuing to do so.[30] In October or November, they wrote again in the same tenor: Gregory had deposed Henry and forbidden his subjects to obey him, and the Germans had been subjected to Rudolf by papal authority (through Cardinal Bernard's judgment). They warn that if he now fails them, 'heaven and earth are witness above us that we are unjustly ruined.'[31] The last two letters, written in November or December, 1078, and at the beginning of the next year, rehearse the measures of Gregory and Bernard similarly, and strongly threaten Gregory with divine punishment should he rescind those earlier actions.[32]

Gregory's reaction to these protests is highly instructive. We are told that he made no response whatever to the first complaint,[33] and indeed, his first relevant letter after the Lenten Synod (dated 1 July) reaffirms his intention to arbitrate between the two kings, urging all Germans not under ban of excommunication to labor on behalf of the assembly where the dispute was to be settled.[34] In his next pronouncement on this matter (October), Gregory complains that some persons have hindered that assembly from convening.[35] And that he continued in his acknowledgment of the two kings despite the increasingly heated protests we have mentioned is indicated by the fact that he received vows of assistance from Henry's envoys as well as from

---

[29] Bruno c. 108, p. 97ff.
[30] *Ibid.* c. 110, p. 99ff.
[31] *Ibid.* c. 114, p. 107ff.
[32] *Ibid.* cc. 115, 112, pp. 108f, 101ff.
[33] *Ibid.* c. 109, p. 99.
[34] *Reg.* 6.1 (389f.).
[35] *Reg.* 6.4 (397).

128

Rudolf's both at his November Synod (1078) and in his Lenten Synod the next year (February, 1079).[36]

The extent to which practical politics dictated the Pope's hesitancy in recognizing Rudolf as sole king and his continued willingness to negotiate with Henry is not at all clear. Henry had won a great victory over the Saxons in 1075, and his forces in the period after his first excommunication (1076) remained strong. Among the great temporal princes, only Wratislav of Poland stood beside him; but his followers in the spiritual order were more numerous. The Archbishops of Cologne, Trier, Prague and Bremen, the bishops of Eichstädt, Naumburg, Osnabrück, Utrecht, Verdun, Lausanne, Freising, Constance, Augsburg, Basel, and Strassburg, and the Abbot of St. Gall, among others, came readily to his support. Moreover, the citizens of some cities, like Mainz, whose bishops had joined Rudolf, remained loyal to the King and expelled their spiritual leaders. But Rudolf's strength was also very great. Dukes Berchtold of Carinthia, Welf of Bavaria, Otto of Nordheim, Boleslas of Poland, Ladislas of Hungary, and the Count Palatine Frederick were all in his army. They were joined by the premier bishop of Germany, the Archbishop of Mainz, by the Saxon prelates Werner of Magdeburg and Werner of Merseburg, by the Archbishop of Salzburg, and the bishops of Worms, Würzburg, Passau, and Metz, together with the Abbots of Hirsau and Reichenau. Siegfried of Mainz, Adalbert of Worms, Adalbero of Würzburg, and Altman of Passau were all temporarily expelled from their sees by Henry or by pro-Henrican forces in their cities early in the period; and in 1079, Abbot Ekkehard of Reichenau was imprisoned by Henry and his monastery put under the administration of Abbot Ulrich of St. Gall. Still, the power of the expelled bishops remained considerable, and Rudolf was able to draw further support from Swabia and Burgundy, where some sentiment for Henry remained and from Saxony, which was wholly against Henry. The outcome of a conflict, between these two forces must have been far from obvious in 1077-8, and had Roman authority taken no juristic action against Henry or in favor of Rudolf at that time, Gregory's delay in recognizing Rudolf and his negotiations with Henry could be explained as a 'wait and see' policy.

And yet, by mid-November, 1077, Rome had taken a very definite position toward each royal claimant. Gregory himself had declared Henry excommunicate and deposed, and, on papal commission, Cardinal Bernard had renewed that ban against Henry and acknowledged Rudolf as rightful king. It would appear — indeed, it did appear to the Saxons — that a consistent policy had been followed, and that the dispute had been resolved. There was no apparent occasion for temporizing; and yet Gregory did temporize for nearly

---

[36] *Reg.* 6.5b, 17a (401, 428).

three years without in any way acknowledging the decision of his legate. A definite policy had been established by Gregory and his legate, but the Pope himself refused to maintain it.

Were this ambivalence dictated primarily by the uncertain balance of military power in Germany, the moment for ending the 'wait and see' policy was oddly chosen. The conflict had gone well for Henry in 1079; he was able to advance far into the territory which Rudolf had once held securely, and to effect a temporary truce advantageous to himself. That truce was shortly broken. At the beginning of 1080, little more than one month before the beginning of the Lenten Synod where Gregory issued his second edict against Henry and declared in favor of Rudolf, Henry won an important, though not decisive, victory over his enemy in the battle of Flarchheim (27 January), the first in the series of victories which ended with Rudolf's death in the battle of Elster eight months later. One must conclude, therefore, that the second edict was motivated primarily, not by military considerations, but rather by the grave affronts which Henry, emboldened by Flarchheim, immediately offered papal authority.

Gregory's action in this particular incident is important, for it indicates that the weight he placed on moral considerations was far greater than that he placed on the wholly political. The Pope issued the second edict against Henry, not because the war had plainly turned against him, but because he sent as envoys to Rome men whom Gregory had excommunicated, because he corrupted a papal legate with bribes, and because in his personal conduct he was guilty of flagrant and constant disobedience to the moral judgments of the Roman See. (Gregory expressed the same attitude in the next year [1081], when he wrote that he must hold to righteousness even though he was surrounded by enemies and all Italy was threatening to go over to Henry.) His support for Rudolf came, not when the balance of power was patently in favor of the anti-king, but when the conflict had definitely turned against him. One may conclude that his ambiguous relations with Henry and Rudolf were not due primarily to political circumstances, but rather to Gregory's own moral convictions.

We shall discuss below the later history of Gregory's conflict with Henry. For the present, one need say only that those subsequent stages indicate that Gregory continued to observe the same limitations on papal authority over temporal rulers shown in his misunderstanding with the Saxons. His claims to competence over the royal office did not become more complete even after his second bull against Henry (1080) and his declaration in favor of Rudolf. Then, as in the earlier period, Gregory disclaimed authority to raise anyone to the kingship, and further, he explicitly denied that he had done so in the case of Rudolf. Moreover, he continued to disregard the constitutional effects of his deposition of Henry, acknowledging his royal title and negotiating with him towards mutual recognition. In short, he regarded neither his endorsement of a royal candidate nor his deposition of a temporal ruler as in itself definitive (*endgültig*). Gregory's apparent ambivalence and the dispute with the Saxons which it caused show that the views Henry himself and his enemies alike attributed to the Pope were significantly different from those actually held by Gregory; for the Pope conceived his powers over temporal government as being declarative rather than definitive.

II

In order to understand more fully Gregory's view of his process against Henry, one must enquire into the moral context of his political thought.

From the beginning of the controversy with Henry IV until his own death, Gregory maintained one major premise: that as Pope he was the leader of the faithful in active battle against the Devil. It is sometimes maintained that in Gregory's thought, the Church had acceded to the territorial and jurisdictional universality of the Roman Empire, and that as head of the Church, the Pope was in some sense the successor of the Augusti.[37] But Gregory himself never claimed the territorial or jurisdictional universality associated with the Empire, nor did he ever describe himself as the heir of the Caesars.[38] His greatest claims were based rather upon his belief in the moral hegemony of the Papacy over orthodox Christendom, and the earnest conviction that the successor of St. Peter must lead the forces of God against the enemies of God.[39]

---

[37] See the article by P. S. Leicht, 'Il pontefice S. Gregorio VII. ed il diritto romano,' *Studi Gregoriani* 1 (1947) 93-110, where the lack of any knowledge of Roman law on Gregory's part is graphically shown. See Ullmann, *Growth* 276, for the argument to the contrary.

[38] Clearly, Gregory attached some importance to his power of imperial coronation, but his few references to the *Romanum imperium* leave some uncertainty about his precise meaning. As he had before his papal elevation written a letter acknowledging Henry IV as 'Francorum et Romanorum rex' (PL 146.1419: JL 4765), one may tentatively conclude that he did not claim for the papacy the civil authority of the Roman Empire. The problem is, however, not at all clear. See *Reg.* 1.20; 2.75; 4.1, 3, 24 (33, 237, 289, 298, 337); and P. Jaffé, *Monumenta Gregoriana* (Berlin 1865) *Epistolae collectae* nos. 15, 17, pp. 540f, 543. On the power of the Pope to refuse imperial consecration, see Lambert of Hersfeld, *an.* 1069 (ed. Holder-Egger, MGH *SS. in usum scholarum* [1894] 110), the message from Pope Alexander II which Peter Damian delivered to Henry: 'ad haec suis manibus nunquam imperatorem consecrandum fore, qui tam pestilenti exemplo, quantum in se esset, fidem christianam prodidisset.'

[39] This view was strongly set forth by E. Bernheim, *Mittelalterliche Zeitanschauungen* I (Tübingen 1918) 203, 211ff, and, more comprehensively, by a number of students

The importance of this 'political manichaeism' in Gregory's political thought can scarcely be overemphasized, for the concept is distinct in all his judgments upon problems of temporal and spiritual discipline. He complains repeatedly that the Devil has become lord of the world,[40] and that kings, nobles, and even clerics have joined him in undermining the Christian religion, in striving 'against the Lord and against His Christ.'[41] All who professed to be Christians and still refused to obey the Roman See joined the body of the Devil, for they had fallen into the sin of idolatry, into heresy, into paganism,[42] and could no longer be numbered among the true believers. By virtue of their heresy, they were one with the Jews and Saracens, the enemies of God.[43]

Between them and the true believers there was an actual state of war, 'the war of God.'[44] And it was the duty of the Pope to lead the sons of God against His foes, fighting with the sword of the Holy Spirit even unto death.[45] Nor was the warfare to be entirely spiritual. Gregory himself aspired to lead armies against pagans and heretics;[46] he encouraged the Spanish princes in the Reconquista;[47] he urged King Sven II of Denmark and the German princes to lift the material sword 'against the profane and the enemies of God' on behalf

---

who wrote their dissertations under his direction. The clearest statement of the theme is in G. Herzfeld, *Papst Gregors VII. Begriff der bösen Obrigkeit* (Greifswald Diss. 1914), but Herzfeld, curiously enough, did not apply his conclusions to the Henrican conflict. See pp. 60f, 76, 82. The other relevant dissertations approach that controversy from the same point of view. See the work by Sielaff cited above (note 16), the subsequent study by W. Reuter, *Die Gesinnung und die Massnahmen Gregors VII. gegen Heinrich IV. in den Jahren 1080 bis 1085* (Greifswald Diss. 1913), and the other works by H. Krüger, *Was versteht Gregor VII. unter Justitia, und wie wendet er diesen Begriff im einzelnen praktisch an?* (Greifswald Diss. 1910), and E. Weinert, *Die Bedeutung der superbia und humilitas in den Briefen Gregors VII.* (Greifswald Diss. 1920). These somewhat tendentious, but nevertheless suggestive, studies have been in general neglected by students of Gregory's thought. A more recent statement of the same theme, occurs in the article by A. Nitschke, 'Die Wirksamkeit Gottes in der Welt Gregors VII,' *Studi Gregoriani* 5 (1956) 115-219 (esp. 117, 190f, 202), which contains, however, no reference to the earlier works just cited.

[40] *Reg.* 3.15 (277): 'Ecce diabolus palam in mundo dominatur, ecce omnia membra sua se exaltasse letatur ...'

[41] Jaffé, *op. cit. Epp. coll.* no. 1, p. 521. See also *Reg.* 1.42, 7.23 (64ff, 500f.).

[42] E. g. Jaffé no. 28, p. 555: 'Peccatum igitur paganitatis incurrit quisquis, dum christianum se asserit, sedi apostolicae obedire contemnit.'

[43] Cf. Jaffé no. 2, p. 522, *Reg.* 9.2, 4.11 (571, 311) and 2.32 (168), where Philip I of France is judged an enemy of God and the Church.

[44] *Reg.* 1.28 (46): 'et inimicis sanctae ecclesiae bellum Dei secum preliaturus viriliter restiteris.'

[45] *Reg.* 9.35 (623), a frequent figure. See A. Stickler, 'Il gladius nel Registro di Gregorio VII,' *Studi Gregoriani* 3 (1948) 89ff.

[46] *Reg.* 2.31 (166f.) and Meyer von Knonau, *op. cit.* III 311. See also *Reg.* 8.14 (479); Jaffé, *op. cit.* no. 2, p. 522f.

[47] *Reg.* 4.28 (345), *Reg.* 1.7 (to French barons; 11f.).

of the Roman Church;[48] and he commanded the use of secular arms to eject condemned bishops from their former sees.[49] The threat of armed revolt or invasion may also have been intended when Gregory wrote of King Philip I, of France, that if the King should persist in disobedience towards the Roman See, the Pope would 'by every measure attempt with the help of God to snatch the kingdom of France from his tenure.'[50]

In this struggle, the Pope was the commander-in-chief, 'dux et pontifex,' of the faithful; Christian kings were his adjutants. His claims to authority over them were sweeping and comprehensive. In the Church, among the orthodox, the Pope bore secular burdens as well as spiritual,[51] and all in communion with the true Church, owed him their absolute subjection. There were to Gregory's mind several major duties of the Christian king: to feed the poor, to defend the widowed and the orphaned, and to guard the laws of peace and the judgment of equity.[52] But none of them was more important than reverence for the priesthood,[53] and obedience to the See of Peter.[54] In some instances, Gregory added or attempted to add, juristic sanctions to that duty of obedience by requiring oaths of homage from temporal rulers; in them, the princes obliged themselves to obey the Roman see in all things and to render it military assistance in time of need.[55] Those oaths did not, however, impose any general duties other than those Gregory expected of all Christian rulers; whether they were bound to his obedience juristically or not, orthodox

---

[48] *Reg.* 2.51, 6.1 (194, 390).

[49] *Reg.* 3.7 (258f.); Jaffé, *op. cit. Epp. coll.* no. 40, p. 567; Pflugk-Harttung II no. 167, p. 135. See Nitschke, *op. cit.* 193ff.

[50] *Reg.* 2.5 (130): 'Quarum rerum rex vester, qui non rex sed tyrannus dicendus est, *sua dente diabolo* caput et causa est,' and (132): 'Quodsi nec huiusmodi districtione voluerit-resipiscere, nulli clam aut dubium esse volumus quin modis omnibus regnum Franciae de eius occupatione adiuvante Deo temptemus eripere.' The right of rebellion against a wrongful ruler is not explicit in Gregory's letters; his statement to Archbishop Cyriacus of Carthage, *Reg.* 1.23 (39), suggests the course of passive resistence: 'Sed Deo gratias, qui in medio nationis pravae et perversae, fidei tuae constantia velud luminare quoddam omnibus adeo innotuit, ut presentatus regiae audientiae potius definires diversis cruciatibus affici quam precipiente rege contra sanctos canones ordinationes celebrari.'

[51] *Reg.* 1.12 (90): 'Portamus enim, quanquam infirmi ... soli tamen portamus non solum spiritualium sed et secularium ingens pondus negotiorum.'

[52] Cf. *Reg.* 8.11 (530).

[53] *Reg.* 9.37 (630f.).

[54] *Reg.* 1.24, 3.10 (41, 267) and *passim*.

[55] See *Reg.* 1.18a (30f.), 1.21a (35; repeated by Robert Guiscard seven years later, significantly omitting the provision for homage to Henry IV: *Reg.* 8.1a [514f.]); 8.1b, 8.1c, 9.3 (516f, 575f.) and Deusdedit, ed. V. Wolf von Glanville, *Die Kanonensammlung* (Paderborn 1905) 3.324ff. On this development, see G. Ladner, 'The Concepts of "Ecclesia" and "Christianitas" and their Relation to the Idea of Papal "Plenitudo Potestatis" from Gregory VII to Boniface VIII,' *Sacerdozio e Regno* (n. 5 *supra*), esp. 52f.

rulers were subject to the direction and moral jurisdiction of Rome.[56] It is in this context of relationships within the body of the faithful that Gregory's famous letter to William the Conqueror must be set. Just as all the world is illumined by two lights, the sun and the moon so, he wrote, creation is governed by two divers offices, the apostolic (i. e., episcopal or papal) and the royal; and the Christian religion is so ordered that the royal office is governed by the apostolic office and by God.[57] It has been suggested that this statement accompanied a demand that William render an oath of homage to the Papacy.[58] But it concerns us more that the basis of the statement and of the supposed demand was the same: obedient to the judgment of the Apostolic See, William had waged war against Harald of England, vanquishing him and acceding to his office with the blessing of St. Peter.[59] It is indicative of his thought that Gregory should address his claim for the supremacy of the spiritual office over the temporal in the Christian commonwealth to a ruler who, on papal commission, had fought against and conquered an excommunicate King.[60]

Gregory's concept of his struggle with Henry IV turns entirely upon the premise that Henry had joined the forces of the Devil, and that Gregory was consequently obliged to rouse the Church against him. In 1076, as he proceeded to the first excommunication of Henry, Gregory compared the King to the serpent of evil and declared that he must raise the sword of vengeance and strike 'the enemy of God and of the Church.'[61] Defending that action, he wrote that Henry had fallen into the hands of the Devil,[62] and that those who (like Henry) refused to heed the command of God were members of Antichrist and must be chastened for their disobedience.[63] He had earlier complained

---

[56] Voosen, op. cit. 238.

[57] Reg. 7.25 (505f.): 'Sicut enim ad mundi pulchritudinem oculis carneis diversis temporibus representandam solem et lunam omnibus aliis eminentiora disposuit luminaria, sic, ne creatura, quam sui benignitas ad imaginem suam in hoc mundo creaverat, in erronea et mortifera traheretur pericula, providit, ut apostolica et regia dignitate per diversa regeretur officia. Qua tamen maioritatis et minoritatis distantia religio sic se movet christiana, ut cura et dispositione apostolica dignitas post Deum gubernetur regia.'

[58] Z. N. Brooke, 'Pope Gregory VII's Demand for Fealty from William the Conqueror,' English Historical Review 26 (1911) 235, 237.

[59] Reg. 7.23 (499f.); Ordericus Vitalis, Hist. Eccles. 2.3.17 (PL 188.285); William of Malmesbury, Gesta Regum Anglorum 3.238 (Rolls Series) II 299.

[60] Wace, Roman de Brut 12353: 'E si saunt Engleiz de veir /A tuz le velt fere savoir / Ke cil sunt escumengié / De l'Apostoile e del clegié.'

[61] Paul of Bernried, Vita Gregorii VII c. 61 (PL 148.73).

[62] Reg. 4.1 (289).

[63] Reg. 4.2 (295): 'Nam sicut illi, qui omni suae voluntati Deum preponunt eiusque precepto plus quam hominibus oboediunt membra sunt Christi, ita et illi de quibus supra diximus, membra sunt antichristi. Si ergo spirituales viri, cum oportet, iudicantur, cur non seculares amplius de suis pravis actibus constringuntur?'

that the simoniac Lombard bishops sought to prostitute the bride of Christ with the Devil,[64] and now he describes Henry and his supporters, principally Wibert of Ravenna (the Antipope Clement III), as members of the Devil, as members of Antichrist, or as Antichrist himself; and the Synod of Brixen, where Henry declared Gregory deposed and secured the election of Wibert, was for Gregory 'the assembly of Satan.'[65] Through them, the world had come to be ruled by the Devil; through them, Satan's conquests were daily increased;[66] through them, the return of the Church to her proper honor, free, chaste, and orthodox, was hindered.[67]

A king—or indeed any person—who lapsed from the true faith into heresy, into the 'sin of paganism,' must be severed from the body of the faithful. He must lose the title 'Christian.' That is clear; but in losing it, must he of necessity lose the title 'king' or the royal office itself? Gregory took three measures against Henry: he excommunicated him; he denied him government, and he forbade Christians bound by oath to Henry to honor those oaths. In other words, he severed Henry from the body of the Church, declared that by ecclesiastical sentence he was no longer king, and separated Christian allegiants from their heretical ruler. Christian orthodoxy and legal tenure of the royal office, however, were discrete in Gregory's mind, and as we shall attempt to show later, removal from one did not invariably produce removal from the other. To be sure, the only true kings were, for Gregory, Christian kings;[68] and only kings who honored the Church obtained their office rightly (recte).[69]

[64] Reg. 1.15: '... sponsam videlicet Christi diabolo prostituere et a catholica fide temptans eam separare nisus est symoniace heresis scelere maculare.'
[65] See especially Reg. 8.5, 4.1, 5.14a, 7.14a (522, 289f., 370, 483).
[66] Reg. 2.37 (173). Cf. Reg. 3.15 (277): 'invenimus dominium diaboli tanto minus duravisse, quanto magis visum fuit exaltari et in christianam religionem prevaluisse.'
[67] Jaffé, op. cit. Epp. coll. no. 46 (Gregory's last encyclical), p. 574: 'Ex quo enim dispositione divina mater ecclesia in throno apostolico me valde indignum et Deo teste invitum collocavit, summopere procuravi ut sancta ecclesia sponsa Dei, domina et mater nostra ad proprium rediens decus, libera casta et catholica permaneret. Sed quia hosti antiquo hec omnino displicent, armavit contra nos membra sua ut omnia in contrarium verteret. Ideo in nos, immo in apostolicam sedem tanta facit, quanta facere a tempore Constantini Magni imperatoris nequivit.'
[68] Reg. 8.3 (519, to Alfonso VI of Leon and Castille): 'gloriabamur te vere christianum regem et ideo vere regem nos habere in parte domini Iesu contra membra diaboli gaudebamus.' Cf. Reg. 4.1 (290, of Henry IV after his first deposition): '... sancta ecclesia ... diversas iniquitates regis, et utinam christiani et vestri, sustinuit...' and Reg. 2.5 (130, of Philip I of France): 'Quarum rerum rex vester, qui non rex sed tyrannus dicendus est, suadente diabolo caput et causa est.'
[69] Reg. 2.30 (164): Writing to Henry nearly twenty years after his accession to the throne, Gregory urges him to let the Church have its due rights, '... et tunc demum regiam potestatem recte te obtinere cognoscas, si regi regum Christo ... dominationis tuae altitudinem inclinas ...'

But not all kings were Christian: Gregory acknowledges Saracen kings and pagan princes and emperors:[70] Though they might not govern rightly, as Christians, they nevertheless governed lawfully, as kings. This distinction is implicit in Gregory's letter to Herman of Metz, justifying his second excommunication and deposition of Henry.[71] There, acknowledging Henry as 'King,'[72] he at the same time wrote: 'In short, any good Christians are to be viewed as kings more suitably than evil princes. For seeking the glory of God, they rule themselves firmly; but seeking their own rather than what is God's, the latter, enemies to themselves, oppress others tyrannically. The former are the body of Christ, the true King, but the others are the body of the Devil.'[73] Gregory does not in this passage or in any other declare that wicked princes might not be lawful rulers; he is rather concerned to say that such princes are incapable of that moral rectitude (justitia) which for him characterized true kingship, kingship patterned on that of Christ, the heavenly King. Saracen, pagan, and heretical princes were under 'the prince of darkness, who is king over all the sons of pride,' but they were still effectual rulers. In short, Gregory did not maintain, as did the later canonist Johannes Teutonicus, that 'there is no empire outside the Church,'[74] for to his eyes there were two empires on earth, that of God and that of Satan.

III

Thus far we have described the general principles which Gregory maintained regarding accession to and removal from the royal office; we must now examine their application in the accession of Rudolf and the process against Henry IV.

Gregory's part in the elevation of Rudolf need not detain us. It was his constant position that kings acceded by the election of God, and that that election was manifested through the normal constitutional procedures of a

---

[70] Reg. 3.21 (287); Reg. 7.1 (459): 'Nemo enim omnium regum etiam paganorum ...'

[71] Cf. Voosen, op. cit. (note 5 supra) 162.

[72] Reg. 8.21, e. g., p. 547: 'Qui ... garriunt auctoritatem sanctae et apostolice sedis non potuisse regem Henricum, hominem christianae legis contemptorem ... excommunicare ...'

[73] Ibid. 557: 'Ad summam, quoslibet bonos christianos multo convenientius quam malos principes reges intellegi decet. Isti enim gloriam Dei querendo se ipsos strenue regunt, at illi non quae Dei sunt sed sua querentes sibimet hostes alios tyrannice opprimunt. Hi veri regis Christi, illi vero diaboli corpus sunt. Isti ad hoc sibi imperant, ut cum summo imperatore eternaliter regnent, illorum vero id potestas agit, ut cum tenebrarum principe, qui rex est super omnes filios superbiae, eterna dampnatione dispereant.'

[74] See the discussion of this text by M. Pacaut, 'L'autorité pontificale selon Innocent IV,' Le Moyen Age 66 (1960) 115. Professor F. Cheyette kindly drew my attention to this article.

given people, through inheritance or election.[75] It is true that he once speaks of persons whom the Church calls to temporal government,[76] and that he wrote to Herman of Metz that Pope Zacharias had deposed Chilperic and substituted Pippin the Short in his place.[77] But, as we have seen, the Pope's actions and the burden of his other pronouncements militate against construing these statements in a strictly constitutional light. Indeed, Gregory wrote explicitly that the German kingship was gained through election,[78] and Henry IV himself had acceded through an election in which Gregory participated before his papal accession.[79] Accordingly, Gregory declined to raise anyone to the royal office without election by the German princes.[80] When, after Henry's first excommunication, the Saxons sent to Gregory saying that they wished to move the election of a new king, he declared himself inclined to favor their proposal.[81] But as we have seen, once the election of Rudolf had taken place and had been approved by the papal legate, Cardinal Bernard, Gregory himself refused to accept it as a definitive settlement of the German dispute. When at last he did acknowledge Rudolf as rightful King of the Germans (1080), he specifically declared that Rudolf had been elected without his counsel,[82] and he later wrote more strongly that Rudolf had not entered the royal office by his 'command or counsel.'[83] In this instance, therefore, Gregory did not claim, as Benzo of Alba wrote, the power to bestow the royal office upon whomever he chose.[84]

---

[75] *Reg.* 1.32, 5.10, 7.21 (59, 362, 497). See Voosen, *op. cit.* 174. Compare his more forceful assertions toward Hungary and Dalmatia, where he claimed the power to bestow the royal office by virtue of his feudal tenure over those lands. On Hungary, see *Reg.* 2.63, 70 (218, 230); on Dalmatia, the oath of Swonimir, as given by Deusdedit, cited note 55, *supra*.

[76] *Reg.* 8.21 (561).

[77] *Reg.* 8.21 (554). See F. Kern, *Gottesgnadentum und Widerstandsrecht im frühen Mittelalter*, 2nd ed. by R. Buchner (Münster 1954) 50 n. 103.

[78] Bruno, *op. cit.* c. 91, p. 85.

[79] *Reg.* 1.19 (32): 'Quod ipsum [Henricum] in regem elegimus ...'.

[80] Paul of Bernried, *Vita Gregorii VII* c. 77 (PL 148.80).

[81] *Reg.* 4.7 (305).

[82] *Reg.* 7.14a (484).

[83] *Reg.* 9.29 (613).

[84] However, one cannot fully accept Sielaff's suggestion that Gregory's acknowledgment of Rudolf was merely 'Drohpolitik' designed to secure Henry's repentance. (*op. cit.* n. 16 *supra*, 95ff.). Gregory may have been reluctant to receive Rudolf as king because of uncertainty as to his standing on the issue of simony (*Reg.* 2.45: 183f), a suspicion Rudolf made dramatic efforts to dispel (Paul of Bernried, *Vita Gregorii VII* c. 87: PL 148.86). An interesting new approach to the powers Gregory claimed in this instance is offered by W. Berges, 'Gregor VII. und das deutsche Designationsrecht,' *Studi Gregoriani* 2 (1948) 139-209, especially 193ff. Otto of Freising's description of the crown Gregory is supposed to have sent to Rudolf is still a curious element in the fabric of Gregorian thought (*Gesta Frederici* 1.7 :

His process against Henry shows further that Benzo's second point—that Gregory presumed to remove from the kingship anyone who displeased him— is equally inaccurate; for he explicitly left the question of Henry's removal from office to the German electors.[84a]

It was Gregory's position that kings might not interject their judgments into the constitutional structure of the Church,[85] and though the converse is nowhere explicitly stated in his correspondence, he appears to have accepted it as well. Father Stickler has demonstrated that Gregory did not use the image of the sword in the political sense.[86] Before Stickler, Voosen maintained that his excommunication of Henry was not constitutive, but declarative, and more important, Kern saw Henry's deposition in the same terms.[87] These highly suggestive delimitations of Gregory's thought indicate that in Gregory's eyes, the whole of his action against the German King took place within a moral or ecclesiological rather than within a political framework.

Scholars have in general observed a tension in Gregory's thought between the lapidary statement of the *Dictatus Papae*—'Quod illi [i.e. papae] liceat imperatores deponere'[88]—and the Pope's actions towards Henry after the

---

MGH *SS. in usum schol.* [1912] 23). The meaning of the inscription Otto preserves—'Roma dedit Petro, Petrus diadema Rudolfo'—is unclear. Accepting its historicity, one may perhaps assume that Gregory acted either as representative of the Romans in acknowledging Rudolf as 'rex Romanorum,' or as lord of Saxony in investing a temporal ruler for that land, just as he invested the king of Hungary. (See *Reg.* 8.23 [567]: 'Idem vero magnus imperator [Carolus] Saxoniam obtulit beato Petro...'). Still, in *Reg.* 7.14a (486), he acknowledges Rudolf as king over the whole *regnum Theutonicum*, not merely over Saxony, and the first possibility would therefore seem to be the more likely.

[84a] *Reg.* 4.3.299: 'Hoc tamen videtur laudabile, postquam certum fuerit *apud vos* et omnino firmatum, quod eius filius a regno removeatur, consilium ab ea et a nobis requiratur de inventa persona ac regni gubernacula.'

[85] This was, of course, the basis of the Investiture Conflict. Gregory also applied the principle to ecclesiastical legislation. See A. Werminghoff, 'Bruchstück,' *Neues Archiv* 27 (1902) 673: 'Quam [regulam apostolicam] utique in sui regni provinciis inventam nec Ludovicus [Pius] mutare qualibet ratione debuit aut potuit sine auctoritate et consensu sanctae Romanae et apostolicae sedis, quia quamvis imperator et devotus tamen erat laicus sed nec episcoporum quisquam quia non est illorum novam in ecclesias solo suo magisterio vel arbitrio regulam introducere...'

[86] *Art. cit. supra* n. 45.

[87] Voosen, *op. cit.* 281, 283. Kern, *op. cit.* (note 77 *supra*) 200. Kern's conclusions are largely drawn, however, from post-Gregorian canonists.

[88] *Reg.* 2.55a c. 12 (204). On this line, see K. Hofmann, *Der 'Dictatus Papae' Gregors VII* (Veröffentlichungen der Sektion für Rechts- und Staatswissenschaft der Görres-Gesellschaft 63; Paderborn 1933) 141ff. For more recent judgments on the general character of the *Dictatus* see Hofmann's article, 'Der *Dictatus Papae* Gregors VII als Index einer Kanonessammlung?' *Studi Gregoriani* 1 (1947) 523-537, and the very perceptive comments of S. Kuttner, 'Liber Canonicus: A Note on *Dictatus Papae* c. 17,' *Studi Gregoriani* 2 (1947) 387-401. As we do not yet know precisely the contents of the collection for which the *Dic-*

ban of 1076. For, as we have seen, Gregory's policy towards Henry in the years 1076-1080 was one of great forbearance. An attempt to resolve that tension has been made by suggesting that the first excommunication was in reality a suspension from office, and that the second, in 1080, was definitive. However, Voosen and Reuter have shown very clearly the difficulties of this solution. The terms in the later decree are precisely the same as those in the earlier: in both, Gregory denies government to Henry, absolves his Christian subjects of their allegiance to him, declares him excommunicate, and prays for his repentance. To be sure, he adds the acknowledgment of Rudolf as King in the bull of 1080, but that in no way affects the terms of the sentence against Henry.[89] In both decrees, Gregory avoided the word 'depose' as regards his action towards the King, but the verb occurs with reference to it in his correspondence in 1076 just as it does in 1080.[90] There is, in short, nothing to indicate that the character of the 1080 deposition and excommucation was definitive while the 1076 sentence was provisional; to the contrary, there is much to indicate that the one was as definitive, or as provisional, as the other.

Had Gregory intended the 1080 decree to be definitive, his actions in the five years which followed it would be full of open contradictions. For example,

---

tatus were headings, it is clearly impossible to attribute any definite meaning to those short and deceptively crisp statements. Professor Kuttner has kindly directed my attention to a recent comment on the *Dictatus Papae* by R. Morghen, 'Ricerche sulla formazione del Registro di Gregorio VII,' *Annali di Storia del diritto* 3-4 (1959-60) 35-63, esp. 38ff., which disputes the conclusions of Hofmann and Borino and accepts the *Dictatus* as statements of papal doctrine which were complete in themselves. See also Additional Note, p. 148 *infra*.

[89] Voosen, *op. cit.* 260ff. Reuter, *op. cit.* (note 39 *supra*) 10ff, 40, 59ff. Earlier than these authors, K. Mirbt had established the identity of the two actions in 'Absetzung Heinrichs IV.,' *Kirchengeschichtliche Studien: Festschrift Hermann Reuter* (Leipzig 1890) 95-144. On the 'provisional' nature of the earlier decree, see Sielaff, *op. cit.* 37ff, 60, and P. Sander *Der Kampf Heinrichs IV. und Gregors VII. (1080-1084)* (Strassburg Diss. Berlin 1893) 155f. Cf. A. Brackmann, 'Gregor VII. und die kirchliche Reformbewegung in Deutschland,' *Studi Gregoriani* 2 (1947) 16: (of the 1080 decree) 'Dieser Beschluss brachte das Ende der Verständigungsbereitschaft des Papstes. Von dieser Fastensynode des Jahres 1080 an gab es für ihn nur den Kampf.'

[90] *Reg.* 4.3 (of 1076, p. 298): '... cur sit anathematis vinculo alligatus et a regia dignitate depositus ...' *Reg.* 8.21 (of 1080, p. 551): 'Quis nos Henricum ... deposuisse et excommunicasse reprehendat ...' It should be noted that in the earlier letter Gregory made provision for Henry's 'reinstatement' in the royal office. One may also observe that the terms of the later may have been made as strong as possible to confirm Herman of Metz in the Gregorian camp, for in 1081 he is known to have been wavering between the papalists and the imperialists. See Gebehard of Salzburg's letter to Herman (MGH *Lib. de lite* 1.262): 'quamnam potissimum in magno illo potestatum certamine rationem sequandam esse putaret.'

he continued throughout to refer to Henry as 'rex.' Certainly, as in the earlier period of the controversy, he sometimes mentioned him as 'rex dictus.' But one must observe that this term merely indicates that Gregory did not consider a king not in communion with the Roman Church to possess the moral virtues of Christians, true kings; it is in fact an acknowledgment that Henry held the royal title.

There were other positive actions which would have been very curious if the 1080 deposition had been intended as a constitutional removal from office. The earliest was Gregory's famous Easter prophecy, about one month after the second bull had been issued: We are told that Gregory predicted 'quod, si usque ad festivitatem sancti Petri Heinricus non resipuerit, mortuus erit aut depositus.' [91] Had the second deposition been intended to be definitive, this prophecy would have been nonsensical.

Again in 1083, Henry advanced towards Rome, declaring that he wished to receive the imperial crown at Gregory's hands. The Pope at first accepted this proposal with one qualification: Henry must secure release from excommunication by public action.[92] Henry then entered negotiations with the Roman nobles and won a promise from them that they would secure his imperial coronation by Gregory or by a pope elected in his stead.[93] Confronted by this threat to his authority in Rome itself, Gregory appears to have modified his earlier decision and to have agreed to meet his enemies before a synod in the autumn. His stated purpose was to restore harmony between the pontifical and the royal offices.[94] That synod was not held in November, as scheduled, but there is a report which indicates that Gregory's curious ambivalence continued. We are told that envoys of the Pope met at the monastery of St. Mary in Pallaria, probably between 4 December 1083, and 31 March 1084,[95] and that they there submitted the dispute to trial by ordeal. The anti-Gregorian author of the sole account which mentions this trial states that a young boy was plunged into cold water four times, and that each time, despite attempts of the envoys to drown him, he floated in the water, a sign

---

[91] Bonizo, *Liber ad amicum* 9 (MGH *Lib. de lite* 1.616). For the variants of this prophecy, see Meyer von Knonau, *op. cit.* III 258 n. 46. See Reuter, *op. cit.* 18ff.

[92] Bonizo, *Liber ad amicum* 8 (614). See the discussion in Sander, *op. cit.* (note 89 *supra*) 206ff.

[93] MGH *Const.* 1 no. 442, p. 651. Ekkehard, *Chronicon an.* 1083; Sigebert of Gembloux, *Chronicon an.* 1083 (MGH *SS.* 6.205, 364).

[94] *Reg.* 9.29 (613f), and Jaffé, *op. cit. Epp. coll.* no. 23, p. 549f.

[95] Sander, *op. cit.* 219ff. See also G. B. Ladner, 'Two Gregorian Letters on the Sources and Nature of Gregory VII's Reform Ideology,' *Studi Gregoriani* 5 (1956) 299 n. 29. The text concerning the process is printed as an addendum to the chronicle of Hugh of Flavigny in MGH *SS.* 8.460f.

predesignated to indicate God's judgment in favor of Henry. The witnesses of the trial vowed to keep its results secret.[96]

Without further corroboration, one must accept this account *cum grano salis*. Yet, in the light of Gregory's willingness to negotiate with Henry, it allows of a fuller appreciation of three measures taken by Gregory in the following year. Though Gregory excommunicated in general terms all those who hindered persons from coming to St. Peter or to the Pope, he did not explicitly mention Henry in the ban (1084).[97] Later in the same year, when Henry restated his desire to receive the imperial crown, Gregory agreed to perform the ceremony himself should Henry do suitable penance; otherwise, he would deliver the imperial crown to the King, sending it out of the Castel Sant'Angelo on a pole.[98] Finally, we are told that, shortly before his death, Gregory released Henry (*dictus rex*), Wibert, and other '*principales personas*' from the ban of excommunication, provided that they acknowledge his special power as vicar of SS. Peter and Paul.[99]

If the decree of 1080 had been final in Gregory's eyes, these extraordinary measures—the prophecy, continued acknowledgment of Henry's royal title,

---

[96] *Ibid.* 461: 'Ad tale miraculum sunt stupefacti, et nesciunt quid agere debeant. Sunt modo consiliati ac fidem inter se dederunt, si res ista in propatulo esset, regi per aliquem hominem, ut nec unus illorum audeat dicere sine communi consilio et sine consilio papae. Nam ipse accepit fidem ab omnibus, ut nullus audeat dicere.' The general desertion of Gregory by the cardinals early in 1084 is possible, but not certain, corroboration of this account. One must admit, however, that the armies of Henry may have decided their defection more effectively than the judgment of God. See Meyer von Knonau, *op. cit.* III 525 n. 7.

[97] Reuter, *op. cit.* 88f.

[98] Bernold, *Chronicon an.* 1083 (MGH *SS* 5.438): 'Domnus tamen papa sinodum tribus diebus sollemniter celebravit, et ne Heinricum specialiter iterum anathematizaret, vix a sinodo exoratus, omnes tamen excommunicavit, quicumque aliquem ad Sanctum Petrum vel ad papam venientem quoquomodo impedirent. Sed iam advenit terminus, ad quem Romani, nesciente papa, Heinrico se effecturos iuraverant, ut aut Gregorius papa eum incoronaret, aut alius, quem ipsi illo expulso eligerent. ... Adveniente igitur termino Romani papae de iuramento manifestaverunt, dicentes, se Heinrico iurasse, non ut papa illum sollemniter regali unctione incoronaret, set tantum simpliciter, ut ei coronam daret. Annuit igitur papa eorum votis, ut eos a iuramento absolveret, videlicet ut Heinrico si vellet, cum iusticia, sin autem cum maledictione coronam daret. Unde Romani mandaverunt Heinrico, ut veniret ad accipiendam coronam cum iusticia, si vellet, sin autem, de castello sancti Angeli per virgam sibi dimissam a papa reciperet.'

[99] Paul of Bernried, *Vita Gregorii VII* c. 102 (PL 148.94): 'Interea pontifex beatus Gregorius super his quos excommunicaret, requisitus, si quam dispensationem facere vellet, respondit: Praeterea Henricum regem dictum et Guibertum apostolicae sedis invasorem, et omnes illas principales personas quae aut consilio aut auxilio favent nequitiae vel impietati illorum, omnes absolvo et benedico, quicumque me hanc habere specialem potestatem in vice apostolorum Petri et Pauli credunt indubitanter ...' It is important to recall that Gregory's immediate sucecssor did not repeat the excommunication of Henry.

and willingness to negotiate with him, the offer to surrender the imperial crown so that the imperial coronation could be performed by 'Antichrist' (Wibert), and the conditional retraction of the ban of excommunication against him—would have been grave inconsistencies. One must observe further that Gregory never dealt with the anti-king Herman of Salm, whom the Saxons elected after Rudolf's death, even though Herman declared himself willing to march to the defence of the Apostolic See,[100] and that he never made any effort to secure the election of a rival to Henry. As Reuter suggested, his proposal to papal legates in 1081 that a new election be moved is tentative and does not exclude the possibility that Henry himself might be advanced in the proposed action.[101]

One further argument against the interpretation of Gregory's edicts as final is found by comparing the text of Gregory's depositions of Henry with depositions of bishops, which he considered genuinely definitive. In the latter, one observes the same elements as are in the bulls against Henry: excommunication of the condemned, release of his former subjects from their obligations to obey him, and the sentence of deposition. There are also two regular elements which do not occur in the decrees of 1076 and 1080: the provision that the deposition is final—'sine spe recuperationis'—and the provision for election of a new bishop by canonical electors.[102] These last elements do not occur in either decree against Henry. To be sure, the election of Rudolf was acknowledged as a *fait accompli* in the bull of 1080, and it is clear from Gregory's other letters that he believed a new election (like that of Rudolf) should have been held if Henry proved totally unrepentant. But the Pope himself did not provide for that measure. The omission of the phrase 'sine spe recuperationis' is even more suggestive of Gregory's thought. In a letter to the German faithful written to justify his first edict of deposition, Gregory clearly states his view. Before issuing the edict, he writes, he had warned the King that should he persist in his wrongful acts, he would deserve not only to be excommunicated until he rendered due satisfaction, but also to be stripped of all royal honor without hope of recovery (*absque spe recuperationis*).[103] Gregory did not here claim for the papacy the power to effect that

---

[100] Meyer von Knonau, *op. cit.* III 464.

[101] *Op. cit.* 62f.

[102] With reference to clerical cases, the term 'absque (*or* sine) spe recuperationis' occurs in *Reg.* 2.62, 5.14a, 6.10, 8.18 (21f, 369, 411, 540). Cf. *Reg.* 8.18 (540 'inrevocabili iudicio'), *Reg.* 2.23 (155 'absque spe futurae reconciliationis'), *Reg.* 3.2 (245 'et imperpetuum depositum esse censemus'), *Reg.* 3.1 (243 'ut inrecuperabiliter ab episcopali officio semotus'), *Reg.* 2.54 (199 'absque ulla unquam spe reconciliationis ab omni episcopali honore deposuimus'). For the provision concerning new elections, see *Reg.* 8.18, 3.2, 3.3, 3.1, 5.11, 8.13, 3.8 (540, 245, 247, 242f, 364f, 533f, 258).

[103] Jaffé, *op. cit. Epp. coll.* no. 14, p. 538: 'quae quidem horrenda dictu sunt, pluribus autem

final deposition, and the omission of the technical phrase 'sine spe recuperationis' in the two formal edicts of deposition indicate very strongly that he did not see himself as exercising it. The first edict states that Gregory 'denied' Henry powers of government; the second declares that the Pope 'removed' them from the King. But neither was specifically an irrevocable sentence.

If, in Gregory's judgment, Henry deserved to be permanently removed from the royal office, and if the papal powers were insufficient to secure his removal, one must ask what power could effect the just deposition of an unjust king. It seems probable that Gregory believed such a deposition could be performed only by divine action or by the judgment of St. Peter, whom 'Jesus Christ, the King of glory, established as prince over the kingdoms of the world.'[104] For Gregory, although there was a close relationship between the comprehensive power of St. Peter and papal authority, the two were not identical.[105] But, casting his decrees in the form of letters to St. Peter (the second was addressed to St. Paul as well), whose vicar he was, Gregory sought the final ratification of his action by heavenly judgment.[106] He acknowledged circumstances under which the pope might rely in vain upon the merits of St. Peter,[107] and stated the premise that divine judgments often differed from those of men.[108] Just as he himself sometimes overturned the judgments of his own vicars, so, he appears to have thought, St. Peter might reverse the decisions of his.[109]

---

nota et in multis partibus divulgata, propter quae eum non excommunicari solum usque ad condignam satisfactionem, sed ab omni honore regni absque spe recuperationis debere destitui, divinarum et humanarum legum testatur et iubet auctoritas...'

[104] *Reg.* 1.63 (92). Cf. his warning to Philip I of France, *Reg.* 8.30 (543): 'Ac maxime enitere ut beatum Petrum in cuius potestate est tuum regnum et anima tua, qui te potest in celo et in terra ligare et absolvere, tibi facias debitorem ...'

[105] Cf. Jaffé, *Epp. Coll.* no. 18, p. 544: 'Benedicat vos ille, ex cuius gratia mihi dictum est ad corpus beati Petri in die ordinationis meae: "Quodcunque benedixeris, benedictum erit, et quodcumque solveris super terram, erit solutum et in caelis."' *Ibid.* no. 31 (558), 'qui videlicet postquam iudicium tanti huius negotii in manu beati Petri commissum est, nichil aliud vobis testibus intendimus nisi ut per iustitiae semitam incedamus.' *Reg.* 4.2 (293): 'De aliis autem rebus, super quibus me interrogasti, utinam beatus Petrus per me respondeat, qui sepe in me qualicunque suo famulo honoratur vel iniuriam patitur.' The use of the subjunctive in the last sentence was surely intentional.

[106] *Reg.* 3.6 (255): 'Qualiter autem aut quibus pro causis beatus Petrus anathematis vinculo regem alliga*verit* in cartula, quac huic inclusa est, plene potestis cognoscere.' Cf. Ullmann, *Growth* 284.

[107] *Reg.* 2.31 (165): 'quia si te ut oportet non diligo, in vanum de misericordia Dei meritis beati Petri confido.'

[108] *Reg.* 3.4, 8.9 (248, 527); *Reg.* 7.8 (469): 'Verum quia omnipotentis Dei inestimabilis providentia omnia iuste et sapienter disponit, iudicia eius, nimirum recta consilia ipsius equitatis et misericordiae plena nobis sunt, fratres equanimiter ferenda.'

[109] On Gregory's action, see T. Schieffer, *Die päpstlichen Legaten in Frankreich* (Berlin 1935) 106f.

In fact, Gregory explicitly appealed to St. Peter for final corroboration of his sentence, perhaps in battle[110] or, as evidence from the 1083-4 negotiations suggests, in trial by ordeal. In 1075, he had warned Henry to observe the example of Saul, whom God, 'in whose hand and power is all kingdom and empire,' cast down;[111] again, after issuing the first edict against the King, he threatened him with "wrath and vengeance of divine judgment."[112] And the words with which he concluded the second decree make his meaning plain. Addressing SS. Peter and Paul,[113] he prayed:

> Act now, I ask, Fathers and Most Sacred Princes, that all the world may perceive and understand that, if you can bind and loose in Heaven, you can on earth withdraw from and grant to anyone according to his merits empires, kingdoms, principalities, dukedoms, marquisates, countships and the possessions of all men. For you have often taken patriarchates, primacies, archiepiscopacies, and episcopacies from the wicked and unworthy, and have given them to religious men. If you judge of spiritual things, what must one believe of your powers in secular matters? And if you will judge the angels who rule in all proud princes, what can you do with regard to their servants? Let kings and all princes of the world now heed how great you are and what you can do, and let them fear to disregard the command of your Church. Implement your judgment as regards the said Henry so quickly that all may know he falls not by chance, but by your power; may he be confounded—O that it were to repentance— that his soul may be saved in the day of the Lord![114]

In this prayer, Gregory attributed the power to dispose of temporal as well as spiritual offices to SS. Peter and Paul, but he did not claim it for the Pope, their vicar. It is clear that Gregory left the definitive deposition of Henry to divine judgment.

---

[110] *Reg.* 7.14a (the second excommunication of Henry, 486): 'Ipse autem Heinricus cum suis fautoribus in omni congressione belli nullas vires nullamque in vita sua victoriam optineat.' Cf. *Reg.* 3.7 (258).

[111] *Reg.* 3.10 (267). See also *Reg.* 2.63 (to Geisa of Hungary, 218): 'Quod quia consanguineus tuus [Salomo] a rege Theotonico non a Romano pontifice usurpative obtinuit dominium eius, ut credimus, divinum iudicium impedivit.' Cf. *Reg.* 8.3 (to Alfonso VI, 520): 'Ipsum quippe regem sapientissimum Salomonem incestus mulierum turpiter amore deiecit et florentissimum regnum Israel Dei iudicio pene totum de manu posteritatis eius abrupit.' See Sielaff, *op. cit.* (note 16 *supra*) 33f.

[112] *Reg.* 4.1 (291f.).

[113] Some authors—for example, Carlyle and Pacaut—have assumed that these concluding remarks were addressed to the bishops in synod, rather than to the Apostles. But there is no change of address from the beginning of the letter to the end; and in any case, the reference to bishops as 'principes sanctissimi' instead of 'fratres' or 'patres et fratres' would have been extraordinary. See A. J. Carlyle, *History of Medieval Political Thought in the West* IV (3rd impression, London 1940) 201; Pacaut, *La théocratie* 87.

[114] *Reg.* 7.14a (487).

IV

We are now in a position to sum up the major points of Gregory's thought concerning Church-State relations and, addressing ourselves to the original problem, to assess the meaning of the specific measures Gregory took against Henry IV and of his actions at Canossa.

Gregory's political and ecclesiological thought was cast entirely in terms of a conflict between the forces of Antichrist and the forces of God, whose earthly leader was the Pope. Within the Christian community, the Pope held directive power over all persons and consequently over all offices exercised by Christians, including the kingship. But temporal offices were in the last analysis discrete from the Church; they were like threads which might be woven into the fabric of Christendom or pulled out from it, retaining their integrity in either case.[115] The power to grant or to withdraw the legal powers of the kingship was attributed, therefore, not to the Papacy, but to divine judgment. The Church might cast wicked rulers out from the body of the faithful; but, having acknowledged them as members of the Devil, it had no further power over them, no power to depose them from the offices which they exercised wrongfully, but, at the same time, lawfully.

Of the three measures Gregory took against Henry, excommunication is surely the easiest to understand. It was simply the removal of a recalcitrant sinner from the Church, and it had no intrinsic political implications. Gregory had considered Henry excommunicate in 1074, before the beginning of their dispute, but he did not then regard his royal title as being tainted in any way.[116] Indeed, the distinction between this religious sanction and the political measures he adopted is illustrated by Gregory's own statement that at Canossa he restored the King to communion but neither restored him to the kingship nor enjoined his subjects to resume their obedience to him.[117] The second measure, the release of Christian subjects from their vows of

---

[115] This point is clear in Gregory's famous statement on the origin of the royal power in his second letter to Herman of Metz, *Reg.* 8.21 (552): 'Quis nesciat reges et duces ab iis habuisse principium qui Deum ignorantes superbia rapinis perfidia homicidiis postremo universis pene sceleribus mundi principe diabolo videlicet agitante super pares, scilicet homines, dominari ceca cupidine et intollerabili presumptione affectaverunt?' Gregory was concerned here to demonstrate that kings within the framework of the orthodox church were dependent for salvation upon the sacramental offices of the priesthood.

[116] See *Reg.* 1.85 (121). Similarly, he wrote to excommunicate canons concerning an excommunicate count, all of whom he still considered in possession of their offices. Jaffé, *Epp. coll.* no. 38, p. 565f.

[117] *Reg.* 7.14a (484). See Hofmann's book (note 88 *supra*) 150ff; Fliche, 'Grégoire VII' (n. 1) 374.

fidelity to Henry, is a logical, but as we have said, not a necessary, elaboration. On the apparent principle that Christians ought not to be subject to the 'synagogue of Satan,'[118] Gregory freed them from the necessity of obeying a heretical ruler. Subjects had, therefore, the option of rejecting their ruler or rejecting their faith.[119] Just as Gregory released subjects of simoniac bishops and priests from their obligation of obedience[120]—without, it should be added, encouraging them to rebellion—so he also attempted to preserve the spiritual welfare of Christians from the moral danger of wicked kings by delivering them from their subjection. The final measure, deposition, was, as we have attempted to show, a declarative act, rather than a definitive one, and indicated that the king against whom it was directed was no longer a true king in the eyes of the Church;[121] it was in fact a moral, not a juristic, sentence.

In the context of Gregory's thought, therefore, as well as in the context of history, Canossa cannot be viewed as an unique event, but rather as one stage in a legal process which lasted almost a decade. The final confirmation or withdrawal of the kingship, which was the object of that process, was not a real question at Canossa. Gregory appeared there in two capacities: He was the earthly head of the Church, and at the same time, he was the judge whom both Henry and the Saxons had elected to arbitrate their dispute. By virtue of his prelatical office, he had full authority to receive a penitent sinner back into orthodox communion. He therefore freed Henry from the ban of excommunication. In his second capacity, however, he could take no action until both parties in the dispute were present and a full hearing could be held. While acknowledging Henry's title as king, Gregory consequently withheld ecclesiastical sanctions from his rule pending settlement of the case which had been appealed to him. Henry had shown himself morally worthy to return to Christ's flock, but his worthiness of the royal office in the eyes of the Church had not been cleared by the judgment of the German electors, who alone had the power to elevate to the kingship, and of the Pope. At Canossa, when he forbade Henry to use the royal insignia and at the same time he acknowledged him as King, Gregory indicated clearly that he considered Henry suspended, but not irrevocably deposed, from the kingship. For Gregory, the importance of the interview was that negotiations leading to

---

[118] *Reg.* 9.2 (571f), concerning the employment of Jews in the Spanish royal administration.

[119] Cf. *Reg.* 1.35 (57), a threat against Philip I: 'Nam aut rex ipse repudiator turpi symoniace heresis mercimonio idoneas ad sacrum regimen personas promoveri permittet aut Franci pro certo, nisi fidem christianam abicere maluerint, generalis anathematis mucrone percussi illi ulterius obtemperare recusabunt.'

[120] *Reg.* 6.10 (411f), Jaffé, *Epp. coll.* nos. 3, 4, 5, pp. 523ff; Pflugk-Hartuung I no. 47, p. 46 ; Mansi 20.625, *Ep.* 10.

[121] See Kern, *op. cit.* 340.

a just settlement of the dispute might be renewed directly between Henry and himself, since Henry had been delivered from the hands of the Devil back among the sons of God.[122] Canossa was not, therefore, the testing ground of extreme hierocratic theories, but it was simply the beginning of a new stage in a legal process.

Canossa, however, has a higher value for the historian, for the resolution of its ambiguity leads directly to the resolution of the apparent ambiguity which consistently marks Gregory's part in the Investiture Conflict. As Fliche and Arquillière have shown, the essence of that ambiguity is that Gregory acknowledged a man whom he himself had declared deposed to be a lawful king. That ambivalence, one of the invariables in the controversy, was the result, not of indecisiveness, but of settled convictions in Gregory's mind.

It exists even in those most crucial acts, the edicts of deposition against Henry. We have seen that, in the correspondence which followed the first edict, Gregory declared that he had deposed Henry and urged the Germans to receive him back as king should he repent. On the other hand, it has been shown that Gregory prayed for Henry's reconciliation with the Church and continued to negotiate with him and to acknowledge his royal title. And in the later history of the conflict, there is much—Gregory's Easter prophecy of 1080, continued willingness to negotiate with Henry, offer to surrender the imperial crown to him, retraction of the second edict of excommunication, and steadfast acknowledgment of Henry's royal title—to indicate that Gregory himself did not regard his second deposition as a definitive juristic act.

In 1076 as well as in 1080, the emphasis in Gregory's mind was constantly on moral, instead of juristic considerations. His two decrees of excommunication and deposition against Henry were provoked by insupportable challenges to the moral prestige of the Papacy itself. The first was prompted by the Synod of Worms (1076) where, at Henry's instigation, the German episcopacy declared Gregory unworthy of the Papacy, renounced its obedience to him, and denied the supreme jurisdiction of Rome in diocesan affairs. The second followed quickly upon the discovery that Henry had bribed the papal legate, Ulrich of Padua, to render false reports to his papal master. Gregory's anger

---

[122] See Paul of Bernried, *Vita Gregorii VII* c. 77 (PL 148.80). For diverse scholarly judgments on the importance of Canossa, see Sielaff, *op. cit.* 77, Voosen, *op. cit.* 267, Arquillière, *art. cit.* (n. 1 *supra*) 16f, Brackmann (n. 89) 8ff, Fliche, 'Grégoire VII' 375f, *La réforme* 307f. See also Berges' comment on the invitation to the Forcheim assembly which Rudolf sent the Empress Dowager Agnes, *art. cit.* (n. 84) 206: '... das scheint darauf zu weisen, dass der Papst, als die Einladung erging, die Fürsten jedenfalls noch nicht von ihren Eiden entbunden hatte.'

was so great that he deposed Ulrich on the spot; immediately thereafter, he moved the deposition of Henry and the recognition of Rudolf.[123]

In the more usual circumstances of the controversy, however challenging, Gregory without exception recognised Henry's royal title, and declared his eagerness for the King's reconciliation with the true Church, which latter was the condition for renewed negotiations in 1074, the preliminary condition satisfied at Canossa, the condition Gregory set for his coronation of Henry in 1084, and the condition upon which, in his last days, Gregory provisionally lifted the ban of excommunication against the King. However, Gregory's constant acknowledgment of Henry's royal title and his refusal of his own power to set another in Henry's place was as frequent an element in the history of the conflict as were Gregory's insistent and prayerful entreaties that Henry turn from his wrongful government and accept once again the direction of the Roman Church. From the penance Henry rendered to papal legates in 1074 to his first excommunication, from the first ban to Canossa, from Canossa to the second ban, and from the second decree to the time of Gregory's death the tacit rejection of absolute powers over temporal government and the determined assertion of Rome's moral headship within the body of the faithful were Gregory's Scylla and Charybdis.

It was the combination of political and moral thought which produced the apparent ambivalence in Gregory's whole conduct in the dispute, and which was epitomized in his actions at Canossa. At the important interview, he was able to acknowledge Henry as king, since he was in fact lawfully king; he was able, at the same time to observe that he did not restore Henry to the kingship, since it was beyond his competence to bestow the royal power. Henry's definitive deposition or restoration did not fall to the Papacy, but to divine judgment as manifested in war or in full judicial process. The seeming inconsistency between the Pope's thought and his actions, which appears if one assumes him to have been an absolute papal supremist in theory, is therefore resolved if one sees his thought in moral terms, in terms of the struggle between the world and the Church which allowed him to recognise a wrongful king as a lawful king.

It is quite clear from the writing of Gregorian partisans that the hierocratic views which came to fulfillment in the thought of Innocent III and, even

---

[123] Gregory's attitude towards the bribery of a papal legate can be estimated from his remarks concerning Herman of Bamberg's attempts to buy a favorable judgment from the Roman See. *Reg.* 3.3 (to Henry IV, 247): 'Symoniacus enim ille Herimannus dictus episcopus hoc anno ad synodum Romanam accessisset, in itinere substitit et premittens nuntios suos cum copiosis muneribus noto sibi artificio innocentiam nostram et confratrum nostrorum integritatem pactione pecuniae attemptare atque, si fieri posset, corrumpere molitus est. Quod ubi preter spem evenit, iam de damnatione sua securior festinanter retrocessit...'

more, in that of Alexander IV, were present in Gregory's intellectual circle. But Gregory himself did not adopt those views, and his thought was midway between them and the rigid dualism of other thinkers. In this context, it is perhaps significant that Gregory's own last words, 'I have loved justice and hated iniquity; therefore I die in exile,' were contradicted by a bishop who heard them: 'O Lord,' he said, 'you cannot die in exile, for in the stead of Christ and His apostles you have divinely received the nations and the ends of the earth as an inheritance and a possession.'[124] Spiritual meaning, of course, is not far from this response. But neither are the lofty claims to universal dominion so foreign to Gregory himself, claims to temporal and spiritual supremacy based on a text which not once appears in Gregory's works: 'I have this day set thee over the nations and over the kingdoms, to root out, and to pull down, and to destroy, and to throw down, to build, and to plant' (Jeremiah 1.10). For Gregory, the world and the Church were not yet identical; between them there was still the struggle of good and evil for men's souls, the contest between Christ, the Head of the Church, and Satan, who was master in the world.

University of Minnesota

---

[124] Paul of Bernried, *Vita Gregorii VII* c. 102 (PL 148.95): 'Ubi vero in extremo positus erat, ultima verba ejus haec fuerunt: "Dilexi justitiam et odivi iniquitatem; propterea morior in exilio." Episcopus respondisse narratur: "Non potes, Domine, mori in exsilio, qui in vice Christi et apostolorum ejus divinitus accepisti gentes haereditatem et possessionem terminos terrae."'

Additional Note. Morghen, *art. cit.* n. 88 *supra*, argues that, as the *Dictatus* seems to imply, Gregory claimed the power to depose kings definitively, and that this claim derived from the doctrine of cogent necessity, which warranted papal intervention in the trial of bishops, and also from the authority which Gregory assumed over feudal relationships. See esp. p. 42ff. — Another recent comment to which Professor Kuttner has directed my attention occurs in J. Bernhard, *La Collection en deux livres (Cod. Vat. lat. 3832)* I (Strasbourg 1962) 587 and *passim*, where the author concerns himself primarily to affirm Gregory VII's indebtedness to the *Collectio* for the thoughts expressed in his *Dictatus*, but not to discuss the content of the latter.

V

The Structure of Holiness In Othloh's *Vita Bonifatii* and Ebo's *Vita Ottonis*

The interview between Christ and the Grand Inquisitor, which Dostoyevsky portrays in *The Brothers Karamazov,* may seem a strange point from which to begin a discussion of eleventh and twelfth century ideas. However, the encounter raises in sharp detail one matter that is central for us: namely, the pressures of institutional growth on the church's primitive ethos. The Grand Inquisitor's intricate argument that he had "corrected" Christ and allied with Satan so that Christ's ideals of peace and freedom could survive and be realized recalls many analogues to the mediaevalist's mind. One thinks of disputes that tormented Cluny and the Franciscan Order. All the issues involved in this ceaseless and, in some ways tragic, dialectic between ideals and experience center on one issue: their nucleus is holiness. Without resorting to the Inquisitor's cynicism, or to the insistence of some modern scholars that canonization has been yet another trophy of *Realpolitik,*[1] we can point to a number of changes in the way in which the visible church has thought about this subject. We are dealing with typology in process. It is well established that the early church considered the martyr as the epitome of holiness, and that, a little later, the type of the desert Father became dominant. In the Latin West, around the eighth century, people thought of bishops when they thought of holiness, and, beginning in the twelfth century, the religious gained a precedence that they have not lost until the present day. In an intricate and fascinating manner, each stage absorbed the traits of the earlier ones. The examples that will be studied combine the quest for martyrdom, the idealization of the ascetic life that is also the learned life, and the episcopal *magisterium.* The relative paucity of women and of diocesan clergy among those venerated as saints indicates persistent traits, both positive and negative, beneath this sequence of incremental change, which, of course, had its roots in the slow, collective experience of western Europe.

The structure of holiness that we are to consider had historical meaning because it had a place in the sequence of typologies just indicated: it held its dominance between the eighth and the twelfth centuries. This is our first ground-rule. We have a second: holiness was not yet defined by a tried and established juridical process. We are about to discuss St. Boniface and St. Otto of Bamberg. Apart from isolated and exceptional cases in the tenth and eleventh centuries, the latter was one of the first whose credentials were re-viewed by the papal court in a process bearing all the marks of canonization as we know it. And yet, just as much as did Boniface and his biographer, Otto belonged to the earlier age, when the juristic review was rough and im-provised, and the recognition of holiness owed its integrity to Scripture and the Fathers.

Any concept is made up of parts. Holiness is no exception to this rule. Despite the fullness of Latin hagiographical literature, and despite the ex-traordinary care and lucidity with which that literature has been edited and analyzed, there is still room for study of sanctity, as a concept, in terms of its structure. A synthetic analysis would certainly require preliminary dissec-tions of a large and representative sample of biographies. In this paper, I mean to suggest a few directions indicated by two biographies written in eleventh- and twelfth-century Germany.

Since they treat of missionaries, St. Boniface and St. Otto of Bamberg, analogies with St. Paul were natural. The Apostle of the Gentiles also made a direct contribution to the concept of sanctity as set forth by Othloh of St. Emmeram and Ebo. His distinctions between appearance and reality—in terms of the visible and the invisible, the flesh and the spirit, the animal and the spiritual—drew a sharp line between man's outer existence and his inner life; and, raised to the higher level of true and false knowledge, this distinc-tion was fundamental to our authors' understanding of holiness. Theology gives us the analytical categories needed to describe the structure of the con-cept: namely, the necessity, conditions, possibility, manner, and proofs of holiness. These formed unconscious agenda for Othloh and Ebo, and they gave hidden centers of gravity for unspoken assumptions. On each of the five counts, they returned to the Pauline distinctions, with an emphasis on spiri-tuality that was only to be expected in works intended to serve as apologetics for monasteries against the encroachments of princes and worldly bishops.[2]

Othloh is known, on the one hand, as a monk whose peculiar visions sup-ply titillating examples of abnormal psychology, and, on the other, as a highly competent student of theology and classical learning. Both his "psychopathologische Deutung" and his skill in divine and secular phi-losophy have been extensively treated by Helga Schauwecker in her recent study.[3] His biography of St. Boniface, however, has never received a thorough discussion, and we shall have to digress to locate it in his life and *oeuvre*.

The reason for neglect is doubtless the very reason for the *Vita*'s im-portance: namely, since Othloh was writing about a man who died three hundred years before his own day, he could provide no eye-witness accounts, but instead relied entirely on eighth-century materials. The brethren of Fulda originally commissioned him to revise the biography of St. Boniface by Willibald. The resulting work in fact combines elements from several narra-tive accounts contemporary with St. Boniface, and quantitatively, well over half of Othloh's work consists of letters that passed between Boniface and the popes of his day. As Hauck wrote, the biography by Othloh, "was originally intended to be nothing other than the stylistic improvement of an old, clumsy work. But here, too, the commission pressed the author further. . . . With their study [i.e., the study of letters to and from Boniface], he gained the insight . . . that the writing of history must as far as possible be grounded on primary sources. From this point of view, he not only smoothed out the form of the old biography, but he enlarged it with letters, and thereby created the first extant biography that rests essentially upon documentary material."[4] As we shall see, the use of sources was highly purposeful; it expressed convictions thoroughly rooted in Othloh's life, and in the intersection of his views with the experience of Fulda.

Othloh was born in the diocese of Freising (ca. 1010). After receiving an education, excellent for the day, at the monasteries of Tegernsee and Hersfeld, he entered the circle of Meinhard, bishop of Würzburg, and gained a fair reputation as a practitioner of the liberal arts. He made forays into monasteries for the purpose of studying books kept in their libraries. During one of those excursions, to St. Emmeram in Regensburg, he fell ill. On vowing to become a monk he miraculously recovered, and, in 1032, he entered the monastic life. For the next thirty years, Othloh was able to pursue his studies at St. Emmeram, and to develop skills in versifying, in rhetoric, in penmanship, and, not least, in polemics, of which he was extremely proud. Through much of that time, however, the monastery engaged Bishop Gebehard III of Regensburg (1036–60) in an intermittent conflict over property. New forms of the transfer and tenure of property were evolved to give the monastery a firmer grasp on its lands and emoluments; but Gebehard persisted in his "avarice." Over the years, Othloh came to see the struggle as a sign that the world was hastening toward its end, and as one of the reasons why men were afflicted with many disasters in his day, and why the rulers of the church should turn from their "immeasurable vanity" and seek ways in which God could be brought to cease his blows and show mercy to His people.[5] Gebehard's successor, Otto, found Othloh such a thorn in his side that the monk was forced to leave St. Emmeram and to seek asylum at Fulda, where he remained for four years. During that time, he composed several works, including the *Vita Bonifatii*. Subsequently, he returned to St. Emmeram, by way of Amorbach, and remained there until his death (ca. 1070).

Othloh discovered a familiar scenario in motion when he arrived at Fulda. The monks there were struggling with the archbishop of Mainz over the Thuringian tithes when Othloh came upon the scene. This conflict was a persistent one, and yet the monks had reason to hope that it might be resolved in their favor if an appeal were made *blande suaviterque*. The new archbishop, Siegfried (1060–84) was not only, as his predecessors had been, the successor of St. Boniface, who had founded Fulda and so esteemed it that he wished to be buried there rather than in Mainz, and whose relics still guarded the monastery. He had also been monk and abbot at Fulda. Siegfried had adapted all too well to the conventions of his see, gaining the support of the imperial court in his efforts to encroach upon the tithes rendered to Fulda and Hersfeld. He was so relentless and successful in this effort that, in 1065, Pope Alexander II joined forces with Fulda and, in 1068, forced him to return to the monastery holdings sufficient to restore its wealth to the level maintained when he had been abbot. Undaunted, the archbishop continued his efforts, and his persistence was rewarded by a synod held at Erfurt in 1073, which rejected the pleas of Fulda and Hersfeld and upheld Siegfried's.[6]

The matter bore the more heavily on Fulda because of its vulnerability to imperial intervention. At Christmastide 1052, as part of an agreement between Pope Leo IX and Henry III, Fulda, "and some other places and monastic communities which are said to have been given of old to St. Peter," were transferred from papal to imperial control.[7] During the regency of the Empress Agnes, and after Archbishop Anno of Cologne replaced her, the ominous possibilities of the transfer became obvious; for between early December 1056 and mid-December 1062 at least nine monastic properties were transferred by imperial authority to the control of bishops. This flagrant and repeated violation of traditional monastic privileges and liberties, and other arbitrary administration of proprietary ecclesiastical institutions of the Empire, forecast ruin for the monastic establishment or church whose representatives could not gain the favor of the regent. Abbot Egbert of Fulda saw the direction of things and, even in the pontificate of Leo IX, he sent records about St. Boniface to Rome as part of an effort to defend the prerogatives of his community,[8] an effort that gained, in 1057, a confirmation of privileges from Pope Victor II. Episcopal encroachments, sustained by the imperial regency, had advanced several stages by the time when Othloh arrived at Fulda, and Egbert had been succeeded as abbot by Widerad, a man in whom the brethren had little confidence.

A ceremonial dispute brought all these strands together. Convention gave the Abbot of Fulda the privilege of sitting beside the Archbishop of Mainz, the Metropolitan of Germany, in assemblies. Bishop Hezil of Hildesheim contested this privilege, and at Christmastide 1063 a street battle between his retainers and Widerad's brought the matter to a head before the imperial court. Although a panel of inquiry found Hezil's followers at fault, they went unpunished, whereas Widerad and his case were brushed aside. When news of the melee and subsequent indignities reached Fulda, the monks protested furiously against Widerad's feeble efforts. They sent emissaries to plead the case of Fulda before the imperial court. But their envoys received harsh judgments; Widerad was granted asylum at court and the power to end the monastic uprising in any way he chose. The initial question of protocol remained menacingly open.

The monks were "afire with the pain of the recent wound and with the memory of past wounds."[9] Since their formal legation had been spurned, they were in need of another means, more circuitous perhaps than direct recourse, by which to present their case to secular and ecclesiastical princes.

They had two ends in view: first, to gain a strong patron at the imperial court; and second, even if that dignitary were a bishop, to uphold the traditional monastic liberties from episcopal control. Siegfried of Mainz naturally came to mind. While the exact date of Othloh's *Vita Bonifatii* is not known, a date of 1063–64 is plausible in this historical context. Othloh mentions that the brethren had recalled Egbert's plan for a new biography of their patron, and that they would not let him decline the commission. This reversion to the plan of an effective abbot, the petulant insistence of the monks that Othloh describe the favors of Boniface toward Fulda, and the utter omission of any reference to Widerad indicate that the *Vita* may have been written in 1063–64, while the anger of the monks was hot, and Widerad had taken refuge among their enemies at court.

In his *Liber de tentatione*, Othloh wrote that biographies of saints should be read so that, by imitating holy exemplars, one could master the flesh and avoid the terrors of the Last Judgment.[10] In the *Vita Bonifatii*, he repeated his confidence in the didactic function of hagiography[11]; and his treatment of the documentary evidence put at his disposal by the monks indicates the particular lessons that he wished to teach. Othloh himself referred to his purposes in the prologue to Book 1. He wrote that he considered Boniface's correspondence of utmost importance, since the letters set forth most clearly the nature of Boniface's relations with the papacy; a description of his missionary activities and of his episcopal administration; an indication of the veneration which he received from Carloman and Pippin; and finally information as to his endowment of Fulda "with possessions and special tithes." The letters, therefore, were not simple glosses or ornaments; they comprised an integral part of Othloh's characterization, as well as of the historical facts deployed in that portrayal.[12]

It must be said at the outset that Othloh reproduced the texts of the Bonifatian letters accurately. He included thirty of them. With some exceptions, he arranged them in correct chronological order;[13] and, though he (or the copy that he consulted) suppressed some formulaic titles, statements, and datings,[14] the texts are exact and complete. The telling point is in the letters omitted. Some omissions are not important: for example, the two letters of Gregory II, and the three of Zacharias that exist in the *corpus* as we have it, but that do not appear in the *Vita Bonifatii*. They merely confirm, or repeat, information included in materials that Othloh did reproduce. Other omissions fall into a different category. Only three letters by Boniface himself were included, and one of them was, in effect, a synodal record. Othloh specifically excluded the Anglo-Saxon part of the Bonifatian correspondence, in order, he said, to avoid tiring the reader, "maxime cum nobis sufficiant nostra. Nostra autem dico, quae pro patribus nostris, Germanis scilicet, salvandis scripsit vel ab ullo scripta recepit."[15] This means, of course, that hagiographical importance of the letters, apart from their contents, lay in their origins and in their relevance to German ecclesiastical matters. Of the thirty letters which the *Vita* contains (including a spurious cession to Fulda attributed to Othloh), only two were issued by laymen: the edict that Carloman issued from the *Concilium Germanicum,* and the alleged grant of Pippin to Fulda. The three letters of Boniface have already been mentioned. It should also be observed that all of the three were addressed to the apostolic see, and that one of them is the *iuramentum* that Boniface submitted before his episcopal consecration. The remaining twenty-five letters were issued by the papal curia, seven of them under Gregory II, five under Gregory III, and thirteen under Zacharias. Sixteen of the letters were, or could have been thought to have been, received by Boniface; the remainder, not by him, were issued on his behalf to laymen, princes, and clergy. It is quite apparent that Othloh selected letters for inclusion so as to present, not Boniface in his own words and in the totality of his life, but Boniface in his functions as missionary and as the premier bishop of Germany, preaching and governing on the commission and under the direction of Rome, and with the filial support of secular princes. The inclusion of forged and genuine documents regarding Fulda served the purpose of his commission: namely, the demonstration of Fulda's extraordinary privileges that tied it, through Boniface, to the apostolic see.[16]

Omissions from other materials at Othloh's disposal also indicate his guiding motives. He alleged that one of his main purposes in consulting texts other than Willibald's life was to enlarge what Willibald had to say about miracles. Indeed, he did appropriate three miracles from the Mainz *Vita;* but he omitted a fourth miracle related in the same source (c. 12). Two of the appropriated miracles (the vision of St. Michael and the prophecy concerning Adelher's bequest) strongly underscore Boniface's role as defender and augmenter of monastic property. The third (the vision in which St. Boniface orders the removal of his body from Mainz to Fulda) was an essential part of the encomium to Fulda. The omitted miracle, a miraculous draught of fishes during the translation of Boniface's body, said something about sanctity, but nothing about Othloh's apologetic goals.

A second omission concerns the *Vita Sturmi,* a biography of Fulda's first abbot which Othloh quarried extensively. Othloh knew from that text that a bitter controversy divided Lull, Boniface's designated successor as bishop of Mainz, and Sturmi. Yet, writing within the walls of Sturmi's monastery, Othloh not only left out every trace of their dispute, but even took occasion to describe Lull (both in his own text and in the papal letters that he included) as a worthy and devoted disciple of Boniface. He underscored the closeness of their relationship by his description of the last interview between the two men, in which Boniface, as the master and friend, entrusted ecclesiastical and personal obligations to Lull.[17] This treatment of the bonds among Boniface, Lull, and Sturmi indicates an effort to revise the past according to the ideal relation that the monks of Fulda needed, and apparently wished to establish, with Siegfried, an effort indicated another way by the prominence given Mainz in the substance of the biography, both by its division into two books (the first treating of events before Boniface acceded to Mainz, the second of later events), and by the materials furnished to illustrate the subordination of Cologne to Mainz.

A third omission bears on Boniface's relationship with his contemporary popes. Othloh included two documents that indicated significant differences between Boniface's wishes, or actions, and Roman practice. Pope Zacharias denied Boniface the privilege of installing his own successor,[18] though Boniface did in fact consecrate Lull as bishop of Mainz under conditions that are unclear.[19] On another occasion, Zacharias declared himself astonished to hear that Boniface had ordered the rebaptism of those baptised by illiterate priests who garbled the sacramental formulae, and he admonished him to teach "as the holy fathers teach and preach."[20] Othloh followed Willibald, however, in leaving out all reference to Pope Stephen II, the last pope under whom Boniface served. From the Mainz *Vita,* he knew of the controversy that arose between Stephen and Boniface when the latter questioned the pope's right to consecrate a bishop in an archidiocese not his own without the consent of the bishop ordinary, a dispute that was inconsonant with Othloh's portrait since it could not be proven to have ended, as could the other two, in reconciliation.

Finally, a cluster of omissions illustrates Othloh's attitude toward the intervention of secular powers in ecclesiastical affairs, and indeed suggests how incompatible his monastic ideals were with the imperial church of his day. He avoided the word "patrocinium" in appropriating passages from the Mainz *Vita* and the Vita *Sturmi* which describe secular protection of the church. In this regard, it is also worth observing that Othloh omitted the Mainz author's description of an interview in which Pope Stephen "gave the power 'patrocinandi' " to Pippin; Boniface's reference in the *Vita Sturmi* to the royal defence of Fulda; Carloman's declaration, in the *Vita Sturmi,* that he transfered the site of Fulda "whole and entire" from his legal control; and the final provision in *ep.* 56, in which, without synodal approval, Carloman imposed penalties for pagan practices on the precedent of an act of Charles Martel. Othloh was intent on describing secular rulers as men who were devout sons of the church, disciples, rather than masters. Omissions such as those indicated suggest that, while Othloh acknowledged that secular princes could have a part in the elections of bishops, in the erection of episcopal sees, in the summoning of synods, and in the execution of synodal decrees, he rejected the view that rulers were privileged to act in affairs of religion on their own authority, or in a superior role. This attitude is also illustrated by an addition that Othloh made to his known sources. Carloman and Charlemagne appear as model princes, the latter obviously out of chronology. Among Boniface's contemporaries, Carloman took the palm for his personal devoutness and his support of the monasteries, even when he was beset by enemies on all sides. But Carloman had one further claim to distinction in Othloh's eyes, which he carefully inserted: "He chose the best part, which was not taken from him. For he relinquished kingdoms full of earthly power, and going to Monte Cassino, in which the strictest discipline of monastic life was then held, he was made a monk there."[21]

Othloh's selection and editing of materials tells a great deal about the deliberateness with which he constructed hagiographical models for emulation by his contemporary prelates and princes. But they also contribute fundamentally to an understanding of the concept of sanctity that informed his entire reconstitution of the past; for both his use of sources and his understanding turned on a fundamental distinction between appearance and reality, corresponding with the line that he drew, as Schauwecker has shown, between *divina* and *mundana philosophia*. That distinction, in turn, was central to many particulars, including the troubling fact that miracles had ceased at the tomb of St. Boniface.

Through Boniface's merits, many had obtained miraculous benefits for the interior man—in the remission of sins—and for the outer man—in the lifting of physical infirmities. The lapse of these benefits, Othloh said, was not due to God's inclemency or to any weakness in Boniface's intercessory powers before God, but rather to infidelity expressed in the negligence of divine service, in the incorrigible malice of the inhabitants of the land, in the ingratitude of those who, when miracles came to pass through the intercession of saints, neither rendered appropriate praise and thanks to God and His saints for them, nor even kept them in remembrance.[22] The distinction between the apparent world of the body and the authentic world of the spirit, that Othloh applied to a contemporary quandary, recurred in the documents that he incorporated into the *Vita*.

In one letter (*ep.* 82), Pope Zacharias admonished the German clergy with the words of Luke 12:4f., following them with a conflation of 2 Cor. 10:4f. and Eph. 6:10, distinguishing between body and soul, and carnal and spiritual weapons.[23] Boniface himself—who knew how wolves could masquerade in sheep's clothing[24]—confessed that, while he had been able spiritually to keep his vow to abstain from association with unworthy clerics, he had been unable physically to avoid them when he waited upon the Prince of the Franks.[25] For Othloh, the distinction pervaded every aspect of his story. It appears, rather conventionally, in passages that describe how Boniface, through studies, grew in virtues, and how this inner strength was externally manifested in priestly orders; how Boniface declined, first, an abbacy, to follow his vocation as missionary, and, second, an episcopacy, to obey his commission from Rome;[26] and how Boniface always sought *lucrum animarum* instead of *lucrum temporale*.[27] It appears most dramatically in the distinction between the apparent death of Boniface and his companions, and the corresponding victory of the pagans, and the real martyrdom, the *passio gloriosa,* of the "saints" attended by the spiritual and, not much later, the physical destruction of their slayers.[28]

In terms of Othloh's hagiographical purposes, the distinction was particularly cast as the higher antinomies of true and false. The specious piety of

Ananias and Saphira[29] was a scriptural analogue of the perjury which Boniface encountered, and for which he foretold a condign punishment;[30] of the effort of Aldebert to masquerade as an angel of the Lord in human form,[31] a hypocrisy that Boniface wished to end with perpetual imprisonment; and of the false story concocted by the people of Utrecht in an attempt to retain Boniface's body, which was unmasked by a miraculous pealing of the church bell.[32] Othloh understood Boniface's life and work chiefly in the light of this sort of pairing. On the one hand, there were the "fables and vain prodigies and signs," the false visions, and the fabricated relics of heretics.[00] On the other hand, there were the miracles, associated with Boniface, the visions authenticated by purgation, the relics bestowed by the apostolic see upon Boniface, those to which he had recourse in his last hour, and the primary and secondary relics of Boniface himself. On the one hand, there were heretics, false Christians, false priests, false bishops, false prophets, and pagans—pagans, not merely in Germany, but even in Rome, performing their detestable and pernicious rites in the shadows of the apostles' tombs.[34] On the other hand, there stood the orthodox: namely, the apostolic see and those (including especially Boniface) in communion with it and faithful to its order and doctrine. The former presumed to call themselves apostles, though they were members of Satan and precursors of Antichrist;[35] they called themselves holy.[36] But "apostolic holiness" remained among those who did not arrogate it to themselves,[37] though they granted the title "holiness" to others. It remained among the true imitators of Christ, who, following Him in carnal tribulation, carried His death in their bodies in such fashion that His life was also manifested in their bodies, and that they might be glorified by the catholic faith.[38]

The didacticism that informed Othloh's apologetic purpose intersected the exemplarism of theology. It was well and good to describe Carloman's generosity toward monasteries for the profit of those worthy to be edified by good examples and for the confusion of those who, contrary to their best knowledge, persisted in confessing God with their mouths while opening "the ears of their hearts" to love of worldly life.[39] Still, Carloman's benefactions were part of a wider exemplarism centering on Boniface. Just as Abraham is said to be the father of all those who believe in Christ because of the merit of his faith and obedience, merit to be imitated by all, Boniface can be called father of all the inhabitants of Germany in that he begot them through preaching, confirmed them by example and, in charity, laid down his life for them.[40] Those who failed to heed his example must forswear their evil ways lest death come, leaving no time for repentance.[41] Their wicked doings would weigh especially upon bishops who ignored the authority of his examples, which became a testimony of their damnation, as demonstrated by the Gospels and the prophet Ezekiel.[42] The immediate issue was monastic property; but soteriology was prior to that, and it was rooted in the theology of the apparent and the real, of the obvious and the hidden, of the outer and the inner man.

Naturally, the holiness that informed Othloh's exemplary model, Boniface, was also rooted in that theology of salvation. Thus far, we have examined the purposes for which Othloh wrote the *Vita*, and the selection and use of texts in the service of those ends. We have also indicated two kinds of theological tension that profoundly characterized Othloh's thought, and particularly his view of holiness: namely, the tension, first, between apparent and real, in its various Pauline formulations, and, second, between the ideal, or exemplar, and the actual. We have discussed (1) the way in which Othloh built up a characterization appropriate to the needs of the moment, and (2) dialectical aspects of his theology. It remains to suggest that both matters expressed an underlying structure of assumptions about holiness that can be described within the five categories that we mentioned earlier.

1. *Holiness is necessary.* From what has already been said, it is apparent that holiness is necessary to salvation. But, as a quality derived in men and original in God, holiness is also essential to the operations of grace and, hence, to providential history. The "venerable holiness" of Boniface derived from the "wonderful power" of God, as did the "holiness" of the gospel codex that Boniface raised against his slayer,[43] and it was part of the encounter with God that effected his vocation to the monastic life, his resolution to go as a missionary wherever grace directed, the conversion that through grace he achieved, and the assistance that, *divino nutu* or *divino affatu,* he received from ecclesiastical superiors or princes.[44] The papal letters, which Othloh allowed to carry much of his story, add some useful observations. God called Boniface to his missionary labors.[45] He assisted him, sent an angel before him to prepare his way, and strengthened his preaching by divine inspiration. As the kingdom of God approached and the world drew toward its end, divine mercy commanded that Boniface not only preach, but also preside over the entire province of the Gauls.[46] The eschatological and soteriological dimensions of necessity coincided in the third dimension of ecclesiology and, of course, in Boniface's role in the church. For unity, as a divine perfection, was also a note of the church, "one body," composed of many abounding in grace and striving to preserve unity of spirit in the bond of peace and charity, a unity manifested, in the Bonifatian letters, by faithful obedience to St. Peter and his see.[47] Othloh himself expressed this sense of unity in his anagogical application of Old Testament prophecies to his own day, and in his insistence that the foundation stones of the church were the earliest fathers, whose canons and definitions should continually govern ecclesiastical affairs and, who, as the canons themselves said, still lived in their establishments.[48]

2. *Holiness is conditional.* As Othloh developed his characterizations, holiness was conditional in two ways. In the first place, it presupposed the ability to distinguish between true and false. It rested, posteriorly, on knowledge as faith, and specifically on the "agnitio Christi," or the "agnitio

veritatis," or the "agnitio verae fidei."[49] Through his preaching, Boniface
made people know the light of Christ,[50] and he was able to see the seeds of
the divine word that he scattered in the hearts of the faithful germinate and
bear fruit.[51] Pagans, heretics, and false Christians were defective, or entirely
lacking in this recognitive capacity. In the second place, holiness was
necessary, anteriorly, if men were to become cooperators with grace. The
stages of Boniface's career are in fact benchmarks of a process by which a saint
conveyed the faith handed down from Peter and Paul and the other apostles
to the popes,[52] and the discipline transmitted from Gregory the Great to
Augustine of Canterbury and thence to the Anglo-Saxons,[53] and by which he
consequently moved from his initial vocation, through priesthood, prelacy,
and martyrdom, to become for men a patron before God, and, through faithfulness, the father of the inhabitants of Germany, as Abraham was father of
all believers in Christ.

3. *Holiness becomes possible.* Othloh recognizes that holiness derives from
God through the grace of vocation, that it infuses a providential necessity
into the lives of individual persons, the cosmos, and the church, and that it is
conditional on faith and necessary for works. But how does it become possible? The examples of contemporary princes and prelates indicate that hearing
the Word of God and knowing the prescripts of the canons is not enough in
itself to procure holy actions, nor, perhaps, is even a holy life. Contemporary
bishops and rulers see the better but approve and do the worse. Othloh used
the example of Boniface to teach that holiness became possible through
obedience to the Scriptures, to the canons, to St. Peter, to the Roman see
endowed by God with the power of binding and loosing, and to the vicar of
St. Peter.[54] For Othloh, Boniface exemplified the need to obey and to
enforce canonical faith and order as it came from Rome. Following Willibald, he wrote that Gregory II, after consecrating Boniface, gave him "a
book in which the most sacred laws of ecclesiastical institution, digests from
assemblies of bishops, were contained." But then, departing from his source,
Othloh stated that Gregory gave Boniface the book, "ordering that both the
clergy and the other peoples to be subjected to his rule be instructed in such
institutes."[55] Boniface's journies to Rome; his consecration and change of
name by papal action; his resort to Rome for advice in greater and lesser
aspects of ecclesiastical government; his adherence to "the tradition of the
Roman Church";[56] his astonished disbelief of the possibility that Rome
could judge against the canons[57]—all comprise one aspect of Othloh's
portrait. Another is formed by Boniface's preaching, and especially by the
disciplinary actions often associated with synodal judgment, through which
he reformed an unwilling and corrupt clergy "according to the statutes of the
sacred canons." As Pope Zacharias wrote to him, "according to the institutes
of the canons, all have been bent to obey you."[58] Faith and order were parts
of the same composition. Holiness was not possible outside the hierarchic
church in communion with Rome—certainly not for the pagans, or for the

false Christians, false priests, and false bishops against whom Boniface called synods and gained sentences of deposition, excommunication, and imprisonment.

4. *Sanctity is divine love expressed in different modes.* Carloman, in his patronage of monasteries, and the companions slain with Boniface manifested holiness in particular modes. Othloh, to be sure, described Boniface most fully of all the *dramatis personae.* To him, as a scholar, Boniface's excellence in literary studies while a young man was of particular interest. It indicated, he thought, that Boniface was "full of divine power," for it led to a multiplication of virtues in him.[59] His preaching to the pagans, his correction of erring Christians, his construction of monasteries and churches, his endowment of them with possessions, his institution of good pastors in them and, finally, his martyrdom as an extension of his other testimonies to the divine word were all, in Othloh's presentation, episodic manifestations of the same holiness, as wisdom, of the same love of Christ through which Boniface became a missionary, the divine love through which the saint bore pain for the sake of Him who suffered for men, the charity that informed obedience and without which prophecy, tongues, understanding, faith, and works profited nothing.[60]

5. *Sanctity can be proven authentic.* Without this assumption, Othloh's hagiographical techniques would not have served his didactic purpose. He went to great lengths to provide demonstrations, objective in his own mind, of Boniface's sanctity. We see this effort in his use of texts, particularly of the Bonifatian letters, his descriptions of Boniface's dealings with princes and of his dependence upon Rome, his declared purpose of garnering miracles other than those narrated by Willibald, his comments on the general acknowledgment of Boniface's learning and worthiness of the heavenly sacrament, as leading to his priestly ordination,[61] his extensive reflection on the circumstances of Boniface's death and burial. Indeed, among the proofs still solicited in a canonization process are the writings of the *servus Dei,* the public recognition of his sanctity, testimonies of ecclesiastical superiors, miracles, the cause of witness (or martyrdom), the circumstances of death, and the conditions of the body (or relics). There was certainly every reason for Othloh to provide as many testimonials to Boniface's sanctity as he could, for he had to persuade his readers that miracles at St. Boniface's tomb had lapsed through the infidelity of recent times, and not because Fulda's intercessor before God had become as ineffective as her abbot before the imperial judges.

The dialectical binary structure that, for Othloh, defined holiness came to a resolution in the capacity of holiness for proof. Othloh did not understand Boniface in the complexity accessible through twentieth-century psychology, and it is doubtful whether he conceived of him as a unique personality. Certainly, the characterization lacks reference to physical appearance, temperament, motivation, or existential ambiguities. He did not feel moved to supply what his sources lacked. As testifier to divine truth, Boniface is less important than his testimony. He is circumscribed by determinants external to himself and, as we have said, these are necessary (divided into binary categories, such as saved and unredeemed, called and reprobate, transitory and eschaton, unity and separation), conditional (divided into categories of faithfulness and infidelity, knowledge, and ignorance), possible (divided into categories of obedience and disobience, reform and deformation, tradition and novelty), and modal (divided into love and estrangement from the life of God). The capacity of holiness for proof united these elements. For it posited that the ambiguity between apparent truth and real truth could be objectively resolved and that through the plain evidence of history authentic truth was taught by example.

Here, Othloh's thought discloses the hermeneutic tautology of any *a priori* pattern. In itself, the dialectic between apparent and real could not be resolved. As holiness could be manifested only by those capable of it, so its manifestations could be correctly read only by those already comprehended in unity, faithfulness, obedience, and love. Othloh appealed to the bar of history—from bishops and princes ill informed to bishops and princes better informed—although he fully recognized that disbelief might deafen "the ears of their hearts" and blind their inner eyes to exemplars of holiness. A monk, as *miles Christi,* had no need to be reminded of the warfare in the world between Christ and Satan, who transformed himself into the likeness of an angel of light, especially a monk acutely vexed, as was Othloh, by the Tempter in many visions. It was not astonishing that miracles lapsed at Boniface's tomb through the faithlessness of the day; for even Christ, in His own country, had been unable to do wonders through the disbelief of many.[62] The duty of the saints, united by imitation to Boniface and to Christ Himself, was to hold fast to their inner vision, to admonish, rebuke, testify to the hidden truth, and, if need be, endure the glorious passion.

Nearly 100 years after Othloh's *Vita Bonifatii* (that is, between 1151 and 1159), Ebo composed his life of Otto of Bamberg (1060/62–1139). While Ebo drew from a number of earlier writings—including at least some portions of Otto's correspondence, annalistic materials and a biography (the Prüfening *Vita*) written 1140–46—the substance of his account came from recollections of Otto's own companions, especially one named Ulrich of St. Egidius. Consequently, textual criticism of his deployment of materials is not so apt a means of detecting Ebo's frame of reference as it is in regard to Othloh's, and there is the additional difference that we do not have a *corpus* of writings by Ebo in which to locate his biography. Ebo's place in history depends on this one text. When all differences have been taken into account, close similarities do remain. Some of them are fortuitous. Otto and Ebo lived in the same region of Germany as Othloh, and both of them had been educated in the same curriculum as he, blending pre-Christian rhetoric and history with patristic theology. Before his conversion to the canonical life,

Otto, indeed, is said to have made a considerable fortune teaching the children of Polish magnates.[63] Both biographies were written on behalf of monasteries chosen by the subjects of the biographies as burial places. Both had a didactic, or apologetic purpose—namely, the defence of monastic possessions—which they characterized as a struggle of monastic spirituality against the worldliness of bishops and princes. Both examined the enigma of holiness in the setting of missionization and martyrdom.

For our purposes, the most important similarity is the appearance, in Ebo's account, of a concept of holiness much like the one set forth in the *Vita Bonifatii*. The dyad of inner and outer is, if anything, more pronounced in Ebo's work than it is in Othloh's. In particular, Ebo knew of crypto-Christians who lived in pagan territory for many years without benefit of Christian rites,[64] and disclosed their true commitment when Otto appeared among them. There were other examples. In Ebo's mind, spiritual richness and temporal wealth were related. One of Otto's principal characteristics was that he was prudent in economic matters. He became rich as a teacher; he served a niece of Henry IV "as another Joseph"; he demonstrated extraordinary managerial abilities as that emperor's master of works at Speier; and his stewardship at the imperial court led him once to decline election as bishop. After his accession, he had a keen eye for other men of practical acumen.[65] He smoothed his diplomatic negotiations with splendid gifts to ease the passage to love of heavenly goods by way of earthly;[66] and, in his zeal for building chapels, churches, and monasteries, he also looked to the future and took care lest the new establishments fall into want.[67] This knowledge of interior and exterior things, this conduct of the outer man that expressed the inner care of Otto's soul, had a counterpart in the monasteries that, under Otto, experienced wonderful increases of interior and exterior profit, and in the experience of those whose conversion was strengthened by seeing Otto's exceeding abundance of temporal and spiritual increase.[68]

Still, the correlation between inner and outer was not inevitable. It was desirable, but not necessary, that outward signs of spiritual dignity correspond with inner grace,[69] and that baptism, as an outer dedication, foreshadow the dedication of the heart.[70] Pagans made the mistake of identifying divine favor with sensual magnificence. They lavishly adorned their shrines with carvings and precious metals. How could they accept, as an emissary of the most high God, a man who came to them barefoot and in sackcloth? They sent him away with ridicule, teaching him the lesson that pagans were animals, entirely ignorant of spiritual gifts, and that they were not to be reckoned as men except in their external bearing.[71] St. Paul's distinction between the animal and the spiritual man (1 Cor. 2:10–16) lay behind this judgment, as his exposition of idolatry, the confusion of creature and Creator (Rom. 1), inspired Ebo's comments on the errors of native Pommeranian cults.[72] Ebo agreed that without knowledge of his creator, any man was a brute animal. Ignorant of the God who made them and coupled with senseless beasts of burden in the worship of something beyond sensory perception, the pagans became, like animals, incapable of rational service of the living God.[73] Pagans could not distinguish between appearance and reality. They accepted opulence as an expression of invisible power, for, lacking spiritual gifts, they also lacked the ambiguously hidden and disclosed wisdom of divine revelation and thus they were able to consider placing side by side temples of Otto's God and theirs.[74] This view provides a telling contrast with Otto's conception of the sacred, for he shrank from "the foulnesses of idolatry" as from pollution.[75] and commanded his new converts to avoid the unconverted in all things, and especially to segregate their burial places from those of the pagans.[76]

The pagans were not alone in defective understandings of hidden truth. Otto, "the light of the Church" (3.26; p. 140) shone as the sun among other bishops,[77] for the spirituality that he expressed in his preaching missions and in his establishment and endowment of churches and monasteries was contradicted by their devotion to worldly concerns, such as the building of castles, towns, and town walls.[78] Indeed, the connection between spiritual and temporal eminence that Ebo did accept ran into difficulties on this score. Just as Othloh had to acknowledge that miracles ceased at Boniface's tomb, even though Boniface was still a powerful patron before God, Ebo had to acknowledge that, through the misplaced values of recent bishops and magnates, monastic temporalities had decayed, even though monastic discipline and virtues continued, even though Michelsburg was still adorned with Otto's relics "as though with pearls" and sheltered by his heavenly patronage.[79] Feeling he was writing "with the cooperating grace of the Holy Spirit,"[80] Ebo was confident that the story was not yet over, and that a terrible retribution was laid up in God's providence for Christians who ignored the gospel as well as for pagans who rejected it and that a great glory was stored there for the servants of God.[81] The cutting edge of the Last Judgment was part of the didactic exemplarism by which Ebo pointed out both Otto's devout care of monasteries and the great company of spiritual sons begotten there by him, sons who would attend Otto with their prayers in this world and accompany him before the King of kings in the glory of the resurrection.[82]

Confidence in retributive justice indicates that, behind Ebo's dyad of inner and outer, real and apparent, spiritual and animal, there was a wider conceptual structure resembling Othloh's concept of holiness. Let us take up each of our five points, in the same order as before.

1. *Necessity.* Expectation that scores would be settled at the Last Judgment posits necessity on the side of right, necessity expressed in different ways through cosmology, soteriology, and eschatology. Here, as in Othloh's *Vita,* the assumptions of unity and universality are included in that of necessity. The entire world is created, aging, and bound under sin.[83] Cosmic senescence and human redemption were parts of the same movement, and the providence informing the first was, for the second, the vocation by which God predestined and called some to eternal life.[84] God had formed Otto in

the womb as His servant, as the light of the gentiles;[85] men entered the monastic life by way of vocation.[86] The necessity of vocation to individual conversion, and to works done by men through the spirit of adoption, had a wide historical dimension; for it was eschatologically necessary that the gospel be preached in all the world for a witness to the gentiles before the end came.[87]

The sense of a guiding and unseen unity in history also shaped Ebo's understanding of the relation between the church's manifestation as a visible community and its authentic character as an invisible communion, in which the saints, through their relics, intercession, and canonical regulations were contemporaries in the eternal present of the body of Christ. They were united in time and out of time by charity, "the bond of perfection."[88] This interplay between apparent and real made vestments and sacraments more than signs; it made them symbols, filled with the power of the divine love that they represented.[89] It established identity between widely separated historical events, such as Otto's own *gloriosus transitus* and the martyrdom of St. Paul, whom Otto "strove to imitate before all others" giving them the same *dies natalis*.[90] It drew Christ into the ceremonials of the visible church, whether the dedication of a soul, as His temple, through baptism[91] or the dedication of a church. The latter was mimetic and mnemonic: a ceremony that must be observed with all devotion, in that it forecast the image and shadow of the heavenly dedication. Christ, the true pontiff, will have completed the temple that He built with the living and chosen stones from the beginning of the world to the end of time. Then, He will celebrate the longed-for and perfect solemnity to which the transitory acts of men direct the inmost desires of all the church's sons.[92]

2. *Conditionality.* The inner necessity of grace gave the preaching and the practices of saints an authenticity lacking to pagans and faithless Christians, despite outward show. But it was conditional in much the same ways as it was in Othloh's conception. It was conditional upon knowledge (or recognition), and it was a condition for works of holiness. Ebo adduced examples of converts who lapsed, and of pagans who obdurately rejected the yoke of Christian faith to which the entire Roman world had submitted, and who remained content to be abortive offspring, estranged from the church. For him these illustrated how slender the bonds of faith might be.[93] The "agnitio Christi" might come through human instrumentality, as it did through Otto's preaching,[94] but, ultimately it came through the infusion of divine grace, through spiritual adoption. Ebo frequently used the metaphor of illumination to describe that event. He was able to apply to Otto the words "lux gentium," an epithet originally applied to St. Paul.[95] But he knew that Christ was the "true light" and that God, "the Father of lights," had sent Otto to declare salvation to the ends of the earth so that the dark hearts of the gentiles might be irradiated with the light of faith.[96] The interplay between light and darkness recurs throughout Ebo's biography, when he refers to conversions as light scattering the shadows of idolatry or ignorance, to those

blinded by the devil so that they could not see the true light, and to the miraculous restoration of physical sight.[97]

This imagery was appropriate in view of Otto's devotion to St. John the Evangelist (as well as to St. Michael the Archangel);[98] it was also a convention in Christian rhetoric. In any case, it expressed the derived character of holiness, which did not inhere in the animal man and which, in fact, was opposed, not only by the devil's malevolence,[99] but also by what would now be called common sense: i.e., by the pagans' awareness that, if they abandoned their religion and took up that of "the German god,"[100] they would subvert their fatherland and their ancient laws.[101] It was this condition, working against odds, that made prayer, not merely an aspect of Otto's personal piety, but a dramatic element in Ebo's narrative.[102]

Holiness was conditional upon illumination, and necessary for the works holiness. The people of Stettin lapsed into apostacy when they became convinced that a plague could be lifted by sacrificing to their ancient gods.[103] Others wavered. But Otto, persisting in his faithfulness was no backslider. He achieved his building schemes. He reformed corrupt monasteries and infused new life into them. He converted the Pommeranians, precisely because he had responded in faith to God's election of him, and therefore was attended by divine grace, preceded by God's mercy, and inflamed by the fire of divine love.[104]

3. *Possibility.* When he thought about how holiness became possible, Ebo, like Othloh, thought in terms of a *magisterium spirituale* overseen by Rome.[105] Though the paradigm of one flock and one shepherd was deeply woven into the conventions of theology, the investiture conflict no doubt left its mark on Otto's understanding of church order, and hence on Ebo's account of his work. Ebo described Henry IV, Otto's greatest early patron, in a favorable light, but he also characterized Otto as attending scrupulously to canonical regulations and to the judgment of the apostolic see. For three years after the Emperor designated him as bishop, Otto delayed consecration, Ebo said, to prepare himself for the spiritual and temporal administration of his see. That there was a reason other than the need for study is indicated by Ebo's reference to the conflict between Henry IV and Ruothard of Mainz and by the shadow of simony that fell upon him because of his long and faithful labors in the royal court.[106] To clear his title, Otto went to Rome and abdicated, only to be recalled and consecrated by Paschal II, consecrated, the pope wrote, "as though by St. Peter's own hands."[107] When he undertook his missionary journeys, he secured papal sanctions and acted as a papal *missus,*[108] and he carefully observed the privileges of bishops through whose sees he travelled.[109] Certainly, the reform that he instituted in his own diocese was designed to elevate the level of spiritual devotion, and also to enforce on others the same obedience that marked his own sanctity.[110]

The emphasis on hierarchic order was part of the way in which Ebo understood the Christian ambiguity of freedom and bondage. Freedom from physical bondage formed part of Ebo's story.[111] It stood as a counterpart in the external world of Otto's work of conversion in the spiritual world. And yet, the spiritual freedom of converts was characterized exactly by submission to the yoke of Christ, to the yoke of the Christian faith,[112] expressed by careful adherence to the order and judgments of the visible Church.

Ebo was fascinated with Otto as a builder of churches and monasteries, and this attraction to the problem of form-giving also expressed itself in a fuller awareness of the possibility of holiness—that is, of holiness becoming—than we have found in Othloh's *Vita*. Consciousness of process, as the succession of organically related forms, was an important characteristic of twelfth-century German religious thought. It appears, not only in the historical works of Otto of Freising, but also in mystical perceptions, such as those of Anselm of Havelberg, and in apocalyptic visions, such as those of Gerhoch of Reichersberg. Otto, master of the works at Speier and builder of churches, is the counterpart of Christ, building through time His celestial church of living stones, and the sense of directed and progressive movement intrinsic in the analogue of architecture appears throughout Ebo's biography, both in his descriptions and in his metaphors. His description of the life and work of Otto as a *peregrinatio*, and not simply of his missionary journeys, is one instance, closely related to the metaphor of the way.[113] Ebo characterizes Otto as a good tree, flowering before it bears fruit,[114] as a fruitful olive tree;[115] and the metaphor of seed scattered abroad to produce a harvest often appears.[116] With their prayers, his spiritual sons surround him as beautiful flowers in God's sight.[117] These organic analogues—together with the additional one of Otto's fecund spiritual paternity—indicate several things about the way in which Ebo understood the becoming of holiness. They indicate that he considered it a dynamic process by which something that is not comes into being; that the means of becoming is subsumed in the goal; and that the process affirms its beginning as it moves towards its end. In other words, the metaphors of growth express a dynamic aspect of the same tautological conception that Ebo cast in another way as the mimetic pairing of heavenly temple and earthly church, and yet again as the light that Otto saw and by seeing, became.

4. *Manner*. As we have seen, charity was the bond of perfection that gave the church the necessity of its unity, and it was a condition for works of holiness. It was also the substance of this dynamic movement. For, as in Othloh's mind, so in Ebo's the ways in which holiness was articulated were all modes of divine love. Though this metaphorical reasoning had not yet been elaborated into a concept of progressive creation, Ebo concurred with Othloh in considering all the ways in which holiness became all modes of divine love moving toward an historical and eschatological end. Ebo understood Otto's apostolate—that is, his missionary labors as an extension of his episcopate,[118] endeavors undertaken, as was the office of preaching, solely for the love of Christ.[119] Entering his see as bishop-elect, he was inwardly aflame with divine love. As missionary, he strove to realize the breadth of the holy love that had been let into his heart by the Holy Spirit, and that was

with divine love. As missionary, he strove to realize the breadth of the holy love that had been let into his heart by the Holy Spirit, and that was expressed in one way by very detailed regulations on pagan practices to be avoided. He was moved by that love than which man has no greater when he stood ready to lay down his life for his flock; in his quest for martyrdom, "the most ardent lover of Christ thirsted to pour out his sweet life for Jesus, the most sweet."[120] More than Otto's own devotion was at issue; for, in his episcopal offices and in his apostolate, he was urged on by the power of Christ's own love; he was full of God who is love. Animated by this love, his very countenance revealed the light within him. His face shown with angelic brightness.[121]

5. *Proofs.* We have now come to the proofs of holiness. In a limited way, Ebo used two kinds of evidence that figured very prominently in Othloh's *Vita.* He incorporated eight letters from Otto's correspondence, only three of which were from Otto himself and, consequently, adduced writings of the *servus Dei* and the commendatory testimonies of his ecclesiastical superiors.[122] The burden of his evidence, however, fell into other categories. In the first place, he gave considerable emphasis to argument by analogy, perhaps with St. Peter[123] and St. Stephen, the protomartyr,[124] but particularly with St. Paul and with Christ. We have already indicated that the latter analogues were rooted in Ebo's mimetic conceptions of the spiritual world. In so far as analogues constituted proof, it was important for Ebo that Otto's missionary work replicated that of the apostle of the gentiles so closely that he too could be called the "light of the gentiles,"[125] received as though he were an angel of God,[126] and commemorated on the Feast of SS. Peter and Paul. The analogue with Christ was even more amply developed with regard to Christ as "true pontiff," as builder, and as the archetypal martyr who laid down His life for others. Ebo was ready to press similarities rather far, and not only by reference to Otto's entrance into his see with bare and blood-stained feet, or to the devout care for the sick and poor by which he offered up a sacrifice of toil and sweat.[127] Describing how Otto took leave from his followers when setting out on his second missionary journey, Ebo drew a specific parallel between Christ, the great high priest, taking leave of His friends before His Passion, and Otto, arrayed in full pontificals, going forth in search of martyrdom,[128] just as, later, when he was certain (though wrongly) that he would be killed by pagans at Stettin, he again went forth alone vested in full pontificals.[129] Ebo saw a second, even more striking parallel when Otto returned. He happened to re-enter Bamberg on Easter day. He was received as a "new apostle," returning as a victor after he had destroyed the gates of death among the barbarians. He entered his church, Ebo wrote, amidst a noble triumph, greeted by the antiphon, normally addressed to Christ, *Advenisti desiderabilis.* Alleluias resounded, and it seemed to everyone as though they had been receiving Christ risen from the dead.[130]

Of course, it was not enough that these analogues existed; they must also be generally recognized. To supply that requirement, Ebo included a long series of acknowledgments by others of Otto's holiness, ranging from Anselm of Speier's early perception of an extraordinary divine grace in his countenance,[131] through the testimonials that he received from popes, to the honors accorded him by Henry IV and other secular princes,[132] to the processions in which the people crowded upon him to kiss his hands, hallowed by almsgiving, his feet, consecrated by preaching the Gospel of peace, and his footsteps, a devotion foreshadowed in the unanimous acclamation of him as bishop.[133] Otto's holiness was apparent to all Christians.[134]

Finally, Ebo presented the evidence of Otto's works. The achievements of Otto's episcopate and apostolate were important as evidence, particularly in that he was able to bring them to fruition, since efficacy demonstrated the general rule that God perfected the works that He inspired.[135] Miracles carried authority that was equally convincing, and the concentration of miracles in the last book indicates the aura and the evidential base with which Ebo wished to authenticate his account of Otto's last years and death. Of all the miraculous events described by Ebo, only one was performed even indirectly by Otto himself.[136] The others were premonitory, or admonitory, revelatory, confirmative, or punitive.[137] They testified, without Otto's own agency, to the divine favor that he held, as also did miracles performed at his tomb.[138] In the evidence of works, Ebo certainly included Otto's efforts to achieve martyrdom.[139] Though that persistent effort failed, Otto yet died in a manner that, in itself and in the universal grief that it caused, composed a holy triumph of his glory.[140]

Materials bearing on the lives of saints intersect four areas of mental effort: history, rhetoric, liturgy, and iconography. In the present essay, we have examined the ground that those areas had in common and the language of metaphor and analogy that enabled hagiography to speak for them all. This unity existed because holiness, the thread running through the whole fabric of thought, had an absolute exemplary character, inseparable from the theology of salvation. Drawing on two monastic biographies of bishops, written in Fulda and in Bamberg nearly a century apart, we have been able to describe holiness as a concept made up of clearly identifiable parts. To be full of God was not to be full of *je ne sais quoi*. Theology, particularly the doctrine of substances, had not yet become sufficiently refined for either of our authors to discuss sanctity, as Thomas Aquinas did, in terms of the "connaturality" of the elect with God. The keystone of the structures that we have examined was the assumption that holiness was imparted to man by an act of grace that established mimetic likeness, or the capacity for such likeness, between him and God, and that that likeness consisted in knowledge or in faith as a kind of knowledge. It was also assumed that holiness had a social, or collective character. For visible church, as a vessel of holiness, possessed a spiritual magistracy, both by the continual presence of the Holy

Spirit, and by a tradition of faith handed down by Christ to the apostles, and by them to the bishops of Rome and to those in communion with, and obedience toward, the see of Peter.

We have examined ramifications of two fundamental distinctions. Those distinctions—between appearance and reality, and falsehood (or illusion) and truth—were sharpened by our authors' conviction that they were caught up in a war that was both temporal and spiritual between the forces of worldliness and those of righteousness. Under the category of necessity, we have described the symmetrical pairing of plurality and unity, of reprobate and called, the derived holiness of man and the original holiness of God. Under the heading of conditionality, infidelity was matched against faithfulness, and ignorance against knowledge. The category of possibility brought to light a pairing of disobedience (among false Christians as well as among pagans) and obedience toward the Roman see. When we considered the manifestations of holiness, we distinguished between acts which expressed estrangement from the life of God and those which were modes in which, through human agency, divine love articulated itself. Finally, in examining the proofs of holiness, we came to the tautological nature of our structure. For the evidence of grace could rightly be read only by those who had received grace; it was holy to the holy. And this returns us to the principle of ultimate unity running through degrees of likeness formed by knowledge of God.

The binary structure of thought through which these assumptions were articulated rested on even more fundamental principles. The philosophical components consisted of two kinds. Some of them were transcendent: for example, those of unity and universality, and spiritual virtues (such as wisdom). Some were immanent, as was the informing principle of divine love. There were also historical components derived from the Old Testament, as recast by the gospels and St. Paul, and among these can be mentioned creation, sin, election, fall, sacrifice, reconciliation, and judgment. As a system of binaries, the system achieved unity through its philosophical base of exemplarism. From this point of view, the dialectical tension between appearance and reality (or false and true as Othloh and Ebo understood it) mediated and resolved in a love that sanctified the profane, had come to our authors through often circuitous routes from the Latin and Greek fathers, Plotinus, St. Paul, and Plato. The symbolic universe within which they worked, as a conglomerate of disparate elements, permitted variant conceptions of the structure and functions of holiness even in their own day. Later in the procession of ideas, the incorporation of new philosophical elements opened profoundly new alternatives. Neoplatonic exemplarism shaded into St. Thomas's careful and brilliant reconciliation of opposites. And the historical modalities of divine love were recast in the doctrine of continual and progressive creation, so easily confused with pantheism, taught by Meister Eckhart and his followers.

University of Chicago

Notes

In writing this essay, I have drawn upon an earlier effort that I prepared as a master's candidate at Cornell, in 1957, and on seminar research done at the University of Chicago, in 1974. It is a particular happiness to acknowledge the dialogues in which I engaged as a student with Professor Theodor Mommsen and, as a teacher, with Miss Joan Luft, and MM. Michael La-Plante and Michael Ricks. The conceptualizations here set forth derive from a wider study, now in process, provisionally entitled, "I Am Thou: The Tradition of Mimesis and the Culture of Revolution."

1. On canonization as an aspect of ecclesiastical politics, see, for the twelfth century, M. Schwarz, "Heiligsprechungen im 12. Jahrhundert. Beweggründe ihrer Urheber," *Archiv für Kulturgeschichte* XXXIX (1957), 49ff, 53; and, in general, P. Delooz, *Sociologie et Canonisations* Collection scientifique de la Faculté de droit de l'Université de Liège, XXX (Liège, 1969), pp. 400 and *passim*, including his appendix on the monetary cost of the canonization process in the twentieth century. A series of articles on concepts of truth and falsity, especially as regarding relics, also has a considerable bearing on the content of this paper. See, especially, H. L. Mikoletzsky, "Sinn und Art der Heiligung im frühen Mittelalter," *MIöG* LVII (1949), 87 and *passim*; H. Fichtenau, "Zum Reliquienwesen im früheren Mittelalter," *MIöG* LX (1952), 63ff, 76; K. Shreiner, " 'Discrimen veri ac falsi.' Ansätze und Formen der Kritik in der Heiligen-und Reliquienverehrung des Mittelalters," *Archiv für Kulturgeschichte* XLVIII (1966), 5ff, and, by the same author, "Zum Wahrheitsverständnis im Heiligen-und Reliquienwesen des Mittelalters," *Saeculum* XVII (1966), 138f, 141, 145ff; and K. Guth, *Guibert von Nogent und die hochmittelalterliche Kritik an der Reliquienverehrung, Studien und Mitteilungen zur Geschichte des Benediktinerordens. Ergänzungsband* XXI, (Ottobeuron, 1970) x: 72ff, 95ff, 108ff. See also a discussion by K. Bosl, H. Fuhrmann, A. Nitschke, and H. Patze, "Die Fälschungen im Mittelalter. Überlegungen zum mittelalterlichen Wahrheitsbegriff," *HZ* CXCVII (1963), 529–601.

2. The magisterial work of Rudolf Otto rightly hovers before anyone who writes on the subject of holiness, but it will be apparent that a phenomenological approach to that subject, such as the one here attempted, leads to emphases and categories that Otto discounted. Two of R. Otto's points have a direct bearing on this essay: first, that the holy is an *a priori* category that does not originate in sensory experience (trans. J. W. Harvey, *The Idea of the Holy*, 2d ed. [London, 1950], p. 112) and, second, that man can not recognize the holy unless he is first like it in a way not open to all human beings (p. 160). Much of what R. Otto wrote concerning the sense of urgency, illumination, and ardent love pertains to the materials here discussed. And yet, his reliance on mystical categories produced in his reflections an almost exclusive emphasis on the authenticity of the experience of the holy for the person who has it. On the whole, he did not consider holiness as an attribute of communion, or community or, consequently, as a conception belonging to inherited collective wisdom. For Othloh and Ebo, and presumably also for their subjects and readers, the church was holy, because it was one, catholic, and apostolic, and holiness was described by and embedded in its doctrine. R. Otto's discussion of mystical aspects of the experience of the holy—the *mysteriosum. tremendum.* and *fascinosum*—of the erotic element, the aridity, the feelings of annihilation and guilt has little applicability to these biographies, and consequently, his central concept of the numinous is recognizable, in them, only by its adumbrations. Othloh and Ebo were much concerned, however, with the importance of holiness in the unfolding of human experience, and this posited assumptions regarding predestination and eschatology that, in the main, R. Otto left aside. They were also concerned with personal holiness in the context of the communion of saints, and, consequently, they thought in categories that R. Otto did not include at all in his frame of reference—for example, hierarchic order, orthodoxy of faith and practice, and the evidential base indicated by our fifth category. Finally, the dialectical binary structure of holiness, as set forth in these biographies, is present only by implication in R. Otto's discussion, pitched as it is at a high level of theoretical abstraction without reference to temporal variations, although it would need to figure in a specialist treatment of hagiography in the eleventh and twelfth centuries.

As expressions of a rhetorical tradition, saints' lives have structure in a literary sense. They have been arranged according to classifications proper to literary criticism, such as panegyrics, historical (or factual) accounts, romances, epics, and hagiographical cycles (cf. H. Delehaye, *Les Passions des Martyrs et les Genres littéraires* [Brussels, 1921]; R. Aigrain, *L'Hagiographie. Ses Sources, ses Méthodes, son histoire* [Paris, 1953]). In this connection, scholars have also studied the use of *topoi* and stereotypal outlines for different categories of saints (cf. R. S. Farrar's discussion of the lives of confessors and virgin martyrs in "Structure and Function in Representative Old English Saints' Lives," *Neophilologus*, LVII [1973], 83–93). Lately, Peter Brown has approached holiness as a matter of function within a particular social structure (especially, "The Rise and Function of the Holy Man In Late Antiquity, *Journal of Roman Studies* LXI [1971], 80–101). In the present essay, structure is meant, not in a literary or sociological sense, but in a conceptual one, and the effort is made to locate the idea of holiness in the larger symbolic universe of two authors.

3. *Otloh von St. Emmeram. Ein Beitrag zur Bildungs- und Frömmigkeitsgeschichte des 11. Jahrhunderts* (Munich, n.d.), esp. pp. 43f.

4. A. Hauck, *Kirchengeschichte Deutschlands* (Leipzig, 1920), III: 945f. See also J. Lechner, "Zu den falschen Exemptionsprivilegien für St. Emmeram (Regensburg)," *Neues Archiv* XXV (1900), 628; E. Dümmler, "Über den Mönch Otloh von St. Emmeram," *Sitzungsberichte der kgl. Preussischen Akademie der Wissenschaften zu Berlin* XLVIII.2 (1895), pp. 1095f. See also Schauwecker, *Otloh*, p. 43.

5. Cf. *De cursu spirituali*, in B. Pez, *Thesaurus anecdotorum novissimus* (Augsburg, 1721), III.2: 260. See Schauwecker, *Otloh*, pp. 11f.

6. Max Herrmann, *Siegfried I. Erzbischof von Mainz, 1060–1084* (Jena, 1889), pp. 16ff. G. Meyer von Knonau, *Jahrbücher des deutschen Reiches unter Henrich IV. und Henrich V.* (Leipzig, 1894), II: 188ff.

7. *Herimanni Augiensis chronicon*, MGH SS V: 132 (A.D. 1053).

8. Othloh, *Vita Bonifatii*, preface, ed. W. Levison, *Vita sancti Bonifatii*, MGH SS in usum schol. (Hannover-Leipzig, 1905), p. 111 (hereafter VB).

9. Lambert of Hersfeld, *Annales*, MGH SS V: 164 (A.D. 1063).

10. J. Mabillon, *Vetera analecta* (Paris, 1723), col. 114B. On the general objects of hagiography in this period, see B. de Gaiffier d'Hestroy, "L'Hagiographie et son Public au XIe Siècle," *Miscellanea historica in honorem Leonis Van der Essen* (Brussels, 1947), I: 135–66. This essay originally formed part of Fr. Gaiffier's *these* at the École des Chartes (1926), and he drew his materials primarily from Flanders and the Low Countries.

11. VB 1.39, 2.16; pp. 154, 202.

12. VB 1, prologue, 1.40, 1.44, 2.16; pp. 113, 154, 157f., 201f.

13. *Epp.* 21, 60, 61, 57, 58.

14. E.g., after the signatures in *ep.* 59, at the conclusion of *ep.* 28, and *epp.* 45, 60, 87, 88.

15. VB 1.44; p. 157.

16. Cf. VB 2.12, 2.13, 2.15; pp. 195ff., 201.

17. Cf. A. Göpfert, *Lullus der Nachfolger des Bonifatius im Mainzer Erzbistum* (Ph.D. dissertation, Leipzig, n.d.), pp. 16f.

18. *Ep.* 51, VB 2.2; p. 166.

19. Othloh presented no evidence that Zacharias's prohibition was reversed. In *epp.* 86 and 87, VB 2.12–13; pp. 194, 197, 199, Lull is still mentioned as a priest. Cf. Levison, VB, p. 45, n. 2.

20. *Ep.* 68, VB 2.3; p. 169.

21. VB 2.18; p. 204.

22. VB 2.32; pp. 215f.

23. VB 2.5; p. 179.

24. *Ep.* 59, VB 2.4; p. 171.

25. *Ep.* 86, VB 2.12; p. 194.

26. VB 1.3, p. 119. VB 1.6; pp. 121f. VB 1.10; p. 125.

27. *Ep.* 25, VB 1.20; p. 133. Cf. 1.30; p. 143.
28. VB 2.25, 28; pp. 209f., 212.
29. *Ep.* 16, VB 1.14; p. 128.
30. VB 2.20; p. 206.
31. *Ep.* 59, VB 2.4; p. 171.
32. VB 2.29; p. 213.
33. *Ep.* 59, VB 2.4; pp. 171, 173.
34. *Ep.* 50, VB 2.1; *ep.* 51, 2.2; pp. 162, 167.
35. *Ep.* 59, VB 2.4; pp. 172f., 176.
36. *Ep.* 57, VB 2.10; p. 192.
37. Cf. *ep.* 59, VB 2.4; p. 171.
38. *Ep.* 77, VB 2.8; *ep.* 80, 2.9; pp. 185, 188.
39. VB 2.16; p. 202.
40. VB 1.44; p. 158.
41. VB. 1.39; p. 154.
42. VB 1, prologue; p. 114.
43. VB 2.27; p. 211.
44. VB 1.1; pp. 117f., 2.22; p. 207. 2.23; p. 208. 1.6, 35; pp. 122, 148.
45. *Ep.* 51, VB 2.2; p. 168.
46. *Ep.* 60, VB 2.7; p. 181. *Ep.* 45, VB 1.34; p. 147 (Cf. 1.5; p. 121). *Ep.* 57, VB 2.10;
p. 191. *Ep.* 21, VB 1.21; *ep.* 43, 1.31; pp. 134, 144. *Ep.* 58, VB 2.11; p. 193.
47. *Ep.* 82, VB 2.5; pp. 178f.
48. VB 1, prologue; p. 114.
49. *Epp.* 21, 28, VB 1.21, 27; pp. 134, 139.
50. *Ep.* 88, VB 2.14; p. 200.
51. VB 2.21; p. 206.
52. *Ep.* 80, VB 2.9; p. 186.
53. *Ep.* 50, VB 2.1; p. 162; *ep.* 80, 2.9; p. 186.
54. Cf. *ep.* 16, VB 1.14; p. 128.
55. VB 1.15; p. 129.
56. *Ep.* 45, VB 1.34; p. 147.
57. *Ep.* 50, VB 2.1; p. 163.
58. *Ep.* 88, VB 2.14; p. 200.
59. VB 1.1, 2; pp. 117ff.
60. VB 1.16; p. 122. VB 2.25; p. 210. *Ep.* 50, VB 2.1; p. 163.
61. VB 1.3; p. 119. See also the description of popular veneration of Boniface's corpse,
2.29–31; pp. 213ff.
62. Matt. 13:58. VB 2.32; p. 215. Professor Barbara Rosenwein recently completed a
doctoral dissertation on hagiographical exemplarism at Cluny in the tenth century which
provides interesting points of comparison: *Piety and Power: Cluniac Spirituality in the Time of St.
Odo* (Ph.D. dissertation, University of Chicago, 1974).
63. Ebo, *Vita Ottonis,* 1.1, ed. J. Wikarjak, Monumenta Poloniae historica, n.s. VIII.2
(Warsaw, 1969), 10 (hereafter VO). On older scholarly studies see A. Hofmeister, *Das Leben
des Bischofs Otto von Bamberg* (Leipzig, 1928), and bibliographical references in the *apparatus
criticus* of Wikarjak's edition, parts of which were prepared by Casimir Liman. See also E. von
Guttenberg, ed., *Das Bistum Bamberg,* Germania sacra II (Berlin, 1937), I.1: 115–38. J.
Petersohn, "*Apostolus Pomeranorum.* Studien zur Geschichte und Bedeutung des Apostelepi-
thetons Bischof Ottos I. von Bamberg," *Historische Jahrbuch* LXXXVI (1966), 257–94.
Eberhard Demm, *Reformmönchtum und Slawenmission im 12. Jahrhundert. Wertsoziologisch-
geistesgeschichtliche Untersuchungen zu den Viten Bischofs Ottos von Bamberg,* Historische Studien
CCCCXIX (Hamburg, 1970). Demm did not use the Wikarjak edition. Consequently, his
views on Ebo's use of sources vary from those here stated, particularly regarding the use of the
Prüfening *Vita.* See ibid., pp. 15f.
64. Cf. VO 2.9, 3.6; pp. 70, 104f. Cf. 3.7; pp. 107f.

THE STRUCTURE OF HOLINESS 155

V

65. VO 1.3; p. 12. VO 1.4; pp. 13f. VO 1.19; 2.3; pp. 35ff., 58.
66. VO 2.4; p. 63.
67. Cf. VO 2.18; 3.26; pp. 89, 140f.
68. VO 1.9; pp. 21f. VO 1.4; p. 14. VO 1.19; p. 35. VO 3.17; p. 126.
69. E.g., the pallium, VO 1.12; p. 26.
70. VO 3.12; p. 112.
71. VO 2.1; p. 53.
72. E.g., VO 3.1; pp. 91ff.
73. VO 2.11; p. 72. Cf. 2.1; p. 53.
74. VO 3.1; p. 94.
75. VO 3.2, 5; pp. 96, 103. See Demm, *Reformmönchtum*, pp. 59f.
76. VO 2.12; pp. 73ff.
77. VO 1.20; 2.1; pp. 37, 49.
78. VO 1.16; 2.12; 3.24; pp. 30, 73, 137. Cf. on Boleslaus, 2.4; p. 62.
79. VO 3.27; p. 145.
80. VO 1, prologue; p. 4.
81. VO 3.15; p. 122. Cf. VO 2.8; pp. 67f.
82. VO 1.21; p. 42. Demm, *Reformmönchtum*, pp. 18f.
83. VO 2.1; p. 49.
84. VO 2.5; p. 64. Cf. Rom. 9:18–23. VO 3.3; pp. 97f. Cf. Rom. 10:15.
85. VO 2.16; p. 80.
86. VO 1.21; p. 41.
87. VO 2.1; pp. 91f. Cf. Matt. 24:14.
88. VO 2.3; 3.17; pp. 59, 83, and passim. Cf. Col. 3:14.
89. E.g., VO 1.18; 3.19; pp. 34, 128.
90. VO 3.27; p. 145.
91. VO 3.12; p. 112.
92. VO 1.22. Cf. reference to Otto's death, 3.25; pp. 46, 138.
93. VO 3.6; p. 106.
94. VO 2.12; 3.1; pp. 74, 93.
95. VO 2.16; p. 80. Cf. Acts 13:47.
96. VO 3.16; p. 124. Cf. 1.20; p. 37. Otto, in restoring discipline at Michelsburg, "velut aurora pulcherrima et lucifer matutinus ad discutiendas et illuminandas prisce conversationis caligines celitus effulsit."
97. VO 2.9; 3.23; pp. 71, 134. VO 3.16; p. 124. VO 3.21; p. 131.
98. VO 3.24; 3.26; pp. 137, 140. Otto established monasteries in honor of St. John at Michelsfeld and at Mullersdorf, 2.3; p. 58; 1.17; pp. 31f.
99. VO 2.14, 18; 3.16; pp. 78, 89, 124.
100. VO 3.1; p. 94. Cf. Demm, *Reformmönchtum*, p. 66.
101. VO 2.7, 11; pp. 67, 72.
102. E.g., VO 1.20; 2.11, 18; 3.2, 6, 15, 16, 19, 23, 26.
103. VO 3.1; p. 92.
104. VO 1.9, 18; 3.14; pp. 21, 33, 119f., and passim.
105. VO 1.20; p. 37.
106. VO 1.9; p. 22. VO 1.11; p. 24.
107. VO 1.14; p. 28. Cf. 1.11; p. 25.
108. VO 2.3, 4; 3.3; pp. 56, 63, 97.
109. VO 2.3; 3.3, 23; pp. 60, 99, 135.
110. Cf. VO 1.10; p. 23, where Otto applied St. Peter's words in Luke 22:33 to himself. Ulrich of St. Egidius uses the same passage of himself in his discussion with Otto, 2.3; p. 57.
111. VO 2.13; 3.2; pp. 77, 94ff. Cf. Acts 12:6ff. VO 3.12, 16; pp. 112ff., 125.
112. VO 3.1, 4, 16; 2.5, 18; 3.3, 6.
113. VO 2.2, 3, 12; 3.24; pp. 55, 56, 73, 137, and passim. Cf. Demm, *Reformmönchtum*, p. 52.

114. VO 1.2; p. 11.
115. VO 1.16; 3.26; pp. 30, 143. Cf. Ps. 51:10; Jer. 11:16.
116. E.g., VO 3.23; p. 135. Cf. the description of the new church at Kammin as a "novella plantacio," 2.5; p. 65.
117. VO 1.21; p. 42.
118. VO 2.12, 18; 3.1, 27; pp. 73, 86, 91, 145.
119. VO 3.9; p. 109f.
120. VO 1.9; p. 21. VO 2.12; p. 73. VO 3.13; p. 117. VO 3.23; p. 135.
121. VO 1.9; 2.3; pp. 21, 56. VO 1.17; p. 33. VO 2.3, 18; pp. 60, 89.
122. From Paschal II; VO 1.10, 12, 13, 14; from Otto: 1.15, 20; 2.12; from Wignand: 2.16.
123. VO 1.10; p. 23. Cf. Luke 22:33. Demm, *Reformmönchtum*, p. 88.
124. VO 2.3, 18; pp. 60, 89. Cf. Acts 6:15.
125. VO 2.16; p. 80. Cf. Acts 13:47. Petersohn, *"Apostolus Pomeranorum,"* pp. 268ff.
126. VO 1.16; 2.4, 18; 3.23; pp. 30, 63, 89, 133. Cf. Gal. 4:14.
127. VO 1.9; p. 21. VO 1.25; p. 139.
128. VO 2.3; p. 59. Cf. 3.16; p. 123, where Otto quotes Jesus' words before Pilate as in John 18:37.
129. VO 3.15; p. 121.
130. VO 2.18; pp. 88f. This view of Otto's return was very explicitly shared by several other contemporary authors. See Petersohn, *"Apostolus Pomeranorum,"* p. 258.
131. VO 1.5; p. 15.
132. VO 1.3–4, 6–7; 2.18; 3.13, 23, 24; pp. 12ff., 87, 115ff., 133ff.
133. VO 2.3, 4, 18; pp. 60, 62, 89. VO 1.8; p. 19.
134. VO 2.2; p. 55.
135. Cf. VO 2.15; p. 79.
136. VO 2.10; p. 71. Cf. 3.21; p. 131.
137. VO 3.19, 25; pp. 127f., 138. VO 1.19; 3.1, 12, 14; pp. 36, 94, 113f., 119f. VO 3.11, 17; pp. 111f., 126f. VO 3.16, 22; pp. 122f., 132f. VO 2.6; 3.1, 22; pp. 65f., 94, 133.
138. VO 3.27; p. 143.
139. VO 2.1, 3; 3.14, 15, 23; pp. 50, 56, 119, 121, 135.
140. VO 3.26; p. 142.

Otto of Freising's Quest for the Hermeneutic Circle

Otto of Freising was a man of contradictions. Some of them touched the familiar disparity between thought and action. As a Cistercian and former abbot of Morimund, he applauded Gregory VII's struggle for the freedom of the Church. And yet, as bishop, he witnessed, encouraged, and performed acts contrary to the Gregorian reforms. In his writings, he preached peace and the vanity — indeed, the misery — of earthly things. And yet, as bishop, he was regularly in armed conflict with other princes, including his own brothers. He enlisted as a crusader and served, at least nominally, as a field commander. In the *Gesta* he chose to celebrate Frederick I as a prince of peace, though they had been together on a crusade during which Barbarossa had burned a Greek monastery on impulse, as an act of vengeance, and though — as the letter by which the emperor commissioned Otto to write the *Gesta* indicates — Frederick vaunted himself on his virtuosity in causing misery through sieges and the carnage of battle. Far from being indifferent to the things of this world, our Cistercian bishop assiduously rebuilt his episcopal see and endowed it with precious goods of many kinds; and the register of his official acts, fragmentary as it is, reveals an enterprising man frequently negotiating advantageous exchanges of property, engaging for the sake of gain in legal affairs from the level of village life to that of the Empire, and taking every precaution to see that the temporal resources that he had gotten for his church were secured by papal or imperial decrees.

Neither was consistency one of Otto of Freising's virtues as a historian. The disparities between his world history, the *Chronicle*, and his later work, the *Deeds of Frederick Barbarossa*, are striking in themselves. Eschatology provided the main organizing principle for the *Chronicle*, but it figures not at all in the *Deeds*, where, instead of *delectatio morosa* over the impending Last Judgment, one finds a vivid excitement over the achievements of Otto's own day, and an expectation of yet brighter accomplishments. Even more remarkable than the broad contrast between the two works, however, is the fact that each treatise contains major incongruities. Considerable efforts

An early draft of this paper was delivered before the Rocky Mountain Medieval Conference in 1977. I am grateful to the Conference, and especially to Professors Harry Rosenberg and Roger Reynolds, for the privilege of speaking there. I am also under an obligation to the Institute for Advanced Study, under whose hospitable roof the initial research was done, and to the National Endowment for the Humanities for a grant that enabled me to work at the Institute. The paper has benefited from the kind and incisive suggestions of Professor Bernard McGinn.

have been made to explain the personal situations that gave rise to this disharmony. The contention of the present essay is that the inconsistencies tell us not only about the external circumstances in which the bishop wrote, but also about a cognitive strategy that persisted throughout the fifteen years of his literary work, to which both the eschatology of the *Chronicle* and the philosophy of the *Deeds* testify.

One can think of a work of art as something finished, crystallized and complete in itself. Or one can think of it as encasing a hermeneutic process, a circle in which the parts and the whole mutually illuminate one another, a sequence of events through which a critic can reexperience the making of the work and actually understand the making better than the artist did at the time of composition. I suggest that Otto regarded his own texts in this second way, and, moreover, that he considered apparent incongruities not as defects externally induced, but as evidence of tactics inherent in the process of verifying theories over a long space of time. Considered in this light, the two texts make up a continuous essay in self-criticism. By attending to the linkages between Otto's eschatology and his philosophy, I hope to clarify the differences that do exist between the two works, especially with regard to the Investiture Conflict.

Of course, to think in this way is to query some very ably defended assumptions about Otto's work. One of them is that the *Chronicle* and the *Deeds* mark entirely different historical interpretations, and that they are actually incommensurable. Among recent authors, Peter Munz has held, cogently and vivaciously, that, in 1156–57, Otto experienced "an intellectual, if not [a] spiritual, revolution" that fundamentally altered his view of the past and set the *Deeds* quite apart from the *Chronicle*. I shall have to reckon with this position, and, because the discussion will center on Otto's philosophical convictions, I shall also need to examine the propositions that, by contrast with Augustine, Otto was not a metaphysician, but rather a historian preoccupied above all with power. I shall, however, be concerned only by implication with the vexed question of whether Otto was a man of originality, or a bit of a muddler, following where others led, either by philosophical cogency or by political might.[1]

---

[1] Peter Munz, *Frederick Barbarossa: A Study in Medieval Politics* (Ithaca, 1969), p. 133, and "Why Did Rahewin Stop Writing the *Gesta Frederici*? A Further Consideration," *English Historical Review* 84 (1969), 775, 777 f. In spite of the disparities between the *Chronicle* and the *Gesta*, some authors feel able to regard the *Gesta* as a continuation of the earlier work. For example, Franz-Josef Schmale, in Adolf Schmidt, trans., and F.-J. Schmale, ed., *Die Taten Friedrichs oder richtiger Cronica* (Berlin, 1965), p. 15 f., and Anna-Dorothée v. den Brincken, *Studien zur lateinischen Weltchronistik bis in das Zeitalter Ottos von Freising*, Diss. Münster (Düsseldorf, 1957), p. 221. The matter is also discussed, without resolution, in the excellent work by Gottfried Koch, *Auf dem Wege zum Sacrum Imperium: Studien zur ideologischen Herrschaftsbegründung der deutschen Zentralgewalt im 11. und 12. Jahrhundert*, Forschungen zur mittelalterlichen Geschichte 20 (Vienna, 1972), p. 183 ff. Two of the most comprehensive efforts to harmonize dissonances are the elegant articles by Josef Koch, "Die Grundlagen der Geschichtsphilosophie Ottos von Freising," in Walther Lammers, ed., *Geschichtsdenken und Geschichtsbild im Mittelalter*, Wege der Forschung 21 (Darmstadt, 1965), pp. 321–349, and Eberhard F. Otto, "Otto von Freising und Friedrich Barbarossa," ibid., pp. 247–277. On J. Koch's essay, see Hans M. Klinkenberg, "Der Sinn der

This stance is possible, in part, because the revision of the *Chronicle* actually coincided with the writing of the *Deeds*. Between 1143 and 1147,

---

Chronik Ottos von Freising," in Josef Engel and Hans M. Klinkenberg, eds., *Aus Mittelalter und Neuzeit: Festschrift Gerhard Kallen* (Bonn, 1957), p. 64. On the question of whether the *Gesta* as completed by Rahewin was itself further revised, see Franz-Josef Schmale, "Die Gesta Friderici I. Imperatoris Ottos von Freising und Rahewins," *Deutsches Archiv* 19 (1963), 168–214. Schmale provides a review of earlier literature on the subject and concludes that, while the edition by Waitz (as revised by Simson) is basically reliable, "eine Neuausgabe der Gesta dringend erwünscht ist, damit die Gesta in der bestmöglichen Gestalt benutzbar wären, befreit von allen Entstellungen durch die Humanisten und die unnötig komplizierten Vorstellungen der bisherigen Herausgeber" (p. 214; see also pp. 172 f., 200 f., 202 ff., 210 ff.). Students of Otto are divided into two camps: those who consider that Otto perfected an interpretive theory or a historical genre, and those who, while not deprecating his achievement, still find flaws. Since the object of the present paper is to examine difficulties and inconsistencies, I shall now refer to several eminent members of the other side. Cf. Wolfram von den Steinen, *Der Kosmos des Mittelalters von Karl dem Grossen zu Bernhard von Clairvaux*, 2d ed. (Bern, 1967), pp. 337 f.; Werner Kaegi, *Grundformen der Geschichtschreibung seit dem Mittelalter* (Utrecht, 1947), p. 6, emphasizing the simplicity of Otto's interpretation; Brincken, *Studien*, pp. 220, 228; Leopold Grill, "Bildung und Wissenschaft im Leben Bischof Ottos von Freising," *Analecta Sacri Ordinis Cisterciensis* 14 (1958), 281–333; and Joseph Schmidlin, "Die Eschatologie Ottos von Freising," *Zeitschrift für katholische Theologie* 29 (1905), 445, 447. For an explanation of some reasons behind this divergence, see Klinkenberg, "Sinn," pp. 63, 67 n. 12. Klinkenberg's own resolution is ibid., p. 69.

The question of originality reared its head early in studies of Otto, and the more recent publication of works about Otto and his contemporaries has not let the matter rest. Bernheim's argument that Otto was not original in any area, and that he owed his entire system of thought to Gilbert de la Porrée, got very short shrift from Schmidlin, who devoted much of his life to a study of Otto's eschatology and philosophy. Schmidlin argued that even though Otto took over a great deal, especially from Gilbert, he still exercised an independent judgment and made some original contributions. Ernst Bernheim, "Der Charakter Ottos von Freising und seiner Werke," *Mittheilungen des Instituts für oesterreichische Geschichtsforschung* 6 (1885), 14. Joseph Schmidlin, "Die Philosophie Ottos von Freising," *Philosophisches Jahrbuch* (Görres-Gesellschaft) 18 (1905), 315, 320 ff., supplemented more fully in *Die geschichtsphilosophische und kirchenpolitische Weltanschauung Ottos von Freising*, Studien und Darstellungen aus dem Gebiete der Geschichte 4, 2–3 (Freiburg i. B., 1906). Otto's editor, Adolf Hofmeister, concluded his exhaustive review of the matter crisply: "Otto von Freising war gewiss nicht der Mann, die geistige Entwicklung in neue Bahnen zu leiten." "Studien über Otto von Freising, II," *Neues Archiv* 37 (1912), 764. See also ibid., p. 767: "Selbständig ist er, wenn wir von der Eschatologie im besondern absehen, nur auf dem Gebiete der Geschichtsauffassung, und auch hier hat er nicht eigentlich neue Bahnen gewiesen." Hashagen argued that Otto represented an epoch, and a mode of thought, that had already ended. And, consequently, tied as his work was to the documents and attitudes of the past, it was quickly brushed aside by more advanced achievements. Justus Hashagen, *Otto von Freising als Geschichtsphilosoph und Kirchenpolitiker*, Leipziger Studien aus dem Gebiet der Geschichte 6,2 (Leipzig, 1900), p. 99. Lately, Josef Koch has reviewed the lines of the debate, and determined that Otto did achieve something new; he combined metaphysics and theology into a true philosophy of history in which man was the free, creative agent. "Grundlagen," esp. pp. 321 f., 327, 349.

On the distinction between Augustine's use of the term *civitas Dei* and Otto's, another aspect of the old/new debate, see the interpretation in Johannes Spörl, "Die 'Civitas Dei' im Geschichtsdenken Ottos von Freising," in Lammers, *Geschichtsdenken*, pp. 301 f., and esp. p. 312. Otto's departures from the eschatological models of Augustine are emphasized by Norbert Grabe, "Die Zweistaatenlehre bei Otto von Freising und Augustin. Ein Vergleich," *Cistercienser-Chronik* 80 (1973), 34–70. See also R. A. Markus, *Saeculum: History and Society in the Theology of St. Augustine* (Cambridge, 1970), pp. 162–165.

Otto brought to fruition his first work, an effort to explain the ways of God to man through eschatology, in the *Chronicle* (or *The Two Cities*). Ten years later, he began the second, an experiment in reading history under the light of philosophy. He intended to set forth this reading in a comprehensive account of Frederick Barbarossa's reign to date. His earlier work, and its interpretive difficulties, were very fresh in his mind; for, in 1157, about the time when he began the *Deeds*, he had just completed a revision of the *Chronicle*. When Otto died, he left drafts of a preface and two books for the *Deeds*. The last two books were prepared — partly or largely from his materials — by his chaplain and secretary, Rahewin, who had also assisted him in writing the *Chronicle*.

More than facts, interpretation was involved; and, given the sequence of events, one can recognize the possibility that the interpretive strategy in the *Deeds* was framed, not merely to suit the panegyrical function of the work, but, more profoundly, to reconsider the burden of the earlier argument, which Otto had so recently worked through again.

Still, there is the problem of consistency. Contrasts between the two works, especially those concerning the Investiture Conflict, make it hard to escape this well-flogged question. Imponderables have always clouded the issue. Otto left the *Deeds* truncated. The absence of philosophical excursus in the second book is so much at variance with the general procedure described in Otto's preface, and with the actual content of the first book, that one may doubt whether he lived to complete his design even in Book II. Rahewin provides another caution when he describes Otto on his deathbed. The bishop, holding the manuscript of the *Deeds* in his hands, gave it over to learned and religious men, asking them to examine what he had written about Gilbert de la Porrée and to correct, as they thought best, such comments in favor of Gilbert as could give offence.[2] He then made a profession of his own faith. If changes *were* made in that extensive and crucial section on philosophy, we do not have Otto's exact words. If changes *were not* made, we have a text about which the author felt deep anxiety in his last hours. A severe critical examination would also point out that further changes could have been introduced by Rahewin himself, or by Ulrich and Henry, respectively the imperial chancellor and notary, to whom he submitted the entire *Deeds*.[3]

A careful thematic revision would have smoothed away the remaining incongruities, and, consequently, their persistence is evidence that we have Otto's texts much as he left them, that is, as works in progress. Otto gave

---

[2] Georg Waitz and Bernhard von Simson, eds., *Ottonis et Rahewini Gesta Friderici I. Imperatoris*, MGH SSrG (Hanover and Leipzig, 1912), 4.14, p. 251 (cited hereafter as *Gesta*). For a later edition, see Georg Waitz, Bernhard von Simson, and Franz-Josef Schmale, *Ottonis Episcopi Frisingensis et Rahewini Gesta Frederici, seu rectius Cronica*, Ausgewählte Quellen zur deutschen Geschichte des Mittelalters 17 (Berlin, 1965), p. 542 (identical with the Schmidt-Schmale translaion referred to in n. 1, and cited hereafter as Schmale, *Gesta*). Some chapter numbers in Schmale's edition vary from those in Waitz-Simson's.

[3] See Schmale, "Gesta," p. 178.

some credence to this position when he wrote that he made few changes during the revision of the *Chronicle;*[4] and he may have been speaking of the entire work, as well as of the apocalyptic exegesis in its last book, when he said that some things were to be read, not as affirmations, but as conjecture and quest, left for appraisal to the definitive judgment of wiser men.[5] Certainly, he would have thought that the *Chronicle* and the *Deeds* were provisional statements if he put them in the general course of history as he described it. On these propositions, let us examine the problem.

1. THE MASTER PLAN AND ITS DILEMMA

The eschatological line of argument in the *Chronicle* is crisp and clear. Difficulties appear only at the second glance. Behind the confusion of passing events, Otto describes one steady goal in the *Chronicle.* The world moves toward the moment when the city of man will be destroyed and the city of Christ transformed and exalted into its heavenly state. Each stage *en route* ambiguously fulfills what went before and anticipates what will follow. Thus, the Church was foreshadowed among the Israelites, and latent in the Roman Empire until, under Constantine and Theodosius I, it achieved the visible form that God intended for it. As the Church rose, the Empire declined, even from the time when St. Peter was martyred in Rome. When Otto looked at his own times, he saw plainly that the Church was the great stone uncut by human hands prophesied by Daniel, and that the Roman Empire, translated to the Germanic peoples, was part of the colossus of world monarchy that it was in the process of destroying. Gregory VII's actions against Henry IV and Calixtus II's dealings with Henry V revealed that the stone had grown to mountainous proportions,[6] that the old forms were passing

---

[4] The view that — as he himself says — Otto introduced few and minor changes during his revision entered historiography almost before the beginning of modern historical studies, with the article by Roger Wilmans, "Über die Chronik Ottos von Freisingen," *Archiv* 10 (1851), 131–173, esp. pp. 142–144, 169–172. It has held sway, except for the challenge issued by Mohr (below, n. 6). See Bernheim, "Charakter," pp. 34 f.; Walther Lammers, "Ein universales Geschichtsbild der Stauferzeit in Miniaturen," *Alteuropa und die moderne Gesellschaft: Festschrift Otto Brunner* (Göttingen, 1963), p. 174. For the argument that the Regensburg Diet of 1156 was the moment when Otto determined that the time of sadness was over, see Henry Simonsfeld, *Jahrbücher des deutschen Reiches unter Friedrich I.,* 1 (Leipzig, 1908), 479 f.

[5] Adolf Hofmeister ed., *Ottonis Episcopi Frisingensis Chronica sive Historia de duabus Civitatibus,* 2d ed., MGH SSrG (Hanover, 1912), 8.35, p. 457 (cited hereafter as *Chron.*).

[6] *Chron.* 6.36, 7.16, pp. 305, 331 f. This striking metaphor, which is central in Otto's exposition, has an antecedent in the writings of Gregory VII's companion, Humbert of Silva Candida. See his text, *De sancta Romana ecclesia,* in Percy Ernst Schramm, *Kaiser, Rom und Renovatio,* 2 (Leipzig, 1929), pp. 132 f. For a discussion of this text, and of the place of the Empire in eschatological writings of the tenth and eleventh centuries, see Heinz Löwe, "Kaisertum und Abendland in ottonischer und frühsalischer Zeit," *Historische Zeitschrift* 196 (1963), 537 f., 560. Otto's use of the metaphor is also discussed more or less in passing by Horst Dieter Rauh, *Das Bild des Antichrist im Mittelalter: Von Tyconius zum deutschen Symbolismus,* Beiträge zur Geschichte der Philosophie und Theologie des Mittelalters, Texte und Untersuchungen, N. F. 9, (Münster, 1973), pp. 313, 339 f. But Rauh is not concerned to unravel Otto's understanding of the

away with the Empire, and that the new order of spiritual purity was supplanting it in the hierarchic Church and, especially, in monastic orders. The translation of power, wisdom, and — in monasticism — religion[7] from East to West had reached its furthest possible limit. The Church already had all that was promised it except what could come only outside of time: that is, immortality. As it was, the Church stood forth as the image of the heavenly kingdom, one of the "visible things" by which one could perceive the "invisible things" of God. But, as the Investiture Conflict proclaimed, it was also poised on the brink of the unutterable persecutions and sufferings that Antichrist would inflict upon it. And yet, even the eschatological narrative in the *Chronicle* is inconsistent,[8] a mark of how Otto's thinking progressed and shifted in writing and in revision.

When Otto read the long sequence of events before him, he found many troubling questions. If he rightly saw the direction of things, how could one explain the lapses of prophecy in the Old Testament? Why did God delay the Incarnation of Christ, and hence allow Gentiles through many ages to perish in unbelief?[9] Why did He blind the Jews and submit the early Church

---

Investiture Conflict or, consequently, to define what the metaphor meant for Otto in that setting. See ibid., pp. 329 f., 341.

On the importance of the Investiture Conflict for Otto as the moment in the eschatological drama when the unity of Church and Empire disintegrated, or at least when the Empire disintegrated with catastrophic results, see Amos Funkenstein, *Heilsplan und natürliche Entwicklung: Formen der Gegenwartsbestimmung im Geschichtsdenken des hohen Mittelalters*, Diss. Berlin (Munich, 1965), p. 107; Kaegi, *Grundformen*, p. 12; Lammers, "Geschichtsbild," p. 213. Schmidlin thought that the Conflict served Otto as a catalyst of ideas, much as the fall of Rome had served Augustine (*Weltanschauung*, p. 10). See also Johannes Spörl, *Grundformen hochmittelalterlicher Geschichtsanschauung: Studien zum Weltbild der Geschichtsschreiber des 12. Jahrhunderts* (Munich, 1935), pp. 34 f., "Civitas Dei," p. 315; and Hashagen, *Geschichtsphilosoph*, p. 61. This centrality led Klinkenberg to consider *Chron.* 7 as containing a hermeneutic key to the entire work ("Sinn," p. 71).

Walter Mohr has underscored the importance of the Conflict for Otto by proposing a fascinating new approach to the relation between the *Chronicle* and the *Gesta* based on Otto's discovery of a pseudo-Sibylline text, "Zum Geschichtsbild Ottos von Freising," in H. Rahner and E. von Severus, eds., *Perennitas: Festschrift P. Thomas Michels, O.S.B.* (Münster, 1963), pp. 274–293.

[7] *Chron.* 7.35, p. 372.

[8] For general studies of two of Otto's organizing principles without reference to Otto himself, see Roderich Schmidt, "Aetates mundi: Die Weltalter als Ordnungsprinzip der Geschichte," *Zeitschrift für Kirchengeschichte* 67 (1955/56), 288–317 (on the twelfth-century, see pp. 298–300); and two works on the same subject, A. van den Baar, *Die kirchliche Lehre von der translatio imperii bis zur Mitte des 13. Jahrhunderts*, Analecta Gregoriana 78 (Rome, 1956), and Werner Goez, *Translatio imperii* (Tübingen, 1958), esp. pp. 111–130 on Otto, pp. 117 ff. on the *translatio sapientiae* (comparing Otto's views with those of Hugh of St. Victor), and passim. The most complete discussion of the *translatio* motif in Otto remains that by Schmidlin, *Weltanschauung*, pp. 21, 68 ff. On Otto's several chronological systems, Mierow aptly remarked: "It is evident therefore that Otto developed a plan of division for himself, and not from a single viewpoint," in Charles C. Mierow trans., *The Two Cities: A Chronicle of Universal History to the Year 1146 A. D.* (New York, 1928), p. 32. See also Brincken, *Studien*, p. 223; Hashagen, *Geschichtsphilosoph*, pp. 34 ff.

[9] On Otto's discussion of the lapse of prophecy, see Schmidlin, *Weltanschauung*, p. 92; on why

to persecution, forcing it to lie hidden within the city of man until the time of Constantine? All these phenomena severely tested Otto's theory, and to their number we must add the Investiture Conflict.

For it was difficult to bring the facts of that dispute and its aftershocks into line with a theory that history was the story of the papacy's ascent, and, indeed, of an ascent in which secular government was the gradual loser; that the coming world order was to be monastic in broad outline; and, finally, that the series of popes was continually sustained by the prayers of Christ.

Educated, as he had been, in the critical methods of early scholasticism, Otto realized that hypotheses had to be tested as well as affirmed. Drawing on the different strands of his learning, the bishop recognized two categories of objection to his eschatological reading.

The first set of objections concerned his allegorical reading of history. On scriptural and patristic authority, he defended his search for significance beneath historical events. The objection arose over the question of whether God were responsible for the evil that befell, and was still to befall, the Church. Otto adduced the intriguing argument that, by the same creative act, God made the light which He pronounced good and the shadows without which there could be no evil. The bishop withdrew from this dangerous ground to the safer one of divine inscrutability. No evils occurred, he said, without God's permission and without serving the good of the whole.[10]

The second category of objections involved the always difficult correlation between the Church as it is and the Church as it will be.[11] Though he maintained, sometimes in extreme language, that the two were analogous and, after a fashion, identical, Otto encountered disparities between the facts that he described and the theories that he espoused. Those disparities became especially troublesome when Otto took up the particular subject of relations between the Empire and the papacy as tested in the Investiture Conflict. He found it impossible, and perhaps undesirable, to choose between two contending allegories: that is, on the one hand, his eschatological concept of the Church as Daniel's great stone demolishing the Empire, and, on the other, the Christological one of a duality of sacerdotal and royal persons dividing and coordinating the offices of Christ in the Church. One stone or two swords (or persons)? Not to choose invited confusion. To choose meant excluding either the expectancy that gave the sufferings of his time sacred hope, or the aspirations, close to Otto's heart, that centered on the Empire. In this case, as in others, Otto declined to choose. However, he did recognize his predicament, and, as he appraised the careers of Gregory

---

God allowed the world to lie in ignorance so long before the Incarnation, ibid., pp. 94 f.; Funkenstein, *Heilsplan*, pp. 105 f.

[10] *Chron.* 8.prol., pp. 392 f. On the very careful organization of Book 8, see the outline of the discussion in Schmidlin, "Eschatologie," pp. 449 ff. *Chron.* 7. prol., 8.3, 8.20, pp. 308, 395 f., 422 f.

[11] *Chron.* 4.prol., p. 183.

VII and Henry IV, he drew out with diagrammatic clarity the ambiguities that played against each other in his mind.

Beyond these two specific sets of objections, Otto's theory of impending eschatological doom, and his own *ex post facto* contention that events proved the theory, ran into obstacles, for while miseries continued, so did the world, the hierarchic Church, and the Empire; and, moreover, the rupture between papacy and Empire opened in 1075 appeared to have been closed in a new and fruitful era of collaboration.[12]

Otto's efforts throughout the *Chronicle* to test his hypotheses and to respond seriously to objections characterize a man who had a guiding vision of the origin and direction of human life, and who also worked steadily to improve it. In the last analysis, as Otto recognized, his work reflected his own unhappy state of mind, which, in turn, took form in the mold of contemporary events.[13] This recognition indicates the same probing temperament, the same continual quest. Otto determined that the eschatological structure in the *Chronicle* was, at least partly, the response of his mind to a finite situation that had passed. But crucial objections to his hypotheses remained unanswered. Soon after he completed the second version of the *Chronicle*, in a happier frame of mind, he attempted a new approach to history in the *Deeds*, not on eschatological, but on philosophical, grounds.[14]

2. Traces of a Metaphysical Hermeneutic

It is easy to overlook the fact that Otto's exposition in the *Chronicle* contained several elements that could be used again in a philosophical mode, elements that emerge as a palimpsest beneath the eschatological overlay and later rise full blown in the *Deeds*. Alongside Otto's somber eschatological narrative of divisions among men and the decline of the world caused by sin, there runs a second, quite different narrative. Such was the complexity of his thinking that he was also able to teach that, in some fashion, all men were one, and that the history of the world traced the ascent of man through the developing powers of human reason. Accordingly, we find in the *Chronicle* evidence of a sense of progress and an attachment to philosophy that figured prominently in the *Deeds*. How did the ascetic's dream of the Last Things coincide with the philosopher's dream of progress?

To be sure, Otto understood "reason" and "philosophy" as tools of Christian discipline, and mankind's advance as a cumulative growth in wisdom

---

[12] Cf. *Chron.* 3.6, p. 142.

[13] *Chron.*, ep. ad Frid., p. 2 f.

[14] Otto appears to have regarded philosophy with the mixture of fear and fascination that had been conventional since the time of the apologists. He recognized that, in the remote and not so remote past, Origen and Abelard had been misled by their excessive attraction to philosophy, and that the Emperor Julian's learning had not kept him from actions unsuitable either for a philosopher or for a prince. He knew that philosophy pandered to those who, given over to the delights of the world, were all too susceptible to arguments that enabled them to deny the faith (*Chron.* 8.4, p. 398; see Hashagen, *Geschichtsphilosoph*, p. 8). And yet, he plunged ahead with it himself.

that would be fulfilled in heaven. Hints of this attitude appear in the *Chronicle* (4.14) when the bishop praises the Egyptian hermits, followers of St. Antony, who, he writes, studied philosophy in the desert and won fame through their signs and apostolic miracles, and in his recollection of Boethius's *Consolation* as a very useful philosophical work on the contempt of the world. Christian asceticism thus saturated Otto's conception of philosophical subjects, including especially appearance and reality. This dyad concerned him above all in his effort to detect meaning hidden in events.[15]

Otto was not content with the simple identification of events with scriptural prophecies. He required a broader, metaphysical rationale, and this need enmeshed him in differences among the leading lights of his intellectual world. By appealing to events, Otto betrayed his allegiance to Orosius, from whose *Seven Books of History against the Pagans* he profusely quoted. But Otto also followed Orosius's patron, St. Augustine, who refused to identify specific events and persons with the eschatological predictions found in the Scriptures; he followed Boethius, whose teachings on the stable forms underyling the mutable world left little place for eschatology;[16] he followed Dionysius the Areopagite (through the good offices of Hugh of St. Victor), whose stable metaphysical order likewise crowded out eschatological progression. Could the Orosian strain be harmonized with the others? At any rate, the impact of Augustine, Boethius, and Dionysius the Areopagite on Otto's thinking gave the dyad of appearance and reality both an ascetic and a metaphysical content.

From Otto's perspective, philosophy, history, and theology were differentiated parts of a common endeavor to find release from the deceptions of this life, one broad effort to distinguish true from false, and, thereby, to pass from visible to invisible things.[17] Otto was quite aware, however, that in each

---

[15] One should therefore avoid placing an extreme interpretation on Grabe's distinction between Augustine as a metaphysician and Otto as a historian. Grabe, "Zweistaatenlehre," p. 58. The metaphysical content of Otto's texts is also one measure of his departure from Orosius. Cf. Markus, *Saeculum*, pp. 164 f. I am in substantial agreement with Schmale, *Taten*, pp. 8, 10.

[16] In the *Chronicle*, Otto refers twice to Boethius, once in his dedicatory letter to Rainald of Dassel, when he says that he agrees with Boethius that the greatest consolations amidst his troubled life are to be found in the philosophical disciplines (including grammar, logic, and geometry, p. 4), and again, when he records Boethius's philosophical work "on the contempt of the world" (the *Consolation*), texts by him that were "useful to the Church of God" (*On the Trinity, Against Nestorius and Eutychius*), translations of Aristotle's works into Latin, and his commentary and introduction to the *Topics* (5.1, p. 229 f.). For explicit references to Otto's use of Boethian materials, see the notes below concerning philosophical discourses in the *Deeds*. In general, see Frederick P. Pickering, *Augustinus oder Boethius? Geschichtsschreibung und epische Dichtung im Mittelalter — und in der Neuzeit*, 2 vols. Philologische Studien und Quellen 39, 80 (Berlin, 1967, 1976). Pickering considers Otto of Freising in 2:104–118. While he is concerned to establish Otto's debt to Boethius, notably with regard to the concept of *fortuna*, the philosophical orientations that we are discussing are peripheral to his theme (see esp. p. 118).

[17] On the parallel between the passage from visible to invisible in theology and philosophy, *Chron.* 2.8 and 4.prol., pp. 76, 180. On the parallel between the distinction between true and false in philosophy and history, see *Chron.*, ep. ad Rainaldum and 2.8, pp. 4, 76. On the fusion of symbolism, scholastic philosophy, and grammar in Otto's mind, Johannes Spörl, "Vom

of the three branches progress in knowledge depended on the capacity of the knower. Working with figurative signs as they did, philosophers could be distracted from authentic knowledge by failing to go beyond their search for natural causes; historical writers too could misread the signs around them; theologians could wander in heresy and ignorance, self-assured that they held to the truth.[18] Otto's philosophical heritage thus led him to exalt reason; his heritage of ascetic self-doubt led him to discount it.

The bishop's esteem for reason conjured up a magnificent vision. Through reason, the dominant element in their humanity, all men were one, and the course of history was the gradual advance of man's collective mind in wisdom. All men alike were the image of God in their reason, through which they mimetically participated in God, the principle of wisdom, goodness, and being.[19] Because there were degrees of participation (and thus of likeness), there were also higher and lower levels of knowledge, which would carry over, among the saints, into the heavenly ranks.[20] But, since all were united in their common humanity, it was possible to follow Augustine in considering all men to be one man, and history, as the education of mankind. "A person," Boethius had written, "is an individual substance of rational nature,"[21] and the fact that Otto retained this philosophical concept of personal separateness within a natural unity had important consequences for his history. It permitted him to identify mankind's advance in reason as a mimetic transformation running more fully and widely as the times progressed. As we shall see, it also figured in the interpretive apparatus of the *Deeds.*

In remotest antiquity, Otto wrote, men did not use their reason. Moved by greed and unchecked by religion or law, they prowled hither and yon like wild beasts. Only after Ninus, the Assyrian, who founded the world monarchy by profaning the earth with human blood, did the light of reason begin to shine in laws and government. The human mind was still too weak to

---

Weltbild Ottos von Freising," in J. A. Fischer, ed., *Otto von Freising: Gedenkgabe zu seinem 800. Todesjahr* (Freising, 1958), p. 11.

[18] On the figurative interpretations of philosophers, see Otto's reference to Plato's *Timaeus* (*Chron.* 8.8, p. 401). Abelard expressed a common position, apparently shared also by Otto, when he wrote that Plato and other philosophers, like prophets and theologians, spoke figuratively through parables and enigmas, to make their doctrines more appealing to the reader, and thereby to make the *arcana philosophiae* more accessible to him. Abelard, *Introductio ad Theologiam* 1.17, 19, PL 178:1019, 1021 f. On the danger of going astray, concerning philosophers, *Chron.* 8.4, 20, pp. 398, 422; concerning historians, Otto's own ambiguities; concerning heretics, *Chron.* 3.prol., p. 130. Sacred knowledge, of course, was the point from which Otto judged other peoples. On *agnitio Christi*, with reference to the pre-Christian Romans, see *Chron.* 2.34, p. 108; to the Muslims, see the very odd account in *Chron.* 7.7, p. 317 f.; to the Jews, see *Chron.* 3.10, p. 146, and passim. Regarding the conversion of the Jews in the Last Times, see *Chron.* 8.7, pp. 399 f., and Robert E. Lerner, "Refreshment of the Saints: The Time after Antichrist as a Station for Earthly Progress in Medieval Thought," *Traditio* 32 (1976), 112.

[19] *Chron.* 7.prol., p. 307. This entire prologue is an exercise in the blended allegories of philosophy and theology. See below, nn. 51, 71.

[20] *Chron.* 8.29, p. 439 f.

[21] *Gesta* 1.prol., p. 9.

comprehend the highest precepts of life. The law was given to man in that infancy of the world, and later, in the progress brought about by collective life, the application of wisdom through legislation, and the inquiries of philosophers, the minds of men were prepared to grasp the laws of Christ.[22] Even then, wisdom continued to enlarge as its temporal focus passed, with world monarchy, from East to West. Otto considered that it had reached an unprecedented height and diversification in his own time.[23]

To be sure, the tragic drama described in the *Chronicle* was not simply this rise from bestiality to spirituality. At every advance, there was menacing conflict. Demons had no power to change human nature, but they could confuse minds, occupying the parts of the body close to the seat of reason and dazzling the eye with secret machinations and hidden seeds of nature.[24] Before Christ's advent, Satan had deceived the entire world, except the Israelites.[25] The philosophers, even Plato who grasped the doctrine of the Logos, lacked knowledge of what salvation required.[26] Satan was still bound in the minds of his imitators, the reprobate,[27] awaiting the moment when, under Antichrist, the city of Christ would suffer its last, and worst, persecution by sword, falsehood, and deception.[28]

Trial by deception would cease, when sitting in the minds of His elect, the Lord judged the world.[29] But movement and mimetic transformation would not. There is perhaps no need to stress the endless movement and contortions of form that the suffering of the reprobate involved. But what of beatitude? The promise of heavenly reward contained action, but that action imparted form untainted by the perishable round of generation and decay. The blessed would see and not grow tired, love without satiety, praise without weariness, rejoice without any admixture of sadness. They would also move in a second way. For, according to the diversity of gifts, they would receive different places in the celestial hierarchy, higher and lower degrees of illumination and hence of beatitude. As their holiness enlarged, they would progress and ascend through the orders of spiritual enlightenment: that is through degrees of likeness to God.

From what has been said thus far, we can identify the philosophical substratum discernible through the eschatology of the *Chronicle*. It consists of

[22] *Chron.* 1.6, 3.prol., pp. 44 ff, 130. Concerning the primitive state of man, see Funkenstein, *Heilsplan,* p. 104.

[23] Otto connected this advance intimately with speculative grammar. His references to Priscian, and his application of grammatical rules in the effort to disclose eschatological secrets about the saints in "the book of God's most wise foreknowledge," witness to that conviction (*Chron.* 5.prol., 4, 8, 32, pp. 226, 235, 448 ff.). In 1157, he wrote that grammar was the first step toward philosophy (*Chron.,* ep. ad Rainaldum, p. 4).

[24] *Chron.* 1.26, p. 60.

[25] *Chron.* 3.prol., p. 130.

[26] *Chron.* 2.8, p. 78.

[27] *Chron.* 8.2, p. 394.

[28] *Chron.* 8.1, p. 393.

[29] *Chron.* 8.17, p. 415. On the end of the world "without end," see Schmidlin, "Eschatologie," p. 445.

Neo-platonic doctrines of mimetic transformation that Otto found affirmed by Boethius in philosophy, by Augustine in theology, and by Dionysius the Areopagite in contemplative spirituality. Still, even ratified by such great authority, this philosophical orientation gave Otto no final assurances.

It has sometimes been held that Otto was preoccupied with power — that, for him, history was above all the history of power.[30] On the interpretive level, this is true only in the limited sense that Otto classed the vicissitudes of kingdoms among the major signs which manifested invisible realities. On that level, it would be more accurate to say that he was preoccupied with form. Despite his inconsistencies with regard to periodization, despite the incongruity between facts and theory, he held steadfastly to the Boethian doctrine of form, which, indeed, made up a large part of his didactic strategy. But, for Otto, the philosopher's heart was restless until it rested in God. The ascetic content of philosophy was reinforced by such moral *exempla* as those of the Egyptian hermits and Boethius, and, with the Areopagite, Otto looked forward to the end of rational progress, that highest moment of knowledge when, transformed and absorbed into God, man could have by grace what the Son of God had by nature.[31] To form the reason was also to be conformed with the Image of the invisible God, in holiness.

In the *Chronicle,* Otto of Freising portrayed holiness on the grand scale, not in the biography of one man, but in the career of mankind. History — the acts that man performed and recorded and, remembering, imitated — was both a reflection and a manifestation of God " 'in whom we live and move and are.' Without Him we neither live nor move nor are, since what was made is life, not in itself, but in Him."[32] Otto considered man's reason to be the hallmark of human nature, and he portrayed human achievements both in government and in wisdom as expressions of it. But beyond reason and its works there were the facts that it was given and, moreover, that it was given for a specific purpose that was ultimately disproportionate to human faculties. "Every man is capable of reason to the end that he may know his God and not pass over with a blind heart the things that He has made, or attend to them with deaf ears."[33] As capacity for the knowledge of God, reason enabled the wise man to do even more, to free himself from the variable and disordered movement of temporal things and to fix himself foursquare in the steadiness of virtues,[34] but at the cost of realizing that, in themselves, men were nothing and knew nothing, and that they existed

---

[30] Joseph Staber, "Eschatologie und Geschichte bei Otto von Freising," in Fischer ed., *Otto von Freising: Gedenkgabe zu seinem 800. Todesjahr,* p. 119.

[31] *Chron.* 8.10, p. 405.

[32] *Chron.* 8.10, p. 405. "Habet quippe solus Deus vitam in semet ipso, qui ex se, a se, in se vivens aliunde vivere non accipit, cui est vivere quod esse, nec aliud esse quam vivere, quia ipse est vita, et sic vita, quod ab eo omnis vita. 'In ipso enim vivimus, movemur et sumus,' sine ipso nec vivimus nec movemur nec sumus, quia quod factum est non in se, sed in ipso, vita est."

[33] *Chron.* 7.prol., p. 307. "Omnis homo capax ad hoc rationis est ut auctorem suum Deum cognoscat factaque sua ceco corde non transeat, surdis auribus non audiat."

[34] *Chron.* 1.prol., p. 6.

through God's mercy and spoke through His grace.[35] So conceived, history, the collective advance of mankind, expressed the sacred. That was especially true of the saints, living not their lives but Christ's, whom God honored as His collective Image,[36] and who, throughout the generations, incrementally and always imperfectly formed the Church, the Bride and Body and City of Christ.[37]

These relatively few maxims, drawn from Scripture and interpreted in Boethian terms, gave Otto the principles that he needed for a coherent story of man's life in the world. From the moment when he was cast out of Eden, man had lived a pilgrimage. At every moment, he suffered, moving toward his goal. Those who lived at the end of time and surveyed the whole course of things could see that there was an informing pattern running through the immense fabric.[38]

And still, Otto's way of looking at evidence in terms of formative processes posed enigmas that his proofs could not riddle out. If he proposed necessity, he also had to thread his way between determinism and freedom. If he resorted to man's actual experience of holiness, he ran up against the bottomless enigma of appearance and reality, haunted by the twin specters of self-deception and of Satan disguising himself as an angel of light. If he rested much weight on the possibility of holiness in the Church, he encountered the radical, hidden, and anxious disparity between the pilgrim Church and the heavenly Jerusalem.

Anxious uncertainty was thus a condition of mankind's progress in knowledge, just as sin was of redemption. What Otto said regarding one internal problem can be applied to them all. How was it possible, he asked, that the Savior of all wished to be born at the end of time, leaving all the nations in previous ages to perish in their faithlessness? Such a question, he said, was beyond the boldness of man to investigate. As St. Paul wrote,

'O the height of the riches of God's wisdom and knowledge! How incomprehensible are His judgments, and His ways past finding out!' (Rom. 11:33) What, therefore, shall we do? If we cannot understand, shall we be silent? And who will answer

---

[35] *Chron.* 3.prol., p. 134 f.

[36] *Chron.* 4.4, p. 190. On the problem of holiness in Otto's works, see the brief remarks in Manfred Müller, *Beiträge zur Theologie Ottos von Freising* (Mödling, 1965), pp. 32–35.

[37] *Chron.* 6.36, p. 305, and passim. On the general importance of the themes of soteriology and Christology in twelfth-century historical writing, see Spörl, *Grundformen*, p. 19. Otto's reflections on the subject have a particular interest because of the veneration that he has himself received as a saint, both shortly after his death and from the fifteenth century onward. On that account, he figured in Maximilian I's glorification of the Hapsburg dynasty (which included the canonization of Otto's father, Leopold III [IV], in 1485, and his proclamation as patron saint of Austria), an effort which also brought about the rescue of Otto's works from neglect. On Otto's posthumous reputation, particularly in the fifteenth century, see Alphons Lhotsky, "Das Nachleben Ottos von Freising," *Europäisches Mittelalter: Das Land Oesterreich. Aufsätze und Vorträge*, 1 (Munich, 1970), pp. 29–48. Lhotsky provides some information concerning the use of Otto's writings by authors in the twelfth and thirteenth centuries, on which, see also Brincken, *Studien*, pp. 222 f.

[38] *Chron.* 1.prol., 2, pp. 7, 38. Cf. ibid., 4.4, p. 189.

the gainsayers, keep the attackers at bay, and, finally, with the reason and force of words, silence those who wish to destroy the faith that is in us? Thus, we cannot comprehend the hidden counsels of God, and yet we are commonly driven to give account of them. . . . And so it happens that, when we speak of theological matters, lacking terms cognate with the things themselves, we, who are men, use our words, and, speaking of so great a God we use human words the more confidently, since we do not doubt that He understands the device that we have made. For who understands better than He who created?[39]

To sum up this part of the discussion: In the *Chronicle*, Otto of Freising betrayed several traits of mind that conflicted with his eschatological narrative and that, without eschatology, reappeared in the *Deeds:* (1) a concept of history as the progressive formation of mankind in wisdom (which was also holiness), (2) confidence in philosophy as a major instrument of man's rational progress, (3) awareness that restless self-criticism and conflict were conditions of human progress, and (4) commitment to the Neo-platonic philosophy of form, as conveyed by Augustine, Dionysius Areopagitica, and, especially, Boethius.

In the *Chronicle*, the eschatological context gave the Investiture Conflict its meaning. That context — and therefore the meaning that derived from it — posed difficulties even at the time of first writing. The course of events after 1147 made it increasingly difficult for Otto to persist in holding that, under Gregory VII, the Church had smitten and destroyed the Roman Empire, the last of the world monarchies. Indeed, the position of the Roman Church could not be seen as it was described in the *Chronicle* if one were troubled, as the *Deeds* suggest that Otto was, by lapses of the prophetic spirit, as in St. Bernard's preaching and Eugenius III's encouragement of the Second Crusade, by the uncertain voice of the Holy Spirit as witnessed in a series of divided papal elections, by the failure of the pope's temporal power over the city of Rome even to the killing of pilgrims by his enemies in St. Peter's, by the divergence between the rapacity of papal legates and the ascetic spirituality of monastic orders, and by the clear ascendancy of the Empire.

To say this much is also to say that the splendid vision, rendered in the *Chronicle*, of a world increasingly guided by monastic holiness had also dimmed. For, in 1146, Otto wrote inspired by a series of popes who either came from monasteries or fostered the monastic life. By 1157, the series had faltered and Otto had had much to lament in the pontificate of his brother Cistercian, Eugenius III, including a sharp papal rebuke to Otto himself.[40]

---

[39] *Chron.* 3.prol., p. 130 f.

[40] The apotheosis of monasticism, and the ascendancy of the Church over the Empire, figure very large in Otto's discussion of his own time. It is not necessary to attribute their prominence exclusively to a monastic ethos. It is undesirable to do so, and thereby to omit the fact that Calixtus II (1119–1124) was the first pope since 1073 not drawn from the monastic life. Honorius II (1125–1130), his successor, was also elected from the secular clergy, but he gave papal sanction to Prémontré and to the Templars. Innocent II (1130–1143) was a monk, and, after the very brief pontificates of Celestine II (1143–44) and Lucius II (1144–45), the series of

Perhaps one had judged too soon and precipitately read prophetic utterances into somber times, without recognizing the promise of good that lay hidden in the shadows and that was ripening toward maturity. The world did not end. Times changed for the better. Another tool of interpretation was available: there were ancient precedents illustrating that one could pass from historical acts, and even from fables, to the sublime secrets of philosophy without reference to allegory and tropology. By this method, events could also be read figuratively, as signs of eternal truths; and there were crucial points at which the philosophical search for the causes of things, and its method of avoiding falsehood and knowing truth[41] intersected with and illuminated the invisible things of God.

3. THE RECONSIDERATION

Even while he maintained that fundamental change in patterns of thought divided the *Deeds* from the *Chronicle*, Peter Munz recognized that the radical shift from pessimism to optimism, which he posited was "psychologically almost implausible" and explicable, if at all, only in terms of influence exerted by Frederick Barbarossa and his advisor, Rainald of Dassel. It is my contention that no such change occurred, at least on the deep level where the commitments of metaphysics and faith were identical, and I shall now indicate some lines of continuity. Munz advanced a valuable argument for the integrity and completeness of Otto's views as set forth in the *Deeds*. I entirely accept his insight, but I wish to approach both the *Chronicle* and the *Deeds* as a coherent whole in terms of their internal arguments.

The first book of the *Deeds* has a rather odd feature, for, while it is intended to celebrate the reign of Frederick Barbarossa, a large part of it concerns apparently extraneous matters: St. Bernard's assaults on Abelard and Gilbert de la Porrée. The incongruity is even sharper because Otto not only described events in some detail, but also inserted discourses on the philosophical points at issue. Otto anticipated objections, and he left, in his prologue, a response to the criticisms (1) that the book as a whole lacks unity and (2) that the philosophical sections are not integrated with the historical. His response to the first criticism is that, "If deeds of an ecclesiastical or secular person from other realms are inserted along the way, they will not be thought matter foreign to this [main] concern; for the story of all kingdoms or peoples returns to the state of the Roman commonwealth as though to a fountainhead." His answer to the second objection is, as previously indicated, that the higher things of philosophy were not extraneous to the simpler

---

monastic popes continued with Eugenius III (1145–1153). To a man writing in 1146, nothing might have seemed more obvious on historical evidence — without resort to mysticism — that that the monastic life had become predominant in the Church and that the Church, in the hands of monks elevated to the throne of St. Peter, had achieved predominance over emperors. In the *Gesta*, Otto included Eugenius's rebuke to him and ten other prelates for sanctioning Barbarossa's translation of Wichmann from the see of Zeitz to Magdeburg (2.8).

[41] *Chron.* 2.8, p. 76. *Gesta* prol., 1.4, pp. 12, 16. Schmale, *Gesta*, pp. 120, 128.

matters of history's "plain diction," since they carried the mind to hidden truths.[42]

When we consider the locations and subjects of the philosophical discussions, we can understand what Otto meant, and how they bear on what he wrote in the *Chronicle*. There are only three such passages. The first occurs in the midst of the account of the Investiture Conflict;[43] the second, in the narration of Gilbert de la Porrée's trial, which Otto introduced with a discussion of Peter Abelard's doctrines, trial, and condemnation;[44] the last, to which we have already referred, appears in Otto's vindication of the Second Crusade.[45]

Despite the wide-ranging content of Book I, the only conspicuous discussion "of an ecclesiastical or secular person from other realms" without apparent relation to the Empire is precisely that of Gilbert de la Porrée. Externally, it appears remarkably intrusive. It interrupts Otto's account of the Second Crusade, coming immediately after the departure of Conrad III and Louis VII and their arrival in the Holy Land. The section required Otto to break his chronological sequence, falling back, first, from 1147 to 1142, when he introduced Gilbert, and, again, to about 1120, when he brought Abelard on the scene. Finally, the interpolation is long. It amounts to thirteen chapters (out of seventy) and, in length, to nearly one-quarter of the entire book.

On Otto's own authority, we are warranted in thinking that this extensive discussion and its strategic location in the narrative were not accidental, but, rather, that the bishop intended through them to illuminate his account of the Empire. Instead of an intrusion, we have a play within a play.

I contend that this is true of all three philosophical excursus. To state this case, I must consider two questions. Are these excursus interrelated at all?

---

[42] *Gesta* prol., p. 12. Schmale, *Gesta*, p. 118. "Si qua vero ex aliis regnis aecclesiasticae secularisve personae gesta incidenter interserta fuerint, ob huius negotii materia aliena non putabuntur, dum omnium regnorum vel gentium ad Romanae rei publicae statum tamquam ad fontem recurrat narratio." Munz, *Frederick Barbarossa*, p. 140. For arguments similar to Munz's, see J. Koch, "Grundlagen," p. 328, and, emphasizing Otto's alleged *Reichsmetaphysik*, Spörl, *Grundformen*, pp. 43 ff. See also Spörl's reconsiderations in "Civitas Dei," pp. 318 f. For reservations concerning the function, or even the presence, of a *Reichsmetaphysik*, see Kaegi, *Grundformen*, p. 8; Klinkenberg, "Sinn," p. 67. On the differences and similarities between the two works, see also above, n. 1, and Kaegi, *Grundformen*, p. 13.

[43] *Gesta* 1.4–5, pp. 15–22. Schmale, *Gesta*, p. 126 ff. Otto's debt to grammar and logic has been repeatedly emphasized. See Hofmeister, "Studien, I.," p. 151 n. 6, and "Studien, II.," pp. 732 f.; Schmidlin, "Philosophie," p. 160, on grammar. On logic, with its freight of ontology, Schmidlin, "Philosophie," pp. 163 f., 323, 407. On Otto's use of certain rhetorical topoi, see Leonid Arbusow, *Liturgie und Geschichtsschreibung im Mittelalter* (Bonn, 1951), pp. 32 f. The most recent, and one of the best, discussions of the three excursus to which we are turning, is that of J. Koch, "Grundlagen," pp. 328 f., 341 ff., who also argues for their conceptual relationship.

[44] *Gesta* 1.54–55, pp. 75–80. Schmale, *Gesta*, pp. 238–248. For arguments to the effect that Gilbert exercised a normative influence on Otto's theology, see Bernheim, "Charakter," pp. 5–9; Schmidlin, "Philosophie," p. 313; Hofmeister, "Studien, II.," p. 644; Grill, "Bildung," pp. 320 f.

[45] *Gesta* 1.65–66, pp. 91–93. Schmale, *Gesta*, pp. 266 f.

What can they tell us about the movement, and the consistency, of Otto's thought?

Turning to the first question, it would be possible to argue that the three excursus have little to do with one another, since each deals with a special problem and leads to a conclusion quite detached from the others. Indeed, this would appear to be undeniably the case if one took account only of the subjects treated: the distinction between the simple nature of God and the compound nature of created substances, the assumptions underlying Gilbert de la Porrée's doctrine of personality as applied to the Trinity, and, finally, the difficulty of reconciling the goodness of God with the horrendous catastrophe of the Second Crusade. Otto explicitly referred to his first and longest excursus — set into his account of the Investiture Conflict — as a departure from his theme, and one could perhaps regard the other two as learned *obiter dicta*, illuminating two moments — the trial of Gilbert and the failure of the Crusade — that happened about the same time but that had nothing else in common.

Let us look again, paying attention to context. Objectively, the events have nothing in common. But they all struck close to Otto's heart. The Investiture Conflict seared his family with its ferocity. The trial pitted Gilbert, a man whom Otto particularly esteemed, against Bernard of Clairvaux, the most eminent figure in Otto's own religious order. The Crusade inflicted on the bishop's own body the dangers and suffering of defeat, and, on his mind, gnawing doubts concerning the original inspiration for the enterprise and the fervent support that it had received from those two other Cistercians, Bernard and Pope Eugenius III.

Thus, the excursus appear, almost as miniatures, at points that held vivid meaning for Otto, and that were associated in his own life and spiritual quest. We can therefore assume that the discussions were rather more than idle exercises, and, indeed, that they belonged to a wide effort to reason out the deep perplexities with which the three events beset him.

Bearing subjective association in mind, we can also detect a common strategy of thought that is both narrative and hermeneutic.

On the narrative level, the excursus serve the general purpose and theme that Otto set for himself. The purpose was conventional, and even trite: Otto intended the *Deeds* to edify readers, inciting them to virtue and appealing especially to those who delighted in the subtle reasoning of philosophic discourse (prol.). The theme was the amelioration of the times, and the first book, in which our excursus occur, was to have been but a prologue to an account of Barbarossa's magnificent achievements.

Thus conceived, there are some obvious connections between the three sections under review and the didactic line in the *Chronicle*, which affirmed the collective progress of mankind in wisdom. Set into the account of Henry IV's troubles, the earliest of them explains that mutability is in the very fabric of human nature. This discourse was intended to teach the princes of the earth to keep their own roles in perspective by ever comparing the ceaseless ebb and flow in human life with the eternal sameness of the Creator (1.4). Here, Otto pitches edification in philosophical abstractions. In the *Chronicle*, Otto had likewise used his grandfather's lamentable fate for edification, but in an ascetic vein. Reviewing Henry IV's deposition in 1105 (Otto wrote in the earlier work), some believed that this affliction came toward his life's end to prove, and not to condemn, him. They affirmed that, by alms and many works of charity, he had earned from the Lord the grace of being punished in this world (and not in the next) for his excesses and wanton conduct as king.[46]

The excursus on the Second Crusade likewise serves Otto's general purpose and theme; it edifies the "little brethren of the Church" who were dismayed by the miserable failure of the expedition by asserting the benefits that the disaster brought with regard to the souls redeemed and the punishment of pride and disobedience that followed from it (1.65). A connection is apparent with the ascetic theme in the *Chronicle* that mankind advanced as it learned through suffering.

For further clarification, Otto referred his reader to St. Bernard's *De Consideratione* (2.1–4). There, the didactic theme is raised to an even higher level, one that obviously appealed to the bishop. Bernard argued that the Crusade resembled military defeats recounted in the Old Testament, routs into which the Israelites had marched relying on the promises of God. God punished their sins; He tested their obedience; and, because He appeared to have deceived His people, He opened his name to reproach. But God's justice never voided His promises. Bernard preached the Crusade, he wrote, obedient to the command that God had uttered through the pope. His conscience is clear, and this is his defense — and the defense that he offers to those (including Otto) who took up the Cross at his urging — against those who mistakenly judge actions by results. For, in obedience, he has deflected upon himself reproaches that men might have hurled against God. He glories in companionship with Christ, who said through the Psalmist, "the reproaches of them that reproached thee are fallen on me" (KJV Ps. 69.9). Otto would easily have filled in the words of this verse that Bernard omitted: "for the zeal of thine house hath consumed me."

Finally, what Otto says about Gilbert de la Porrée in the *Deeds* quite obviously bears on the view stated in the *Chronicle* that the progress of rational wisdom had achieved an unprecedented height in his own day. To Otto's mind, Gilbert was a man of an intellect powerful almost beyond comprehension, even by the learned, and, equally, of extraordinary moral uprightness (1.48.52). His doctrine, trial, and vindication clearly fascinated Otto for their own sakes, but also for what they taught, generally, concerning the advances of mankind toward Barbarossa's illustrious reign (prol.) and, specifically, concerning the fallibility of wise and holy men in deep matters, so long as they were burdened down in this world by the corruptible

---

[46] *Chron.* 7.11, p. 322 f.

body (1.61). The three excursus, therefore, sustain Otto's narrative object of ascetic didacticism and his theme of intellectual progress, both anticipated in the *Chronicle.*

On the hermeneutic level, Otto was concerned with the same major task in all three excursus: that is, he aimed to demonstrate the uniform structure underlying historical transition. His major tool in each instance was the Boethian doctrine of form. To be sure, Otto approached his task from a different point of departure in each excursus. However, the discussions proceed similarly, relating the universal to the individual, and, moreover, developing the argument through contrasts and analogies between the conditional unity among human beings and unqualified unity in the Godhead. Certainly, Otto was convinced that divine and human natures were incommensurable, and that, in its foreignness to the divine essence, the human mind could more certainly say what God is not than it could affirm what He is (1.5). Otto's complicated analogical inference had a special purpose however, thanks to Gilbert de la Porrée himself.

Otto described how, at the climax of his trial, Gilbert was brought to affirm (as he had already written) that the divine essence was not God. Gilbert thereby distinguished between subsistence (divinity) and the subsistent thing (God), in such a way as to hold that each person of the Trinity had specific properties that singled it out from the other two, and that, consequently, did not inhere in the unity of the divine nature (1.58–59). The distinction between nature and person in the Godhead gave Otto an analogue to the distinction between species and person in human beings. The bishop of Freising employed it by way of comparison and contrast, fully recognizing the uncertainties that impaired any attempt of the human mind to contemplate the heights of divine being.

From what has already been said, it is clear that the excursus bear on the two areas of hermeneutic difficulty that Otto encountered when he wrote about the Investiture Conflict in the *Chronicle:* the natures of the good and of the person. Because they are frank exercises in philosophy, the passages also disclose a formal method of thinking about those subjects that Otto did not display quite so self-consciously in the *Chronicle.* The dominant features of that method have already been identified: constant recourse to the Boethian doctrine of form, and the argument by analogy. We have seen that Otto employed these tools to clarify historical events that most intimately concerned him. How was he also able, by using them, to cast new light on the interpretive quandaries that he had encountered in writing the *Chronicle?*

I wish now to examine each excursus individually before suggesting an answer. The nature of the good is the subject of the shortest excursus, that in which Otto performed the breath-taking feat of explaining that, despite the calamities attending it, the Second Crusade was good. Though the excursus is the shortest of the three, its subject is the most fundamental of all. Like Augustine, Otto had to explain evil in such a way as to avoid dualism. He had to define it so as to attribute all things and events to the same source — God, the good — rather than to two independent and warring sources, good and evil. The need for a primordial unity arose on a second count. For Otto also had to reckon with a philosophical maxim: namely, that change was the result and sign of imperfection and, correspondingly, that all change was eventually a decline. In the *Chronicle*, this maxim reinforced the theme of the senescence of the world, but it ran counter to the other theme, in the same work, that no evil occurred in history without benefiting the whole. In the *Deeds*, Otto resolved his ambiguity by applying the Boethian doctrine of form to the experience of change.

Thus, instead of being wedged into the eschatological *Leitmotiv*, so appropriate to it, that characterized the *Chronicle*, the Crusade was used, in the *Deeds*, as a historical example of the logical distinction between absolute and relative good. Only God is truly good, and all things in nature that are called good are so, not because the divine goodness has been divided, but because they derive the name "good" from His goodness. In a relative sense, however, "good" could be understood as something inhering in the perceiver rather than in the object perceived, as henbane nourishes a sparrow, but kills a man, and as one and the same thing may benefit or harm different men. From this point, Otto made a transition by similitude to the conclusion already indicated: though the expedition was not good in the sense of something given by nature, it was good in the sense of utility, since it served the salvation of many souls.[47]

This discussion contains a number of the elements that appeared when Otto took up the problem of good in the *Chronicle*, notably (1) the essential goodness of God and the derived goodness of man, (2) the utility of evils sustained amid the changes of this life, and (3) the power of the reason to detect God's plan for the redemption of the world working itself out in human suffering. But the method of argumentation that Otto employed to sustain these conclusions in the *Deeds* had not been visible in the *Chronicle*. The entire discussion that he built around the *foci* of the universal and the individual is an example of his effort to seek the meaning of change through abstract categories of form and through the mechanisms of formal logic, learned from Boethius. Before he subjected the Crusade to analysis along those lines, however, he had already presented the two other main philosophical excursus of the *Deeds*, both of which bear on his concept of the person.

What, in the *Chronicle*, he sought to explain in terms of the locations of things in an eschatological plan, in the *Deeds*, he sought to explain in terms of the nature of the things themselves. Otto's first two major excursus deal with the same problem: How may an individual be considered both a con-

---

[47] *Gesta* 1.65–66, pp. 90–94. Schmale, *Gesta*, pp. 266 f. Caspar could afford a more pungent observation: "Die Teilnahme Konrads am zweiten Kreuzzug war die grösste Torheit seiner wenig glücklichen Regierung." Erich Caspar, *Roger II. (1101–1154) und die Gründung der normannisch-sicilischen Monarchie* (Innsbruck, 1904), p. 375. See ibid., p. 391.

crete (and unique) entity, and a component member of a universal category?[48] The relevance of these discussions for Otto's understanding of the Investiture Conflict lies in the fact that the individual considered is the person. Otto thereby analyzes what he meant when he said in the *Chronicle* that the Church consisted in the sacerdotal and royal persons.

The doctrines of Gilbert de la Porrée and the controversy surrounding them bore exactly on that matter. For they raised the theology of the person at the highest and most difficult level: at that of the Trinity. In the patristic age, the doctrine of the Church had intersected with the doctrine of the nature of Christ. How could the individual be both singular, standing alone before his Creator and Judge, and a component member of the Body of Christ? How could three persons be one God? In the age of the Fathers, the answers to these questions were mutually dependent. Abelard and, after him, Gilbert reopened the ancient paradox of the Trinity, and so, at the intersection of time and eternity, that of human personality.

It is also instructive to notice exactly how Otto introduced the matter in the specific context of the Investiture Conflict. After describing in broad outline the dispute between Gregory VII and Henry IV, and rounding out the cast of characters with a portrait of Robert Guiscard, Otto turned to the Saxon rebellion. When Henry began to rule in his own right, the king found Saxony tranquil and obedient, but shortly, through youthful arrogance, he stirred up such hostility, Otto said, "that the entire province had moved together against him, united in one body."[49] This observation leads Otto to the moral proposition that it is better to be striving upwards than to be at the peak, from which the only way is down. "For, since man is born to travail, living a brief time — nature tending to dissolution as it is composed of many parts — he can never remain in the same state. If he is on the height, soon he will have to descend. Because of this we may philosophize a bit, since 'Happy is he who can know the causes of things.' "[50]

The Church, in which individuals were compacted in one Body, and the Saxons, moving as one body against their king, brought Otto to the principles of diversity and unity, a philosophical object lesson to princes.

The special subject of this excursus is the growth and decline built into the very fibre of created things and, specifically, into human nature. Otto demonstrates that "humanity" is a universal form. By conforming with one another, individual persons express "humanity," each in a unique fashion. Thus, it is possible to establish both the individuality of men and the unity of

---

[48] These two excursus on the person should be read in conjunction with what Otto wrote concerning the Incarnation, *Chron.* 8.10, pp. 405 f.

[49] *Gesta* 1.4, p. 15. Schmale, *Gesta*, p. 126 f.

[50] Quoting Vergil, *Georgics* 2.490. *Ibid.*, p. 16. "Optime enim a physicis fallaciam complexionum considerantibus dictum cognoscitur: 'Melius est ad summum quam in summo.' Cum enim homo natus ad laborem, brevi vivens tempore, natura tamquam ex multis composita ad dissolutionem tendente, numquam in eodem statu manere valeat, si in summo fuerit, mox eum declinare oportebit. Cuius rei causa paulisper phylosophari liceat, etenim 'Felix qui potuit rerum cognoscere causas.' "

mankind. " 'By participation of species, many men are one,' and, accordingly, we are wont to say, 'The same wine is drunk here and at Rome.' " The humanity of Socrates, in act and nature, conforms with the humanity of Plato. Therefore, although analytically Socrates and Plato are two men, synthetically they can be said to be one man, one in the same universal form, both of them rational and mortal by virtue of the same humanity.[51]

Otto's task was to dissect this subject, explaining the inherent changefulness of creatures that collective bodies — the Church and the Saxons — had brought to mind. His first step was to point out that "humanity," the universal form, was composite, made up of many sub-forms (genus, species, and accidents). Otto's second step was to assert that forms could not exist without material bodies (or subsistent things), which were themselves composite. Thus, an individual person would be made up of a composite form and a composite body, each containing mutually antagonistic parts. Over all, there is the passage of time, through which occurs the swift "flux of forms," some being born as others pass away. In this fashion takes place the "concretion" of forms by which an individual person enters life and grows, and the dissolution of components by which, in the mutability of his nature, his composite unity loosens and, eventually, disintegrates.[52] This lesson applies equally to individual people and to collective bodies.

---

[51] *Gesta* 1.5, p. 16 ff. Schmale, *Gesta*, p. 128 ff. For parallels, see Nikolaus M. Häring, "The Commentary of Gilbert, Bishop of Poitiers, on Boethius' *Contra Eutychen et Nestorium*," *Archives d'histoire doctrinale et littéraire du moyen âge* 21 (1954), 273, 278-83, 294. Also published in Nikolaus M. Häring, *The Commentaries on Boethius by Gilbert of Poitiers*, Studies and Texts 13 (Toronto 1966), pp. 261-62, 269-75, 295-96. Cf. *Chron.* 8.26 p. 433: "Est ergo illius civitatis, quae mater nostra est et sursum est, participatio eius, qui dixit: 'Ego sum qui sum,' et, 'Qui est, misit me ad vos.' Eius, dico, in id ipsum, id est in identitate sua eternaliter et incommutabiliter semper uno eodemque modo permanentis. Cuius quia tunc, cum 'videbit eum, sicuti est,' eternitatis et identitatis vere perfecteque particeps erit, bene dicitur: 'Cuius participatio eius in id ipsum.' " The source of the striking formulation in *Gesta* 1.5, is certainly Boethian, but the exact text has not been identified. As Bernheim noted in "Charakter," p. 3 n. 2, there is an analogue in Gilbert de la Porrée's commentary on *De Trinitate* (PL 64: 1262). Häring, *Commentaries*, p. 72. But since Gilbert spoke of Plato, Cicero, and Aristotle, while Otto spoke only of Socrates and Plato in drawing the point, we can find closer analogues in Boethius's own works. My candidate is in the *secunda editio* of Boethius's commentary on the *Peri Ermeneias*, 2.7, Karl (Carolus) Meiser, ed., *pars posterior* (Leipzig, 1880), p. 137: "atque ideo quoniam humanitas et omnibus hominibus communis est et in singulis tota est (aequaliter enim cuncti homines retinent humanitatem sicut unus homo: si enim id ita non esset, numquam specialis hominis definitio particularis hominis substantiae conveniret): quoniam igitur haec ita sunt, idcirco homo quidem dicitur universale quiddam, ipsa vero Platonitas et Plato particulare." This entire section of the commentary deals with the same matter. See also Boethius's *In Isagogen Porphyrii Commenta* 2.6, CSEL 48, p. 188 ff; and 3.4, p. 209 f. See nn. 19, 71.

[52] For a very detailed analysis of this discussion, see Schmidlin, "Philosophie," p. 407 ff. Schmidlin provides cross references to commentaries by Gilbert on Boethian texts. Consult Nikolaus M. Häring, "The Commentary of Gilbert of Poitiers on Boethius' *De Hebdomadibus*," *Traditio* 9 (1953), esp. c. 27, pp. 201 f., on the text "ex quo fit ut omnia, quae sunt, Deus sint," and, by the same editor, "The Commentaries of Gilbert, Bishop of Poitiers (1142-1154) on the Two Boethian *Opuscula Sacra* on the Holy Trinity," in J. Reginald O'Donnell ed., *Nine Mediaeval Thinkers: A Collection of Hitherto Unedited Texts*, Studies and Texts 1 (Toronto, 1955), pp. 1-98

Otto illuminated his didactic point by contrasting the humanity in individual men with the divinity in the three persons of the Trinity. Whereas "humanity" is composite, the divine essence is simple and, hence, not subject to concretion and disintegration. Indeed, God is the Form from which all being derives, beyond all genus, species, and accidents, immune to the fitful restlessness of created natures and to the cycle of generation and decay.

Having explained — for the edification of overmighty princes — that decay was the inevitable sequel of growth in human affairs, Otto had no immediate need to venture into the difficult issue of how the persons of the Trinity were separate, even though divinity was one. However, this subject was plainly on his mind; for, as I said, he raised it later, in his account of Gilbert de la Porrée's trial. When the time came to orient his reader to Gilbert's disputed propositions, Otto again took up the thread of the argument that I have described concerning the analogue of human personality, and he refined his own position. But, for the moment, he let the matter drop and returned to the collective persons that had first prompted his remarks: the Saxons, the Church, and the Empire, stewing together in the Investiture Conflict.

Let us now consider the third philosophical discourse. Otto used the controversy surrounding Gilbert de la Porrée as an occasion for another effort to unfold a coherent concept of personality.

Otto drags Gilbert into the scene abruptly. He has traced the history of the Empire from 1080, to the preaching of the Second Crusade, the outset of the expedition, and a flash flood that destroyed the German encampment near Constantinople (1147). "But enough of this," he wrote, and, without transition, turned to the bishop of Poitiers.[53]

In deference to sound theological authority and in gravity of habits and life, Otto judged Gilbert to be far superior to Abelard. And yet, no less a critic than St. Bernard had charged that the bishop of Poitiers had erred in teaching that the divine essence was not God, and in holding other doctrines that too sharply divided the persons of the Trinity, on the ground that "every person is, in itself, one thing."[54]

To clarify Gilbert's meaning, Otto returns to the problem of relating the universal to the particular, specifically with regard to the person. His test passage is Boethius's classic definition, "the 'person' is an individual substance of rational nature." "Person" is therefore different from "singular" or "individual." The latter terms may denote indivisible entities, such as a crystal, or a lion, or a soul. But neither a crystal nor a lion possesses a rational nature, and a soul can only inhere in "this" person when it is united with "this" mortal body. Only a unique, actually existing person, with iden-

---

(also published in Häring, *Commentaries*). Funkenstein (*Heilsplan*, p. 100) discusses the passage to explain Otto's conception of the Church's rise to power over the secular monarchy.

[53] *Gesta* 1.47, p. 67. Schmale, *Gesta*, p. 222.

[54] *Gesta* 1.54, p. 76. See the six accusations, *Gesta* 1.52, p. 75. Schmale, *Gesta*, pp. 240, 236, 238.

tifying characteristics that no one else had could satisfy Boethius's definition. But what about God? "All being is from form." In his previous excursus, Otto had used this Boethian maxim, transmitted by Gilbert, to round out his demonstration that God could be called form.[55] Here, as in the discussion of the good, Otto demonstrated that every actual thing (or person) takes its reality and name from a universal form.[56] Gilbert was suspected of error because he appeared to apply this principle to the Trinity, emphasizing the singularity of the persons of the Godhead, and unduly discounting the unity of their nature (cf. 1.58).

Did he in fact err? Otto provided a careful statement of Gilbert's position, emphasizing the ways in which the bishop of Poitiers actually declared the genuine unity of the divine persons, but he cautiously declined to commit himself: "I have set down what he believed. Let others judge what ought to be believed" (1.55). He had a good precedent. Even the Synod of Rheims, presided over by Pope Eugenius III, found it impossible to determine whether three of Gilbert's four disputed propositions were in error, and a verbal elucidation by the pope cleared the fourth of suspicion. Like the Synod, Otto concluded his review of Gilbert's doctrines, dismissing him "in the fulness of honor" (1.61). But, if we are to trust Rahewin, Otto feared that, beneath the mask of impartiality, he had actually written so favorably about Gilbert's doctrines as to invite posthumous censure.

Winding up his philosophical discourse, Otto describes how Bernard attempted to organize the French prelates on his side by framing a common profession of faith, only to gain the enmity of the cardinals who judged his act a tactical manoeuver infringing the prerogatives of the Roman church. Bernard accepted a papal admonition; Gilbert accepted the verbal emendation from Pope Eugenius and went home vindicated, his episcopal dignity unimpaired. "But enough of this," Otto says again, and resumes his historical account of the Crusade.[57]

Gerhoh, the crusty provost of Reichersberg, reproached Otto for subscribing to Gilbert's doctrines.[58] But neither in Gerhoh's writings nor in Otto's can we trace the full range of his commitment. Only these fragmentary excursus survive. The discussion of Gilbert's trial does enlarge upon the apophatic demonstration in the excursus that Otto inserted into his account of the Investiture Conflict. Likewise, his use of the Boethian doctrine that being derives from form supplements his earlier analysis of conformity and composition with regard to human nature.

Let us now attempt to draw these three excursus into a general pattern. Instructed as he was by events between 1147, when he completed the first version of the *Chronicle,* and 1157, when he began the *Deeds,* Otto returned,

[55] *Gesta* 1.5, p. 18 f. Schmale, *Gesta,* p. 134.
[56] *Gesta* 1.55, p. 78. Schmale, *Gesta,* p. 242.
[57] *Gesta* 1.61, p. 88. Schmale, *Gesta,* p. 262.
[58] Peter Classen, *Gerhoch von Reichersberg: Eine Biographie* (Wiesbaden, 1960), pp. 163, 166 f., 184, 410 f.

in the later work, to central problems that he had first encountered when he wrote the *Chronicle* and again, in 1157, when he revised it. Even though he edited his data to suit the tragic, eschatological theme of the *Chronicle*, he still recognized two kinds of difficulties that obdurately surfaced in his discussion of the Investiture Conflict.

The first set of difficulties had been a central concern of his model, St. Augustine: Since God is good and rules the world, how can there be evil? But in the *Deeds* Otto turned not to Augustine so much as to the Boethian doctrine of mimetic form and analytical rules of logic, as set forth particularly in the *De Hebdomadibus*. Thus, Otto was able in the *Deeds* to distinguish God's original goodness from the derived goodness of created species and, moreover, the universal good of a species from the particular good that circumstances might open, by utility, to a given man or class of men. This argument complemented the views on the morphology of change set down in the *Chronicle* that men became good and wise by participating in the principles of Goodness and Wisdom, and that nothing evil happened uselessly: that is, without serving an ultimate benefit that God had preordained for the whole.

Regarding history, his philosophical inquiry into "the origins of things" had one important result. By interlacing eternity with time under the light of philosophy's eternal verities, Otto cast his argument in terms of an imperishable cosmic order rather than in terms of an advancing eschatological plan. Events therefore had meanings that were not tied to their specific locations on the line of eschatological process. Otto was freed from the inexorable sequentiality that had proven so hard to square with the historical data in the *Chronicle*. He had no obligation to multiply the number and depth of recent misfortunes and to dismiss even good fortune for its transiency, by way of affirming that the end of the world was at hand. In the *Deeds* mutability does not appear as the sign of an approaching world conflagration, but rather as the nature of composite, conformable, and concrete persons and, correspondingly, as the nature of such collective persons as kingdoms.[59] On the evidence given in the *Deeds*, there is no reason to assume that the rapid flux of forms, some always being born as others die, will ever cease in men or in their corporations.

The novelty of the *Deeds* is therefore not in philosophical principles, but in the implications that those principles had once they were dislodged from eschatology. There is an obvious connection between this model of change as an indefinite sequence of forms, the later taking shape within the earlier,

---

[59] I cannot follow the argument that Otto's emphasis on corporate unity militated against individual autonomy, and pressed the individual into the background. Schmidlin, "Eschatologie," p. 448; *Weltanschauung*, p. 24. Cf. Hashagen, *Geschichtsphilosoph*, p. 77; Spörl, *Grundformen*, p. 49. J. Koch has presented a cogent rebuttal to this view, "Grundlagen," esp. p. 327. If any further evidence were needed, one would find the germ of a conclusive argument in Otto's doctrine that knowledge of sacred mysteries is incommunicable, *Chron.* 8.35, p. 456 f., as in the election of grace.

and the conception, expressed in the *Chronicle,* of the history of the Church as a series of transformations according to eternal exemplars. The mutability of Henry IV's career, or the failure of the Crusade, exemplified, not the Last Days, but the natural tendency of a created substance to decline, once it reached its height. It represented the Aristotelian principle that, in the generative cycle of nature, things must either grow and reproduce themselves or decay. It was, Otto wrote, what the philosophers called "generation," and what "we" call "making" or "creating."[60] By removing eschatology from the interpretive strategy of the *Deeds,* Otto rendered the Investiture Conflict no more a turning point than any other in the chain of collective forms in transition. Since greater forms were made up by the concretion of lesser, the Church and mankind itself were transfigured by the continual increment of persons as each generation joined its forerunners in the "procession of times," just as, in the *Chronicle,* Otto described the saints, passing from one configuration to the next, as they realized the Image of God, having "one heart and one soul."[61]

As I said, Otto recognized that his reading of the Investiture Conflict also encountered a second category of difficulties. There was an imbalance between his conception of the visible Church as the image of the celestial hierarchy, ruled in this world by the sacerdotal and royal persons, and his characterization of it as the episcopal order, headed by the pope, battering down the last world monarchy. In the *Deeds* he reviewed, in philosophical terms, how one should understand "person."

Without rejecting the sense of "office" or "power," Otto in his two excursus on the "person" reiterates in detail that his thinking ran along a second line. Regarding the Trinity, or men, "person" meant a given rational entity distinguished from all others by its properties, by what Otto called "personalitas." (A particular example of this was "Platonitas," in other words, what made Plato himself and no one else.) Otto's inquiry into the relation of the particular to the universal led him further. Arguing along lines laid down by the Fathers, he was able to see that the persons of the Trinity were one in the divine essence and analogously that, through the composition of forms in their common rational nature, or humanity, mortal persons (such as Plato and Socrates) could be considered "one man."

When Otto wrote of the sacerdotal and royal persons, he therefore had in mind both the functions of office and the men who happened at a given time to be bishop (or pope) and king, and who, though two persons, were yet one man.[62] Once he shook off the narrative requirements of his eschatology,

[60] *Gesta* 1.5, p. 20. Schmale, *Gesta,* p. 136.

[61] *Chron.* 7.35, p. 370. On the *fluxus formarum* and the *processus temporum,* see Schmidlin, "Philosophie," p. 416. In my opinion, it is possibly misleading to apply the word "evolutionary" to Otto's understanding of sequence, and I am also hesitant to emphasize the "empirical-historical" elements in Otto's thought to the exclusion of others. Approaching Otto — primarily the Otto of the *Chronicle* — from this point of view, Funkenstein has, however, produced a very useful interpretive model. *Heilsplan,* pp. 58 f, 97, 117 f.

[62] Nor did he neglect to apply the principle when he described the coronation of Frederick I

Otto was able to characterize the Investiture Conflict as a political and military struggle in which Gregory VII was the chief aggressor and conspirator against the emperor, and in which the definition of the Church had no need to be emphasized. In the *Chronicle*, he had woven the figurative language of allegory about the Church, the destroying stone, the handsome virgin ever bearing a new and handsome issue, even as the Virgin Mary bore Christ its head.[63] In the *Deeds*, Otto sought access to the invisible by way of the philosophy of intelligible form, rather than by allegorical exegesis, and the Investiture Conflict took its place, not as a proving ground for doctrine, but as an episode of collective misfortune from which the Empire gradually regained its powers and moved toward a previously unheard-of serenity under Barbarossa and toward such eminence that even the barbarian or the Greek outside its borders trembled before the weight of its authority.[64]

The implications of Otto's examination of history in terms of nature (understood as a hierarchy of form) led him to the threshold of a remarkable new vision. He had by no means excluded the theological doctrine of the Church as the Body of Christ, but another concept had grown out of his Boethian inference. Through it, he was able to repeat the Fathers in portraying all men as one man; but he was also able to go beyond them by locating the two persons, royal and episcopal, in the Body of mankind, a Body that owed its transfiguration through conflict to ascetic reason. Otto was kept from following the "secularism" of this argument to extremes by the theological matrix in which his thought still moved.

4. POINTS OF INTERSECTION: THE HISTORICAL AND THE HOLY

The discussion has indicated a level of continuity between the "joyful" frame of mind with which Otto wrote the *Deeds* and his conviction, so pervasive in the *Chronicle*, that the spiritual interpretation of Scripture was

---

at Aachen (1152). Later on the same day, in the same church, the very bishops who had anointed and crowned Barbarossa consecrated another Frederick as bishop of Münster. "By this quasi-prognostication, the supreme King and Priest was believed to be in the midst of the present rejoicing in as much as, in one church, one day saw the unction of the only persons who, by the institution of the New and Old Warrant (*instrumenti*) are sacramentally anointed and duly named 'the Lord's christs.' " *Gesta* 2.3, p. 105. Schmale, *Gesta*, p. 288. "Sed et hoc silentio tegendum non erit, quod eadem die in eadem aecclesia Monasteriensis electus item Fridericus ab eisdem, a quibus et rex, episcopis in episcopum consecratur, ut revera summus rex et sacerdos presenti iocunditati hoc quasi prognostico interesse crederetur, qua in una aecclesia una dies duarum personarum, quae solae novi ac veteris instrumenti institutione sacramentaliter unguntur et christi Domini rite dicuntur, vidit unctionem." On this passage, see Arbusow, *Liturgie*, pp. 25 f.; Bernheim, "Charakter," pp. 36 f.; G. Koch, *Sacrum Imperium*, p. 186. See also the mimetic appeal of the people of Tortona to Frederick I: "Imitetur princeps terrae caeli principem, et si in eadem civitate cum superbo humilis inveniatur, non tamen cum superbo humilis puniatur." The Tortonese had something to learn about the Scriptures as well as about Frederick. *Gesta* 2.25, p. 129. Schmale, *Gesta*, p. 332.

[63] *Chron.* 6.36, p. 305.
[64] *Gesta* 1.prol., p. 9. Schmale, *Gesta*, p. 115.

incomparably more "joyful" than the literal.[65] As was natural to a devoted Cistercian in the age of St. Bernard, it was the level on which faith enlightened metaphysics.

At the close of the apocalyptic exegesis that ends the *Chronicle,* Otto wrote that it was important, in discussing great matters, always to leave something for later inquiry. For, he held, if the whole were spread out for all to see, it would appear of little value.[66] My discussion indicates that, in time, Otto himself decided to fill some of the silences that, in the *Chronicle,* he had left surrounding the Investiture Conflict. He examined it through the methods of speculative grammar, instead of apocalyptic exegesis; he described it in the narrative form of *iocunda historia,* instead of tragedy; and, occasionally, he trimmed his evidence to suit the celebratory object of the work.

The philosophical excursus enlarged upon terms and conceptions that appeared less distinctly in the *Chronicle;* the characterization of the parts taken by Henry IV and Henry V in the struggle was softened; the magnitude of the Conflict, in relation to other events was diminished; and, finally, its meaning changed with Otto's interpretive strategy.

One can, however, regard the accounts as complementary. They open to us two perspectives from which Otto considered the problem of transformation, and particularly, they define transformations with reference to man's chief end, beatitude, both in time and out of time. For it was in this respect that Boethius's philosophy appealed to him, teaching, so he thought, the same contempt of the world that Otto wished to portray through the mutability of earthly things,[67] and likewise that Dionysius the Areopagite, learning from St. Paul secrets opened to him when he was rapt to the third heaven, was entitled to be called "the divine philosopher."[68] In the *Deeds,* the historical level stands alone, without allegory. But it retains, and indeed brings into the open, a philosophical structure that had lain not far below the surface in the *Chronicle* in Otto's allusions to Augustine, Boethius, and Dionysius. Refreshed by a fortunate turn of events, inspired by a new commission, Otto applied the Boethian doctrine of intelligible form to the morphology of change. As in the *Chronicle,* Otto proceeded from visible things to invisible truths, according to the principles that, as he said in the earlier work, enabled man to act as the image of God by seeking truth, not only outside himself in other creatures, but also within, in reason, the light of God's countenance set upon him as a seal.[69] Through the reason that made him the image of God, man participated in the wisdom, goodness, and being of God, and through the progress of knowledge across the ages, mankind was transformed into a great, collective image of its Creator. In the *Deeds,* by his discussion of the good and of the person according to the

[65] *Chron.* 8.26, p. 436.
[66] *Chron.* 8.35, p. 457.
[67] *Chron.* 7.prol., p. 309.
[68] *Chron.* 8.30, p. 442.
[69] *Chron.* 7.prol., p. 307.

methods of speculative grammar, Otto (a) defined the derivative nature of man, and of earthly good;[70] (b) established both that each person was unique and that, through their humanity (primarily their rational nature), all persons could be called one man;[71] and (c) demonstrated that every person, being composite, moved first in growth and then inevitably in decay, and yet that collective man had in recent times moved toward the height, from ill to good, advanced through strife by "the spirit of the Pilgrim God."[72]

How fragile and malign had been the holiness of individual men, such as Epiphanius, who destroyed St. John Chrysostom,[73] and St. Bernard who assailed Abelard and Gilbert, the advocates of reason, and preached the Second Crusade. How obscure was the holiness manifested by contemporary popes. In contrast, the passage from the darkness of the Investiture Conflict to the radiant dawn of the present had been extraordinarily imposing, the ascent of what Frederick I was pleased to call "the holy Empire."[74]

The differences and the similarities between Otto's treatment of the Investiture Conflict in the *Chronicle* and in the *Deeds* point to another factor. Holiness and the perception of holiness were distinct. Otto himself recognized that the tragic cast of the *Chronicle* expressed his own bitterness of spirit in hard years, and that the brighter tone of the *Deeds* similarly reflected his happiness in a time of joy and peace. Behind the modes of transformation in the two works was the change in Otto's mind. Given his selective use of evidence, and the truncated state in which he left the *Deeds*, it would be wrong to seek completeness in either work or fundamental consistency between them, and hence to deny Otto the credit due his faculties for self-criticism. It would also be wrong to discount either the complex models of interpreting transition that he left behind him, or the extraordinary difficulty of the task, as he conceived it, or his recognition that uncertainty at every stage was the condition of advancement in holiness through reason.

In conclusion:

I. Otto's experiences between 1147 and 1157 (notably those centering on the Second Crusade and papal diplomacy) produced a change from the eschatological mode of the *Chronicle* to the philosophical one of the *Deeds*,

---

[70] God is form. All being is from form. *Gesta* 1.5; 55, pp. 19, 78. Schmale, *Gesta*, pp. 134, 244.

[71] A person is the individual substance of rational being. The species is the form of individuals and the ultimate likeness. *Gesta* 1.55, p. 77. Schmale, *Gesta*, p. 242. See also the axiom that, because of their participation in species, several men are one. *Gesta* 1.5, p. 17. Schmale, *Gesta*, p. 132 ff. See above, nn. 19, 51.

[72] *Gesta* 1.prol., pp. 9–11; Schmale, *Gesta*, pp. 114 ff.

[73] *Gesta* 1.61, p. 88. Schmale, *Gesta*, p. 260.

[74] *Gesta* 2.50, p. 158. Schmale, *Gesta*, p. 384. See Alois Dempf, *Sacrum Imperium* (Munich, 1929), esp. pp. 247 f., relating Otto's thought to that of St. Bernard, Hugh of St. Victor, and others. G. Koch, *Sacrum Imperium*, excellently describes how the concept of the *sacrum imperium* took shape from the eleventh century onwards, being woven together from many elements: the Salian concept that the ruler held a divine mandate, electoral practice, rights of conquest, Byzantine thought and practice, and materials offered by ancient Roman literature and Roman law.

sharply indicated by the diminished importance of the Investiture Conflict in the later work. By changing expository modes, Otto also markedly changed his portrayals of Gregory VII and Henry IV, indicating that, over the years, his judgment had shifted in favor of the king. There is reason to think that the shift occurred, not merely because the *Deeds* had a panegyrical object, but also because the Roman Church had not fulfilled the promise of the Danielic stone, as Otto had expected in 1147. It cannot be assumed therefore that judgments on parties to the conflict that Otto issued in the *Chronicle* illuminate those in the *Deeds*.

II.   It also cannot be assumed that Otto wrote the *Deeds* in an entirely different mode from the one employed in the *Chronicle*. Otto loosely threw the eschatology of the *Chronicle* together with another structure of thought which, in his altered cast of mind, he proceeded to reexamine in the *Deeds*. This second cluster of organizing principles comprised a doctrine of form in which eternity and its image, time, were reciprocally in one another. By virtue of the power of God, which ramified through the "flux of forms," change was always for the good. Indeed, beneath the instability of human existence, there steadily ran an ancient, semi-Christianized pattern of cumulative advancement through reason, the faculty through which all men were one man, and all saints constituted progressively through time one Image of God. In the *Deeds*, the "one man" comprised by all human beings performed the same functions as the "one Body" comprised by Christians had done in the *Chronicle*. While the same principles appeared in the *Chronicle* and the *Deeds*, their implications in the later work were startling, due to the simple fact that eschatology played no role. The implications of indefinite progression were more apparent in Meister Eckhart's generation than they were, or could have been, to anyone at the middle of the twelfth century.

III.   Otto recast ancient doctrines on the provisional character of knowledge, defining it explicitly as a historical phenomenon.[75] In so doing, he was among the first to attempt the extremely difficult task of combining the closed hierarchy of form taught by Augustine, Boethius, and Dionysius with the open progression of experience. There is, he argued, an enduring formal order of being; the course of events follows a divine plan; the morphology of change combines the order and the plan. And yet, personally, institutionally, and socially men are passing through a series of transformations, through time and eternity, toward an end without end. It was far from clear to Otto what kind of hermeneutic could satisfy the still contrary demands for closure and for openness. And yet, in a sense far different from what Otto intended or foresaw, this concept of the ceaseless transformation of man from lesser to greater degrees of ascetic illumination was one of the most potent legacies bequeathed by him and his generation to European society. It was, and has remained, the goad of militant minorities.

UNIVERSITY OF CHICAGO

[75] *Gesta* 1.prol., p. 11. Schmale, *Gesta*, p. 118.

INDEX

Abelard, Peter: VI 221,222,227,229, 235
Abraham: II 629;V 139,141
Agnes, Empress: V 134
Alcuin: II 623,635;III 145,153,158
Alexander II, Pope: V 134
Alexander IV, Pope: IV 148
allegory: VI 213,221,233. See also analogy; metaphor
Ambrose, Bishop of Milan: I 7,10,20-29,41-51;II 655,680,681,692
analogy: I 3;II 583,591-3,599,606, 609,615,616,630,647,651,669,693; IV 121;V 149;VI 225
Ananias: V 139
angels: II 604,631,672,679
animality: II 612;V 144,145,147; VI 216. See also human nature
Anno, Archbishop of Cologne: V 134
Anselm of Havelberg, Archbishop of Ravenna: V 148
Anselm of Speier: V 150
Antichrist: I 39;IV 133,134,141,144; V 139;VI 212,217
apostolic succession: I 32,34,38; II 597,665,674,699,706;III 152,156, 157
Aquileia, Synod of (381): I 41
architecture: II 592,593,596,599, 651,655. See also tomb
Arianism: I 13-15,23,24,26,30,36, 38,45;II 644,656,671,680,691
arts, liberal. See liberal arts
arts, medical: II 592,594,596,600-5, 617-21,641,642,654-6,678,701. See also physicians; surgery
arts, verbal: II 592,596,598,600-5, 617
arts, visual: II 591,603,605,617; See also painting
asceticism: II 606,607,652,653,665, 667,671,697,709
Athanasius, Bishop of Alexandria: I 6, 14,17-19,24,25,28,30-33,36,37,38
Athens: III 145,146,153,158
Augustine, Archbishop of Canterbury: V 141
Augustine, Bishop of Hippo: I 9,17,20; II 584,607,614,629,632-5,643;III 153,157;VI 208,215,216,218,220, 225,234,236
Aurelian, Emperor: I 8

baptism: I 31,32,35,36,39,41,48; II 598,629,630,631,632,639,642, 663,671,672. See also pagans;sacraments
Bede: II 635
Benedict of Nursia: II 603,607
Benzo of Alba: IV 136,137
Bernard of Clairvaux: VI 220,221,223, 224,229,230,235
Bernard of St. Victor's, legate:IV 125, 126
Bernard, cardinal-legate: IV 124-8
bishops, as angels: II 679
bishops, monastic opposition to: V 133,134,139,142,145
Boethius: VI 215,216,218-20,225, 226,230,231,234,236
Boniface, Archbishop of Mainz: V 131-143,145
Brixen, Synod of (1080): III 155; IV 134
Bruno of Magdeburg: IV 123,126
Byzantium: II 588,589

Caesaropapism: I 4-6,14,15
Calixtus II, Pope: VI 211
canon law: I 13-26,33,34,37,38;II 598,605,608,616,635,638,688,693, 698,699,701,702,703,705,708;III 149,150,157;IV 122;V 140,141
canons regular: V 143
Canossa: IV 144,146,147
Cardinals, College of: III 155,156
Carloman the Elder: V 135-7,139
Charlemagne, Emperor: II 608,656; III 145-8
Charles Martel: II 673
Charles the Bald, Emperor: II 588, 593,649,666,683,685,688,689,691-4
Charles the Fat, Emperor: II 621,622, 627
Chilperic I, King: III 144
Chilperic III, King: IV 136
Christians, false: IV 131;V 139,141, 142-6,151
Cistercian Order: VI 207,234
Clement III, Antipope. See Wibert, Archbishop of Ravenna
Clovis, King: II 598,649,655,656,663, 671-4
"conciliarism"; II 709;III 152,157,158
Concilium Germanicum: V 136